Crinoline to Calico

Crinoline to Calico

NAN HEACOCK

The Iowa State University Press / Ames

1977

© 1977 The Iowa State University Press
Ames, Iowa 50010. All rights reserved

Composed and printed by
The Iowa State University Press

First edition, 1977

Library of Congress Cataloging in Publication Data

Heacock, Nan, 1903-
    Crinoline to calico.

    I. Title.
PZ4.H4318Cr   [PS3558.E13]   813'.5'4   76-30665
ISBN 0-8138-0065-X

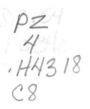
Contents

Preface

ALTHOUGH this story is fiction, it is based on historical and biographical events. My mother's parents and foster-parents were among the very early settlers in the vicinity of Anita, Iowa. Mother's tales of them and their neighbors form the skeleton of fact upon which the fiction is built. As confirmation for these family legends I have used a book my mother had, *Compendium of History and Biography of Cass County, Iowa,* which contains much firsthand information gathered directly from the settlers. Material for the History appears to have been collected over a period of several years prior to publication in 1906; my mother knew many of the people mentioned and spoke of them frequently. In fact, I know more about a number of them than the author of the History.

However, Mother's memories of the Civil War were hazy, and as the History covers the period in considerable detail, with dates, places, and the itinerary of both the Fourth Iowa and the Twenty-Third Iowa, I have used it to assure accuracy. I have also cross-checked with other histories, particularly *The Great Rebellion, A History of the Civil War in the United States,* which records almost every encounter of the Civil War.

My mother, Cassie Dobbs Peters, was born in Henry County, Illinois, in 1860. While she was still too young to remember the trip, her parents, Porter and Tabitha Dobbs, took her and her sisters to Cass County, Iowa, in a covered wagon. They stopped about two miles from the present Anita and Grandmother Dobbs took my mother and her sister Bell to the cabin of William and Dinah Peters for a drink of water while Grandfather and the other girls went on to find a camping spot for the night. Grandfather had intended to go on to California, but instead took a claim somewhere near the Peters farm on Section 30 of Grant Township, which at that time was part of the old Turkey Grove Township.

My mother and her older sister Bell were daughters of Porter Dobbs; the other three girls who came with them to Iowa were Grandmother's daughters by former marriage. However, settling in Iowa did not quench Grandfather's "gold fever" and a few years later he went to Idaho in the "gold rush." He found a partner, staked a claim, struck gold, and wrote that he would sell out and come home. But across the bottom of the letter he scrawled, "I don't trust my partner." He was never heard from again. Grandmother kept the farm as long as she could, then adopted out her girls, keeping with her only the youngest, born after Grandfather had left for Idaho. She went to work cooking at the stage station for Mrs. Lewis Beason, where, when the railroad at last came through, Lew Beason platted the town of Anita. When Porter Dobbs had been missing for seven years, Grandmother had him declared legally dead and married D. F. Gaylord, a widower, who had several children by former marriage. Grandmother had a daughter and a son by him, the boy the youngest of her ten children.

Since the girls were adopted by neighbors, they were able to keep in touch. In fact, the girls were an excellent excuse for a good bit of visiting among the various families. And by that time there were roads—of a sort—and numerous occasions for community get-togethers.

The older girls must have been nearly grown by the time Grandmother gave up her home and they probably married within a few years.

William and Dinah Peters took my mother, a youngster of around five or six years. After her own father was declared dead, Grandfather Peters adopted Mother legally as he and Dinah had no children, and when he died he left her a share of his very considerable estate. Grandmother Peters' share also came to her eventually.

Grandfather Peters [Jonathan] was born in a poor farm in Wales, ran away at the age of fourteen, and educated himself in the London bookstalls. He subsequently studied for the ministry, for medicine, and for law. I don't think he ever practiced in Iowa, though he had been "called to the bar" in England and had practiced there long enough that he did not come to this country empty-handed. He lived in Pittsburgh for a time before going to Iowa, but I don't know what he did there.

Grandmother Peters [Castle], the daughter of a wealthy Pittsburgh glassmaker, was a thoroughly spoiled young lady. Jilted in her teens, she spent eleven years in her room grieving for her lost love. This practice of seclusion was considered in those times quite proper and most romantic.

Eventually her father got fed up with her foolishness and ill temper and they had a terrific row, after which she vowed she would marry the first man who asked her, "even if he is a nigger." She dressed and went to a ball where she met William Peters, proposed to him the same night, married him within the week, and went with him to Iowa, where she spent the rest of her life hating Iowa and hating him. Or so she said. However, from my mother's stories of them, in spite of their cat and dog life, I have the feeling they were deeply devoted to each other. Grandfather was a rather stern, aloof sort of person—never demonstrative—yet he was a kind man and of ironclad integrity, whose word was as good as his bond and his bond better than purest gold. But under the rather cold exterior was a violent temper and when his wife pushed him too far, as she frequently did, he whaled the tar out of her and more than once dragged her around the house by her hair. However, no one but Mother ever knew of their fights and she never told anyone but me.

Publicly, the two of them always presented a carefully united front and no one who knew them would ever have believed that a cross word could pass between them.

Though Grandmother Peters could neither read nor write, for years she served as doctor and midwife to all her neighbors for twenty miles around, and in the days when there were no roads and only horses and wagons for transportation, that was quite a "fur piece." A devil in her own home, she was regarded as an "angel of mercy" in her community and no woman was ever more universally respected. She was unkind, even cruel, to my mother as a child, yet the croup story is true; Mother remembered it and told it many times. I gathered that as Mother grew older they became more companionable, and I'm sure that in her later years Grandmother became very dependent on Mother. They lived under the same roof for thirty-seven years and I suspect that something of Grandmother rubbed off on Mother, for during the twenty years I lived with my parents, many of Mother's little philosophies were prefaced by, "My mother used to say . . ."

The principles and attitudes of Grandmother and Grandfather Peters influence me even today. In my infancy my bedtime stories were tales of life in western Iowa when the Peterses lived in a thatched-roof cabin and Indians camped on the creek in winter. The Indians did come to the house to beg and the incidents I have related actually happened. Grandfather did haul his wheat a hundred miles to Des Moines and bring back lumber for his fancy frame house. And Mother attended the first school in Anita, taught by E. E. Major, who later went to Chicago, studied medicine, and eventually practiced in Anita for many years. After Grandfather died, the farm was sold and Grandmother and Mother moved to town.

In details pertaining to farming, farm life, and the work of the farmer's wife, I have drawn largely on my own experience. When I was small we lived for a time on a farm near Mammoth Springs, Arkansas; in 1908-1909 conditions in the Ozark foothills were still rather primitive. Later, I spent my vacations on my sister's farm in Iowa, about fifty miles from Anita, and though everything else had changed, the topography was the same as in my mother's childhood. From 1925 to 1927 I lived in a log cabin on a ranch in Wyoming where I cooked on a black iron cooking stove, hung the milk in the well and my wash on the barbed wire fence, stored vegetables in a cellar dug into a bank, and had no meat but game. We were forty miles from town and two miles to the nearest neighbor and telephone. Horses were the only transportation, oil lamps our only light. Our carriage was a spring wagon and in winter we put the wagon seat on the wood sled. I've seen worse storms than those described in the story.

From 1947 to 1958 I had my own farm on Montana Mountain in northwestern New Jersey. I raised my own vegetables and meat, cured and smoked my own hams and bacon, milked my own cows, churned my own butter, and made my own cheese. I canned, jellied, pickled, and preserved from early spring until late fall. I have pieced numerous quilts and made numerous rag rugs. And since my farming has been mostly do-it-myself, I have done things farmers' wives do not usually have to do. I not only did chores night and morning seven days a week in any and all weather, but I dug postholes and ran fence wire and, on occasion, felled trees and cut them up for firewood. And I have played midwife to everything from biddy-hens to bossy cows.

I have helped to bring up eight children besides my own daughter and I nursed them through tonsillectomies, appendectomies, measles, mumps, whooping cough, chicken pox, cuts, burns, bruises, and broken bones, and through it all my standbys were the old remedies Grandmother Peters passed on to Mother and Mother passed on to me.

Once the children were grown and on their own, I came home to Tennessee, where the winters aren't so long and cold and where living is a little less costly. High Noon Hollow boasts eighty-five acres; my house is in a "holler," where I can "lift up mine eyes unto the hills"—which are always beautiful—and where on a hot day it is always cool up by the waterfall. I drive to town when I have to; when my friends want to see me, they come to High Noon. I have four ponies, four milk goats, two dogs, and I refuse to count the cats. I live the way I want to live, do the things I want to do, and have many interests. If you ever come to Middle Tennessee, call me and I'll tell you how to get here. Otherwise, you wouldn't find it and I'd miss the pleasure of your company.

NAN HEACOCK

The books listed are in my own library. Since my research has gone on intermittently over a period of more than thirty years, I cannot list all the other books I have consulted.

Harper's Weekly (52 issues in two bound vols.), 1861, 1862; Headly, J. T., *The Great Rebellion, A History of the Civil War in the United States,* vols. 1, 2, Washington, D.C.: National Tribune, 1898; *Compendium of History and Biography of Cass County, Iowa,* Chicago: Henry Taylor, 1906; Charnwood, Lord, *Abraham Lincoln,* Garden City, N.Y.: Garden City Publishing, 1917; Mencken, H. L., *The American Language,* 4th ed., New York: Alfred A. Knopf, 1937; James, Marquis, *The Life of Andrew Jackson,* Indianapolis: Bobbs-Merrill, 1938; Kouwenhoven, John A., *Adventures of America, 1857-1900, A Pictorial Record from Harper's Weekly,* New York: Harper & Brothers, 1938; Sandburg, Carl, *Abraham Lincoln, The War Years,* 4 vols., New York: Harcourt, Brace & World, 1938; Leech, Margaret, *Reveille in Washington, 1860-1865,* New York: Harper & Brothers, 1941; Beard, Charles A. and Mary, *The Beards' Basic History of the United States,* Garden City, N. Y.: Doubleday, 1944; Woodward, W. E., *The Way Our People Lived,* New York: E. P. Dutton, 1944; Catton, Bruce, *The Army of the Potomac,* 3 vols.,

Garden City, N.Y.: Doubleday, 1952, 1953, 1962; Sloane, Eric, *American Barns and Covered Bridges,* 1954, *Our Vanishing Landscape,* 1955, *American Yesterday,* 1956, New York: Wilfred Funk; McGinnis, R. J., ed., *The Good Old Days,* New York: Harper & Brothers, 1960; Catton, Bruce, *The Centennial History of the Civil War,* 3 vols., Garden City, N.Y.: Doubleday, 1961, 1963, 1965; Morison, Samuel Eliot, *The Oxford History of the American People,* New York: Oxford University Press, 1965; Morris, Richard B., *Encyclopedia of American History,* New York: Harper & Row, 1965.

To
Those who come after me
Lest they forget
Those who went before

PART I

I Take Thee

1 8 5 4

1

W H I L E Castle twisted and fidgeted, Jonathan sat hunched forward, elbows on knees, the lines held loosely in his hands. From time to time he clucked to the horses as they clomped up hill and down, sometimes following a fairly well-defined trail, more often making their way across trackless prairie where Jonathan guided them by nothing more than an occasional squint at the sun. Castle was tired, bone tired. Since dawn they had jounced along in the covered wagon and every jounce hurt her pride more than it hurt her unaccustomed body. The seat was of hardest board with only a narrow strip for a backrest. And the backrest did more harm than good for with every jolt of the wagon it gave her aching back a vicious dig. Twisting again to avoid it she pulled her leghorn bonnet forward to shade her eyes.

"How much farther is it?"

"I don't know."

"When there isn't any road, how do you know where to go?"

"I don't."

She stared at her husband and her black brows drew together like storm clouds. "Do you mean to sit there and tell me you don't know where you're going? Just wandering around? . . . Where is your farm? How can you find it if you don't even know the way?"

"When I see what I want, I'll stop. This country is all open to settlement. I can take what I want wherever I find it."

"Where is the town?"

"We left it this morning. Remember?"

As if she could forget! "I don't mean the town we left. I mean the one we're going to."

He shook his head. "Kanesville is the only town of any size in this part of

3

the state.[1] Fort Des Moines is the nearest settlement this side of Dubuque and Dubuque is over on the Mississippi.''[2]

Castle gave an impatient flounce. "I don't know what you're talking about. There have to be towns!"

"None you would recognize as such. There are a few settlements, but I have no desire to live in any of them."

"Well, we can't live right out in the middle of this . . . wilderness!"

"Why not?" Jonathan turned to look at his wife. Above the black beard his lips smiled and his black eyes danced. "I'll build you a cabin—you'll have a roof over your head. You may not like it but it'll be the only roof for miles around so you'll have no less than your neighbors."

"There'll be neighbors?"

"Very few and widely scattered. We've seen a couple of cabins. That smoke to your left is either a cabin or an Indian campfire."

"Indians? They'll scalp us!"

He chuckled. "I doubt it. The Pottawattamies are a shiftless, harmless lot from what I've been able to learn about them. Don't worry. That's a cabin. Too much smoke for an Indian fire."

Castle dismissed the Indians. "You still haven't told me where we're going."

"Truthfully, my dear, I really don't know. Certain things are necessary: the soil, the right lay of the land, water and timber. A house can be changed, moved, replaced, but you can't change land and water. The farm I buy now we'll have to live on and work for the rest of our lives. If I make a poor choice now we'll have to work harder for a poorer living. So, however far we have to go, however long it takes, I want to be sure I find the right place."

"But I want to live where there are people and . . . and . . . "

"Then you shouldn't have asked me to bring you to Iowa." Jonathan smiled at her and Castle flushed.

"You're no gentleman!" she accused angrily.

"Did I say I was?" he asked innocently. "But then you're no lady."

"I am so!"

"Are you, Miss Castle?"

She didn't trouble to answer. She'd settle that score later. This was not the time or the place. She searched the prairie for some sign of life. The smoke, whatever its origin, was out of sight now and there was no other evidence of habitation. Were there no towns? Would they really be miles from anyone in this emptiness?

Western Iowa is a land of rolling hills, some a little higher, some a little lower, but few too steep for the plow. Nowhere are there the monotonous levels of the tablelands, for the landscape rises and falls like the swell of some gigantic sea. The soil is deep and generous, the many streams clear and cool, most of them edged with timber. In winter the snow lies long and heavily upon the face of the land and the wind whips down from the north in a cold fury. But in summer the days are long and hot. And when heat waves dance in the noonday sun, the corn shoots up inches overnight.

It was spring when Castle and Jonathan Gayle first saw the rolling hills of Iowa; the snow was gone and the prairie grass was turning from brown to green. Yet in Kanesville that morning there had been a nip in the air. Now, well past noon, the sun was warm, almost too warm. And Castle was hungry. She had been hungry all day. They had spent the night at a dreary clapboard hotel with dingy sheets and lumpy bed. Breakfast had been hasty and scanty. The cold food Jonathan had brought for their nooning had been greasy and tasteless, a poor substitute for the piping hot dinners at Homeplace.

When they dressed that morning, Jonathan had packed his black broadcloth and donned coarse baggy pants and a cheap blue shirt, well-worn boots, a shabby vest, and a rough, ill-fitting jacket. He looked like a common day laborer. . . . Only he didn't. Castle studied her husband for a moment. Somehow the way he held his head, the careless ease of his big body, the neatly brushed hair and beard, the level look of his dark eyes were not "common." Yet what a picture they must have made leaving town in the covered wagon: buckets and pots dangling under and around, a coop of squawking chickens tied on the back, and an angular yellow cow trailing behind. Luckily few people had been about at that ungodly hour and the few men they had passed had taken no notice of them.

In the weeks since her marriage Castle's whole world, her whole concept of life as it should be lived, had been turned topsy-turvy. For Mallory Castle Talbot was the older granddaughter of Major Hunter Talbot, owner of one of the largest and best glasshouses in the Pittsburgh area. Though the major was an army man with a game leg, acquired at the battle of New Orleans, his brother, Captain Timothy Talbot, was a man of the river — owner of a fleet of steamboats plying both the Ohio and Mississippi rivers.[4] With his headquarters in St. Louis he made frequent trips up to Pittsburgh and down to New Orleans, and wherever he went he sold Talbot glass, carried on Talbot steamboats.

As a child, Castle had often gone to the glasshouse with Major Hunter and sometimes one or another of the glassblowers had made her some fragile toy of spun glass. The engraved goblets and cutglass bowls that graced the Major's table were so much a part of her daily life, it never occurred to her that they were both beautiful and valuable. As commonplace to her as silver, china, and linen, it never entered her head that the world was largely populated by people who did not drink from Talbot crystal. That she had only begun to learn on the trip to Iowa.

If she had known how far it would be . . . what the journey would be like. . . . But she hadn't had the foggiest notion. Nor had the trip from Pittsburgh to St. Louis on the big Talbot riverboat given her any inkling of what was in store for her, for the boat had been the last word in luxury and elegance; there had even been a neat little mulatto maid to help her into her hoops and stays, button her up the back, and do her long, heavy hair.

But the boat from St. Louis to Kanesville had been small and stuffy, devoid of either luxury or elegance. In addition to a few other passengers, it had carried a varied assortment of freight, including several pens of hogs as well as Jonathan's team. Nor had there been a maid, so she had been forced to dress without assistance except that her husband had buttoned her up the back. But sometimes he had gone up on deck before she had finished dressing and then she could only wait in the cramped smelly cabin until he remembered and came to her rescue.

She had wanted to give him a piece of her mind more than once! That she had not done so was due largely to the fact that this new husband of hers was still something of a stranger. As yet she was not at all sure she would come off winner in a battle with him. Too, flying into a screaming, shouting rage in a more or less public place was something she had never done and could not do. At Homeplace, with only the family and servants about, she had shrieked and thrown things with gusto and abandon whenever she was annoyed, knowing full well that her conduct would be carefully ignored by the entire household and under no circumstances mentioned outside the walls of the sprawling white house. Certainly not beyond the grounds! This present situation was something else, and whatever her grievances against Jonathan, they must wait until a more propitious time.

She sighed, too engrossed in her own thoughts to be aware of the searching look her husband gave her. So far Jonathan had been more amused than annoyed by his wife's frequent and obvious efforts to hold her tongue and swallow her temper. He had been warned and knew better than to expect that her present docility was permanent. There would be explosions and he would deal with them when they came. He was more troubled by her long sullen and abstract silences. What went on in that agile brain of hers when she sat staring blankly into space? He reminded himself that she had been too much alone those years she had spent in her room pining for her lost love; in the same breath he wondered if even now she might still be grieving for the dainty fop who had jilted her in her youth.

Jonathan had known few women and none of them well. No woman had ever stirred him as Castle did. It was a strange feeling, a feeling he did not understand and could not repress, and it troubled him. He found it difficult to talk to her and since he feared to say too much, he said too little and that almost gruffly. Every time he touched her, or even her billowing skirts, the rush of emotion that swept over him left him all but gasping. He had no intention of making an ass of himself. Pitfalls enough in the sudden and unpremeditated marriage without that. Not that he regretted his marriage — far from it. But neither was he blinded by his wife's beauty, if beauty it might be called.

While he filled and lighted his pipe he surveyed his wife as she sat beside him, stiffly uneasy, her unseeing eyes gazing ahead across the prairie. Under her bonnet the copper colored hair framed a triangular face with brows like raven wings above hazel eyes which, in anger, were almost as yellow as a cat's. The red mouth, too wide and too full, turned downward at the corners in lines of bitterness. The skin of her face and neck, always carefully shielded from the sun, was not white but almost olive. Here was none of the ethereal fragility of Miss Sarah, her gentle, ineffectual little mother, nor the glowing pink and white and gold of Marybelle, her younger sister. In the drawing room of the wide, porticoed house at Homeplace,

Major Hunter had shown Jonathan the portrait of his long dead and greatly loved wife where it hung above the mantel.

"In looks, Castle resembles Miss Mallory, but I'm afraid she's more like me." The old man shook his head ruefully. "I spoiled her. I couldn't help myself. She so reminded me . . ." He ran his hand through the lion's mane of white hair. "She was a girl-child, how could I be hard on her? I had lost my son, her father. . . . Then that young whippersnapper . . ." The cane he carried to ease his game leg thumped the floor. "You know how it is. If a young man is disappointed in love he can drown his sorrow properly, or run away to sea. But a young lady. . . . She spent eleven years in that room of hers and if it was hard on her, it was harder on the rest of us! Aunt Lucy was the only person who could ever do anything with her." Turning he laid a strong wrinkled hand on Jonathan's arm. "There's good stuff in the girl. There has to be!" The old man chuckled and his eyes danced. "Think you're man enough, my boy?"

"I'm man enough," Jonathan had told him. He hoped he would be.

Castle twisted and hunched her shoulders, straightened and shook herself, and Jonathan realized his pipe had gone out. Stopping the team at the top of a rise he studied the scene about them while the great grey horses rested and blew the dust from their nostrils. He knocked out his pipe, shaved tobacco from the plug, and refilled and lighted it. This was all good country; the virgin soil waited to be plowed and planted. Any part of it would be a good farm. Then he shook his head at his own thoughts. No, not yet. He knew what he wanted and it would be folly to settle for less. He would need fields for hay and grain and pasture for his stock; there must be ample running water; and no farm was complete without a proper woodlot. All these were necessary and all must be grouped for easy accessibility. Two days — a week — did it matter? He had waited all his life and come nearly half way across the world, why should he hurry now? Within a few days he would choose the spot that would be his home. There he would till his fields and raise his family. For Jonathan wanted children — sons — as he wanted land. His wife would not find the new life easy, but she was young and strong and healthy and he was sure she had capacities and powers she had never been called on to use. Heretofore her energy and ability had been throttled, stifled in the attempt to fit her to the fixed pattern of a society lady — for her an unnatural pattern and one to which she had never been able to conform.

The red sun dropped behind the hills and left the western sky glowing pink and amber. Jonathan guided the team among the trees bordering a small stream and brought them to a stop.

"We'll camp here for the night," he said as he swung down over the wheel. "You may as well make up the bed in the back of the wagon while I unhitch and take care of the stock."

Castle stiffened and stared at him in unbelief. "You don't mean . . . sleep here?"

He was unbuckling the harness. "We won't find a better place tonight. It's past sundown."

She had no answer. Never had she heard of respectable people spending a night in the woods. Hunters and trappers and runaway slaves from across the Ohio, yes, but decent people slept at home in their beds or visited friends or relatives.

"Your feather bed and the quilts are behind you on that chest," Jonathan continued as he pulled the collar from the near horse. "Better get the bed made while you can see. It'll be dark by the time we've had supper."

"You're telling *me* to make the bed?" Castle was incredulous. "I've never made a bed in my life! I'm no servant."

"No, that you aren't. But I was under the impression you were my wife."

"Wife! I'd certainly never know it!"

"Apparently not. So far you haven't done much to earn the title." With that he turned and led the team through the woods to the stream.

She stared after him indignantly. Fine husband he'd turned out to be! Dragging her all over the country, that awful boat, that horrid hotel, and now this disgusting covered wagon. Even expecting her to sleep in the woods and telling her to make the bed!

When Jonathan returned with the horses slobbering almost on his shoulder, Castle was still sitting stiff and straight on the wagon seat. He staked the horses then held a hand up to her.

"Get down. You aren't accomplishing anything there. I have to milk and feed. You can gather firewood."

With her husband's assistance she climbed down, though every muscle protested each movement. She shook herself and tried to limber her arms and legs while Jonathan untied the chicken coop, set it beside the wagon, and gave the hens corn and water. He led the cow to the stream and when he returned Castle was standing where he had left her.

"What about some wood?" He asked impatiently. "Surely you can pick up a few sticks. You'd be better off to move around."

"I won't pick up sticks! Cookie never carried a stick of wood in her life and why should I? If I'm not as good as she was . . ."

"Cookie had work to do. Cooking for the family and a house full of servants is a big job and there are always a couple of little black boys around to carry wood. The more wood they carry, the less mischief they get into. You'll only have to cook for two and for a while we'll be eating very simply. There'll be no little black boys to carry wood and I'll have work of my own to do. If you expect to eat regularly, there may be times when you'll have to bring in a few sticks yourself."

"I won't! And if I picked up sticks now I'd soil my hands and tear my skirts."

"You tore your skirt getting out of the wagon. Tomorrow, put on one of the calicos."

"Calico! How you talk. As if I'd wear calico!" She was wearing her new buff mull and it was a pity she'd torn it. Now she wouldn't be able to wear it again and she had few enough gowns. The others she had worn on the trip from Pittsburgh had been hastily remodeled relics of her youth and none would ever be worn again as the silk was old and splitting along the folds and gathers. There hadn't been time for her and Aunt Lucy to make a proper number of gowns. Just as soon as they were settled she'd have to do some sewing. . . . What had he said?

"What did you say? What do you mean, 'one of the calicos'?"

"I explained to Miss Sarah and Aunt Lucy that silk would be unsuitable for everyday wear in this country. Since there wasn't time for additional fittings, Aunt Lucy ran up a few calicos by the same measurements as the gown you're wearing. I hope your trousseau meets with your approval."

"How dared you go behind my back?" She stamped her foot but the slipper was thin and the ground rough. "I wouldn't be caught dead in calico!"

"I hope you won't be caught dead in them, but you'll wear calico gowns or run around in your petticoats. In your trunk are just two more black silks and two alpacas."

"You're a skunk!"

"Even so, you may as well take off your bonnet. You're staying the night—I hope."

Jonathan crouched with his head against the cow's flank and squirted milk into the pail while Bossey ate her supper. Castle moved off around the wagon and he called, "Don't go far. I haven't time to look for you if you get lost."

Castle had no intention of going far enough to get lost. She wanted to get in the wagon and look in her trunk, but she couldn't get back up without help. Calico? Impossible! Aunt Lucy would have refused to make them. Yet if he had told the truth, she would have to wear them. How long would two silks last? The mull was torn and the alpacas were winter gowns. The contemptible cur! She moved to the edge of the woods and sat on a fallen log. It was almost dark. If she stayed there, he'd think she was lost and he'd have to look for her.

Jonathan didn't look for her. The animals cared for and the bed made, he built a fire, put corn pone in one spider and side meat in another, and wedged the coffee pot between them. Castle endured it as long as she could but the aroma of coffee and side meat was too much for her empty stomach. By the time supper was ready, she was waiting by the fire. Jonathan poured the coffee into tin cups and dished up the food in two pie tins.

"Sit down on that stump before you spill something. And tomorrow, put on a calico and leave off those hoops. You'll have to learn to help."

"I won't leave off my hoops! A lady is never seen outside her chamber without hoops and stays."

"Who do you think would see you out here?"

"*You* would!"

"Why should it matter if I saw you without hoops?"

"You're a man, aren't you?"

For a moment he studied her. "You'll find that I am."

With her bonnet hanging down her back and her slippers tucked under her skirts, Castle balanced cup and plate—food had never been more welcome. When she asked for a second cup of coffee her husband shook his head.

"It might keep you awake this late in the evening. We'll be making an early start and you need your rest."

She rose, set her cup and plate on the stump, and swept over to the fire where she picked up the pot and poured her own coffee. Jonathan might make her wear calico but he wasn't going to keep her from having as much coffee as she wanted. Nor did she admit that the handle of the pot had reddened her palm. Back on the stump she sipped her coffee, then sniffed uneasily.

"Must you tie the cow and horses so close to the wagon?"

"Wouldn't it be foolish to give them to the Indians?"

"Indians? Here?"

He shrugged. "Who knows where they are? Until recently this was their hunting ground. They're in the habit of roaming about as they please.[5] They could turn up anytime, anyplace." He sat on his heels by the fire, the light flickering across his dark bearded face as he bent to stir the coals and add wood.

"What if Indians stole the horses?"

"We'd walk. But the stock is safe as long as they're staked within rifle range of the wagon. You'd better go on to bed. You've had a hard day and tomorrow will be no better."

"But it just got dark!"

"And it won't be light when we get up in the morning." He spoke with his pipe between his teeth while he shaved tobacco to fill it. "I want to be on the trail by sunup. I'll come to bed as soon as I finish my pipe. Come, I'll give you a hand up."

He set her foot on his knee and took her hand, showed her where to step and how to hold, and up she went over the tailgate. She would not have believed she could do such a thing but it had been rather fun and Jonathan had done his part very cleverly. Only a faint light from the campfire filtered through the canvas wagon cover, but as soon as Jonathan turned away, Castle opened her trunk. If she couldn't see, she could still feel. The things she would need for the trip had been packed on top and she had not bothered to look further. Now she pawed down and down: night dresses; chemise; petticoats; silk—two bodices, two skirts; alpaca—the same; calico. Calico!

She pulled and tugged until she dragged out a garment and took it to the opening at the back of the wagon where the light from the fire touched the grey print. Without a doubt, calico. Aunt Lucy had made it as though it were the finest silk because only the best was fitting for a lady. How could she be a lady in a calico gown? Aunt Lucy would be so shamed! Castle closed the trunk and sat wearily on the bed her husband had made. Her shoulder blades felt raw, her back ached, her limbs ached. She ached all over. Amanda used to rub her before she went to sleep. What was she doing now? And Aunt Lucy and Miss Sarah and Major Hunter? They didn't love her or they wouldn't have permitted her to marry Jonathan and leave home!

She struggled painfully out of her clothes, peeling off one onionlike layer after another. Once in her nightdress she gave herself to the comfort of the feather bed. At long last her tired body was still, but her mind would not rest. If only . . . if only . . . if only dear, dear Garland hadn't run off with that trashy little Griselda! And after their glorious engagement ball and her trousseau from Philadelphia and all the parties and dinners and dances. . . . She had been so happy when she thought she was going to marry. Garland.

The morning of her wedding day she had set out gaily, envied she was sure by every girl she knew, for she was seventeen and was marrying Garland Delacroix, the richest and handsomest young man in all Allegheny County. Old Isaac had polished the harness buckles until they sparkled in the sun and the carriage was like a mirror. As the horses pranced down the drive the servants had gathered to see them off. Then in the palm-banked church she had waited with her bridesmaids while the guests whispered and rustled in anticipation. Waited until the girls' happy chatter fell to uneasy silence and the guests craned their necks curiously. Waited endlessly and grew faint with long standing in her too-tight stays. Waited while a gnawing dread tore at her vitals. Then at last when she could have borne no more, a spindly little boy in a ragged straw hat brought the Major a note. She had not dared to ask what it said, for the Major, his face grey, turned to her without a word, without even giving the boy a penny. Sick with bewilderment and humiliation she had allowed him to lead her back to the carriage.

And now she was waiting for her husband, a black-bearded stranger whom she scarcely knew. Her marriage to Jonathan and the preceding two weeks of their engagement were a kaleidoscope, much of it fuzzy around the edges. But one incident stood out: the row over the servants. Quietly but firmly antislavery, Major Hunter had staffed his house with Negroes he had bought and freed. Manse had been the first. He had found the Major on the New Orleans battlefield and after carrying him to the dressing station he had stayed to care for him at the risk of being taken as a runaway slave. That threat had been averted when Manse's owner was paid a whopping price for him. By the time Major Hunter was able to travel, Manse had lined up a few other purchases for his new master and Old Isaac, his wife Aunt Lucy, and her small daughter Callie had been added to the entourage. Later on a trip downriver with the Major and Captain Tim, Manse had found a girl he could not live without, and at Homeplace his new wife had taken charge of the kitchen, muttering, "Kin see dis hyur fambly needs fattin'n up!" And she had been doing her best at it ever since. Then, long years afterwards, in Memphis on a business trip the Major had inadvertently passed the slave auction and seen eight-year-old Amanda weeping on the block. He had brought her home and put two-year-old Castle in her arms. "She's yours, girl. Take care of her." And Amanda had taken care of her. Until Castle married Jonathan.

During the mad two weeks of her engagement, Castle had given considerable thought to the question of which of the servants she wanted to take with her, or rather, which she might inveigle into going with her. Amanda, of course. That required no consideration. Nor did the older ones. Wild horses could not drag them from Homeplace. But she had grown up with their children and grandchildren. Some had played with her and Amanda, some with Marybelle. Which ones did she want, which ones might be willing to leave their homes and families? . . . Then one evening Jonathan and the Major were discussing plans for the trip and the Major said he had told Captain Tim to arrange passage for Castle and Jonathan. Castle asked how the servants were to travel and was told that they would not. Not any of them. Not even Amanda. Though Iowa was a Free State, there as everywhere Negroes would be suspect and too many slave catchers were anxious to collect the rewards for runaways—or better yet, catch a nonrunaway who could be sold down the river to the deep South. Around Pittsburgh the Talbot Negroes were well known and no slave catcher would dare lay a hand on one of them. But in Iowa they would be strangers among strangers, fair game for anyone out to make a grab. Nor would Jonathan be prepared to provide for them at the outset of his venture in a new and unsettled country. So Castle and Jonathan would go alone and servantless.

Castle had argued and coaxed and wept in despair but both men had been obdurate. She would have called off the wedding then and there only it would have been too embarrassing. Besides, the Major would not have stood for it. He not only wanted her married, he had taken a fancy to Jonathan. So on the morning of their departure she and Jonathan had stood together in the drawing room with Anne and Bob Middleton as matron of honor and best man, while the rector of St. Stephen's united them in the bonds of holy matrimony in the presence of Miss Sarah, Major Hunter, Marybelle, and all the servants. No guests had been invited to the wedding breakfast, and though it broke Cookie's heart, the wedding cake had been a simple three-tiered affair but iced within an inch of its life. At parting, Amanda had wept in Castle's arms and Aunt Lucy had held her close while tears ran down her wrinkled black cheeks. Then straightening her shoulders, "Lamb, youah husban' a-waitin'," and hiding her face in her white apron she had turned away. Praise be, Aunt Lucy would never know she had slept in a covered wagon out in the woods!

When she opened her eyes Castle thought the wagon seemed darker than before and propping herself on her elbow she looked out the back. Jonathan was hunched by the fire poking his pipe with a twig. What would he do when he came to bed tonight? So far he had done nothing, sleeping beside her as though he were alone. But tonight he had looked at her . . . so . . . when he said she would find he was a man. She wriggled and squirmed. Would he kiss her? Make love to her? Say pretty things like a gentlemen in the novels Anne Middleton had read to her? She wasn't sure she wanted him to kiss her, though she had liked it when Garland kissed her. And a few of the other young men. Only nice girls didn't kiss—very often. She wondered what nice wives did, and snuggled deeper into the feather bed. Then she heard her husband clear his throat and knock out his pipe. He'd be coming . . .

His bulk loomed in the doorway at the back of the wagon. He came in carelessly, undressed as casually as though there were no witness to his disrobing, then climbed into the bed as though no wife lay there. A moment later he turned and covered her mouth with his. No man had ever kissed her like that and she struggled instinctively. Jonathan held her and the fight drained away leaving her limp and yielding. Never again would she doubt that he was a man and her husband. His hard thighs were hot against her cool flesh, his hard arms held her fiercely. Her hands brushed his shoulders and found them smooth as satin, but his hairy chest was horrid. She touched him curiously, gingerly, frightened and shamed by the pounding of her heart and the hot flood sweeping over her.

This was not love as Anne's novels had painted it. Her mother had warned her that a wife must "submit" to her husband's peculiarities, however reluctantly, lest he take up with some "common" woman who actually enjoyed those things. If Jonathan guessed that she liked his love making, would he think her common? Yet how could she behave like a lady and merely submit gracefully when she was slipping into a deep and timeless void?

Later he kissed her again, then rolled over and was soon snoring. She was disappointed and disillusioned. In the novels the gentlemen were so charming, so gallant, and they always made such pretty speeches. Jonathan hadn't said he loved her or that she was beautiful or an angel. He hadn't said anything at all. If he didn't love her, why . . . ?

"Jonathan, Jonathan!" she whispered close to his ear. "Jonathan, why didn't you *say* anything?"

"Huh? Uh? Oh! What is it?" He rose on his elbow only half awake.

"You didn't say you love me . . . or anything."

"Good God, woman! This is no time for fancy phrases. Go to sleep! It'll soon be morning."

"But why . . . did you . . . if you don't love me?"

"I married you, didn't I?" Jonathan dropped back on the pillow. "Someday I'll tell you, but not tonight. Go to sleep."

They were rolling by sunup, jouncing along on the hard board seat with the backrest rubbing Castle's shoulders. A rifle stood propped against the seat and on the floor lay another gun with a longer barrel. Several times rabbits darted ahead of the team but Jonathan ignored them.

"Why don't you shoot a rabbit?" Castle asked. "We could have it for supper."

He shook his head. "It's the breeding season. They aren't fit to eat."

"Why do you have two guns?"

He threw her an amused glance. "The one on the floor is old Betsy, my varmint gun. She's a smooth bore muzzle-loader and she'll take a charge to stop an elephant. This," he patted the blue barrel by his knee, "is the finest rifle money can buy, made by a master smith. It'll take the eye out of a rabbit as far as I can see the critter. For bear or wolf I'd use Betsy. For food I'll use the rifle so the meat isn't damaged. When our house is built, Betsy will hang over the door—just in case she's ever needed in a hurry. She'll always be loaded and I'll change the charge often enough to keep it dry. But old Betsy is tricky. In an emergency she might save your life, but she'd just as soon kill you as a bear. The rifle is safe enough if you know how to handle it, but until you do, let them both alone. Never touch either of them unless you're in real danger.''

Castle eyed the long barrel suspiciously. "As if I'd go near the silly things!''

''Don't—unless it's necessary.'' Then he smiled. "You'll have plenty of rabbit this fall. We won't have meat until we raise it. Meanwhile, we'll eat game. I hope you'll like it.''

All that day and the next and the next—for a full week—they traveled, eating by campfires and sleeping in the wagon. Miles and miles they rambled on, a few times coming close enough to some settler's house for Castle to take in some of the details: log cabins or soddies; rail fences enclosing barn lots; sallow women in hoopless calico, patched and faded; men lean and hungry looking, their faces as worn as their clothing. And always swarms of children. The settlers and their houses were as depressing as the vacant land. Surely where they were going there would be respectable people, ladies and gentlemen, not just riffraff.

Then, at last, coming over a rise Jonathan stopped the team. As a man returning from a long journey recognizes the lineaments of the "hills of home'' from a distance, so Jonathan saw and knew as from long acquaintance that place which would be his own. The clean, flowing creek, the small grove of hardwoods, the gentle undulation of the land, all were as he had known they should be. Letting the horses blow he filled his pipe and studied the scene that lay spread out before him. The house there, on a spot high enough and far enough from the creek for good drainage. Behind it and nearer the creek would be the place for the stock barn he would build— eventually. The well should be near the back door, the corncrib and granary near the stable. There would be ample space for all the necessary outbuildings. Along the creek was plentiful pasture where the stock would have water year around. Beyond the creek was a long, easy north slope where he would plant his orchard, with a row of hives along the fence. And surrounding it all would be the fields for corn and wheat and oats and hay. Yes, here was his home—the home for which he had worked and waited and come so far: across an ocean and over the rivers and mountains and plains of half a continent. But none of that mattered now. He had come home.

2

C A S T L E sat on a slab bench in front of the cabin that had been her home for the past week. Behind the house was a stream bordered by a stand of tall trees, but from where she sat there was nothing whatever to see but the prairie rolling away to the horizon under a sky of cloudless blue. This was what she had come to! For this she had traveled long, miserable miles and longer, more miserable days and weeks. Jonathan had finally made his choice and they had camped in the wagon while he cut the logs for the cabin; then men had come from all around to lay up the log walls and set the roof poles in place. Afterward Jonathan had laid the thatch since he was the only one who knew how. With the roof completed he had put down the puncheon floor and built the overtall stick-and-clay chimney that stuck up like a sore thumb at one end of the cabin. He had made the furniture, too: a prairie bed of willow poles, a table of hewn slabs, four splint-bottom chairs, and the shelves in the corner to hold their food and pots and pans. A heavy timber formed the mantel over the fireplace and along one wall was a row of pegs for their clothes. The bench by the door had been intended for the washpan and water bucket so that Jonathan could wash up outside in summer, but Castle had taken immediate possession and while her husband went about his work she spread her calico skirts on the bench and dreamed of better days—specifically, the day of the Middleton Ball.

She had lived the day over and over and still did not know what had set the Major off like a firecracker that night. In the afternoon he had found Amanda crying in the hall—the silly ninny—and thumped his cane and shouted. But the Major thumped and shouted as easily as he breathed and it meant little more. As she had been kicking Amanda's shins since the two of them raced with the hounds and the other black children, why make a fuss about it on that particular day? Could it have had something to do with Marybelle? That was equally incredible, for Marybelle had always come home for the Middleton Ball and when she arrived she always made a duty call on Castle—two minutes and a sisterly peck—and that was the last they saw of each other until the whole thing was repeated when Marybelle left to go back to Baltimore. So what could Marybelle have to do with the Major's explosion? Besides, Marybelle's husband, Drew Coleman, hadn't come and Susan and Rebecca had stayed at home with him, which Castle had considered a blessing, so there had been no occasion for her to yell at them to get out of her room. Miss Sarah and the Major always made such a to-do over the little beasts, but Castle loathed them. Even more than she had loathed their mother at that age. Nothing was sacred to them, not even her room. *She* had no children, why should she be pestered by her sister's brats? Of course, if she'd had Garland's two sons she could have taken Marybelle down a peg. She had overheard her mother telling Marybelle the boys looked just like

15

Garland. Drat Miss Sarah anyway! She and Marybelle had always chattered like magpies.

From the time Marybelle came home the two of them had been closeted in the sewing room with Aunt Lucy, making the gown Marybelle was to wear to the ball that night. Catch *her* making such a fuss over a bit of sewing! But Marybelle had always been clumsy as a cow with a needle. Aunt Lucy had never been able to teach her the first thing about proper sewing. Castle would gladly have made the stupid gown for her sister just to show her how it should be done, but if she had, everyone would have thought she had forgotten Garland. It wasn't right and it wasn't fair. Marybelle was much too pretty for a married woman with two children. Marybelle always had been much too pretty, all dressed up in frills and ruffles like an overgrown doll, while Castle's hair had been slicked back in tight braids, her gowns ugly dark blue or brown pinafores, just because Miss Sarah and Aunt Lucy said she was a tom-boy and didn't take care of her clothes. But it was Marybelle who would go to the Middleton Ball while her elder sister sat at home twiddling her thumbs. If only she could go! If only she could see Garland again! But she couldn't face him and hear him say, "Miss Castle, I want you to meet my wife," and see that prissy Griselda hanging on his arm. Never! Not if she lived and died right in her own room! And that was how it would be, for they were at every party, every picnic, every sociable. She couldn't even go calling on her friends without the possibility that Garland would walk in with Griselda. And never, never, never would she look at or speak to Griselda!

Rather than risk such an encounter she had closeted herself in her room from the day old Manse had carried her up the wide stairs in her bridal gown and laid her on the high tester bed, her bridal veil trailing the floor—the veil Mallory Page had worn and which Castle had afterwards ripped to shreds and thrown in the fire. She had not even left her room when Marybelle and Drew were married. When it was over, Marybelle had kissed her goodbye in her room. Why Drew had married her and how he could stand to live with her was too much to figure out. Likely he'd stayed at home to have a little peace and quiet and his important business was just an excuse.

As always, Castle was sitting in her favorite chair by her one un-shuttered window when Miss Sarah slipped in quietly and spoke in tones reserved for the hopelessly afflicted.

"I've been neglecting you, dear . . . we've been so busy . . . Marybelle's gown, you know . . . would you like to see it? . . . Shall I bring the Bible and read to you a while?" Some of Miss Sarah's Bible stories were almost as good as Anne's novels, but Castle was in no mood for stories so she merely ignored her mother's suggestion. "I was going to take a nap, but I'm afraid I'm not very sleepy. . . . We're having supper early. When you're through with her, would you mind if Amanda helps Marybelle dress? Amanda is so clever and Marybelle's maid is new and not very well trained."

Castle continued to gaze out the window while Miss Sarah sat perched on the edge of her chair as though poised for flight. She was never quite sure when it was safe to sit in the presence of her elder daughter.

"Perhaps I'd better go . . . there's so much to do . . . the ball . . .''
She rose and shaking down her skirts straightened her slight body and
drifted from the room as quietly as she had come, closing the door carefully
behind her.

Later Amanda brought Castle's supper tray and put it on the table
beside her chair. "Kin Ah git yuh sumpun else, Miss Castle?'' Castle un-
covered the dishes and sniffed disdainfully. "Hit awright, ain' hit?''

"I should send it back to the kitchen! Though I suppose I wouldn't get
anything any better.''

"No'm, not t'night yuh wun't,'' Amanda agreed and withdrew hastily.

Castle attacked the tray with relish. One disadvantage of having her
meals in her room was the difficulty of getting second helpings. She was well
under way when Major Hunter knocked and without waiting for the invitation
he knew he would not receive, came in tapping his cane jauntily.

"Good evening, my dear. Having your supper early, I see. Quite right.
You'll need plenty of time to dress.''

"Dress?'' Castle echoed between bites.

"Certainly. For the ball.''

"You know perfectly well I'm not going.''

Major Hunter fingered his cigar. Castle hated cigar smoke in her room.
No use getting off to a bad start this time. "Why not go? Do you good. See
your friends. Get out of that ridiculous black stuff you wear.''

"My mourning?'' Castle touched the high collar of her black silk gown,
ran a hand down the long sleeve. "And what do you suppose people would
say if I left off mourning and went to a ball?''

"They'd forget your . . . er . . . unhappy love affair if you'd give them
a chance. Come, come, girl! Isn't it time you had done with this nonsense?
Get dressed and come to the ball with Marybelle and me.'' He slipped the
cigar back in his waistcoat pocket. Later.

"People forget? How can *I* forget?''

The Major strode the length of the room, the cane that eased his game
leg making only a muffled thump on the thick carpet. Those who knew him
well could judge his temper by the sound of his cane, and had Castle been
listening she might have been warned. At the far window he folded the
shutter in and looked out across the garden and tree-shadowed lawn.

"A man is at a disadvantage with a lady. He can horsewhip a low-down
scoundrel of a man, or he can shoot a gentleman who isn't a gentleman. But
what does he do with an ill-tempered harridan who is a fool?'' Turning from
the window he swung back toward his granddaughter. "Castle, you've not
only immolated yourself for your stubborn pride, but you're sacrificing the
rest of us as well. For years you've behaved abominably and your conduct
grows worse every day. Your treatment of your mother is intolerable and
your mistreatment of Amanda is insufferable. The situation cannot continue.
I have a duty to the other members of this household.'' He stood facing her,
his feet planted, his cane clasped before him in both hands, his head with its
shock of white hair bent above her. "I want you to go to the Middleton Ball
tonight.'' His voice made the statement a command.

"Well, I won't, so there!" Castle drank her coffee with an air of indifference, but her eyes were yellow and her black brows were drawn together.

"Young lady, *you are going!*" the Major thundered. "I've had enough of your mooning around like a lovesick calf!" Her head snapped up but he continued before she could speak. "You're a fool! A stupid, brainless fool! The whole miserable affair was your own fault in the first place!"

"What *are* you talking about?"

"You know what I'm talking about! I know the whole disgraceful story! You tricked that young nincompoop into proposing and then tried to drag him to the altar. Because he got away you're bound to spend the rest of your life a sour old maid!"

Castle drew herself up indignantly. "This is a fine time for you to disapprove of my engagement to Garland!"

"Disapprove, bah! Would I have approved had I known you threw yourself at his head? Didn't Miss Sarah or Aunt Lucy ever tell you that no young lady ever accepts a gentleman until he has declared himself at least three times? To think that a granddaughter of mine . . ."

"Can I help it I'm your granddaughter?"

"None of your impertinence, Miss! Haven't you sense enough to know I'd have shot that young whelp if his father — God rest his soul — hadn't informed me of your trickery? Haven't you the wit to know that MY honor was involved? How can I hold my head up with you pining for a man who never loved you? I won't be shamed to my grave by an old maid granddaughter. It's a woman's duty to marry and bring up a family and that's what you're going to do!" The cane pounded the floor in an echoing crescendo as the old man roared out his ultimatum. "If you can't find youself a husband, I'll find one for you. And by God, you'll marry him! Now get dressed. You're going to the Middleton Ball if I have to drag you bodily in your chemise!"

Castle leaped up so suddenly her hoops caught on the arm of the chair. Jerking free she faced her grandfather. "All right! I'll go to the damned ball!" she shouted, her face livid. "I'll go to the ball and I'll marry the first man who asks me — even if he's a nigger!"

Major Hunter slammed out of the room and Castle plopped back in her chair, her clenched fists pounding the arms. She had loved Garland so . . . and he had told on her, the sneaky tattletale! The Major had known it all the time. . . . Oh, horrors! If Garland had told his father, he might have told Griselda — and anybody and everybody! No, no, of course not. He wouldn't. Garland was a gentleman. . . . How dared Major Hunter talk to her like that? She'd show him! He couldn't call *her* a sour old maid! She'd go to the ball and she'd get married . . .

"Amanda! Amanda! Where is that dumb darkey? AMANDA!"

"Ah's comin', Miss Castle. Ah's comin'."

"Coming, coming! I want you *here!* Get my gown. I'm going to the ball!"

Amanda gaped incredulously at mention of the ball. "Ball? Whut ball, Miss Castle?"

"The Middleton Ball, numbskull! Get my gown and hurry up about it."

"You ain' got no ball gown, Miss Castle. You ain' had no ball gown made sin Lawd know when."

Castle stood in the middle of the floor while her hands pushed at the knot of hair on the back of her neck. The girl was right. She had no ball gown. The gowns she'd worn as a girl hung in the dressing room, but they would be hopelessly out of fashion. Certainly she couldn't whip up a ball gown in a couple of hours. Why, Aunt Lucy and Marybelle and Miss Sarah had been working for weeks on Marybelle's gown. . . . Marybelle's gown!

"In the sewing room," she told Amanda. "My new gown is in the sewing room. Go on! Get a move on!" Amanda stood with her mouth open, eyes rolling. "Simpleton!" Castle shouted and reached for something to throw. Amanda ducked and ran. Silly thing. Of course it was Marybelle's gown and Marybelle would be furious. But she had other gowns and she was already married. Amanda was to help Marybelle. . . . Well, Amanda could dress her first and she'd be out of the house before Marybelle missed the gown.

Chemise, stays, hoops, and ten stiffly starched petticoats. Amanda did her hair with little curls at the sides and a chignon on her neck. Rather youthful, but very fetching. Then the gown. Evidently Marybelle had copied it from the portrait of Miss Mallory for this was the same shade of greenish gold, quite perfect for Castle, though it would have been wasted on Marybelle. The skirt was draped and puffed—what was Marybelle thinking of? She had plumped up since the girls were born and she always had been as dumpy as a meal sack with a string around the middle. Castle had the height to carry it. She glanced down. The skirt was a good three inches too short.

"Push the bodice down, Amanda. Can't you see it's up too high? It makes the skirt too short."

"You got hips, Miss Castle."

"Bother my hips! Get that skirt down where it belongs."

Castle wriggled and Amanda pushed and pulled. "You's comin' out duh top, Miss Castle."

"Say one more word and I'll make your ears ring! I might as well come out the top as the bottom."

"Miss Castle, honey, dat neck so fah down youah ahms you ain' gonna be able tuh keep hit up nowhow. Hit's gonna slip 'n show youah boo-sum foh shuah."

"Get my cameo brooch and pin it to my stays in the front. I'd as soon show my bosom as my limbs." The cameo with its delicate filigree frame was the right touch. Amanda adjusted the dangling cameo ear rings, then Castle stepped back and turned to the girl. "How do I look?"

"Honess, Miss Castle, Ah ain' nevah seen *nobody* look so hansom in all mah bohn days!" Amanda doubled over laughing and clapping her hands in glee. "Lawdy me! Duh gemmuns gonna fit ovah you foh shuah!" Without straightening she turned her head and rolled her eyes. "Ah sho hope Ah ain' roun' when Miss Ma'ybelle axes foh huh gown. But Lawdy, Ah sho would lak tuh see huh face when hit ain' dahr!" Then seriously, "Miss Castle, how come you goin' to dis hyer ball? You ain' bin to no ball sin . . ."

"Shut up! Can't I go to a ball without you asking foolish questions?"

"Yaaaum. On'y Ah reckons yuh cain' stop me wonnerin' how come."

"Never mind that. Tell Manse to have Isaac bring the carriage. He can come back for Marybelle and Major Hunter."

"Ain' hit powahful eahly to staht tuh duh ball? Balls don' 'gin till . . ."

Castle swung the hand mirror and Amanda left hurridly. A fine state of affairs when a lady couldn't go to a ball without her maid asking a lot of silly questions! Did she really look handsome? She preened until Amanda returned and made her announcement.

"Isaac say duh team ain' hitch yit. Say he ain' 'spose mek two trips."

"Blast Isaac! Do I have to go down there and take him apart?"

"No'm. Manse done took keer. Isaac say you gotta wait foh Miss Ma'ybelle and duh Majah. Manse say you ain' wait. Manse ax effen he want you should walk tuh duh ball. Isaac say wooden' look rait. Say two trips no good foh duh hosses, but he ain' goin' let nobudy say he done mek Missy walk tuh save duh hosses."

The carriage was waiting when Manse ushered Castle quietly down the hall and out into the portico. Old Isaac bowed, hat in hand, and Manse spoke casually as though sending his young mistress to a ball unattended was quite the usual thing instead of an unheard of and quite irregular proceeding.

"Sho is a nice night foh a drive, Miss Castle. Isaac tek keer uv you, don' you fret." Isaac nodded gravely and Castle said, "Thank you, Manse," as he handed her into the carriage.

Thunderation! A body couldn't draw a breath without every servant in the house knowing when, where, and how. Likely Aunt Lucy had handed Amanda the gown and scuttled to the kitchen as fast as she could to tell the others and by now it had probably spread to the glasshouse hands! As Amanda had reminded her, it was too early for the ball so she told Isaac to drive around for a while. The old man grumbled, but he drove.

The air was cool and fresh out here in the suburbs away from the smoke and grime of the city. It was good to be out under the trees and the deepening blue of the skies. Since there was no hurry, Isaac let the horses amble along at their own pace, guiding them down little-used country roads, roads Castle had once known well. Now she was not so sure, for here and there were unfamiliar houses, some large, some small. But once they reached the Forty Oaks area, the old houses were the same, as handsome as ever, pink brick and gleaming white under the dark shadows of the tall, spreading trees. At each drive were wrought iron gates which were never closed and around each grounds were vine-covered walls which had not been intended as barriers. Certainly she had scrambled over most of them as a child, for while her father lived they had visited and been visited by all and sundry. At his death, Miss Sarah had gone into mourning, her social life ended, and Castle had been in her teens when Aunt Lucy had persuaded Major Hunter that she could not teach the two girls to "ack lak lil ladies" without entertaining and being entertained. Thereafter, the sisters, escorted by the Major and Aunt Lucy, had attended all the balls, and the finest of all had been her own engagement ball. Well, she'd never have another engagement ball, but she'd get married.

When they drew up at the Middleton door and old Jerocho with his shining bald pate came forward to bow her welcome, Castle felt a thrill of excitement.

"Why, Miss Castle! So glad you could come. Young Miz Middleton will sure be happy to see you." With a smile for the old man, she swept past into the brightly lighted hall and into the arms of Anne Middleton.

"Castle darling! How wonderful!"

"I just couldn't wait for Marybelle—she's so slow," Castle explained hastily, but Anne was not listening.

"Come upstairs this minute—Mother, excuse us, please?"

The elder Mrs. Middleton kissed Castle's cheek. "So glad you came, dear. We've missed you. You'll see Bob later—he's with our attorney at the moment."

Up in the blue guest chamber, Castle was swept by a flood of memories. How she and Anne had chattered when Anne was a bride and she was engaged to Garland! In childhood they had both ridiculed the prissy Garland Delacroix, but when all the other girls goggled bug-eyed at the handsome young gentleman home from college in New England, Anne had remained faithful to her Bob and was therefore free to aid and abet Castle in her conquest. Nor had she ever forgiven Garland for marrying Griselda instead.

"Castle, Castle, whatever happened? I'm dying to hear all about it. . . . But you do look marvelous. And that gorgeous gown! Wait until that sneaky dandy sees you!"

Castle shook her head vehemently. "Oh, no! He isn't going to see me—not with his Griselda! I'll keep out of his way . . ."

"Don't be silly! Walk right up to him and say, 'I hope you have the gout!' Though I can think of better luck to wish him!"

They hugged each other, then arm in arm descended the stairs to find Bob waiting for them with his mother.

"Castle, my dear, you're magnificent! You do know everyone, don't you? Well, nearly everyone. Come . . ."

Only she didn't know everyone. For a moment she wondered if she knew anyone. The room seemed filled with strangers. The names she had known all her life, but the faces . . . were these *old* people the parents of her former friends? Had these young people been mere children before? But there were some whose names were as unfamiliar as their faces. How exciting to be among people who didn't know her! She was sure some of the gentlemen looked after her as she crossed the ballroom with Bob, her skirts rustling as they swirled about her, her head regally high. This was living again! Why in tarnation had she stayed so long in her room?

Major Hunter arrived late with Marybelle pouting in her next best gown. Let her pout! About time she had something to pout about. The Major smiled and nodded across the room as he caught Castle's eye, but she only turned her head and tapped her fan at the tall dark gentleman with whom she'd been dancing. He danced rather badly, but he was quite handsome. His speech was strange, too; she couldn't place it though she could usually tell at least

North from South. Before she could think of a polite way of asking him, Bob Middleton came for her.

"Castle dear, you haven't had refreshments. Come, come, this won't do."

"Who is he?" she asked as soon as they were out of earshot.

"You mean Gayle? Like him?"

"How do I know? I only danced with him once. But who is he? Where does he come from? He's . . . different . . . and the way he talks . . ."

Bob laughed. "He's a lawyer, been around eight . . . ten years. Good practice, doing extremely well. Came here from New York City, but he's from England or someplace. British, anyway. He settled Father's estate and since then he's been looking after me. He's a good man but he's leaving soon and I'll be sorry to see him go. However, he's a lone wolf rather than a social lion, so be nice to him, will you?"

Castle was doing justice to a well-filled plate. "Someone should teach him to dance."

"That, dear lady, is your department, not mine!"

Afterward, Mr. Gayle found her again and as she smiled up at him her glance went past his shoulder. Garland was across the room. Older now, but unmistakably Garland. He smiled and bent his head to catch the words of the dainty little lady at his side. Her nightmare was becoming a reality: Garland with Griselda on his arm. "Miss Castle, may I present my wife?" No, no, she couldn't face it! She must get away before he discovered her. . . . What had her companion been saying? Was he asking her to dance? With Garland leading Griselda onto the floor? Impossible!

"Isn't it rather warm in here?" Castle smiled her sweetest smile and led the way to the veranda overlooking the moonlit garden. For a moment they stood in silence. The fragrance of unseen flowers filled the air and behind the hedge the white bloom of a plum tree hung like a cloud among the darker trees. She had stood on this same spot with Garland. . . . Now he danced with his wife while she had slipped away to hide with a black-bearded stranger. . . . Had he said something? Had she made the right answer? She studied him obliquely. Handsome, yes, his black hair worn fashionably long behind the ears and swept back in a roach above his forehead, accentuating his profile. She guessed he would not see forty again, but under the black cloth of his coat the shoulders were broad and muscular. Yet the hand that rested against the white column was not quite the hand of a leisured gentleman; it was a hard hand, a hand that could hold a horse — or a woman. He glanced down at her and Castle smiled and spread her fan.

"Do you like Pittsburgh?" she asked, hoping to keep him with her until Garland . . .

"Yes, I like Pittsburgh well enough."

"Bob said you came from New York."

"Yes."

Must she do all the talking? "He said you were leaving soon."

"In a week or so."

"Are you going back to New York City?"

"No, to Iowa."

"Iowa?" The word meant nothing. "Why Iowa?"

"It's virgin country. The western part of the state was only opened to white settlement a few years ago."

"White settlement?"

"It was Indian Territory until 1846."[1]

"Are there Indians there now?"

"Some. Most of them have moved on to their new Reservation."

"But why are you going there? Bob said you were doing well here."

Mr. Gayle smiled but his fingers drummed the column impatiently. "Bob seems to have said a number of things. Yes, I've done well here. But there are too many barristers—lawyers—and too few clients."

"Will there be more clients in Iowa?"

"I hope not! I don't want clients, I want land."

"Land?"

"Yes. Now, a section there sells for about the price of a city lot in Pittsburgh, but someday that land will be valuable." There was a different expression in his eyes when he spoke of the land.

"How long will you have to wait before the land is valuable?"

"Not as long as some may think. Meanwhile, a man lives off his investment."

"I don't know what you mean," Castle admitted.

Mr. Gayle smiled again. "Major Talbot lives off his investment in his glasshouse."

"But you're a lawyer."

"My people were farmers."

"You grew up on a farm?"

"On a poor farm. My parents were Welsh cottagers. My father was killed when a stable beam fell because the factor had refused to repair the roof." His voice was tense with pent-up anger. "They evicted my mother from the house where my father was born—and his father and his father's father. They were only tenants though they had paid rent for the same croft for over a hundred years. My mother was . . . she couldn't work, so they sent her to the poor farm. I was born there and my mother was buried there."

"How awful! But you talk like a . . . a . . . a . . . ."

"Gentleman? Yes," he finished for her, his anger gone. "When I was fourteen I ran away to London were I educated myself in the bookstalls. A great and commendable institution, the London bookstalls."

"I thought a lawyer had to study with another lawyer."

"I read law under the renowned Conrad Foley, K.C. Fourteen hours a day without pay. In my spare time I was free to earn a living any way I could. Old Foley probably expected me to starve on a diet of Blackstone and little else, but I fooled him. Once I was called to the bar I stayed in London only long enough to earn passage money to New York." A moment of silence, then, "The garden is beautiful, isn't it?"

"I suppose so. I hadn't thought about it. Anne and Bob and I used to play hide and seek out here when we were little. Before Papa died, that

was. . . . Marybelle can't even remember Papa, but I can. He was Page
Talbot and he was the most beautiful gentleman I ever saw. But I can't
remember Mamma except in mourning though Major Hunter says she was
'fair as a flower' when Papa married her.''

"Did you have a happy childhood, Miss Castle?''

"Oh, I guess I was happy enough. But all the things I liked to do were
unladylike.''

Mr. Gayle laughed outright. "I should think it would be quite stuffy for a
little girl to be ladylike all the time, though I confess I'm not greatly addicted
to ladylike ladies. As a rule they're purely ornamental.''

Suddenly Castle wished he weren't going away. "Are you sure you'll
like it better in Iowa?''

"Quite sure.''

"If I were a man, I'd go away, too.'' If she could go away. . . . "It must
be wonderful to travel.''

"So I've been told, though I never found it so. A man should be a part of
his world with roots as deep as a tree.'' He nodded toward the oaks. "I
should think a woman would want to be part of her world, too.'' Had Bob told
him about her? Castle remained silent and he continued. "I understand
you've been something of a recluse?''

Bob had told him. It would be useless to lie. "Yes.''

"It's a pity to waste your life . . .'' She whirled about and would have
left him but he caught her wrist and held her, and she no longer wanted to
go. "I'm sorry if I'm rude, but this is our first and probably our last meeting,
so hear me out. You have so very much, Miss Castle, and sitting in your room
is such a futile existence. If you were one of the ladylike ladies, it wouldn't
matter. They have nothing to lose but their beauty, nothing to waste but their
youth. But you have so much more . . .'' He broke off, studied her upturned
face and shook his head. "You wouldn't understand if I told you, would you?
You don't know your own worth, your own potential.'' He released her. "If
you wish, we'll say goodbye, but I hope we can part friends.''

"Of course,'' Castle replied automatically, dazed by his outburst. Then
softly, "I won't see you again, will I? You'll go . . .''

"As soon as I complete my arrangements.''

"Take me with you!'' She held her breath as she waited for his answer.
It seemed a long time that he stook looking down at her, almost as though he
had not heard her unseemly request.

Slowly, dancing devils lighted his eyes; he lifted her hand and bowing
low said clearly and distinctly, "Miss Castle, will you do me the honor of
becoming my wife?''

His hand held hers and as her fingers closed on his she drew a deep
breath and murmured, "Yes.''

So she had married him and now here she was and what could she do
about it? Jonathan wouldn't turn around and take her home again and she
couldn't go without him. Go back to Homeplace without her wedded

husband? Unthinkable! Leave her lawful spouse and return to her grand-father's house? Major Hunter would disown her. Yet how could she live here? How could she live in a log cabin in this desolate land without Amanda or Aunt Lucy or anyone to look after her and take care of her? What did people do without servants? She was wearing her last clean garments, and they were no longer clean. Every day Amanda had dressed her in fresh linen and Cally had washed and ironed the clothing she had soiled. Now who would wash her clothes? Would Jonathan? She doubted it. He did the cooking, if you could call it that— cornmeal mush, corn pone, side meat, boiled beans— and her tongue hanging out for one of Cookie's good dinners. Surely if he tried, Jonathan could get someone to do the housework and cooking. Or could he? Where could he find a proper servant? If she could have brought Amanda, or even Little Lucy, Aunt Lucy's granddaughter. If she could have brought *anyone* . . .

There were only three other families in all of Turkey Grove. She had met her neighbors when they came to help with the raising[2] and though the women brought the food and did the cooking, they had not behaved at all like servants. They had not consulted her about anything. Instead, they had given the orders.

"You set!" Indiana Garrison had told her. "This is our party. You can do your share when the next settler comes along."

Castle had "set," too bewildered to do otherwise. The house raising had been exciting, though the women were common as pig tracks. But they had talked to her, which was more than Jonathan did. During the day she had gleaned bits of information about these new neighbors. Lew and Indiana Garrison had arrived in Turkey Grove in 1853 and settled up the creek a few miles. Both were middle-aged and fat, their daughter married and living in Kanesville, their son in California. Tabitha and Solon Crawford lived on Crooked Creek some miles north; their two young sons had worked on the cabin with the men. The Pettit family, who lived a couple of miles down on Turkey Creek, were the nearest neighbors. Mrs. Pettit boasted that her youngest child had been the first white baby born in Turkey Grove. And her with three other children! Why must women be forever having babies? Catch *her* having a passel of brats! . . . But not one of those women would make a proper servant. Indiana Garrison and Tabitha Crawford were so bossy they'd be telling *her* what to do, and Patience Pettit with four children. . . . Surely the servant problem defied solution.

With the house completed, Jonathan was splitting rails for the fence he would need in the fall when the stock could no longer be staked. Perspiration ran down his back, wetting his shirt, and trickled down his cheeks into his beard. He rolled another log in place; with a few strokes of the maul he drove the wedge, then the gluts. When the log split, he went on to split the halves into sections—and the pile of rails grew. His unexpected marriage had delayed him, but if a man managed properly, one year's loss could be turned to another year's gain. The shadows were lengthening and he put aside his tools, stood three rails on end, and tied the tops together. Around these he stood the others, end up so the rain would run off, spaced so air could pass between. The rails well seasoned, his fence would last a lifetime. Tomorrow his plow would cut through the green prairie sod, the chaste, virgin soil of Iowa.

Castle took no heed when her husband came around the cabin wiping his face and neck with his bandanna. He studied her a moment, then rested a hand on her shoulder.

"Come. It's suppertime and I'm tired and hungry. I'll help you tonight but tomorrow I start breaking sod and you'll have to do the cooking and have the meals ready for me when I come to the house. I can't do the cooking and get the crops in."

"I don't know how to cook."

"You'll learn. Come."

"If you wanted someone to cook for you, you should have brought servants." The hand on her shoulder tightened and she tried to shake it off.

"We won't go into that again. Come. I want my supper." Jonathan was growing impatient.

"I'm not a servant and I won't do a servant's work."

Jonathan shook his head wearily. "Castle, this is Iowa, not Homeplace. Here women do their own work. I'm asking no more of you than other men expect of their wives, no more than other wives consider their fair share of responsibility for the home. What would the neighbor women think if they knew you couldn't even boil coffee? You can't boil coffee, can you, Miss Castle?" He smiled sardonically. "Your neighbors would consider you extremely stupid if they knew you couldn't even cook supper for your husband. They'd throw up their hands in horror."

"What do I care about them? They're nothing but a bunch of peasants anyway."

"Then you are also a peasant, my dear. Your husband, your home, your farm are no better than theirs."

"They don't even wear hoops!"

"They have hoops and they wear them when the occasion requires. Are hoops the only difference between a lady and a peasant? If so, they are ladies whenever they choose to wear their hoops." He put his hand under Castle's chin and tilted her head so she was forced to look at him. "Make up your mind to it, if they are peasants, you are a peasant; if you are a lady, they are ladies. You're all in the same boat, whichever boat it is."

Castle snorted and tried to pull away but something about the way he looked at her warned her that this was not the time to cross him. So she rose and followed him into the cabin and under his direction mixed the corn pone while he fried the side meat and warmed up the beans left from dinner.

"Is this all we're ever going to have to eat?"

"Of course not. But I'm no chef and I have to cook whatever takes the least time and effort. We have white flour if you would care to bake, and there are potatoes and a few onions. If you want a change from side meat, there are fish in the stream. If you tried it you might enjoy fishing. Most people do. A little later in the summer there'll be wild fruit for the picking and I'll put the garden near the house so you can have vegetables when you want them. In the fall and winter we'll have game in abundance.''

"A lot of good that does us now! Why don't you kill a hen? I like chicken.''

"I'm sorry, but you won't be eating chicken until late fall.''

"Why not? What was the sense of bringing them if you aren't going to eat them?''

"I brought them to start a flock, and I want every egg for setting.''

"I like eggs for breakfast.''

"You'll have to learn to like mush," he told her shortly. "Chickens and eggs are scarce here now, but in a few years we can have all we want. That is, unless we eat the hens now.''

Castle made no reply. She washed her hands, pinned back the strands of hair which kept escaping from her awkward knot, and sat down at the table. Jonathan served her plate and though she was tired of the same things day after day, she ate heartily. If that was what Jonathan cooked, that was what she would eat, but if he thought she was going to do the cooking, he'd find out!

He was up at dawn and called her before he went to do the chores. "Get up, Castle. There's a pot of water over the fire. When it boils, stir in some cornmeal and salt and when I come in we'll have breakfast." He gave her shoulder a warning shake. "Don't go back to sleep.''

When he came in with the milk she was sleeping as sweetly as a baby. He set the pail on the table and watched her for a moment. One hand was flung up over her head, her triangular face framed in a mass of tawny hair. It would be so easy to give in to her, and so hard to live with her if he did. This time when he shook her he was not particularly gentle.

"Get up! Get up and get my breakfast! And this time you'd better be doing it when I come back!''

"If you wanted someone to cook you should have . . . ," she muttered, snuggling down into the pillow. Jonathan had not stayed to hear. A few minutes later he came in with a bucket of water and an armload of wood. He dropped the wood by the fireplace and stood looking down at his sleeping wife for a time, shaking his head ruefully. Then he emptied the bucket of water over her head. She leaped up, dashing water and wet hair from her face.

"You . . . ! You . . . ! How *dare* you throw water on me!''

"Put your clothes on and get my breakfast.''

"I won't!'' She jerked at the wet nightdress clinging soddenly to her body.

"Castle, I haven't time to cook! Unless I get the crops in we'll all be hungry next winter — you and I and the stock. The only way to get food here is to grow it, and to grow it, I have to plow and plant. If I waste time cooking now, soon there'll be nothing to cook. And for anyone who likes to eat as well as you do, starving would not be a pleasant way to die. Maybe you should try it now instead of next winter." Before she knew what he was doing he took a rawhide thong from his pocket and tied her to the bedpost. ''I can go hungry if you can. This is just to make sure you don't cheat while I'm gone.'' With that he walked out of the house.

She shrieked wildly, hoping he would come back, but she heard him clucking to the horses and when the rattle of the trace chains faded, she knew he was gone. She twisted and turned, trying to free herself, but the bedpost was solid, the knots well tied. She tried to sit on the bed but found she could only lean against the post. Eventually her body began to ache from the strained position, her hands grew numb, her wrists felt raw, and she could think of no more names to call her husband. Of all the foul. . . . She was growing dizzy and his words came floating back to her. ''Unless I get the crops in we'll all be hungry . . . only way to get food is to grow it . . . plow and plant . . . nothing to cook . . . starving . . .''

She was starving. She had had no breakfast and her stomach knew it. Would they really be hungry next winter? Where would they get food if Jonathan didn't grow it? He couldn't run to Kanesville—there was no place to buy food. Maybe he should get the crops in. Maybe doing the cooking wouldn't be as bad as not having anything to cook!

She didn't hear him come. She just looked up and he was standing in the door. ''It it noon?'' she asked and he nodded. ''Get me out of this so I can make us some dinner. Fine thing, you going off with nothing in your stomach!''

So Castle did the cooking, but when her husband asked her to wash his clothes she refused, and he hid hers—all but those she had on. To think of handling his dirty, smelly shirts gagged her. Washing the dishes was bad enough. She held out for three days and Jonathan mentioned neither his clothes nor hers. She had to have clean clothes. The gown she was wearing was stiff. The thought of washing soiled clothing was sickening, but the thought of wearing that filthy gown another day was even more sickening. Apparently the only way she could get anything clean was to wash her clothes herself—and her husband's into the bargain.

After supper that night she asked, ''Where are my clothes? I can't wear these for the rest of my life. I stink! Fill the pot before you go to bed so I'll have hot water in the morning.''

''You're doing the family wash tomorrow?''

''I am. Where's the soap? This is only a sliver.''

''In that box under the shelves. The first rainy day I'll build an ash pit so you can leach lye for another batch before this is gone. With plenty of lye, you can make hominy in the fall, too.'' He filled the pot over the fire and piled the family wash at the foot of the bed. ''How are the candles holding out?''

''How should I know?''

''The candle mould is on the top shelf. When we're down to the last dozen let me know and I'll show you how to make them. I like to read in the evening and the firelight hurts my eyes. Here are the sadirons. Tomorrow night I'll show you how to use them.''

''You know a lot, don't you?''

"It's a good thing I do. With your limited knowledge you'd find survival difficult, Miss Castle." He smiled at his wife, took a coal from the fire, and lighted his pipe. "You'll catch on. In a few years you'll be the best housewife in Turkey Grove."

"As if that would be any distinction!"

She did catch on. Jonathan soon taught her enough about cooking to keep them from going hungry. He showed her how to rub the clothes without rubbing the skin off her knuckles and how to handle the sadirons so she wouldn't burn herself—or the clothes. But never once did she iron a shirt until he needed it, and never once did she iron two shirts or two gowns the same day. She did cook and wash and iron, and on occasion she even swept the floor, but she hated the work and hated her husband with every stroke, with every burned finger and blistered palm. Her hands would be ruined, and her face, too, forever working over the hot fire. Yet through it all she donned her hoops when she rose in the morning and took them off only when she went to bed at night. A lady she had been born and a lady she would remain, no matter what. When the weather was pleasant she spent most of the day sitting on the bench in front of the cabin, and though she gazed out across the prairie, the prairie was not what she saw.

So many long years she had spent with her hands in her lap, looking out her window across the lawn of Homeplace. So many years she had pined for her lost love. . . . Garland, Garland! Why, why? All that summer while the other girls had watched, green with envy, *she* had been the one he had escorted to all the parties and picnics and balls. He had been so handsome, with his beautiful waving brown hair and the lovely mustache above his dear laughing lips. They had had such gay times together, riding in his carriage, dancing, feeding each other tidbits, standing close on shadowed verandas— how could she have guessed there was anyone else? What did she know of a senator's daughter in far off New England? He had complimented her, flattered her, said all the pretty things a gentleman can say to a lady and she. . . . She had used every trick in a well-stocked bag! But surely, surely he had loved her as much as she loved him! Yet he had married Griselda the day he should have married her, and she had gone home to her room, alone and lonely. And all those years no one had ever spoken a cross word to her until that night when the Major had told her it was all her own fault.

3

J O N A T H A N only came to the house to eat and sleep. This was his land and the fulfillment of his dreams: his plow cutting into the deep prairie sod that had lain waiting for centuries, waiting for him and for sons who would come after him. The long generations of crofters who had been his forebears had tilled soil they could never own, but this land was his, and it would belong to his sons and to their sons. Down through all the years to come it could not be taken from those of his blood who followed in his footsteps behind the plow. He stopped the team and let them blow, and while they rested he picked up a handful of earth and felt the tilth as it ran through his fingers. This was soil to gladden the heart of any man who knew what soil should be. And Jonathan knew, knew in his mind and his heart and his bones.

He clucked to the team. The grass in the meadow bordering the stream was already lush and green and he was late with his plowing. Before the summer was over he would break every possible inch of sod even though much of it would lie fallow over winter. For sod broken this summer and left to the frosts of winter would be more easily prepared and yield a better crop another year. Once a field was plowed and harrowed he planted as quickly as he could, then went on to the next. When it was too late to plant, he would still continue breaking sod until the corn was up. Then would come the endless hoeing, with little time for anything else until the corn was laid by.

For Castle, that was a lonely summer and she looked forward eagerly to the letters from home. The first time Jonathan brought the mail he gave her a letter and sat down to read his newspaper. When he turned the page she was still holding the letter, unopened.

"Sorry, my dear. I forgot your handicap. Tell me, how was it that Marybelle went to the Female Academy, while you never even learned to read and write?"

"I wouldn't learn. Nobody could make me. Major Hunter said I was a girl-child and it didn't matter anyway."

"You wouldn't learn? Why, pray?"

Her eyes were almost yellow in remembered anger. "Oh, that fine sister of Mrs. Delacroix—from Boston she was—came to call and she said Marybelle was so pretty she'd have no trouble getting a fine husband. Then she saw me and said, "What's this, the ugly duckling? Well, if a girl isn't pretty, sometimes she has brains. Send her to the Academy for a couple of years and if worse comes to worst she can always teach school."

"So?"

"So I wouldn't learn to read and write."

"I don't understand . . ."

"Well, my land! If I couldn't read and write I couldn't teach school, could I?"

The mails were as regular as could be expected with the nearest railroad four hundred miles away and the trip requiring four weeks by stagecoach, wagon, and single buggy.[1] And the nearest post office was at Cold Spring,[2] a distance of twenty miles, with several fords and over an all but nonexistent track.

Miss Sarah wrote rambling letters full of motherly counsel, all of it impractical, much of it absurd in the circumstances. Castle was particularly annoyed when her mother asked veiled questions about her "condition," for her husband always smiled over those passages. The brief epistles from Major Hunter were a different matter. Addressed to Jonathan, they were intended for Castle, too, and she listened to them in heavy silence, hearing again the old man pounding his cane as he spoke. Marybelle wrote occasionally, for she had forgiven Castle when she met Jonathan. But since the two sisters had never had much in common, her letters were rather stiff and contained little of interest to Castle. Anne Middleton's letters she enjoyed most of all, for Anne wrote as she talked, chattering on paper of people and events once part of Castle's life. Sitting with her husband in the wavering light of the candle, closing her eyes and listening to Anne's recital of the latest scandals or newest romances, she could forget Iowa and imagine herself back in her room with Anne.

Though the letters were welcome, answering was a chore. Jonathan wrote at her dictation and while Anne's letters were answered promptly, only his insistence kept up the correspondence between Castle and her family. She could find nothing to say to them. She had told her mother of the neighbor women and their children but she had seen none of them since the house raising and she couldn't tell her mother that. She couldn't tell her of this all but uninhabited country. She could never tell her that she cooked and washed and ironed, burning her hands and scorching her face over the hearth fire, living and eating no better than the Negroes in the slave cabins Major Hunter had told about. Nor could she tell her that Jonathan cared for nothing but his farm and his books; in the fields all day and reading all evening, he seldom spoke a dozen words to her. Those were things she did not want her mother and the Major to know. Nor did she want them to know that her feather bed rested on a corn shuck mattress, that her slab table was set with heavy ironstone plates and steel knives and forks. She had not forgotten the unkind thing Major Hunter had said that night, but he was still the Major, and she loved him more than anyone in the world. Except Garland . . . And Garland had told on her, the skunk! She would never, never forgive him, even though he begged her on bended knee.

Toward the end of summer she grew uneasy. Either she had miscalculated or she was going to have a baby. She couldn't read the almanac, and keeping track was difficult. She might have made a mistake. Certainly she had trouble enough without getting in the family way. If necessary, she'd do something. Once she had stood unnoticed at the sewing room door while Callie told Aunt Lucy about old Sobel, the crone who gathered roots and "yarbs" in the woods and hills. When old Sobel's former master had sold her child she had vowed she would never have another, and she had kept her vow. Castle had heard how she had done it, and if Sobel could, so could she. She wouldn't have a baby and that was that.

Fall came and the trees along the creek were a painted picture in their flaming colors. But here there were mere patches of timber while at Homeplace the mountains had been a riot of color stretching into the distant blue and purple haze, each outline less distinct than the one before until hills and horizon merged. Here there were no mountains, not even hills worthy of the name. And there could be no mistaking the line that divided prairie from sky. All summer Jonathan had been working so they would be ready for winter when it came. He had dug a well and walled it up and hung the well bucket on a pulley so it was easy to draw water. The milk kept sweet for days in a covered lard pail hanging in the cool dark depths near the water. He had built a stable for the horses and cow, with a lean-to for the hens, and the barnlot fence was up. By midsummer they had had vegetables and there were more in the garden to be stored under the haystack for winter use: turnips, carrots, squash, pumpkins, and plenty of potatoes. Jonathan had showed his wife how to braid the tops of the onions so she could hang them from the roof poles within easy reach. He had built a granary and a corncrib and both were filled, and he had showed her how to steam the whole grain wheat overnight for a welcome change from cornmeal mush for breakfast. Now she could watch the leaves turn and drop without fear, for they would not be hungry when winter came.

On a crisp frosty morning when Jonathan came in with the milk he said, "I'll have to make a trip to Kanesville for supplies."[3]

"With all the food . . ."

"We need some things we can't raise: coffee, tea, sugar, saleratus, molasses, salt—and clothing. Later, if we want white flour, I'll have to take wheat to the mill. But Bossey is about dry, so you won't have to milk her." He reached for a towel to dry his dripping face and Castle handed him one out of the basket. "You'll be all right," he muttered behind the towel.

"What do you mean? If you're going to Kanesville, so am I! You can't expect me to stay here alone."

"Someone has to stay, and you can't very well go to Kanesville while I stay."

"But I want to go! I want some new gowns. I can't wear these forever."

"When those are past mending I'll buy material for more—just like them."

"I won't wear them! I'll put on my silks and wear them every day!"

"Then you'll have no silks, and there's always the possibility that someday you'll go someplace where you'll want to wear silk." Jonathan sat down and Castle put the dinner on the table. "You have no need for silk dresses at the moment," he continued between bites. "Proper dress is in accordance with your mode of life. Silk gowns in a log cabin would be as out of place as calico in a drawing room."

"I don't belong in a log cabin! I belong in a drawing room!"

"Hummm. I was under the impression you asked me to bring you here. But that's beside the point. You have no warm winter clothes. You'll need underwear and flannel petticoats, good stout shoes, a heavy cloak and a couple of shawls, a hood and various other items, depending on what they have in stock in the stores.''

Already the nights were chilly and in the end Castle decided it would be no pleasure traveling and camping for a week each way, to say nothing of the humiliation of riding into town in the covered wagon. So Jonathan went to Kanesville and Castle stayed at home. At least she wouldn't have to cook for him for a while. She wouldn't have to do anything she didn't want to except look after the cow and the chickens. She could have eggs for breakfast and after breakfast she could go back to bed.

The afternoon Jonathan left she sat by the fire until she was hungry, then warmed up the leftovers from the night before. Not many dishes to wash, either. They could wait until she had fed the chickens and cow and brought in a bucket of water. She'd have to go out and shut the chickens up later, so she came back and sat by the fire again, thinking of Homeplace and all she had lost when she married Jonathan. Half dozing, she forgot the time until a coyote yipped, which sent her scurrying to the hen house. She'd done without eggs too long to let coyotes get the hens now. Too, there were all those nice young cocks. She would have eaten them long ago, but Jonathan insisted on waiting until they were big enough to make a good meal. On the way back from the hen house, Castle became acutely aware that she was alone. Nor was the night as silent as it had always seemed heretofore. All summer the crickets and katydids and cicadas had filled the night with a sort of background of sound, but now only a few were left and each individual song became loud and insistent, punctuating the stillness as surely as the yip of the coyote that sounded again from somewhere beyond the the woods and was answered from far out on the prairie. Then some wild creature went crashing through the plum thicket and a night bird called from the trees along the creek, while the wind rustled their tops and a dust devil tumbled a handful of leaves across the barnlot. Castle stood rigidly listening, then dashed for the cabin and bolted the door behind her. She built up the fire with lightwood until the glow touched the farthest corners of the room, but still she was alone. Jonathan's chair by the table was empty. Incredible that she should want Jonathan, yet at that moment she wanted him more than anything in the world. Even sitting by the table with his nose in a book, he was far better than being alone.

For several days she did as nearly nothing as possible. Then one morning an Indian came toward the house from the woods. He had to be an Indian, for he wore buckskin pants and nothing else except some ornaments around his neck. Castle's first impulse was to slam the door and bolt it, but if she did he might take the cow and chickens. Then they'd have no milk, no butter, no eggs, and no tasty young cocks. Would he scalp her? He was alone and apparently unarmed. But he could scalp her with a penknife! She'd let him see she had a gun. He wouldn't know she couldn't shoot it. Jonathan had taken his rifle but Betsy hung in her usual place over the door. Castle lifted the muzzle-loader gently from the pegs and stood it gingerly at the foot of the bed where it was within reach of her hand and in plain sight from the door.

With the gun in place, she turned back to the door. Seeing her the Indian raised his hand in some sort of signal, and when he arrived at the doorstep he folded his arms and made an unintelligible speech. Castle shook her head and he unfolded his arms and made various gestures. Again she shook her head. Then he went through the motions of eating — that she understood. But what did Indians eat? She had little food in the house and she didn't want him to know their provisions were in the woodshed. Jonathan had said Indians would steal anything they could carry away. Afraid to turn her back lest he stab her, she nevertheless turned her back and picked up the vegetables she had brought in for her own dinner. The buck shook his head and pointed toward the outbuildings. Afraid to go with him, she was more afraid to refuse. He led her to the corncrib, pushed his finger between the slats, and touched an ear of corn. If all he wanted was corn for meal, she'd gladly give him a basketful just to get shut of him.

Castle unfastened the door, took the split-oak basket from the peg and stepped in, then realized she was trapped with the Indian blocking the only exit. With quick strategy she handed him the basket and motioned for him to help himself. He obligingly took the basket and stepped in — and she stepped out. It was all she could do not to lift her skirts and take to her heels, but with her heart pounding she walked slowly to the house without looking back. Once inside she dropped the bolt and leaned against the door, for her knees were shaking until she could scarcely stand. She wanted to crawl under the bed and hide, but she knew she would have no peace unless she actually saw the Indian leave. Her knees might shake, but carry her they must. The ticking of the clock was as loud as hammer blows while she waited, her face pressed to the small high window.

At last the buck emerged from the crib, his basket heaped high. Jonathan wouldn't like it that she had let him take so much corn, and a good basket, too. If only he would go! After closing the crib he examined the peg that held the door. Jonathan would have to make a better latch. Frantic when the Indian disappeared behind the crib, she clung to the window, tense, scarcely breathing until he reappeared on the other side and returned to shake the door again. He turned away. Would he come to the house? No, he was going the other way. To the stable? — the cow shed? — the hen house? He had passed them all. God be praised, he was heading toward the woods!

Castle watched him out of sight among the trees, then flung herself on the bed and sobbed with relief. Suddenly she was sick, so sick she barely got the door unbolted in time to save having to mop the floor. All day the very thought of food turned her stomach, yet she dared not stay in bed lest the Indian return. She kept listening and listening and every whisper of sound sent her scurrying to the window. The hours dragged and the day seemed endless. This time she didn't wait until the last minute to care for the cow and chickens, but she couldn't shut the chickens up until they went to roost and it seemed they would never get through scratching. She looked out the window every few minutes and by the time they were all in it was almost dusk. She was tempted to take a chance on coyotes rather than go out and find an Indian lurking in the shadows. But coyotes were the more certain threat, and taking a pine knot from the handful Jonathan kept for emergencies, she braved the gathering darkness, realizing too late that the burning brand only made her a more conspicuous target for an Indian arrow.

There were neither Indians nor arrows and she returned safely to the cabin. Afraid to sleep, she went supperless to bed, but slept the night through and wakened ravenously hungry. With the coffee grinder on her lap she gave the handle a few vigorous turns before the first whiff of the strong fresh aroma set her racing out behind the house. What on earth was the matter with her? She had a cast iron stomach and she had eaten nothing to upset her or make her bilious. Great God Almighty! Was she going to have a baby? She had wondered before about it. Now . . . cook and wash and iron and do all the rest of the work and take care of a baby—out in this wilderness? Oh, no! Let other women have babies if they wanted them. She didn't want a baby and she wouldn't have a baby!

Before the day was over, Castle was sure she would die. The Indians could have taken the cow and chickens and burned the cabin over her head and she would not have lifted a finger. All because she had married Jonathan. All because Major Hunter had called her a sour old maid. She wished she'd stayed an old maid! Well, she might die, but she wouldn't have a baby. That was one thing Jonathan couldn't make her do.

He was gone over two weeks and Castle had not entirely recovered when he returned. She had stayed in bed most of the time since her illness, but morning and night there were the chickens and cow to look after, water to be carried in, and if she ate at all she had to prepare her own food. She was scattering corn for the hens when Jonathan drove in and backed up to the wood shed. He leaped over the wheel and went to her where she stood with a basket of corn on her arm. One look at her face and he raised his hand to strike, then let it fall with a gesture of helpless rage.

"I could kill you, but what good would it do? I hope you enjoyed yourself."

"Enjoyed myself? With Indians all over the place? You should be ashamed, going off and leaving your own wife . . ."

"Wife! Damn my wife! Taking advantage of my absence to behave like a slut!"

"How dare you . . ."

"How dare I? Why, you fool, you weak-minded imbecile, do you think I don't know what you've done? It's written all over you! I might have had a son!"

Jonathan flung away from her and Castle looked after him in amazement. How did he know? Well, there was nothing he could do about it now. She'd had *her* way for once!

But Jonathan could read the almanac even if his wife couldn't. He had taken for granted she would want a child as much as he, and he had been waiting for her to break the good news. Now she had repudiated her own flesh, destroyed her own and his posterity. From the looks of her, she had all but destroyed herself. Yet he could feel no pity; she deserved whatever she had suffered. Only she might have died. Fortunately, she had not and for that he was grimly thankful. Nor was he greatly perturbed by her encounter with the Indian. When she attempted to repeat her story during supper he silenced her with a gesture.

"Eat your supper. An Indian should have been no surprise to you. I've told you they are scattered about the country and can show up anytime, anyplace. If they've camped on the creek for the winter, we may as well get used to them and try to get along with them. So far, the Pottawattamies have been peaceful and given no trouble, but they're a lazy lot and if you let them frighten you into giving them everything they ask for, we'll end up feeding the tribe. Give them corn when they come for it, but small amounts and small ears. And don't let them see that you're afraid of them. Cowardice is the most contemptible of sins in the eyes of an Indian. So don't quake in your boots every time you see one."

"He didn't know I was afraid!"

"You let that buck take a good split-oak basket and all the corn he could carry."

"He could get it as good as I could. Why should I wait on him?"

Jonathan found the Indians camped along the creek beyond his east meadow. The band was a remnant of a once large tribe, and for all their dirt and poverty they received Jonathan with dignity. After accepting gifts of corn and beans and plug tobacco and salt, the peace pipe was smoked all around. Thereafter, in theory, they were friends and whenever Jonathan met one of them they greeted each other with a hand raised in the sign of peace. Sometimes he stopped at the camp to powwow with the old men, partly out of curiosity, largely because in an emergency the more he knew about them the better he would be able to deal with them. For the same reason, whatever he learned he passed on to his wife, but no amount of information could allay Castle's fears. One morning a strapping buck came to the house to ask for a loaf of the white bread she had just baked, a delicacy no Indian could resist. Hands and face still smarting from the heat of the fire, she handed over a loaf of bread fearfully and reluctantly, then watched from the window to be sure the Indian had actually gone.

"There isn't a bit of use in me baking with them around," she muttered disgustedly. "I declare, they smell it baking a mile away!" One of her red flannel petticoats hung on the line and as the Indian passed he reached out and took the skirt. At sight of him calmly walking off with her warm red wool petticoat, Castle dashed out the door and half across the yard after him.

"Give that back, you low-life beggar!" she shouted. "Give me that petticoat this instant!" She stamped her foot in rage. Turning, the Indian offered the petticoat as though he had never had any other intention. She snatched it from his hands, her eyes snapping. "Stealing the clothes right off my line under my very nose! And right after I gave you a loaf of bread!" She pointed to the loaf, knowing he understood only her gestures. "Ingrate, that's what you are!"

The Indian grunted and taking a thong strung with bits of bone from around his neck he offered it with the air of one conferring a costly gift, a gift in return for the gift of bread. That done, he marched off as though nothing had happened. Castle stared after him in amazement. She had been so angry she had forgotten to be afraid and now she was astonished at the buck's calm acceptance of her outburst.

"Dirty, greasy red Indians! They needn't think they can scare me! I guess I know how to handle them. I'll show them!"

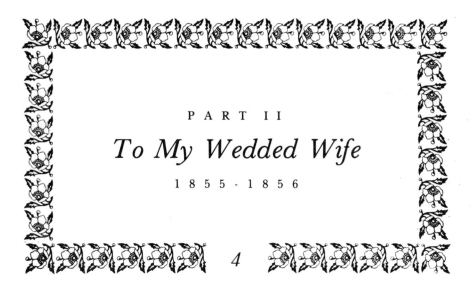

T O W A R D winter, Ed Pettit rode up to the door at dusk and called, "Hello, there! Anybody home?"

Castle smoothed down her skirts, tucked back the stray whisps of hair, threw a shawl around her shoulders, and stepped outside.

"Good evening, Mr. Pettit. Won't you come in?"

"Evenin', Miz Gayle. Can't take time to visit this trip. I been gone since dinner and I'm already late for supper."

"If you want to see Jonathan, he's at the stable."

"Now, ma'am, why would I want to see him when I can set here and look at you?" Ed grinned and the humor in his twinkling blue eyes lighted his freckled homely face. "Stopped by to let you know we're getting new neighbors. Family name of Olson is taking a whole section a couple miles below my place. They aim to hold the raising this coming Thursday."

"How many in the family?" Castle inquired. Ed would expect her to take an interest in the new neighbors.

"Mr. and Mrs. and four boys: two big'uns like the Crawford boys and two not so big—about like mine. You won't forget to tell Jonathan about the raising?"

"I'll tell him soon as he comes in. How are Patience and the children?"

"First rate. Patience ain't husky but she gets around."

"I don't know how she does it all."

"I don't neither. But women are smart that way. Well, I got to get along or she'll think I got lost. Reckon we'll see you at the raising." He touched his hat, clucked to the horse, and rode off at a trot.

Castle looked after him, her mouth puckered scornfully. Such people! Chilled from standing in the wind, she poked up the fire, stirred the kettle of meat and potatoes, then held her hands to the warmth of the blaze. Ed Pettit said women were smart. Jonathan didn't think *she* was smart. Why couldn't he be nice to her? Sometimes there was a look in his eyes. . . . Anyway, he was much handsomer than any of the other men around. When he came in she told him of the new neighbors and the house raising while he washed up.

"Honestly, these people! They haven't a mite of pride — or manners, either. Ed Pettit sat his horse while I stood! And he was riding bareback on a plow horse."

"He'd covered twenty miles bareback on that plow horse to get word out about a house raising for a man he'd met only a few days ago."

"He didn't have to, did he?"

"If he didn't, there'd be no raising."

Castle tasted the stew and added salt. "The women all brought food to our raising. I been thinking what to take. Chicken would be nice."

She put the plates and knives and forks on the table while Jonathan dried his face and combed his hair and beard. His wife watched him out of the corner of her eye. He had never shaved and his beard was as soft and silky as a woman's hair. It looked fine when it was combed and neat, and he always kept it carefully trimmed.

"I could shoot a few prairie chickens or perhaps a wild turkey. One of the Indians got one the other day," Jonathan said as he eased the backlog over.

"Any of the men can shoot prairie chickens or a turkey. I want to take a couple of those Dominick cocks. They're big enough to kill. . . . Let that fire alone. I just got done poking it."

"All the fire is at the front. You have to keep the backlog burning, too. And you can't have Dominicks. We don't have enough for a raising."

Castle put the supper on the table and Jonathan helped himself. After pouring the coffee she sat down and filled her plate. But the more she thought of it, the more she wanted to take real chickens to the raising. It was the one thing she was sure no one else could take.

"I don't know why you're so stingy. A couple of cocks wouldn't make much difference."

"Not to nine men and all the women and children at a house raising. No one else will be taking chicken so you'd have to take enough to go around. You'd need at least a dozen cocks." How could she be so dense? "Make a pot of baked beans and roast a haunch of venison. Brown some turnips with the meat. That would be tasty."

"If I can't take Dominicks, I won't go!"

"Very well. I'll go without you and tell the ladies why."

In sudden fury Castle sprang up and dashed her plate in her husband's face. He rose and stalked out the door, returned, and washed his face and beard while she stood laughing at him. He hung up the towel, whipped around the table, and slapped her face so hard she sat down on the hearth, her skirts only inches from the fire. Snatching them to safety, her hand struck the Dutch oven; clutching the heavy lid she lifted it to hurl at her husband, but he was on her, wrenching the lid from her hand.

"Break that and you'll bake without an oven!" he hissed. "I'll not drive two hundred miles for another!"

Her free hand found the poker and brought it down across his shoulder. He swore and snatched it from her, but she clawed his face. In a mad rage he grabbed her and shook her, shook her until her heavy hair fell about her face, until her head wagged and wobbled and the wind went out of her lungs and the firelight whirled and swayed drunkenly. He jerked her to her feet and flung her on the bed and while she lay limp and gasping, he stripped off her clothes and his own. She tried to push him away but his mouth covered hers, his hard body pressed her down, and the hot blood surging up wiped out pride and reason and will. She hated him! But she could not fight both his strength and her own desire.

At the house raising, Indiana Garrison asked, "For goodness sake, Jonathan, what happened to your face?"

He laughed and lied like a gentleman. "I chased the cow through a plum thicket."

A few weeks later another house raising took place when Josh Marker brought his wife and son from York State and took forty acres on the creek a mile or two below the Garrison's. Jonathan gave Castle the news as they sat by the fire after supper, he with his pipe in one hand, a book in the other, she with her hands in her lap.

"The raising is day after tomorrow, and you are not taking Dominicks."

She ignored the insult. "Why couldn't they have taken land next to ours? It'll be the same old story: too far to walk and you never have time to take me visiting."

"A man chooses the spot he thinks is best suited to his needs and no man considers visiting a necessity. But this Marker hasn't a sou and he can't expect to make much of a living off forty acres. I've heard of starting on a shoestring, but he's starting without one."

"How many acres have you got?" Castle had never thought of it before.

"A quarter section: a hundred and sixty acres. There's open land on all sides of me when I'm ready for more."

"How much do the others have?"

"Crawfords have a quarter section; Pettits have three forties; and Garrisons have forty. But Lew grows only enough crops for himself and his stock. He makes his living hunting and trapping." He shook his head thoughtfully. "Forty acres isn't much of a farm for a man who has a grown son to help him. However, if he can't pay for more than that . . ."

"Why can't he?" Castle unpinned her hair and let it fall about her shoulders. Amanda used to brush it for her when she was tired. Maybe brushing it herself would be restful.

Watching his wife with the firelight on her shining hair, Jonathan explained. "Josh lost his crops three years straight back East. He borrowed money for the trip out here, borrowed to buy his land, borrowed enough to feed them until he makes a crop. His credit must be good! But how can they eat, buy clothing, feed the stock—such as it is—improve the farm, pay taxes and interest, and pay back what he borrowed, all on only forty acres?''

''What do you care?'' Castle paused in her brushing. ''It's nothing to you if he can't pay what he owes.''

''No, it's nothing to me. But I keep wondering if he's courageous or foolhardy.''

Jonathan never found out, for Josh Marker died before he had plowed a furrow in the soil of Iowa. Castle heard the news when, to her surprise, her husband came to the house in the middle of the morning.

''Mrs. Marker wants you to come over and stay until after the funeral.'' He shook the snow off his coat and hung it on the peg. ''Put on a black silk, but take a calico along. There'll be work to do.''

''Why should I go over there and work? I've got enough to do here.'' The breakfast dishes weren't done and it would soon be time to start dinner.

''You won't mind working there. You'll have someone to talk to.''

''Maybe I don't want to talk to her!'' She flounced across the room and sat down at the table. ''Martha Marker is nothing to me. I only saw her at the raising.''

''Markers are our nearest neighbors. I told young Tolly you'd be right over. I don't mind you moping around pining for your lost love when you have nothing better to do, but right now you're needed.'' Castle leaped at her husband but he caught her wrists. ''None of that! You don't want to go over there battered black and blue.''

''I'm not going!''

''I don't want to beat you, my dear, but you *are* my wife and I'm responsible for your conduct.'' He spoke with the hard, cold conviction she was learning to recognize. ''I won't have you shame me publicly. Be as much of a devil as you like when I'm the only witness, but in the eyes of the neighbors you're going to behave as a respectable woman should if I have to beat you every day of your life. Now get dressed.'' He turned her around and gave her a push.

''Why didn't they get Indie Garrison?''

''Mrs. Garrison was with Josh from the time he was taken ill. She's going home to get some rest as soon as you get there. She isn't young and she has rheumatism.''

''There are other women.''

''They have children. You haven't.''

So he was thinking about *that* again. ''Sid and Seth Crawford are big enough to take care of themselves. They're as big as their father . . .''

''Good God, Castle! It's *miles* to Crawfords'! Have you no pride? The fact that Mrs. Marker sent for you is a token of confidence. She *needs* you. What if you were sick?''

''I've never been sick in my life and I don't intend to be. They were fools to come here and they deserve whatever they get. Why didn't they stay in York State where they belonged—with the rest of the blue-belly Yankees?''

Jonathan threw up his hands. ''Is that what you want me to tell Mrs. Marker? I'll have to let her know . . .''

"I thought you were going to hitch up?" Castle rose and untied her apron.

He put on his hat, slipped into his coat, and left without another word. God, what a woman! He had meant it: he would not permit her to shame him. He had been proud of her when he married her and, God willing, he'd be proud of her until he died. What was that proverb about a virtuous woman? A crown to her husband, yes. Like it or not, his wife would be a crown to her husband, and if she were a crown of thorns, that was *his* affair and none of their neighbors' business.

Tolly Marker had found him across the creek cutting wood and Jonathan had brought the wood sled to the barn and left it without unloading it. There were drifts along the creek which the sled could take better than the wagon. Perhaps he could fit the wagon seat on the sled. Castle would no doubt object to riding in such undignified fashion; nevertheless he threw off the wood and fastened the seat in place. He pulled up to the cabin door and his wife came out gowned in black silk and looking very much the fine lady, her cloak over her shoulders, her shawl under her chin. Then she saw the sled.

"Jonathan Gayle, I won't ride on that contraption! You can just go back and hitch the team to the wagon."

"The creek is frozen and slippery and the wagon might turn over in a drift. I'm sure you wouldn't want Tolly Marker to see you headfirst in a snowdrift with your skirts over your head and your pantalets kicking up in the air. That would be most unseemly. And the snow is cold and damp."

Castle began to laugh. "You do beat all! I can just see myself! Only I'm not wearing pantalets."

"Why, Miss Castle! You wouldn't! Go without pantalets? Tck, tck, tck!"

"I'm the one who has to wash and iron them and nobody sees them but me."

"Unless the wagon should upset in a drift. Here, let me wrap the robe around you so the horses won't kick snow on your clothes."

She stayed three days with Martha Marker and worked as she had never worked before. Martha was a tall, spare woman with a long face, and her restless grey eyes made Castle nervous. Why scrub every inch of the house just because her husband was dead? But Martha said it had to be done and Castle was sure that if she missed a spot, Martha would know it. And she didn't want Martha telling the other women that *she* didn't know how to clean a house. So she watched and did as Martha did. More than once Aunt Lucy had told her, "Keep youah mouf shet an' folks won' know you is a fool." So she kept her mouth shut and did whatever Martha told her. Jonathan had taught her to make a bed, wash and dry dishes, wash and iron clothes, sweep and dust, and do a fair amount of plain cooking, yet she spent those three days on tenterhooks lest Martha set her a task she could not perform.

Meanwhile, Jonathan had staked out a corner of his north pasture and he and the men built a split-rail fence around it for a burying ground. Then when they laid Josh Marker in the first grave in Turkey Grove it was

Jonathan who read the burial service from the *Book of Common Prayer*. After supper at Markers' that night, Martha shook hands with Jonathan and kissed Castle's cheek.

"You're such good people! I don't know what me and Tolly would of done without you. It's a real comfort to know we got good neighbors."

"You sure you don't mind staying alone tonight?" Castle asked.

"We got to get used to it and we might as well start now," Martha told her, her spare frame erect, her mouth determined. "You been mighty kind. I can't thank you. But if there's ever anything we can do for you . . ."

"What do you plan to do?" Jonathan asked. "Or haven't you had time to think about it?" He stood at the door, his hat in one hand, the other on the latch.

"I've thought about it. We're going to stay and keep our home. There ain't nothing in York State for us to go back to, and I'd as soon go hungry here as be a pauper there. Tolly ain't but eighteen but he's real strong and he knows how to farm. We'll make out."

"We're reasonably near neighbors; perhaps Tolly and I can help each other."

"Thanks, Mr. Gayle. I reckon I can do the work but I'd be proud to have your advice about some things." Tolly spoke with a man's seriousness.

"Anytime, Tolly. And there'll be jobs on both farms that two men can do more easily than one."

"That's right, too. You just sing out when you've got a two-man job."

Riding home on the sled, the horses trotting on the level stretches and wallowing through the drifts, Castle looked up at her husband and said complacently, "I think Martha likes me. She kept telling me how good I was to come and how much I helped. I did, too."

Smiling, Jonathan rubbed the back of his mitten across his snow-flecked beard. "Of course you helped, and I see no reason why Mrs. Marker shouldn't like you. In this country good neighbors are important," a fact of which he had been totally unaware before his arrival in Iowa, but which was becoming increasingly clear every day he stayed.

At the cabin he helped Castle to the door, then drove on to the stable. She stamped her feet and shook the snow from her skirts before she went in and closed the door quickly behind her. While taking off her wraps she glanced around the room and a strange feeling came over her. The fire had burned low and the embers threw a warm pink glow across the darkness. Moving to the hearth she looked about, savoring the room and the feeling it gave her. She threw a few sticks of lightwood on the fire and again studied the cabin while waiting for the wood to catch. She felt enfolded in the rosy glow of the embers, snug, warm, cozy, and secure, the snow and cold and darkness of night shut out by the stout log walls. The wood flamed up and sent flickering light to the corners of the room and up to the roof poles. Still the feeling persisted and she could not name it.

Jonathan came in, hung up his coat, and crossed to the fire rubbing his hands. "Nice and warm in here. Have any trouble getting the fire going? Seems to be ready for something heavier." He laid on a few larger sticks of wood. "How does it feel to be home?"

"Why . . . why . . . " She looked up at her husband and her eyes were wide. "Being in your own home does feel different. At Markers' I was on pins and needles. I couldn't sleep in a strange bed and . . . well, it was *her* house. It does feel better in your own home, doesn't it?"

He took her in his arms and kissed her gently. "And your own home feels better with you in it."

On a sunny spring afternoon, Jonathan went into the timber to cut a backlog. He begrudged the time it took from his plowing, but a green backlog held fire longer and it was senseless to let the fire go out in the night. Matches were scarce and if the hearth fire went out, it meant starting it with flint or going to a neighbor's for coals.[1] And borrowing coals was considered certain proof that a man was lazy and improvident. When he drove the big grey horse around the corner of the cabin trailing the backlog, Castle, seated on the bench by the door, neither moved nor spoke. At the door he stopped the horse, unfastened the traces, and with a crowbar hitched the log through the doorway and across the floor to the fireplace. There he paused, for the hearth was cluttered with cooking utensils. He put the lid on the Dutch oven and set it aside, moved the greasy spider out of the way, and set back the iron pot half full of beans from the noon meal. With a way cleared he rolled the backlog into place and straightened his long body.

"Castle! Castle, are you going to sweep up this litter?"

Castle was unaware of litter and log cabins and Iowa. As always, when she sat on the bench, her thoughts were far away.

Jonathan took the hearth broom and brushed up the trail of mud and bark left by the backlog. His efforts were wasted, for the room was in complete disorder. The dinner dishes stood on the bare table, the bed was unmade, and articles of wearing apparel—feminine apparel—were strewn about the room, draped over the foot of the bed, hung over the backs of chairs, piled on chest and trunk. Jonathan went on outside and stood beside his wife who still sat as silent and motionless as the slab bench. The horse whinnied and he reached for the bridle, but as he turned, Castle's back straightened abruptly and he glanced in the direction of her gaze. A smudge of greyish white was moving almost imperceptibly along the prairie.

"It's a covered wagon!" she exclaimed without turning her head.

"Yes." Then, "It seems to be swinging this way. You may have guests for supper, Miss Castle."

His tone was sarcastic and she turned to look up at him. He was smiling that slight half-smile of his. She glared at him, then with sudden alacrity rose and swept past him into the cabin, her full skirts brushing his legs as she went. He looked after her with twinkling eyes but said nothing. Though he was anxious to get on with his plowing, should they have guests, it would be no more than common courtesy to declare a holiday. So he led the horse to the stable and mounted the barnyard fence to watch the smudge of white creeping across the green distance. He filled his pipe and chuckled at the thought of Castle galvanized to unwonted activity by the prospect of company. With such a wife, life was sometimes difficult but never monotonous.

The wagon moved slowly, or seemed to. He hoped whoever it was would stop. Castle would enjoy visitors and he could do with a decent meal. She could cook well enough when she took the trouble, and whatever her other failings, she made good coffee.

Castle worked swiftly and effectively. She shook up the feather bed and straightened the corn shuck mattress, beat up the pillows, smoothed the quilts, then gathered up her wardrobe and dumped everything into her trunk. Unfortunately the dishes would have to be washed; if they had guests they would need all of them. She sloshed the plates and cups through a pan of water and dried them hastily. Peering around the doorframe she saw the wagon turn again. Would it go on past and all her work be wasted? Half disappointed, she watched the cavalcade: a man on a black horse followed by the dun-colored oxen and grey wagon, then a red cow trailing behind. The wagon stopped and a woman's blue skirts swung down over the wheel. There were others in the wagon but Castle could not make them out. The man on the horse turned back and stood by the woman, then returned to his place in the lead. The wagon moved on but the woman was coming toward the cabin.

Castle ran to the fireplace. Taking a dipper of water from the pot on the crane she poured it into the beans and stirred them. Beans. But what else? Would Jonathan be able to shoot a prairie chicken on short notice? Or should she ask him to kill one of his cherished hens? The cocks were gone but they had twice as many hens as they had brought with them. Well, no use starting a fight with company coming. Too bad she hadn't baked light bread. There was plenty of flour but she had let the yeast run out. She'd make saleratus biscuit; folks from a covered wagon wouldn't be choosey. The three legged spider stood on the hearth. Too late to scour it now. If Jonathan got a prairie chicken she'd cook it in the stew pot and make gravy. She glanced about the room, stooped, and shoved the offending spider under the bed out of sight. The cabin could stand a good cleaning but a quick going over with the turkey wing duster and the hearth broom would have to do. Once more she went to the door and this time saw that the woman in blue was not alone. She carried a baby in her arms and a little girl clung to her skirts. Children! Was there no escape from them? But these were small; maybe they wouldn't eat too much. If they cried she'd have to grin and bear it.

Her house in a semblance of order, Castle set to work preparing tallow for candles. Already she had learned that in Iowa women took pride in being everlastingly busy. Her mother had disliked being caught doing anything more laborious than a bit of embroidery, but here men might smoke and talk but women's hands were never supposed to be idle. She hated making candles, but Jonathan had been at her for weeks because they were out. Come to think of it, she had rather missed watching him reading by the table in the evenings, the candlelight flickering across his bearded face. He'd be pleased to have candles again, though what he could see in those silly books. . . . She dumped the tallow in the pot and pushed it into the coals, then took down the mould and was setting the wicks when she heard voices. Jonathan came around the corner of the cabin carrying a headless Dominick hen by the feet. So he'd killed a hen. And in the spring when they needed the eggs to set. She'd have something to say to him!

"I hope you didn't kill that hen on my account because I wasn't aiming to stay to supper." The woman's voice was pleasant, her round face under the calico bonnet was jolly and kind. She was short and plump with full breasts and wide hips and although she could not have been much older than Castle, the hands holding the baby were rough and work worn. "The children wanted a drink and it may be a piece to the next crick. And I admit I was hankering for the sight of someone besides my own family, so I thought I'd just stop and set a spell."

"Come on in," Castle invited, moving aside so her skirts wouldn't block the doorway. "We don't get much company so we're glad you stopped."

"And you'll have to stay for supper," Jonathan grinned, dropping the hen on the grass. "She's already lost her head and you can't let such a sacrifice go unrewarded."

The woman chuckled as they went in, the baby turning her head this way and that, staring with round solemn eyes, the little girl clinging to her mother's skirt.

"If you put it that way, I suppose it's obligatory. I'm Abigail Hall. This is Cressy and the baby is Jennifer. She was a year old last month."

Castle dropped a slight courtsey and Jonathan inclined his head. "Castle and Jonathan Gayle," he said and took up the water bucket. "Is your husband with the wagon?"

"Yes, him and my three older girls. That's Evva and Harriet and Thaddeus. They're by former marriage. Only these two are Eli's." Castle placed a chair and Abigail sank into it with a sigh. "My, it's good to set on something that ain't moving!"

"Do you plan to settle around here?" Jonathan asked, filling the pot on the crane and swinging it over the hottest part of the fire. He would need boiling water to scald the hen.

"I'm afraid Eli ain't figgerin' to settle. He's set on going clear to Californy. For my part, I've had a bellyful a'ready. I don't take much stock in these tales of gold in the streets. We've come all the way from Illinoy and I'm that tired of traveling I'd settle most anyplace."

"I'll get fresh water," Jonathan told them and went to the well.

"We came from Pittsburgh," Castle told her visitor.

"Did you now! My, that was a long trip. Did you come all that way in a wagon?"

"Oh, no! We came by boat as far as Kanesville."

"That's over on the Missouri, ain't it? Seems you've already been where Eli's going. He says Kanesville's the jumping off place for Californy. Figgers we'll join up with a wagon train there. But it'll still be an awful long trip— lessen I can get him stopped somehow between here and there."

Jonathan came in with the bucket and Castle held a gourdful of water for little Cressy. She was a pale, pretty child with silvery hair and wide china-blue eyes. She drank and smiled shyly, then ducked behind her mother's chair where she stood peering over her mother's shoulder as Castle held the gourd for baby Jennifer, a brown-haired, blue-eyed roly-poly.

"I'm sorry Mr. Hall didn't stop," Jonathan remarked, "I might have persuaded him to settle here. I agree with you that the tales of gold are highly exaggerated and certainly the goldfields are no place for women and children. This is a good country and it is settling up rapidly. There'll be a stage from Des Moines to Kanesville[2] beginning next month, which means we'll have a market for whatever foodstuffs we raise. The stage station will be at Lew Garrison's, just a few miles from here, and since travelers have to eat, he'll be able to use quite a bit of produce. The stage will carry a certain amount of freight, too, so we'll be able to have goods brought here from the East. It's only twenty miles to Cold Spring, the new county seat, and once the stage is in operation the town will grow that much faster."

"Then you folks like it here?"

"Oh, my yes!" Castle declared stoutly, busily stirring the tallow. "But you've no idea how hard the men worked to get that stage line. They put in half the winter staking the road and bridging the creeks.[3] Jonathan came near having pneumonia twice."

"We couldn't get the stage line without the road," Jonathan explained. "Lew Garrison did the surveying, but the other men all did their share of the work."

"How many other settlers are there around here?"

"There are five families within six miles of us. In a few years you won't know this country. And it's the best corn land in the world. We arrived late last spring and I got a good sod crop."

"Only it looks so bare. I do like timber." Abigail settled Jennifer more comfortably on her lap.

"There's enough timber for logs and firewood and you don't have to clear the fields. You can start plowing as soon as you're ready."

"Could we get a crop this year?" Abigail asked thoughtfully.

"Yes, you could. My plowing is started but not finished. It isn't too late. You could certainly raise enough to feed yourselves over winter. I had a good garden last year."

Abigail's round pod of a belly shook with her laughter. "Mr. Gayle, you just talked yourself into the task of persuading Eli to settle here. I never wanted to go to Californy but another word from me and he'll just get his back up. You work on him and I'll keep mum. Then if you can get him to stay, he can tell me about it like he thought of it himself."

Jonathan laughed. "A delicate situation! I hope I can handle it." He took the pot of water from the crane and went out to scald the chicken.

"Can't I help?" Abigail asked. "I feel right lazy just setting here doing nothing."

Castle protested but Abigail deposited the children outside, warning Cressy not to let the baby put anything in her mouth. Then while Castle prepared the supper, Abigail went on with the candles.

"My, this mould is a handy thing. I have to make dips and it takes forever. You got a real nice place here, only I never seen a roof like this."

"It's thatch, like they have in Wales where Jonathan lived."

"Don't it leak?"

"No, but in rainy weather it smells sort of musty and in dry weather Jonathan is always afraid the sparks will set it afire. That's why he built the chimney so tall."

"I'd settle for any kind of roof to get out of that wagon. And to get out of going to Californy."

"Aren't you afraid Mr. Hall will go on without you?"

Abigail laughed comfortable. "Eli? 'Course not! He'll make camp soon as he comes to a likely spot. He won't go far without me. Besides, I've got his young'uns and he's got mine." When the chicken was tender and the tallow had been poured into the mould she asked, "Want I should make the dumplings while you set the table? You know where you keep things . . ."

"Why, yes, that would be a help."

Castle had not thought of dumplings but now she remembered Cookie's, so light and fluffy they melted in your mouth. Dumplings would be good and she'd watch and see how it was done so she could make them sometime and surprise Jonathan. Abigail mixed up a saleratus biscuit dough soft enough to spoon, then let it ease over the edge of the bowl and cut a knife across it so the globs of dough plopped into the bubbling pot of chicken.

"There." She put the lid on the pot. "Ten minutes and they're done. You're going to have supper right on the dot."

"You can never depend on Jonathan being on the dot. If he isn't late, he's early."

"Men are all alike," Abigail nodded. "There ain't a thing you can do about it."

"I do hope you folks take land nearby," Castle mused. She was so tired of never having anyone but Jonathan to talk to and him with so little to say. Now if the Halls lived near. . . . So far the children hadn't been a mite of bother and the baby hadn't cried once. She wondered what the other girls were like. She couldn't resist asking, "Were you a widow long?"

"Only a couple years. Thaddeus was two when her Pa died. She was named for him, Thaddeus Murray. He was so set on having a boy, when she come a girl we started calling her Thaddeus as a joke and the name stuck."

"But how did you manage, with three children?"

"I farmed the young'uns out and took a job cooking at the hotel. We got along. Seems when the Lord closes one door he opens another."

Mrs. Hall's cheerful acceptance of life on its own terms seemed a strange thing to Castle. If she were left a widow with three children—which God forbid—she wouldn't take it so calmly. And the woman stayed the whole afternoon while her husband and children went on with the wagon. Men had been known to leave their wives, yet she seemed in no hurry and during supper she and Jonathan talked about Iowa: the soil, the crops, the price of land—things which meant less than nothing to Castle. Then when the meal was over Abigail insisted on helping with the dishes and made no move to leave until the last pot had been scoured with wood ashes.

"I did have such a nice time," she told Castle as she picked up the baby, who had been sleeping on the bed. "That was the best meal I've had in years. My, I do hope Mr. Gayle can talk Eli into staying."

"You'll need help getting to camp," Jonathan told her as he shouldered sleepy little Cressy. "And if I don't talk to your husband tonight, he may be gone before I can see him in the morning."

They set out in the direction of the probable campsite and when they topped the first rise, they saw the flicker of a fire among the trees along the creek.

"There! I knew he wouldn't go far. But I was so sick of that wagon and if I hadn't got out he'd of kept going 'til now."

Eli Hall sat on his heels by the fire but rose and came to meet them when they entered the circle of light. His flaming red hair was a mass of curls, his bright blue eyes frank and friendly.

"Howdy, strangers," he greeted them, grinning broadly as he took Cressy from Jonathan. "Light and set by a lonesome widower's campfire. You got no notion how tiresome it gets living alone like I been doing. You folks come far today?"

"Now Eli, you dry up! This here is Mr. Gayle. We had supper with him and his wife. Real chicken and dumplings. Mrs. Gayle is the nicest woman you ever seen and real handsome, too."

"I'll have to rush right over and pay my respects. Been some time since I set eyes on a handsome woman. Glad to know you, Mr. Gayle, and thanks for feeding my wife and young'uns. Abbie does enjoy her victuals. Don't want to die in debt to her stomach."

"The way you talk!" she protested.

Eli carried Cressy to the covered wagon and handed her in. Abigail gave Jonathan a knowing wink as she followed her husband. When Eli returned to the fire he took off his hat, ran his fingers through his fiery hair, and replaced the hat on the back of his head.

"I'm grateful for your kindness to my family," he said seriously. "Abbie's the sociable sort and womenfolks like 'woman talk.' " Jonathan took out his pipe and began shaving tobacco. Eli grinned and took a pipe from his own pocket. "I'd be proud to have you set a spell. I'm sort of a night owl myself."

"So am I. I was sorry you and the girls didn't stop at the house. We have few guests and my wife is sociable, too."

"Never seen a woman that wasn't. Abigail didn't want to leave her friends in Illinoy, but I figger there's gold in Californy and I might as well git my share. Reckon she'll make friends there fast enough."

Jonathan nodded, puffing his pipe. He liked this man Hall, liked his appreciation of the simple kindness shown his wife, liked the easy accustomed way he handled the little girl, liked his friendliness. Why should such a man waste his life looking for gold? Gold was uncertain and dangerous. Land was permanent, something a man could depend on. The two smoked and talked far into the night. Now and then Eli threw fresh wood on the fire and the flames leaped up, lighting the wagon and the surrounding trees. The oxen shuffled about, eager to fill their bellies with the lush grass along the creek. The mare pawed impatiently at the end of her tether because the bite she could not reach looked greener than the grass under her nose. A squirrel, disturbed by the light of the campfire, chattered his annoyance, and from the darkness of the woods the wavering cry of a screech owl sounded now and then. By the time Jonathan knocked out his pipe and rose to go, Eli had decided to preempt the quarter section adjoining the Gayle farm on the south.

At breakfast the next morning Jonathan told Castle, "The Halls are staying. I hope they'll have no regrets. They're fine people, the kind this country needs. And Mrs. Hall is the kind of wife a man needs in this country."

Castle tossed her head and switched her skirts. "And I suppose I'm not! I don't belong here and you know it. I belong at Homeplace and that's where I'm going!"

"And miss the Halls' house raising?"

"What do I care about their raising?"

"As you wish, Miss Castle."

He was so exasperating. He knew she couldn't go home without him and she couldn't miss the Halls' raising after she and Jonathan had persuaded them to settle, could she? But why did he think so much of Abigail Hall? She certainly wasn't pretty. Why, she was as plain as a mud fence! How did she know what kind of wife she was? He thought he was so smart! But try as she would she couldn't work up a really good "mad"; the prospect of near neighbors was too exciting. It distracted her attention from her husband's shortcomings. It would be fine to have neighbors close enough to visit, and maybe the children wouldn't be too bad. The baby had been quiet . . .

As Jonathan rose and took his hat from the peg, Castle laughed. He turned, his brows raised inquiringly.

"If we have near neighbors you won't dare hit me. They'd hear me scream."

"I'll hit you, but you won't scream."

"I will so! I'll scream with all my might and they'll come running and won't you feel fine when I tell them . . ."

Jonathan's black eyes danced. "Won't *you* feel fine when *I* tell them!"

He went out and Castle stamped her foot as she looked after him. He was the meanest man! She wouldn't put it past him to tell on her. He wouldn't care what the neighbors thought of *her!*

5

T H E county was three years old when Eli Hall made camp on Turkey Creek in the spring of 1855. The first settlers had been Mormons who had stopped to recuperate before continuing the long trek to their own promised land.[1] Some twenty families had built cabins on the Nishnabotna River near the site of the old deserted Pottawattamie village and burying ground and established the post office at Cold Spring. By 1852 they were rested and had accumulated enough food for the trip to Deseret and Salt Lake. Soon after the first permanent settler built his cabin, the Mormons continued westward. Within a year or so there were a dozen cabins in the vicinity of Cold Spring and a dozen more scattered about the county, among them the settlers of Turkey Grove.

Now, astride his little black mare, Eli surveyed the scene while from the woods came the plaintive call of a mourning dove. No trees to fell, no stumps to pull. The soil looked good. Where Jonathan had plowed, the dark earth lay moist with dew under the morning sun. The Gayle cabin with its thatch roof and overly tall chimney stood some ways from the creek, facing westward. To the east were the stable and cow shed surrounded by a split-rail fence. North of the house and outbuildings, rows of closely planted young trees had been set, which in a few years would form a sturdy windbreak. If the Gayle establishment lacked beauty Eli was unaware of it, for he saw only the solid construction and planned utility. He found Jonathan at the stable harnessing his team. Eli examined the big greys with admiration.

"Reg'lar draft horses, ain't they?" he asked, patting a broad rump.

"Percherons. Breaking sod is too tough a job for a light team. You'll be glad you have oxen." Jonathan buckled a collar in place and ran his hand over the soft grey nose. "Ready to start plowing?"

Eli grinned. "Not quite. Abbie'll want a house first off. Calc'late I'll locate it down near the creek. She likes trees and it won't be such a piece to fetch the logs."

Jonathan shook his head. "Better not. There's evidence of a recent flood and a creek that floods once will flood again. You can plant trees where you want them; the cottonwoods in particular grow very fast. And since you're getting off to a late start, may I suggest you build a small cabin now and wait until fall for your permanent house? Then you can use your first cabin for your stable. When you get the logs ready, let me know and I'll tell the men."

Eli's grin broadened and he ran his fingers through his hair. "Abbie's real pleased about the neighbors."

"She'll meet them when you put up your cabin. With so little opportunity to sample each others' cooking, the women just dote on raisings."

Eli nodded. "Women are funny that way."

All morning Castle's hands were as busy as the wheels in her head. She not only washed the breakfast dishes, she cleaned the cabin thoroughly. She aired the bedding, scrubbed the floor, wiped down the log walls, and scoured the table and chairs as well as the spider and cook pots. When she was done she glanced about and told herself, "Clean enough for a funeral!" Then she took the candles from the mould, poured another batch and warmed up the leftover chicken and dumplings.

When Jonathan came in for dinner she asked, "When are you going to Garrisons'?" He raised questioning eyebrows. "I need yeast to set sponge. Now the Indians are gone I can bake light bread and eat it myself."

She filled her plate with dumplings. There wasn't much chicken but Abigail had made enough dumplings to feed a regiment and they were good. She picked through the bowl for bites of chicken. Likely she wouldn't get any more until they had young cocks again in the fall.

Jonathan watched her, then glanced about the room, his eyes merry. "I'll see about the yeast," he told her with a straight face.

"Mr. Hall was over, wasn't he?"

"Yes. He's scanning the timber for logs."

"How far is it to their camp?"

"About half a mile. Going calling?"

"Any reason I shouldn't?"

"Wear your sunbonnet. You might get freckled."

"A fat lot of difference it makes out here!"

Nevertheless, Castle wore her sunbonnet. She didn't intend to get parched and leathery like the women she'd seen on the trip from Kanesville. One look told you they had no pride at all. She jerked the bonnet farther over her face. From the top of the rise she could see the camp but it looked a long half mile. Iowa! Such a place! Why anyone in his right mind would live in Iowa from choice was more than she could understand. Jonathan thought it was a fine country, the ornery viper. She hadn't strained her runnet for him. She'd only cleaned the cabin so the Halls would have a good opinion of her, even though they were a bunch of nobodies and at home she wouldn't have looked at them. Nice people didn't come to Iowa; they stayed home where they belonged instead of gallivanting around in covered wagons. Panting and grumbling she trudged on down toward the camp.

The sun was hot and the ground rough and uneven. Creeping vines covered with stickers scraped across her ankles, leaving scratches that stung like nettles. She stopped and wiped her perspiring face on her petticoat. Straightening, she saw Abigail come around the wagon and waved. Seeing her, Abigail waved back and started toward her. Castle was tired enough to drop and spying a fallen tree at the edge of the woods she motioned toward it. Abigail climbed the hill and sat beside her while they fanned themselves with their sunbonnets.

"That was a long walk for you but I'm proud you came. Ain't this a nice camping spot?"

"If you have to camp, it's as good as any," Castle shrugged, glancing about. Trees shaded the wagon and the cow and oxen grazed contendedly. A yellowhammer drummed and a jaybird shrieked his feathered profanity. The cook fire smouldered and smoked while nearby two girls washed dishes in a great tin pan, laughing and chattering as they worked. Smaller figures bobbed about under and around the wagon.

"Them's my girls," Abigail nodded in the direction of the camp, then called lustily, "Evva, you and Harriet come here! Thaddeus! Come meet Mrs. Gayle. Tell Cressy to mind the baby."

Evva was a tall girl of fourteen with a sweet face and straight brown hair in long braids. Harriet, twelve, was freckled as a guinea egg and gangly as a colt. Thaddeus, nine, was obviously the beauty of the family, her black hair a mass of ringlets, her black eyes dancing with mischief. The three shook hands and said, "Pleased to meet you." Then Abigail shooed them away and continued her conversation.

"Well, we're your new neighbors."

"That's why I came. Can't you persuade Mr. Hall to build your cabin somewhere near ours? There's only one field between our house and the land you're taking, and the piece just beyond the field is high ground and good as any for a house."

Abigail's round belly shook with merriment. "You took the words right out of my mouth! We might just as well be near enough to be some good to each other. I'll never know why a man has to go way off in a corner away from everybody to build a house." Abigail studied Castle, then continued. "If we was to locate a likely site up near your place, there wouldn't be any point in him going off the other end of nowhere. But if we wait until he gets a spot of his own picked out, we're licked."

With one accord the two women rose, donned their sunbonnets, and trudged back to the Gayle homestead, Castle's hoops swaying, Abigail's hoopless skirts held in one hand. On the far side of Jonathan's south field they stopped to deliberate. After due appraisal and discussion, Abigail picked up a stick and with Castle at her heels marked off a generous rectangle some hundred yards from Jonathan's boundry.

"There. That's where the house ought to be. Now the stable should be back there a piece and the cow shed . . ."

Castle shook her head. "You want the stable and the cow shed and the hen house all joined together so when it storms you have to shovel only one path. No sense getting lost wandering around in a blizzard."

"Does it storm that bad here?"

"Worse. A man could freeze to death in his own barnyard. Jonathan runs a rope from the house to the stable. He says there isn't enough timber to break the wind. That's why he set the rows of trees."

"They'll look real nice when they get a little bigger. The girls can set ours while Eli is plowing. Goodness, I can see it all right now!"

"Jonathan can locate your well for you, too. He does it with a forked stick."

"Good! I was wondering who we could get. Eli can't witch. Don't it beat all? Just because we stopped at your house for a drink, we're going to be next-door neighbors. I 'spose the good Lord has a hand in things. Does seem so."

Abigail returned to camp and Castle went to the house to get supper.

While she cleared the table she told Jonathan of the plan. He smiled dryly and shook his head as he took a coal to light his pipe.

"When two women put their heads together a man doesn't have a chance. In this case, I cast my vote with the ladies. I've always wished Markers were closer."

"Why? Not so I could go visiting!"

"No, because I could use Tolly's help if it were more easily available. But it's a longish ride each way and I get along without rather than go after him."

"If he helped you, you'd have to help him."

"Tolly works for cash."

"Cash? Where you going to get cash?"

"I brought it with me, Miss Castle. I didn't come without a shoestring, remember? And whatever I put into the farm I get back — with interest."

"*When* do you get it back?"

"When I have enough land under cultivation and stock to fatten on the grain."

"Never mind all that," Castle broke in impatiently. "You going to help persuade Mr. Hall to build over the other side of the south field?"

"I am. Not merely to please you, my dear, but because the aforementioned advantages would be mutual."

"The way you talk! Can't you just speak United States?"

Jonathan grinned. "I try to stick to English for the same reason you cling to your hoops."

Eli's axe rang in the woods from daylight until dark, and when his logs were ready all Turkey Grove turned out for the raising. Since the coffee and staples would be cooked at her hearth and the tables set up in her dooryard, Castle prepared to do the honors as hostess. She was up before daylight and when Jonathan came in with the milk he found her in a fever of preparation.

"Eat and get out of the way," she told him, bustling about among the cooking utensils. "I want the house respectable before anyone gets here." Jonathan washed and sat down and while Castle poured the coffee he helped himself to fried mush and molasses. His wife took her place and continued, "I hope Abigail likes everybody. I want her to feel at home." Jonathan paused between bites to smile at her in broad amusement. "What are you grinning at? She don't know a soul but us. She may feel strange."

Abigail arrived before Castle had done the breakfast dishes.

"Goodness, you're an early bird! I'm not near done my work," she apologized.

Abigail took off her sunbonnet and rolled up her sleeves. "I got four pairs of hands and I left three of 'em to do the chores at camp. Young'uns are a bother, but they're a help, too. The girls will be along later to lend a hand."

"We won't need them," Castle protested. The older girls wouldn't matter but with so many young'uns under foot . . .

Abigail chuckled complacently. "Wild horses couldn't keep 'em away. Thaddy can mind the little ones. She's no good for anything else. Laziest little trollop you ever seen." She shook her head as she swung the broom.

''And what a temper! Reckon it's because she's pretty. The plain ones give less trouble.''

Castle was stunned. Marybelle had been the pretty one and she had always been a perfect little lady. But if she had a lazy, ill-tempered child she wouldn't go around talking and laughing about it. She'd wear the brat out! . . . A wagon was coming and she glanced out to see Martha and Tolly Marker at the barnyard gate. To Abigail she rattled off the list of their neighbor's misfortunes and by the time Martha reached the door Castle was there to greet her.

''Come in, Martha, and meet our newest neighbor, Abigail Hall.''

''Howd'do, Mrs. Hall. We're proud to have you in Turkey Grove. It'll be fine, you and Castle living so close. I wish our house was on this side of the creek, but Josh thought it wasn't suitable.'' A shadow of sadness passed over the long face, but the Hall children were at the door and her grey eyes grew merry in response to their polite greetings. ''My land! You can't complain you got no help around the house!'' she laughed.

Abigail sent Thaddeus to play with Cressy and Jennifer. ''You stay right over there by the fence where we can keep an eye on you. And don't you *dare* cross that field. The men can't be bothered stumbling over you when they're lugging logs.'' Then she set Harriet to peeling potatoes. ''If she starts now she ought to be done by dinner time.''

Harriet grinned unconcernedly and settled herself to the task, a basket of potatoes on the floor, a tin milk pan in her lap. Tolly Marker came to the door and offered to help set up the tables in the yard and Evva went with him, instructing him shyly where and how they should stand, and Tolly looked away and blushed every time she spoke to him. Then Lew and Indiana Garrison arrived. When the wagon stopped, Lew jumped nimbly down from the crosstree and turned to help his wife as she clambered painfully over the wheel. Puffing and blowing she hobbled to the door.

''My rhumatiz always hits me the wrong time,'' she apologized as she dropped heavily into the nearest chair. ''But I was that set on coming 'cause once the stage starts I won't get my nose outside the door for months on end. I ain't as young as I was and not near as spry, but Lew is bound to get that stage line through the county. Now, where is he? . . . Lew, did you bring in them baskets? All right, get along with you. Us women got work to do.''

Lew waved to the women and hurried away.

Castle shook her head at Indiana. ''The men don't give a whoop how much work the Station will be for you, do they? But here, you haven't met Abigail Hall yet. And these are her girls. The others are out by the fence.''

''What, no boys? All girls? Now that's kind of nice, ain't it? My children are such a long way from here. Why do young'uns always leave home?''

''Now, Indie,'' Martha patted her shoulder in passing, ''that ain't the way I heard it. I heard you and Lew as the ones left home.''

An uproar of galloping and shouting drew Indiana half out of her chair in the effort to look out the door. She settled back and waved a reassuring hand at the others, ''Just Knute and Hennie Olson making all the noise they can before their Pa comes and tells 'em to get quiet and keep working. Likely

Axel and Berta ain't far behind.'' Then to Abigail, ''You'll like Berta, but don't die of shock when you see her. She's big as a man but she has the handsomest head of hair you ever seen and a complexion like rose petals.''

Martha nodded. ''She's a real fine looking women. And I reckon Axel ain't so bad even if he does work them boys of his. Just seems to me he's sort of greedy.''

''Does seem so,'' Indiana admitted. ''Though if you was in bad trouble I think he'd help even if it cost him. He ain't mean, just close.''

''We're gabbing too much,'' Martha reminded them, putting wood on the fire. ''We got to get water hot for coffee. What you aim to make it in, Castle? That big iron pot would do. Takes a lot of coffee for a bunch of men.''

''It's the biggest thing I got. . . . Who's that now, Indie?''

Indiana turned again. ''Pettits. Land, how young'uns grow! Mrs. Hall, would you send your girls out to help? Patience has got more stuff than the twins can carry. Patience! Put that child down! He's got legs.''

''She's got no more sense . . . ,'' Martha muttered as she and the girls hurried out. ''Mornin', Ed. Here, Laurel, give me that basket. Luke, let the girls help with them things. Good grief, Patience, you must of thought nobody else would bring anything.''

''Maybe she likes her own cooking,'' Ed grinned as he climbed back in the wagon and headed for the Hall construction.

''Ed! the idea!'' Patience called after him. ''Watch now, don't get underfoot, Josie. . . . Is everybody here? I thought we'd never get started. Indie Garrison! Am I glad to see you! Nothing like a raising to get folks together.'' Patience bent and kissed Indiana's cheek and set the small boy she was carrying on her friend's lap. ''Hold your godchild a minute, will you? Thanks Martha, girls . . .''

''They're Evva and Harriet Hall,'' Castle explained. ''And this is their Ma, Abigail Hall. The little ones are out by the fence: Thaddeus and Cressy and Jennifer.''

''I don't see the boy.''

Abigail laughed. ''No boy. I got all girls. Thaddeus is the one with black hair.''

''Well, that evens things up a bit. My two were the only girls in Turkey Grove. Run on, Josie, and take Cade. Laurel, you help unpack the baskets. Luke, wood and water before you go near the men. Now, what can I do?''

''Set,'' Indiana told her. ''Set here by me and keep out of their way. They got more help than they know what to do with. Set, and give me no back talk. I don't want you working yourself into a decline while my rhumatiz is acting up. I ain't fit to set up nights.''

''Indie is the doctor here,'' Castle told Abigail. ''She brought Cade for Patience.''

''I'm glad there's someone around to call on, though having babies don't bother me much. I shell 'em out like peanuts. And the young'uns are all real healthy, except Cressy. She's had pneumonia twict and near died both times. If she was the kind to spoil, she'd be rotten to the core. But I reckon there's a runt in every litter.''

"Is she the baby?" Patience asked.

"No, Cressy's next youngest. Jenny is the baby and she's real husky though she does have croup sometimes. Don't amount to much."

"Here come the Olsons. And there's Crawfords' wagon. Seems Grampa is the only person in Turkey Grove that won't be here today."

"How is Grampa?" Indiana asked carefully.

"The same. He keeps well but he's getting more deef all the time and he don't see too good." Patience laughed. "Ed says he sees and hears everything that ain't none of his business. He does try Ed so. But the poor old man don't mean no harm. He's just a bit vague."

No one offered any comment. They preferred to discuss Grampa Pettit when his daughter-in-law was elsewhere. The crochety old man made a habit of insulting everyone who came near and they all knew he led both Ed and Patience a dog's life. But he was quickly forgotten as the Olsons drew up with much shouting and laughing.

As she swung easily from the wagon, Berta saw Indiana by the door and called, "Ja, ja, Indie! We be there in the minute." Her load would have staggered a man. Axel followed, a blond giant out of a fairy tale, equally laden. "Nils, Nils, take the care!" Berta admonished her young son. "Those my good dishes that you break I thrash you. Karlie, no. Not by the men yet. Stay!" Then to the women, "That late we are the house is built already. But the big boys, they give the hand. That red cow with the horn off, she is the devil. Through the fence she is and nothing stops. Ja, ja, is good to see the neighbors all to onct. Axel, Nils, the baskets down and you go. Karlie? Where the child is?"

"He saw the other children, Berta. He's all right," Martha said.

"If you don't need me Ma, I'll go look after the young'uns," Evva offered. "Thaddy can mind one or two . . ."

"Yes, go on, Evva. We got help enough here. With so many to play with, Thaddy needs somebody to keep an eye on *her*."

By the time introductions were over, the Crawfords were there. The Gayle cabin was larger than most but Castle wondered how they could squeeze in another set of baskets and another hoop skirt. For today the women all wore their hoops, and calico skirts billowed and rustled over stiffly starched petticoats. Castle would never know how she had been ripped to shreds for wearing her hoops every day, putting on airs and trying to impress her neighbors just because she had been raised in the city with servants to wait on her. So, though they went hoopless in their own homes, the women had all blossomed out in hoops to give the fine Mrs. Gayle a taste of her own medicine.

On the way in, Tabitha Crawford stopped to talk to Evva and the children where they were gathered by the fence, while at the cabin Indiana and Patience drew their chairs from the door to let the Crawford boys through with their baskets. Martha took a quick look around, then motioned to the boys.

"Sid, you can set yours by the hearth, there. Harriet, you'll have to move so Seth can get by to put his under the table. There ain't room anyplace else."

Harriet ducked aside as he passed. Turning, Seth gave her long pigtail a friendly tweek. She looked up and grinned and Seth winked at his brother.

"Girls! Gee willikins! Wouldn't it be nice if they was a little older?"

"They?"

"Shoot, yes! Didn't you see the one with Ma? She's in pigtails, too." Harriet's eyes danced. "I got three sisters ain't in pigtails."

"Yeah? Where?"

"Out there." Harriet jerked her head in the direction of the door and the two boys hurried out. Harriet caught her mother's eye and snickered. Abigail chuckled and when Tabitha came in asking where the boys were going in such a hurry, Harriet told her the joke.

"Serves them right!" Tabitha laughed. "They're smart alecks. Now they're heading across the field at a run. They won't hear the last of this. I'm going to tell the other boys. I'll fix them. I bet it was Seth?"

Harriet giggled. "He pulled my hair."

"Did he now! A boy don't pull a girl's hair unless he likes her."

Harriet blushed and giggled again. "He didn't pull it hard."

"Here, here!" Castle teased. "Sounds like you didn't mind."

"I didn't. The boys in school used to pull my hair back in Illinoy."

"Don't get so set up about it," her mother chided. "You ain't the only girl ever had her braids pulled. Go on out with the others 'till I call you. We'll need you and Evva to wait table."

"It just isn't fair!" Tabitha complained. "You with all those nice girls and only one man to look after, and me with three men and no help. I suppose your husband could use a boy, but what I'd give for a girl!" Tabitha shook her head. "Every woman ought to have a girl or two."

"Ja, ja," Berta mourned, "my two is the graveyard in. So far we leave them, back in Pensywany."

"You got more'n your share of boys," Indiana reminded her.

"Ja, but boys is *boys,* not like girls to company the Mudder."

Tabitha changed the subject abruptly. "What's been done, Castle? Getting here so late, I don't know where to begin." Tabitha's habit of taking charge of everything was a frequent source of irritation to her strong-minded neighbors.

"Never mind beginning," Indiana told her tartly. "It's all done but finishing."

By noon the log walls were up and the men crossed the field to wash up at the horse trough. They found places at the table while the women brought out steaming platters and bowls of food: fresh and smoked venison cooked a dozen ways; baked beans and boiled beans; light bread, saleratus biscuit, corn bread, and muffins; boiled potatoes, fried potatoes, and potatoes browned with the meat; the last of the winter turnips and parsnips and the first of the spring greens. There were jams and pickles and preserves and stewed and dried plums; cookies and molasses cake and gingerbread; and there was coffee topped with thick cream to wash it all down.

For a time the men's knives and forks clattered against their plates with little comment other than an occasional, "Pass me . . ." The morning's work had reduced their stomachs to hollow voids, but as they filled the yawning emptiness, strength and humor returned and they fell to laughing and joking. Then Abigail came out to see what was needed and called to the girls to bring more coffee and meat. Ed Pettit grinned up at her as she paused beside him.

"Think you'll like your new mansion, Mrs. Hall?"

"It's going to be a fine cabin," she declared. "I brought some flower seeds . . ."

"Listen to her!" Ed laughed. "The roof ain't on and she's planting flowers!" Turning he asked soberly, "Seth, I hear you already got engaged to one of the Hall girls?"

The table broke into an uproar. Hennie choked and Sid and Knute pounded him on the back. Patience, ladling coffee for the girls to carry out, smiled over her shoulder at the other women.

"Listen to them! You can't tell the men from the boys."

"Is good to laugh yet, how they work so hard. Ach! Is happy place, this country. But my country too . . . was happy there."

"You ever get homesick, Berta?"

"How say—the homesick?" she shrugged. "My Axel and boys is here. Is my home, this. Old country, my Mudder's home. Same like place you come from back east."

Patience nodded. It would be the same. They had all come from other places, other homes. But Castle wanted to shout that this was not *her* home, nor ever would be. Never, never! Someday she would go back to her own home where a lady could live as a lady should. Yet when the day was over she watched her neighbors leave with a sense of loneliness. It was like a Fourth of July picnic when they all got together, but it was a long time between house raisings. She glanced about the cabin. Everything had been left in order and the room seemed vastly empty after the crowded day. And the empty evening lay ahead: supper to get, dishes to wash, then Jonathan with his nose in a book. The other women had someone to talk to. . . . She threw wood on the fire, straightened, and watched the flames. The other women had someone to talk to because they had children. Even Martha had Tolly when Josh died. If anything happened to Jonathan . . . . but nothing would. Nevertheless, life stretched ahead with all the evenings empty. If she had had a child. . . . How long had it been? Maybe next time. . . . Only babies were such a bother, always crying and getting dirty. If she had no one to talk to, at least she had no brats to annoy her. Perhaps that was the lesser evil.

Now with the Halls living just across the south field she wouldn't be so long with no one but Jonathan around. In the morning she'd go over and offer to help Abigail get settled. That would be the neighborly thing to do. That night as she lay beside her husband in the light of the fire from the hearth, she thought of Homeplace. There, the fireplace in her bedroom had been graced by a lovely mantel and shining blue tiles where firelight danced on chilly evenings as she snuggled under the quilts on her tall tester bed. If only she could go home! Life had been so simple, so easy there. She had been alone, there. Alone in her room, with no one to talk to, no place to go. Only there she'd had the best of everything and servants to wait on her. Now, because she had married Jonathan . . .

"Jonathan! Why don't you build a new house?"

He grunted. "Why should I?"

"Because I want to live respectable."

"I didn't know you expected to stay that long."

"While I'm here I might as well have a decent house." She raised herself on one elbow. "You could build a new house as well as not."

"What's the matter with this one?"

"As if you didn't know! I should think you'd be ashamed . . ."

"I have no wish to impress my neighbors. This cabin is as good as any in Turkey Grove, and if it's no better than the others, that makes no difference to me."

"Well, it does to me! I want a real house with glass windows and a shingle roof and there's no reason why I shouldn't have it."

"Oh, but there is! And you won't get it until you've learned to keep house as well as Mrs. Hall."

Castle gave an angry flounce. "How do you know how she keeps house?"

"I don't have to see it to know. You'd do well to take her as your model."

She sat bolt upright in bed. "ME, take Abigail Hall as my model? Why . . . why . . ."

Jonathan laughed until the bed shook. "Go to sleep. Anyone with your vanity doesn't need a house."

"I do so! You're a dirty, deceiving, underhanded. . . . You tricked me into marrying you! You said you'd do better in Iowa and I believed you. And this is what you brought me to!"

Her cat-eyes blazed but Jonathan continued to laugh. "I've often wondered why you asked me to bring you along. So it was for my money. Too bad I wasn't born rich instead of so handsome. Good night, Miss Castle."

"You . . . you . . . ," she sputtered. But Jonathan turned his back and she suspected he was still laughing. She flopped down beside him and turned her back, too. He was the meanest man!

6

T H O S E first weeks after the arrival of the Halls, Castle had little opportunity to become better acquainted with her new neighbors, but every day she saw them in the fields or about the house and at night their light shining from the doorway kept her company. Somehow Iowa seemed less desolate, less like the end of the earth. Sitting on the bench in the twilight waiting for Jonathan to come in, she heard their voices: Abigail summoning the children from their play, Evva at the fence calling, "Supper's ready, Pa!" And watching the sunset glow fade from the sky, Castle no longer felt herself alone in the wilderness.

Each morning Eli and the oxen were in the fields before sunup, and when a field was plowed and harrowed he moved on to the next, leaving the planting to the rest of the family. Harriet and Thadeus dropped corn and potatoes, Evva and Abigail covered. All worked in an effort to catch up with the advancing season. When the corn came up, they all hoed, but once it was laid by, Castle soon learned what a pleasure and a nuisance neighbors could be.

Abigail was indeed the sociable sort and the girls took after their mother. Singly or by twos and threes they dropped in, staying half the day or all day depending on the work and the weather. Castle found their informal calls entertaining yet disconcerting, since never knowing when they would appear she was obliged to keep her house in a perpetual state of readiness. And when the girls invited themselves to a meal they expected something out of the ordinary, for their mother was still singing the praises of Castle's chicken and dumplings, quite forgetting that she had made the dumplings herself.

One morning Castle awoke in a particularly sour mood. During breakfast everything that could go wrong, did. The coffeepot tipped over and almost put out the fire; the cream spilled and had to be cleaned up off the floor; the mush stuck in the pot and the scorched taste did nothing to enhance its flavor. Worse yet, she broke one of her few ironstone cups. By the time Jonathan left the house she was ready to throw the cooking equipment out the window and herself after it. What was the sense of slaving her life away? The dishes could stay where they were. She was going out and sit on the bench and not lift a finger all day. Then the Halls would see her sitting there and think something was wrong. Fine state of affairs when a woman couldn't sit in front of her own house without the neighbors asking why! The dishes wouldn't wash themselves. She might as well get the dirty work over with. So she clattered them angrily in and out of the dishpan and onto the shelves. She hated sleeping in an unmade bed and it was useless to pat the feather tick without shaking up the cornshuck mattress. Drat the Halls! She might as well make the bed right so if any of them came over. . . . What in tarnation had possessed her to set sponge last night? Now she'd have to work the bread down and bake. Unless she threw the sponge out. But Jonathan knew Abigail baked every other day. . . . Drat Abigail! And Abigail churned when the cream was just blink so the butter would come sweet. Of all the silly ideas! But in another day her cream would be sour as swill and they would have no butter left for supper.

She was churning, banging the dasher up and down with a vengeance, when Abigail called from the dooryard, "You there Castle? I hope you don't mind company. I was up early and got my work done before breakfast so I thought I'd come over and set a spell." She came in and settled herself, drawing her knitting from her apron pocket.

She could get her work done before breakfast with three girls to do it for her! Castle had a good mind to tell her so but decided against it. "I was just thinking I hadn't seen you lately."

"Nice day like this I can't stay cooped up in the house and there ain't a thing I can do outside. Eli don't need us in the field and I've about weeded my flowers to death already."

"Think they'll ever bloom?"

"Oh, my yes! I got a green thumb. Everything I touch grows and blooms like a house afire."

"I never had any luck with flowers," Castle countered. She had never planted a seed in her life but she had no intention of letting Abigail think her ignorant.

"I'll give you some of mine when they're ready to transplant. They got to be thinned anyhow."

Now she'd done it! She'd have flowers to take care of. As if she didn't have enough. . . . She'd just let them die, that's what. "They likely won't live long for me."

"I'll plant 'em for you and they'll live."

The butter was coming and Castle gathered it carefully the way Jonathan had showed her. Seemed funny a man should know about such things, but he'd had to do about everything when he'd lived on the poor farm as a boy. She splashed the dasher up and down gently, turning it slowly. With Abigail watching she was glad she knew how to do it properly.

"You've got a nice batch of butter there," Abigail said admiringly when Castle took it up. But before she could answer, Thaddeus came racing along the south fence shouting at her mother. Abigail sighed in exasperation but continued to knit. "They've lost Jennifer again. I might have knowed I couldn't trust them out of my sight. They get playing and forget the baby. Yes, Thaddy?"

"Jenny's gone, Ma!" the girl panted, her face red and hot, her hair wild.

"Likely I'll have to help hunt. You'd think four girls could keep track of one baby," Abigail complained, putting her knitting back in her pocket resignedly.

"Ain't you frightened?" Castle demanded in astonishment.

"Not any more. Jenny gets lost so often, if I worried about her I'd be in a stew all the time. Since she's walking she's all over the place. Does seem she looks after herself something remarkable."

"But she's so quiet . . ."

"She don't talk much, but you never seen such a busybody."

Remembering stories of babies drowning in wells or creeks or getting lost in the timber, Castle was more excited than Abigail. Putting the butter bowl aside she took off her apron. "I'll help hunt. Something might happen to her."

The girls came to meet their mother and related the places they had looked.

"Start from the house and fan out 'til we find her," she told them calmly.

It was Castle who found the child down in the meadow by the creek, but she dared not call out to let the others know, for Jennifer was standing under Black Beauty's belly. Castle waited in the hot sun, afraid to move or speak, since Beauty was obviously unaware of the child's presence. If the mare were startled she might trample the child without even knowing it. When Jennifer turned and saw her, perhaps she would come. Or would she? Castle had never tried to make friends with her and Jennifer was inclined to keep to herself. Beauty took a step and continued grazing, but Castle held her breath as Jennifer reached out to touch the hind leg as it approached her. Then the child drew her hand back, looked up at the mare's belly, and chuckled quietly. Little devil! She knew well enough what she was doing! Castle wanted to shake her till her teeth rattled—if she had any. Then Jennifer turned and stared at Castle blandly. Castle held out her hands and smiled but Jennifer didn't smile. Instead she turned and walked away, out from under the mare on the far side. Castle called and in minutes Abigail and the girls came running. Evva picked Jennifer up but Abigail turned to Castle.

"My land! You're shaking like a leaf!"

"She was standing under Beauty . . ."

"Beauty wouldn't hurt her."

"Beauty didn't know she was there! Jenny almost took hold of her leg. It might have give Beauty a start . . ."

Abigail plopped down on the ground and took Jennifer on her lap. "I never even thought of that. Maybe you saved Jenny's life!"

Castle went home and worked out her butter but her hands still shook. Why should she care if the brat got killed? She didn't like children and she particularly didn't like Jennifer. The child was stupid, and plain to boot. Plainer even than Evva or Harriet. All she ever did was stare like an owl. Little vixen! The way she had turned and walked away. . . . Horrid brat! But Abigail was convinced Castle had saved Jennifer's life and talked of nothing else for days. Well, she *had* used her head.

On the whole, the Halls were very satisfactory neighbors. However, when the girls came to borrow quilt patterns and recipes for eggless cake and gooseberry conserve, Castle put them off.

"I don't rightly remember," she told them. "I'll look up the receipts and try to find the quilt patterns, but I got no time right now."

Castle prepared an especially tasty supper for Jonathan. She would need his help — and he would be more cooperative if he ate well. While supper was cooking she rummaged through her trunk and found the cookbook her mother had insisted she bring with her. "You won't have servants to do for you. There are so many nice things in it. How to wash black lace and raise the pile on velvet . . . and a good hand lotion. You must take care of your hands. . . . I'm sure you'll find it useful." It was a big thick book so there might be receipts in it, too. When Jonathan finished supper, Castle cleared the table and brought out the book.

"Before you start your reading I wish you'd find a couple receipts for me. The ones for eggless cake and gooseberry conserve." She spoke casually, her face arranged in calm composure, the black brows raised in polite interrogation.

Jonathan looked up at his wife as he took the cookbook from her hands. There was a gleam in his eyes that warned his aid would be dearly bought. He glanced through the book, pausing to read here and there, studying the pictures of ladies making and baking delicacies of all sorts. Then he closed the book on the table and turned to his wife, pushing back his chair and crossing one leg over the other very deliberately.

"So we're to have an economical eggless cake and delicious gooseberry conserve. But why eggless cake when we have plenty of eggs? And have you picked the gooseberries yet? Or would you like me to drop you off on the way to the field in the morning? It's much more pleasant picking in the morning when it's cool."

Castle swallowed her wrath. She needed her husband's help and if she let him pick a fight, she wouldn't get it. Pushing back her hair she tried to speak calmly.

"Is it too much for me to ask you to find a couple receipts?"

"Is it too much for me to ask why? That is, if you don't intend to use them."

"Abigail sent over and I've forgotten . . ."

Jonathan threw back his head and laughed. "You never heard of eggless cake or gooseberry conserve until today! But you wish to impress Abigail with your ability as a cook. A commendable ambition, Mrs. Gayle. Neither would I want it bruited about that my wife knows less than nothing about cookery. My masculine vanity would never survive the humiliation if the guilty truth leaked out. So, Mrs. Macbeth, we will proceed with the crime." He turned to the cookbook, looked in the index, found the page, and turned again to his wife. "Now. I will read each recipe slowly just twice, so put your mind on it."

Castle sat down, propped her head on her hand, and closed her eyes. Jonathan read and she repeated the words after him. Unable to read, she had long since learned to memorize quickly and easily. When the girls came over again she would be able to rattle off the receipts as glibly as you please. She'd have a pencil and paper handy on the mantel shelf for them to write it all down because she'd be too busy . . .

"Another thing, Jonathan. You're handy at drawing and I never could draw a straight line."

"Thank you, my dear, but we can dispense with the flattery. You aren't good at wheedling and I'm not good at being wheedled. Out with it! What more does Abigail want?''

Castle rose and went to the mantel shelf to make sure a pencil and paper were there. Over her shoulder she said meekly, ''Quilt patterns.''

''Quilt patterns. Hummm.'' Jonathan smiled at her back, stroking his beard thoughtfully. He closed the book and pushed it aside. ''Have you ever made a quilt, my love?''

Castle turned so quickly her skirts knocked the poker to the hearth with a clatter. ''I've made more quilts than you can shake a stick at!''

''Did you piece any of those on the bed?''

''I pieced every one of them! The bottom one I made before I was ten years old! Aunt Lucy nearly worked the life out of me — telling me how proud I'd be.''

Jonathan rose and went to the bed, lifted a corner of each quilt in turn and examined it carefully, then went back to the table. ''Take your cookbook. Get your gewgaws out of my way.'' Castle quickly removed salt, pepper, sugar, and spoon holder. From his brass-bound chest Jonathan brought paper and a rule and from the hearth he took a piece of charcoal and sharpened a point. ''If you can make quilts, it's a small matter who supplies the patterns. What design do you want? The same as those on the bed?''

''No, Abigail has seen all them. I know lots of others if I can explain . . .''

Their quarrels forgotten, Castle hung over her husband's shoulder while he drew from her descriptions. And if the results were not replicas of the quilts of her childhood, they at least possessed a certain originality, and she was sure Abigail would be impressed. For a week Jonathan spent his evenings drawing, and to his wife's surprise he made no protest when she asked for another and another pattern. Instead he glanced at her now and then in a way that made her uneasy. He had something up his sleeve, but she had no time to figure out what it might be. He *did* have something up his sleeve — she would have been surprised to know that it was Abigail Hall. Abigail had proved the stimulus he had been hoping for. Once roused, Castle was capable of generating a head of steam that would carry her — where? That was a bridge he would cross when he came to it. Sufficient unto the day. . . . He had worked until nearly midnight finishing the intricate mosaic she called the Bridal Wreath and now he threw down the charcoal and pushed the papers aside.

''That's enough. You couldn't make a quilt like that if your life depended on it.''

''I could so! But I bet Abigail couldn't.''

Next morning as soon as her house was in order, Castle sorted the quilt patterns and hurried to the Hall cabin. Abigail met her at the door, drying her hands on her apron.

''Come on in, Castle. Harriet, you finish the dishes and let Evva get on with the churning. Thaddy, take the young'uns out to play so they won't be underfoot. Cressy, wipe your nose before you go out. Sit down, Castle, I'm that glad you came.''

"I finally got around to the quilt patterns so I brought them over while I was thinking about it." She settled herself and spread her skirts as she handed the stack of patterns to Abigail.

It was Saturday and Jonathan had gone to Garrison's Station with melons and vegetables and wouldn't be back for dinner so she had the day before her. Abigail was delighted with the quilt blocks.

"My, I wish I could make quilts like yours," Abigail shook her head. "You do beat all, the things you can do. That Bridal Wreath is the prettiest thing I ever seen, but I wouldn't even attempt it. The Sunburst is handsome, too, but it wouldn't look like that if *I* made it. I got no patience with anything so complicated. Now that Neck-Tie and the Fan are simple enough I might get them done someday. You know, I think I'll start right in on one of them Neck-Ties. It looks like it would be real fast and easy."

Castle had intended to eat dinner with the Halls but decided to go home and bake an eggless cake. They had plenty of eggs, but she had never baked a cake and the eggless was the only receipt she knew. Jonathan would be that surprised. She could show him a thing or two if she had a mind to. She could do anything Abigail could do. He needn't think Abigail was so all-fired smart.

Jonathan was astounded when she set the cake on the table that evening and announced, "If you'll drop us off down by the meadow Monday morning, Abigail and the girls and I are going to pick gooseberries. We aim to have a picnic and you can stop for us on your way home in the evening. You won't mind taking a cold lunch will you?"

Jonathan managed, "That'll be fine," and tried not to stare at his wife. He wished he knew how Abigail had done it, but since she had, *how* was not important. When he had somewhat recovered from the shock of the cake, which he had enjoyed, he asked, "Were the quilt blocks acceptable?"

"Abigail thinks they're just fine. She's starting a Neck-Tie and I'm going to make a Fan. She says she wishes she could make quilts like mine. She says there ain't anything I can't do."

Jonathan took a book from the shelf but sat down and laid it on the table, pushing the candle aside so the light would not come between him and his wife. He studied her face, animated with pleasure, her eyes glowing, her brows — that personal barometer of hers — up, her mouth no longer set in lines of bitterness. She brushed a lock of damp hair from her forehead and he smiled in amusement as she resumed.

"Abigail says . . ." He chuckled. "What are you laughing at? Don't you believe me?"

"Certainly. I was only thinking how difficult you'll find it to live up to Abigail's good opinion of you."

Castle turned away from him angrily and clattered the dishes into the pan. Why couldn't he have a good opinion of her, too? He always acted as though she didn't know anything and couldn't do anything. The blistering heat of the afternoon had ended in a thunder shower which had brought the temperature down but left the air electric, and now Castle's temper was rising with the barometer. After all her hard work baking that cake . . .

"One of these days I'll go home!" she threw over her shoulder.

Jonathan stepped to the hearth for a coal to light his pipe. "Let me know when you're ready and I'll drive you to Kanesville."

"You'd let me go, wouldn't you? Why don't you say you'd be glad to get shut of me?" She turned to her husband and her eyes were angry and resentful. He returned her gaze with amused indifference, his face in the shadow, the wavering light of the fire striking upward to outline his angular profile.

"I wouldn't say I'd be glad to get rid of you. You wear no noticeable halo, but there are times when I find you amusing. However, I don't want you to feel I'm keeping you here against your will. You did ask me to bring you."

Castle threw a plate. Jonathan didn't trouble to duck and the missile flew wide of its mark, striking the chimney and shattering over the hearth. He set his pipe on the mantel, caught his wife's arm, and whirling her about planted the toe of his boot just under her second hoop. She did not cry out as she would have done before the arrival of the Halls, but as she jerked free she hissed, "Let me be, you polecat!"

Jonathan returned to the fireplace and taking his pipe, relighted it. Between puffs he remarked, "Someday . . . you'll learn . . . not to throw things."

That night they had not been long asleep when they were awakened by frantic knocking. Leaping up, Jonathan pulled on his pants and lighted the candle. He opened the door and found Evva whitefaced and sobbing.

"The baby! She's got croup real bad, and it's all my fault! She'd been playing in the hot sun and when it rained I forgot to put a shirt on her. If she dies—it'll be my fault!"

Castle scrambled out of bed. "Stop your nonsense, Evva. Go on home and do what you can to help your Ma. I'll come soon as I get my clothes on. Go on, now, and stop bellering."

Evva wiped her eyes on her sleeve and trudged off, reassured. Castle turned helplessly to Jonathan.

"Why did they come to me? Why didn't Eli go for Indie?"

"It's several miles to Garrisons'," he reminded her. "Eli would have to ride over and Lew would have to hitch up and bring Indiana. That is, if they could leave the Station unattended. And croup won't wait. Besides, Abigail thinks there's nothing you can't do. Or so you said."

Castle picked up her comb and cast a scornful glance at her husband. "Well, what does she expect me to do now?"

"I don't know. What *can* you do?"

Her head down and hair hanging over her face she paused in her rapid combing. "Don't act so stupid! I can't go over there and tell them I don't know what to do." Witchlike she peered through her hair as she straightened, but Jonathan's face told her nothing and she bent, collected her hair in her hands, flipped it over her head, and swiftly twisted it into its accustomed knot.

Watching her, Jonathan laughed softly. "If you don't know what to do, you won't be much help. Nevertheless, you told Evva you'd go and Abigail will expect you. And she'll expect you to know what to do.''

Castle jerked a petticoat over her head, pulled it down, and buttoned it about her waist. "I never seen a baby with croup in my life. Why can't Abigail nuss her own brats?''

"I told you it would be difficult to live up to her good opinion of you."

"You told me! You told me! Tell me what to do for croup!''

"Castle, you amaze me. How have you managed to live to the comparatively ripe age of thirty and remain totally ignorant of all practical and useful knowledge? Didn't your mother teach you anything?''

"I wouldn't let her!'' she snapped. "Aunt Lucy said I was 'ig'nant as a fiel han.' ''

Jonathan chuckled, then asked, "Was there no sickness at Homeplace? Some of the black babies must have had croup. It isn't uncommon.''

"How should I know? Aunt Lucy took care of the darkies.''

"I have a *Home Medical Adviser* here someplace.'' Not finding it on the shelves, he went to his chest. "Are you sure Aunt Lucy didn't give you any remedies? It's strange she would let you go so far from home with nothing. . . . Here's the book.''

"I don't know what she gave me. I didn't pay any attention. How did I know I'd be expected to doctor the neighbors' young'uns? There's a lot of plunder in the bottom of my trunk . . . wait a minute! There's a box with some bottles . . .'' She threw up the lid and pawed through the contents. "I saw it when I got the cookbook.'' At the bottom of the trunk she found a small chest. "Here it is.'' She gave it to Jonathan. "What does it say on those bottles?'' There were not only bottles, but small jars and boxes, all neatly labeled.

"Turpentine; brandy and rock candy; glycerine and rose water; sulphur and cream of tartar—that's spring tonic. Even *I* know that much. Resin—wonder what that's for? Goose grease—very useful and a large jar. Miss Sarah wrote the labels. Too bad you don't know what the stuff is for.''

"But I do! When I stepped on a nail Aunt Lucy melted resin and lard and made a poultice. The brandy and rock candy is for coughs. Glycerine and rose water is for chapped hands but it stings so bad I'd rather have sore hands. I like tallow better.''

"Hummm, yes. Shepherds rub their hands in sheeps' wool—same thing. Arnica; ipecac; Jamamic rum—I know what to do with that! Blackberry cordial; flaxseed; mustard—a big box of mustard. Linseed oil; sweet oil; castor oil—that I recognize. There's enough stuff here to start a chemist's shop.''

"Turpentine is for cuts and scratches and a few drops on sugar is good for colds, but I'd rather have the cold. You mix sulphur and molasses and eat it for boils. If you get something in your eye, a flaxseed will take it out. Or you can make a flaxseed poultice. Or a bread and milk poultice is just as good. The cordial is for dysentery. When Marybelle had pneumonia, Aunt Lucy used mustard steeps and onion poultices. Sliced onion and sugar steeped on the back of the stove is a good cough syrup and it tastes good, too. Linseed oil is for burns and scalds, and sweet oil is for earache. Only I don't know what to do for croup!"[2]

Jonathan's eyes twinkled. Obviously Castle knew more about home remedies than she realized. "I'll see what I can find in the *Adviser.* Hummm . . . croup . . . croup . . . yes. Contraction, congestion, phlegm; hot towels, emetics—that's the ipecac. Mustard would do. Emergency treatment. . . . Perhaps you won't need that, but I'd better explain it. Now, listen and put your mind on what I say. Sit down and stop fussing with your clothes. They won't care if you're buttoned up the back. Sit down! If you're to be any help to Abigail, you have to know what to do." He read from the book and explained as simply as possible the cause, behavior, and treatment of croup. "Do you understand? It won't do any good to memorize it this time. You have to know what it means."

"I'm no fool! Of course I know what it means! Now, where's that ep . . . ep . . ."

He handed her the bottle. "Ipecac. Put it in your pocket and don't lose it. Shall I go with you?"

"What for? You'd only be in the way." She swung around and snatched her shawl from the peg.

Jonathan watched her go, then climbed back into bed. He left the candle burning and made no attempt to sleep. He was too curious as to how his wife would handle the situation. Nor did he doubt she would handle it.

She found the Hall household in an uproar and Jennifer gasping for breath.

"Other times she come right out of it soon as I got a few hot towels on her," Abigail explained. "Now towels don't do no good and I don't know anything else to do. Jenny's the only one ever had croup."

"She'll be all right," Castle assured her with an air of calm confidence as she threw her shawl over the back of a chair. What was it? Hot towels. Abigail had done that. Ipecac. She'd give her a good dose. It would have to work because she couldn't run her finger down the child's throat no matter what happened. "Get me a spoon and a cup of warm water," she ordered as she raised Jennifer on the pillow. "She's got to puke it up," she told Abigail. "Bring the washpan, Evva. My land, are you still bawling?"

Cressy was at Evva's side, tears running down her cheeks. Evva wiped her eyes on her apron and patted Cressy's hand. Castle turned back to Jennifer and noticed Eli kneeling by a chair in the corner.

"Sakes alive, Eli! Why bother the Lord with things we can take care of ourselves? You'd do more good if you got some wood and built up the fire. We got to have hot water, this towel is cold."

Abigail hurried for another towel, Eli went for wood. Castle shook her head. He must think the Lord didn't have much to do. . . . A couple of doses of ipecac, a few really hot towels, and in an hour or so, Jennifer was sleeping quietly, her breathing still heavy but regular now. The girls went back to their pallets, Abigail set the room to rights, and Eli walked Castle home across the field.

"Such people!" she fumed as she undressed for bed. "I never saw the beat of them. All that fuss over a spell of croup. That ipecac works real good."

Jonathan all but gnawed the quilt to keep from laughing. She was one of a kind, which was just as well. A world overpopulated with Castles would be much too hectic. But one was an experience he would not willingly have missed.

 7

T H E first cutting of hay was stacked, the wheat was harvested, and then the oats. There would be another cutting of hay, and later in the fall the corn would be picked and husked. For a week, during the one brief lull in the summer's work, a camp meeting was to be held at Mill's Grove over on the 'Botnay River.[1] Jonathan told Castle about it at dinner and as soon as they had eaten she hurried over to consult with Abigail. She found Harriet and Thaddeus in tears and Evva with a face a mile long.

"Great grandmother's nightcap! What on earth has happened?"

Abigail smiled wanly over Jennifer's head. "Nothing that ain't happened before. Eli told us about the camp meeting and the girls ain't got nothing fittin' to wear. We got no money for Sunday clothes this year. We'll do good to get winter shoes and wool for stockings and mittens."

"They got Sunday dresses of some kind, ain't they? Well, drag 'em out and let's see what we can do with them. We're going to that camp meeting or bust a hame string."

The Hall family brightened and the girls brought out their Sunday dresses. With her chair by the door to get the light, Castle examined the garments inside and out, turning them this way and that. "I admit they been wore some, but never mind. Aunt Lucy used to make us do our gowns over for the poor people. She and Miss Sarah were forever packing boxes for somebody. We'll pass these down the line a jump and by taking them in we can take out the bad spots. Time they're turned and freshened up you won't know them."

"What about me?" Evva wailed. If I give my blue to Harriet, what'll *I* wear?"

"Hummm. You've growed some and it would be mighty short on you now." Castle held the dress to Evva's shoulders and the others laughed at the four inches of calico below the poplin. Evva tried to laugh but the tears spilled over. "Won't be much too long for Harriet. Look, Evva, I've got a gown I can't wear. I've plumped up some and this one fit me kind of soon to begin with. It's a nice light grey alpaca and we'll brighten it up with some red piping. We can take the waist in and without the bottom flounce it ought to be about the right length. I expect it'll make a real nice dress for you, Evva.''

Evva's plain face was beautiful with happiness. ''You're a wonderful woman, Mrs. Gayle! God ought to be awful good to you.''

''The Lord helps them that helps themselves, child. Now—this yours, Harry?'' She shook her head sadly. ''Don't you know you can't wear green?''

Harriet flushed. ''It looked real pretty on Evva.''

''Evva's got brown eyes and hair. This blue is better for you. Shows up your nice blue eyes.'' Castle looked up and chuckled. ''Making herself pretty is the main aim in life for girls where I came from. You'd never believe how I used to prink! Never mind, we'll do you girls up to beat the cards: wash your hair in egg and put cologne in the rinse and you'll be so fine the boys will all be goggling at you.''

''Castle! You'll make them vain!'' Abigail protested. ''And they're still too young to think about boys.''

''Fiddle-faddle! A girl should be a little bit vain and she's never too young to make the boys sit up and take notice. They'll get married sometime and we want them to be able to take the pick of the pack, not the first one comes along. Here, Thaddeus, nothing like green for a girl with black hair and white skin. A bit of fixing and it'll do. Now for Cressy. Hummm. Brown. Never do. She's too pale. Got to have something light.''

''Good land! You do make a fuss over clothes. Long as they're clean and whole, what difference does the color make?''[2]

''Makes the difference between looking stylish and looking dowdy. A girl ought to make the most of whatever God give her. There, turn around Cressy. You ain't very big. Likely we could get a dress for you out of that bottom flounce from the alpaca. Grey ain't the right color but with blue piping and a white gimpe. . . . They got pantalets, ain't they?''

''They got 'em, such as they are. All but Cressy.''

Evva brought out three pairs of pantalets, two in fair condition, one past mending. Castle looked them over and shook her head.

''Two pairs of pantalets for four girls. Let me think.'' She rubbed her nose and screwed up her face in concentration. ''Don't matter about Cressy. She's little enough to go bare legged and not cause a scandal. But Evva's too old to go without and too young to let down her skirts. Besides, we need that bottom flounce for Cressy. . . . Wait! I got a ruffled chemise that'll do the trick. Yes sirree bob!'' She laughed merrily and took the dress Cressy held. Turning it this way and that she slowly shook her head. ''It ain't worth bothering with. There ain't enough goods in it to do anything with anyhow.'' She picked up the brown dress again. ''Hummm. It ain't what it ought to be, but now Jennifer's walking she don't *have* to wear a white dress and she's big for her age. We'll make the brown for her and pipe it in red and that white baby dress will do for a gimpe. It ain't fit for anything else and it'd be too short for her now.'' She glanced up at Abigail. ''Petticoats?''

Abigail shook her head. ''Not enough and not good enough.''

Castle sighed. "Well, I used to wear eight or ten, but now I have to wash and iron them myself I get along with five or six. I could spare a couple and one of mine would make two . . . three for the girls."

"Castle, you can't give us your good clothes! It ain't right!"

"Now don't argue! No sense letting stuff lay around and rot. If we're all going to that camp meeting, you got to be dressed proper. All right, all we got to do is get to work."

From then until the camp meeting, Castle spent most of her time at the Hall cabin where Abigail and the girls worked under her direction, ripping and basting and pinning. Abigail even turned her own worn blue merino and put on a new collar made from a piece of the ruffle from Castle's chemise. Through it all Castle was so pleasant and agreeable that Jonathan felt he was living with a stranger. She went through her housework like a hot knife through butter and he watched with amazement and amusement but spoke softly lest the miracle come to an untimely end.

One evening he remarked, "I wonder if I owe you an apology. Are you really doing all this out of the goodness of your heart? What are *you* getting out of it?"

"They're riding with *us,* ain't they? What would folks think of *me* if my friends looked like something out of the ragbag?"

"No apology, Miss Castle."

Since the men had refused to take time off from work, they would only attend the meeting on the closing Sunday. The day before was spent in cooking and baking. At sunup the Gayles drove over and Eli stowed Abigail's baskets in the wagon with Castle's. All was in readiness: the girls in their newly made-over finery, Abigail neat in her freshly turned blue gown, Castle stiff and dignified in black silk. Even the men were dressed for the occasion: Jonathan in black broadcloth and ruffled shirt, Eli in his Sunday-go-to-meeting store clothes. Lest something had been overlooked, Abigail went back in the house for a final survey while the girls danced up and down impatiently, shouting they had everything. Eli grinned and mounted his little mare and Abigail returned empty-handed. She shooed the children aside and started to climb into the wagon, but with one foot on the hub she turned to her husband.

"Eli Hall, I wish you'd stay home!" Jonathan laughed and Castle gasped. "He always gets converted," Abigail explained.

"I just get plum carried away," Eli admitted.

"Carried away! Why don't you stay home and behave yourself? You know you got no business going to a camp meeting. I been trying to tell him all along . . ."

"Miss all the fun? I should say not! What if I do get religion. There's no harm in that, is there? Besides, it won't be the first time."

"Nor the last." Abigail clambered over the wheel and settled herself with an air of resignation.

It was a long ride over rough roads in a jouncing, springless wagon, yet to Castle it seemed far less uncomfortable than on the trip out from Kanesville. The weather was fine, and with a light load the horses made good time. Arrived at the camp grounds, the women descended in a flurry of skirts and hoops. Jonathan unhooked the team, then threw the traces over their backs and tied them to the endgate. Eli looped his reins through a spoke in the rear wheel and tossed his saddle into the wagon.

The men followed the women to the tabernacle—a structure of poles roofed with boughs and provided with slab benches. A pulpit of rough boards stood on a raised platform and behind it were chairs for the choir. Wasps droned threateningly and the children were kept busy brushing vicious horseflies away from their bare legs. It was midmorning and hot. On the scantily covered roof the leaves had withered during the week, limiting their effectiveness as shade, and while the women talked they kept their palm leaf fans swishing in time with their conversation.

Elder Bates, from Cold Spring, took his stand before the pulpit and the choir filed up amid much rustling and whispering. The Elder tapped his tuning fork, cleared his throat, and lined the first hymn. The congregation rose and Sister Bates led the singing in a nasal soprano, clearly distinguishable above the voices of a hundred men, women, and children.

> "Come ye disconsolate, where e'er ye languish;
>   Come to the mercy seat, fervently kneel;
> Here bring your wounded hearts, here tell your anguish;
>   Earth hath no sorrow that heaven cannot heal."

A hush followed the hymn, for where was the heart that had not been wounded, where the sorrow that had not hoped for heaven's healing? These men and women were pioneers in a new and hard land, a land that often took more than it gave. They ate their bread in the sweat of their brows, brought forth their children with little aid, buried their dead with a neighbor's prayer. In their faith lay their courage and they clung to it with a desperate need, a heartfelt conviction that God must understand even when they did not.

The Elder read from the Gospel according to St. John, taking as his text the Savior's words to Nicodemus: "Verily, verily, I say unto thee; except a man be born again he cannot see the kingdom of God." After the scripture reading, Elder Bates prayed for peace and plenty, for the abolition of slavery, for a great revival of Christian faith, for a rich harvest of souls saved this day. Then he rose from his knees and in a voice of thunder hurled his text at his waiting congregation.[3]

" 'Except a man be born again . . . he cannot see the kingdom of God!' On this glorious Sabbath morning you stand before the throne of Almighty God, and I ask you, HAVE YOU BEEN BORN AGAIN?" With each shouted word the Elder pounded the pulpit with his fist.

Eli's shoulders began to droop and whenever the Elder's voice rose to shouting pitch, Eli's head sank lower. Abigail reached behind Cressy and took a firm grip on her husband's coattail. Eli glanced at her sideways and grinned ruefully but made no protest. The Elder plunged into hellfire and damnation and Eli groaned aloud while Abigail tightened her hold on his coat. It was a long sermon, but at last Elder Bates reached heaven and set forth the joys of eternal rest in the presence of a loving God and merciful

Father. Then he shouted for sinners to repent and save their souls while there was yet time. Eli slumped forward, elbows on knees, head in hands, and Abigail clutched his coat frantically. The Elder pleaded with those who had seen the error of their ways to come forward and receive forgiveness. Eli groaned and started to rise. Abigail jerked him back to his seat and tried to catch his eye, but he kept his face averted.

Then Sister Bates, who was aiding and abetting her husband by making the rounds of the congregation, paused at Eli's side, bent over him, and asked in a sepulchral voice, "Brother, are you saved?"

Eli could bear no more. Slipping out of his coat he staggered down the aisle in his shirt-sleeves to throw himself on his knees with the penitents. Abigail folded and unfolded his coat. It was so exasperating to have a man act like that. Folks didn't know what a good Christian he was. She half rose.

"I've a good mind to go down there and get him!"

Evva leaned across Thaddy and caught her mother's hand. "Ma, leave him be. It always does Pa a heap of good to get converted."

Cressy had fallen asleep and Abigail stretched her on the bench with Eli's coat for a pillow. Then Thaddeus kept turning and twisting to see who was there until Abigail boxed her ears. "Sit still and stop gaping around!" Thaddeus started to cry and Abigail boxed her again.

Harriet reached across Evva, who held the sleeping Jennifer on her lap, and jabbed Thaddeus. "Look at the Elder!"

"Stop poking me!" Thaddeus snuffled. "I don't want to look at him!"

"Look at him!" Harriet hissed. "Look at his Adam's apple."

Thaddeus wiped her eyes on her petticoat and looked up at the Elder. Jonathan, on the far side of Harriet, had heard the exchange and chuckled audibly. Castle drove a warning elbow into his ribs but he continued to chuckle, and while Elder Bates exhorted sinners to repentance, Jonathan and the girls sat fascinated by the forceful eloquence of his Adam's apple as it jerked spasmodically up and down his scrawny throat. At last the Elder gave thanks for the souls saved and lined the closing hymn.

"There is a fountain filled with blood
    Drawn from Immanuel's veins,
And sinners plunged beneath that flood
    Lose all their guilty stains.
"Lose all their guilty sta-a-ains,
    Lose all their gui-i-il-ty stains!
And sinners plunged beneath that flood
    Lose all their guilty stains."

On slab tables under the trees the baskets were unpacked and the food set out. Crops had been good and homegrown food plentiful. During dinner even Elder and Sister Bates laughed and talked of homely, earthly affairs: of harvest and hunting and pickling and preserving and corn husking and quilting bees, of marriage and birth and death. Elder Bates picked up Jennifer and carried her the length of the table, giving her bites of this and that, laughing uproariously at the faces she made, until Berta Olson took the child away from him impatiently and set her on the quilt with Cade Pettit, where Patience could watch them both. Soon Abigail asked if Jennifer weren't a bother and Patience protested happily.

"Goodness, no! Let her be. She's keeping Cade out of mischief. But how do you ever dress your girls so stylish, Abigail? It's all I can do to keep mine covered."

Across the table, the picture of propriety in her silks and carefully arranged countenance, Castle smiled complacently as Abigail laughed and shook her head.

"I didn't do it, Patience. I got no talent for sewing. Castle bossed the job and you never seen such a hand with a needle. The way she rips a dress apart and puts it back together beats the Dutch."

"Castle Gayle, why didn't you tell me you could sew like that? And you with no girls to dress! I'm going to give a bee and you can just come right along and bring your fashion plates!"

Castle smoothed her skirts as some of the other women turned to listen. "I'll be pleased to come to your bee, Patience, but I got no fashion plates. I just hang a dress on and pin it in place."[4]

"Now, listen to her!" Patience cried. "Who ever heard . . ."

"That's what she does!" Abigail insisted. "You never seen anything like it in all your born days."

"Fashion plates or not, I'm going to have a bee — with Castle the guest of honor!"

Castle was so gratified she almost forgot to eat. It was nice knowing other people appreciated her even if Jonathan didn't. She wished he could have heard them, but he *would* be talking with the men. Women couldn't hold a candle to a bunch of men when they got strung out. Always politics, crops, slavery, and gold. With the Elder spouting, it was likely slavery.

While the women cleared the table and packed the baskets, the men stood under the trees shouting at each other. Solon Crawford was as rabid as the Elder, but Ed Pettit and Jonathan favored moderation. A number of men had other opinions. Across the length and breadth of the land it would have been difficult to find a man who did not have an opinion on the question of slavery. Axel Olson was a lukewarm Abolitionist, but today he could not keep his mind on the discussion; his two older sons had joined the Crawford boys and Tolly Marker by the wagons, and Axel was suspicious of idle boys. Then Elder Bates glanced at the sun and said it was time for the afternoon song service. The song service was a social occasion, the members of the congregation frankly enjoying themselves. For who cared if his voice were rusty from disuse, old and cracked or young and thin, as long as he could pour out his heart at the top of his lungs along with his fellows?

Until nearly sundown they sang, one hymn after another, in joyous abandon. Then the Elder announced, "God's harvest has been good, and our earthly harvest is at hand. We will close our meeting with 'Bringing in the Sheaves.' " And the congregation sang with a will.

The song done, the Elder raised his hand over their bowed heads and pronounced the final benediction. "And now may the grace, mercy and peace of God the Father, God the Son, and God the Holy Ghost, be and abide with you forevermore, Amen." And whatever his human frailties, his hearers received his blessing in humble gratitude.

After corn picking the neighbors gathered once more to raise Eli's permanent house, a story-and-a-half structure, the upper room to be used as sleeping quarters for the girls. Abigail was very proud of her new house and Castle equally envious. The night of the raising she banged the pots around and slammed a sketchy supper before her husband.

"It's too much! They're upstarts, the whole tribe! And to have to put up with their having a better house than I have! All because I married a no-account man without enough pride to provide his wife with a decent roof over her head. I'll never speak to Abigail Hall again. The way she carried on over that house . . ."

Jonathan finished his coffee, laid his knife and fork on his plate, folded his fringed cotton napkin, and slipped it into the horn ring. Then he pushed back his chair and stretched his legs to the fire. "What explanation will you give for your refusal to speak to Abigail?" he asked calmly.

Castle sputtered as she clacked her heels between table and shelves. "I'm going home, that's what! I won't stay here . . ."

Jonathan didn't attempt to explain his reasons for not building a larger cabin. A cabin was a cabin regardless of size. When he built, it would be a frame house, but that was out of the question at the moment. The nearest sawmills were at St. Louis and the freight would amount to more than the house would be worth. His wife's pride would have to suffer until materials became available, and the farm could pay for a new house. A house was not his idea of a capital investment since it would pay no cash return. Hence, when he built, it would be paid for out of earnings, while someone else paid interest on his capital.

And Castle continued to speak to Abigail. After all, Abigail had asked her advice about arranging things in the new house and it wouldn't be neighborly to refuse.

PART III

To Have and to Hold

8

S O L O N Crawford had bought a sawmill in St. Louis and arranged to have it shipped to Council Bluffs, the new name given to the town of Kanesville. However, for some unknown reason, when the boat reached St. Joseph the mill was unloaded there, a hundred miles from Council Bluffs and considerably farther from Turkey Grove! The neighbor men volunteered to help bring the mill home and among them they mustered seven wagons, five teams of horses, a team of Missouri mules, and two yokes of oxen, the oxen to haul the boiler. Eli Hall had offered his wagon and oxen and even agreed that Beauty should go as teammate to Knute Olson's young gelding, but he declined to go along since Abigail was expecting around Christmas and no one knew how long they would be gone. So the party was short a driver. The Crawford boys, with the help of Hennie Olson and a team of Axel's horses, were to build the mill shed and have it ready when the machinery arrived, as it could not be allowed to stand out in the weather.

The only other settlers for miles around were the Newmans, on Troublesome Creek; Hesekiah and his sons kept determinedly aloof from their neighbors, neither asking nor giving aid, so the matter of the needed driver was still unsettled. Jonathan had completed his own preparations for the trip and it only remained for him to make the final arrangements with Eli regarding the oxen and wagon. He told his wife he was going over to Halls' and she promptly announced that she was going along.

"Abigail Hall is no better than I am. If I can stay home and do chores, I don't see why she has to have a man hanging around looking after her. Besides, I want one of the girls to keep me company and do the milking."

Castle disliked old Bossey as much as Bossey disliked her, and while

Jonathan might have forced Castle to do the milking, he couldn't force Bossey to let down her milk. So they set out: she with her cloak flapping in the wind, her calico skirts held high in an effort to keep up with her husband's strides; he watching her with dancing eyes, never changing his gait. Eli saw them and came from the stable while Abigail held the door for them. Castle pushed her chair as close to the fire as she could get, Jonathan sat by the table, Eli tilted his chair against the wall, and Abigail eased herself onto the edge of the bed. The matter of the oxen and wagon was soon settled. Since Eli's wagon was light, Knute would drive it with Beauty and the gelding. Both yokes of oxen would be needed for Solon's heavy log wagon, which would carry the boiler, and each of the other men would drive his own team. Jonathan nodded and lighted his pipe.

"That leaves us just one problem: a driver who can handle oxen. Solon could do it, but he's the only one who knows where we're going, so he can't bring up the rear with the boiler."

Eli was downcast. "I 'spose the oxen would be too slow to lead."

"We have to expect snow and they'll have too heavy a load to break trail."

Eli nodded. "It ain't neighborly of me to refuse to go when the men helped me build *two* houses, but I got to be here if Abigail needs me."

"What would you do if you were here?" Castle demanded.

"There won't be a man or a horse for miles around." He rumpled his hair with a heavy hand. "I got to be here."

"Mercy sakes, Eli, I can look after Abigail as good as you can. Go on with the men and stop your stewing." Jonathan threw his wife a startled glance but Eli was not yet convinced.

"Couldn't you come and stay here? I'd as leave go if you would. Jonathan, put your cow in the shed with mine and the girls can look after her."

Jonathan shook his head. "The house can't stand empty with Indians on the creek. There'd be nothing left." He considered a moment. "We could build beacons and run guide ropes."

In the end, that was the arrangement agreed upon. Harriet would stay with Castle and Evva would look after Abigail. If anything happened she would fire the beacon. Eli, still reluctant, consented to go with the men and Castle and Jonathan returned home. All the way across the field he shook with suppressed laughter and once in the cabin he dropped in a chair and laughed until he held his sides, swaying to and fro.

"What's the matter with you?" Castle demanded peevishly as she removed her hood and hung it on the peg.

"You!" he choked, tears running down his cheeks, his chair thumping the floor as he rocked back and forth on the legs.

"What's so funny about me?"

"You . . . promised to . . . look after Abigail!"

"So? If Martha Marker can stay by herself and I can stay with just Harriet, why can't Abigail stay with Evva to look after her?" She flung off her cloak and slapped it on top of the hood.

"You and Martha aren't in the family way!"

"I should hope not!"

"And you don't know as much about bringing a baby as I do. I've at least played midwife to cows and horses and sheep and hogs. You've never even played midwife to a biddy hen!"

"What's that got to do with it? Eli'll be back before the baby comes."

"No he won't! That's why he didn't want to go. I'm no doctor, but by the looks of her, Abigail isn't far from her time. It's a long way to St. Joseph and we're certain to hit bad weather."

"You mean, she might have it while Eli's gone?" she asked incredulously.

"Certainly! This isn't her first child. She must know about when to expect it. Abigail wouldn't have let Eli refuse to go if she had thought she wouldn't need him. But you so kindly offered to take care of her . . ."

"Good grief! I thought he just didn't want to leave her alone!" She sat down so heavily the chair creaked in protest.

Again Jonathan rocked with laughter. "Castle, Castle, what a pretty pickle you've got yourself into this time! And what I'd give to see you get out of it!"

"Get that doctor book!"

Jonathan put his bandanna in his pocket and stared at his wife. "Doctor book?"

"The one that told about croup. It ought to have something in it about babies."

He studied her in silence. She sat quietly, her hands in her lap, her brows drawn down in concentration, her mouth set determinedly. Jonathan rose and took the book from the shelf.

"Miss Castle, your courage is matched only by your ignorance, yet there are times when you show symptoms of intelligence." Returning to his chair, he laid the book on the table and ran his finger down the index. "Yes, there are several chapters on the subject in question." He found the place, glanced briefly over several pages, then with a last look at his wife, settled himself to his task. He read and explained while she listened intently, occasionally asking him to repeat or expand. When he came to the more gruesome details he paused. "Shall I continue?" She stared at him. "I say, shall I go on with this?"

"You expect me to stop with the baby half way here? Just walk out and say I don't know the rest?"

He burst out laughing again but ran a hand over his face and beard, controlled himself, and went on with the text. Time was short and if Castle had any hope of preparing herself to face the inevitable, she would need all the help he could give her. In the few days remaining before he left, she went about mumbling to herself in a distracted manner and whenever Jonathan came to the house, demanded he look up some point on which she was not clear or some possibility she had overlooked.

"I got to get it right. If the baby *should* come before Eli gets back, there won't be any way to get word to Indie. I'll have to do it myself and I got to know how to do it right.''

''If you're going to do it, you'd *better* do it right!'' So he read and reread until he could have brought the baby himself.

Solon Crawford and his caravan set out the latter part of November and it was after New Year's when they returned. The second of December it began to snow and continued steadily for three days and nights, and the mercury dropped lower and lower. Castle and Harriet spent most of their waking hours at the window watching the white fluff drifting down, obscuring everything beyond the dooryard. Would they see the beacon if it were fired? At night Castle dreaded to sleep and each time she woke she got up and looked out the window, fearful that she would see the glow of the beacon fire, more fearful that it be lighted and she would not see it. She and Harriet did the chores together, for neither would allow the other to venture out alone. Clinging to each other and to the guide rope, they made their way to the stable, grateful to reach that snug refuge, heavy with the warm odor of animals, ammonia, and manure.

Harriet milked and Castle fed, then breaking the ice on the hogshead Jonathan had provided in case of just such an emergency, she filled the water buckets for hens and cow. Their work done, they carried the milk pail between them as they struggled back to the house to stand again at the window watching, always watching. Once the storm was over the whole world was so still it seemed to have stopped breathing. The snow was three feet deep on the level and drifts covered the fences. But above the unbroken blanket of white the tall beacon still stood unfired across the south field. For Castle the suspense was almost unbearable. What if the beacon were lighted? Would she be able to bring the baby safely? Would she fail? Abigail die? the baby die? Such things happened. She dare not fail! She could never face Eli — or Jonathan. She would have to do what had to be done, and do it right!

After loading the wagons in St. Joseph, the men started home, finding their way by landmarks or by the sun, for there were no roads and often no trails. During the storm they moved at a crawl; when it was over, the snow was axle deep in the timber, with men and animals floundering about in the biting cold. At night they camped wherever they found a spot more or less sheltered from the wind, the wagons drawn up to form an additional windbreak for the stock. By day, Jonathan and his big greys or Axel and his mules broke trail. Solon, who had made the trip before, was second in line, shouting directions to the leaders. Tolly, then Knute with the light team, followed, then either Jonathan or Axel, as the case might be, and Eli with the oxen brought up the rear. For a while they made reasonably good time, but on New Year's Eve in a howling storm, the oxen, drawing the heavy boiler, were unable to hold the pace and gradually fell behind without being noticed by the others through the curtain of falling snow. Nor could Eli, shouting against the wind, make them hear his calls. Soon the trail between him and the other wagons was obliterated and by dusk Eli was lost. In the whirling whiteness about him it was impossible to tell in which direction he was heading and for all he knew he might be traveling in circles, exhausting the animals and getting nowhere. Coming upon a grove, he unyoked the oxen and let them seek such protection as they could find; he set out on foot, hoping to overtake the others when they camped for the night, for he was sure they could not be far ahead.

He found no trace of them and when he attempted to return to the wagon he found his own footprints had already been erased by the wind and he had no way of knowing where he had come from. He could see nothing of the grove; veiled in white, without the horizon for a backdrop, the tall trees had melted into nothingness. It was almost dark and the wind-driven snow blinded him, coming at him from all directions. He would die and then what would become of Abigail and the girls? He struggled on and on, his feet so heavy and numb he could barely drag one after the other. Yet he dared not stop; to do so would be fatal. He had to keep moving. At last he saw a flicker of yellow light. The campfire? He listened and heard only the rustle of the snow. The light could not be far or he would not have seen it. Dragging himself toward it, he soon realized it was no campfire. It was a cabin!

When he knocked the door was opened by a squat, dark man, and a woman's voice exclaimed, ''Lord help us, he's near froze!''

For a time Eli was not wholly conscious. The man and his wife rubbed his hands and feet with snow, wrapped him in a blanket, and put him in the far corner of the room. When he had thawed out enough to talk he told them who he was, what had happened, and thanked them for their kindness.

The man nodded. ''Carson's the name. Good thing you seen our light. Lucindy sets a candle in the winder when it storms. Travelers pass sometimes.''

Mrs. Carson ladled up beans and side meat and poured a cup of hot coffee; after he had eaten, Eli slept rolled in a blanket by the fire. In the morning he was as good as new, and with his host as guide they found the oxen in a hollow in the grove where they had sought refuge from the storm. The wagon was all but buried but the two men shoveled it out and with directions from Mr. Carson, Eli set out, reaching Crawfords' the next afternoon just in time to prevent a search party starting out after him. Sid and Seth stabled the weary oxen and Eli went to the house, where Tabitha dried her hands on her apron and lit into him for getting himself lost. The men stayed the night, sleeping in the loft room with the boys, then in the morning got the boiler set up in the shed which was ready and waiting for the mill machinery. As soon as they could be spared, Eli and Jonathan started home, each with his own team and wagon, little Beauty tied behind. The going was slow, for Jonathan had to hold the greys to the gait of the oxen, so it was dark by the time they reached home. The Gayle cabin was dark, but a light shone from the window of the Hall house.

''Want to bet it's a boy?'' Jonathan shouted back at Eli.

''No sense betting with the cards stacked! Abbie's had five chances before this.''

The baby was a girl, born the day before, and Castle thanked her lucky stars it had not come in the middle of the storm. She would not have seen the beacon had it been twice as tall. With a broad grin, Eli bent and kissed his wife, examined the new baby, then knelt by the bedside while the girls hushed their chatter and stood in silence, their heads bowed. Eli rose and kissed each in turn as they crowded around, all talking at once.

"Likely you're hungry, Pa," Evva remembered. "I'll warm up supper for you and Uncle Jonathan."

The men sat at the table and Eli took Jennifer on his lap. Evva dished up potatoes and onions fried together, baked squash, crusty cornbread with fresh butter and plum jam, and coffee as good as it smelled. While they ate the men told of the trip and Eli related his adventure. Like Tabitha, Castle scolded him.

"You must of been plum out of your mind! Tromping around on foot, you might of froze to death and then what would of become of your family?"

"That's just what I was thinking when I seen that light. I'm mighty grateful to that woman."

"I should think so!" Castle shook cornstarch on the new baby's rump and pinned her up with a flourish.

From the bed Abigail said gently, "Never mind, Castle. Eli ain't long on horse sense but the good Lord looks after him." Then to her husband, "What did you say that woman's name was? Maybe we could call the baby after her."

"Her husband called her Lucindy," Eli said with his mouth full. "She might not know it, but it would ease my conscience some. They were real nice folks."

So the new baby was Lucinda, and when it became evident her hair would be as red and curly as her father's, Eli was as proud as a peacock. Castle, knowing nothing about babies and caring less, vowed Lucinda was the most beautiful infant she had ever seen. But she was prejudiced; this was her first godchild, and Abigail insisted it had been a difficult delivery. To Castle, it had been a terrifying and exhausting experience and in the middle of it she had promised herself she would never go through it again. Once safely over, she had brushed aside her fears: bringing a baby didn't amount to anything once you knew how. Abigail was in bed the usual ten days, but she was seldom alone. Castle was in and out all day and news of the baby soon reached the neighbors. Tolly stopped by on his way home from Crawfords', and when he told his mother, she hurried over with a couple of jars of wild strawberry jam. When Axel Olson went to Garrison's Station he dropped Berta off to visit while he was gone, and with her came a basket of sweet buns. Axel naturally told Indiana and she sent Lew over with a smoked haunch of venison. Tabitha Crawford came with all the goodies she could muster, nor would she listen to Abigail's protests that it was too much.

"I just have to make a peace offering, Abigail. To think of you having that baby while Eli was off helping Solon! 'Specially when Eli didn't want to go in the first place and then got lost coming home. My land! When I think of all the things could of happened! It sure is lucky Castle lives so close."

"Eli wouldn't of gone if she hadn't been here. She's such a good woman!"

Patience Pettit managed to come in spite of Grampa and the children.

Castle was bathing the baby and Patience kissed her and Abigail warmly. "Castle, you're a godsend! You come in the nick of time 'cause Cade was the last baby for Indie. She ain't up to it anymore. And don't think you're so far away *I* couldn't send for you!"

"Not *you*, Patience!"

"No, but there's no guarantee. . . . Ain't she the prettiest baby? How'd Eli take it, getting a girl again? The men are all poking fun at him."

Abigail chuckled. "He's used to it by now. And the men don't stop to think the girls ain't all his. Guess he don't either. But he admires her red hair."

"Open that basket for me, Evva, and see if everything is all right. The road is bumpy and it joggled around some."

Evva lifted the cloth that covered the basket and the other girls gathered around to see the contents. "Oh-o-o!" Evva sighed rapturously. From its paper wrappings she lifted a soft little white hood of knitted wool. Carrying it almost reverently to her mother's bed she exclaimed in delight, "See, Ma, ain't it beautiful? It's a present for the baby!"

Abigail fondled the hood then passed it to Castle. "Ain't it the finest, softest wool? Did you ever see such knitting? Wherever did you get the yarn, Patience?"

Castle complimented Patience on both the wool and the knitting but resolved to show both women a thing or two. She'd knit something for the baby. Who had a better right? Jonathan would have to order the yarn for her. Or would he?

He willingly agreed to order the yarn. "They have only coarse worsted in Cold Spring. I'll have the stage driver bring it from Peoria. But shouldn't you do some knitting while you're waiting for the yarn? You may be sadly out of practice."

Castle stood with a plate in her hands and looked at him. "I hadn't thought of that. Where's that stocking yarn you got last fall? You could use mittens and wristlets and I could use winter stockings. Time the baby yarn gets here I'll have my hand in. I'll show Abigail and Patience some *real* knitting!"

Jonathan kept a straight face but he was elated by this unexpected windfall. He had long needed warm sox and mittens, but to date Castle had flatly refused to knit them for him. Now that she had decided to demonstrate her skill, perhaps she would no longer sit with her hands idle in her lap while he went with bare wrists. Yet he was not sure that Castle's success in delivering Lucinda would prove an unmixed blessing, for since that event the men had all been slapping him on the back, praising his wife's courage and competence. Apparently in getting herself out of one predicament she had got herself into another. Without doubt she would henceforth be expected to attend the confinements and other assorted illnesses of her neighbors. There were only two doctors in the county, both at Cold Spring, and the only way to get a doctor was to go after him—a twenty-mile trip each way—and in bad weather, an impossible trip.

So while Castle bustled back and forth between her home and the Hall house, surrounded by an aura of importance, Jonathan kept his counsel. He did not complain that both he and his house were neglected, but neither did he tell his wife that she was a wonderful woman. Castle would have been less annoyed if he had complained. With everybody else singing her praises and taking on over her, it did seem as if he. . . . But when she tried to tell him what the others were saying he silenced her.

"*Abigail* had the baby. That's something you haven't done."

Castle was mad enough to bite him — and Abigail, too.

Slowly the days lengthened as each evening the sun went down a bit farther north. During the day the snow melted and at night long icicles formed at the edge of the overhanging thatch. Then the icicles ceased to form and the receding snow left irregular bare patches which were soon tinged with green. At long last winter was over; the prairie was green and the trees put out tender young leaves. But letters from home reminded Castle that spring had also come to the wooded hills of Allegheny County. Closing her eyes she could see it now more clearly than she had ever seen it when she was there. The hills would be filmed with a hundred shades of pale green — from almost yellow to almost blue — and the steamboats would be riding high on the swollen rivers. At Homeplace, she could see the sprawling Talbot house in the hush of a warm spring afternoon, the peaceful quiet disturbed only by the chatter of blue jays scolding in the sycamore at the end of the long veranda. The white house spread its wings to face the drive and tree-shaded lawn that sloped gently down to the creek where it wound past the old stone wall, the sparkling water tumbling over the rocks from one shallow pool to another. In the long ago days of her childhood, how often had she and Amanda and Little Lief and Bo built dams and castles and caught minnies and crawdads along the creek!

Strange how she could see it all so well now when she'd never even noticed such things when she'd lived there. She had seen, she had known, but it had meant nothing then. Only now when it was too late were the house and gardens and lawns and trees important enough to think about. Would she ever go home? Ever see Miss Sarah and Aunt Lucy and Amanda and Major Hunter again? Ever again hear his cane thumping the floor as he shouted his wrath at whomever happened to be within shouting distance? She would! She would! Somehow, she would!

Miss Sarah had said the Major wasn't well, and he had admitted his game leg bothered him. If something should happen to him. . . . Then a letter came from Anne Middleton; along with the other news she reported that Griselda Delacroix was very ill and the doctors were doubtful if she would live. Castle made no comment when Jonathan read the letter for her but she did considerable thinking afterwards. If Griselda died. . . . If Jonathan let her go home for a visit. . . . Naturally, it would be no more than common courtesy to offer her condolences. And then . . . Well, without Griselda. . . . At least the little bitch wouldn't be hanging on his arm! And with her out of the way, would Garland take her in his arms again? Had he regretted his folly? It seemed only yesterday that she had stood with him on the Middleton verandah, where later, so much later, she had stood with Jonathan. If only he would let her go home for a visit. Once she got there . . .

Jonathan was late coming to supper. The calf had escaped from the pen and the unruly little beast had kicked up his heels and refused to return to the lot. It had required a chase and a tussle to get him and Jonathan was tired, hungry, and cross. Castle, unaware of stock or her husband's weariness, launched her campaign while taking up the supper.

"I'm worried about Major Hunter," she remarked innocently.

Jonathan dried his dripping face, muttering through the towel. "He's getting along in years."

"I'm afraid he's worse off than we know."

"If he were seriously ill, Miss Sarah would say so."

"He wouldn't admit he was sick as long as he could keep his pins under him. Miss Sarah mightn't know and I hate to think I may never see him again." She sighed deeply as she reached for the coffeepot. Jonathan gave her a quick look, filled his plate, and began to eat. Castle waited but he offered no further comment. Taking her place she continued, "I do so want to go home for a visit."

"The crops aren't in yet."

"I know. I don't expect you to go right now. But why couldn't *I* go?" Jonathan's fork paused half way to his mouth, then resumed its journey. Castle shook out her napkin, glanced at her husband, and ventured, "I'm so worried . . .''

He went on chewing and swallowing thoughtfully before he looked up at her. The light of the candle illuminated her too-carefully composed features. "At the moment I think I need you more than Major Hunter."

"You could eat at Halls'."

"Abigail has enough to do caring for her own family."

"She wouldn't mind. Just another place at the table . . ."

"I'd mind. You are my wife, not Abigail."

"But you'd rather have Abigail! Why don't you say it?"

"And you'd rather have Garland Delacroix. Tell me, Miss Castle, are you really concerned about Major Hunter, or have you been daydreaming again? Regarding the possibility that your long lost love may become a widower?" Castle threw down her fork and started to rise. "Eat your supper while we review the facts. You *have* been daydreaming ever since Anne's last letter. Understand, my sweet, you are welcome to daydream to your heart's content — or discontent — but *I* married you, Mr. Delacroix did not. You are *my* wife, whether his wife dies or not. So you are not going home at present, and if Griselda should die, you may never go home. And that is final. I have no intention of allowing you to make a fool of yourself over that ninny a second time."

"Garland is not a ninny and I didn't make a fool of myself!"

"You did, the way I heard it. You needled him into making what you pretended to consider a bona fide proposal and he hadn't the guts to tell you he didn't want to marry you and call the thing off. So after leaving you at the church while he ran off with another girl, he tattled to Papa to save his hide and then gaily danced with his wife while you pined for your lost love. I'd say that was making quite a fool of yourself."

Castle leaped up and her chair went over backwards with a crash. "You're a beast! I won't stay here another minute and you can't make me! I'm going home!"

"Not tonight, so you may as well sit down and finish your supper. I said *sit down!* I will see that you do your wifely duty if I have to wring your stately neck. Is that clear?"

"Don't you ever touch me again!"

"You forget, you're my wife. As your husband the law gives me the right to touch you whenever I see fit."

"The law can't make me stay here if I don't want to!"

"No, but the law will permit me to divorce you if you don't stay. That would be a juicy morsel for Allegheny County to roll under its collective tongue, wouldn't it? I'm sure Garland would be interested, but I'm equally sure the Delacroix family would not 'receive' a divorced woman. Not at Greenbriar. Garland is far too fine a gentleman. No breath of scandal has ever touched his name. No scandal touched *him* when he left you waiting at the church, did it, my dear? Besides, why should he wish to consort with you after I divorced you."

"I could kill you!" she hissed. The words had come unbidden and she acted without thought. Whirling about she snatched the varmint gun from its pegs over the door and setting it to her shoulder, pointed the long barrel at Jonathan's chest. He laughed, pushed back his chair, and crossed one ankle over the other knee. A hand caressed his beard thoughtfully as he smiled at his wife.

"Aren't you being a bit hasty? They hang people for murder, you know. Think how unpleasant it would be to hang by the neck until dead. Publicly, with your petticoats flapping in the breeze. Such an undignified way to die. Particularly for such a fine lady. No doubt it would be in all the papers. They might even print a sketch of you and your petticoats in the Pittsburgh papers. Fine old county family and all that."

Castle let the gun butt drop with a thump; a thunderous roar sounded as the charge tore through the roof, leaving a hole big enough for a cat to crawl through. Jonathan leaped past the table, snatched the gun from his wife's limp hands, and slapped her face with all his strength.

"You fool! You'll have the Halls down on us! I *told* you Betsy was tricky."

Frightened witless by the explosion, sent reeling by the blow Jonathan had dealt her, Castle clutched the back of a chair for support and stood gasping for breath. Before she could get herself in hand, Eli was at the door.

"Jonathan! What happened? We heard a shot . . ."

"Sorry to have alarmed you," Jonathan smiled and pointed at the roof. "I took the gun down to change the charge and let her slip. I'm sorry."

"Good thing it was the roof and not your head! Lordy, what a charge! What is that thing, a cannon?"

"Just an old smooth bore muzzle-loader. Make a good elephant gun—if we had any elephants."

While Jonathan explained the gun's virtues—and vices—and Eli examined the hole in the thatch, marveling and shaking his head, Castle slipped out the door and around the house. She was thankful her husband had distracted Eli's attention from her for she was sure the print of his hand must be plain on her cheek, and she was going to be sick. Her stomach was turning cartwheels. If that gun butt had hit at a slightly different angle, only very slightly different, she'd have had that charge in her own face! By the time she went back in the house, Jonathan was again sitting at the table and Eli was gone. She slipped past, undressed, and crept into bed. Jonathan had a book in his hands but was unaware he was holding it upside down. He was still weak from the fright his wife had given him. She might have killed herself! If only she were capable of loving *him* as much as she imagined she loved Garland! If only she could let him give her the love Garland had never had to give. Yet as long as she thought she loved Garland, she could not seek her husband's love. Poor Castle! Poor misguided, unhappy woman! Eating her heart out for a love that had never been hers, rejecting the love she could have for the asking.

He banked the fire, undressed, and slipped into bed beside his wife. He settled himself and lay quietly for a time, then, sensing that she was not asleep, turned and slipped his arm under her, pillowing her head on his shoulder. To Castle's astonishment, his free hand brushed her hair and his lips touched the cheek his hand had reddened. She waited but he said nothing and after a time she fell asleep, still wondering at this strangely gentle Jonathan. The next day he mended the thatch but the patch was plain to see—for Castle a reminder that she might have been lying in her coffin without a face. Or the gun might have gone off while she held it pointed at her husband. Without trying to decide which was the more terrifying, she pushed both thoughts from her mind. And Jonathan never mentioned the incident.

That year the town of Grove City was platted about ten miles from Cold Spring.[2] Several small buildings sprang up almost overnight; in one of them Jesse Freeman opened a store, though the first stock was decidedly limited. Then a hotel was built and called the Center House and leading citizens proclaimed that one day Grove City would be the county seat. Castle was contemptuous of the new town but greatly impressed when Jonathan came from Cold Spring one day and handing her a bulky package announced that he and Ed Pettit and Lew Garrison had been elected trustees[3] of the newly organized Turkey Grove Township, the second township in the county.

"Why, Jonathan! Ain't that fine! But it's no more than right, seeing you're the only lawyer around." She beamed at him while she picked at the knotted string on the package.

Jonathan pulled off his stiff town boots. "It's the organization of the township that's important and the fact that I was once a barrister had nothing to do with my election."

"Seems to me a trustee would have to know about the law."

"Lew and Ed have no legal training." He slipped his feet into his everyday boots and leaned back with a sigh of satisfaction.

"That's all right. You can tell them what's what," his wife assured him. With the string untied she unrolled the package. "Well, I never! Why didn't you tell me you were going to get goods for gowns?"

"I didn't know it." He took off his white shirt and laid it on his chest. "Do I have a clean work shirt? . . . I've been looking for decent calico for months and this is the first time they've had anything I could endure for the life of the garment. You're not an easy lady to shop for, Miss Castle. I wouldn't care to see you in red—or dark blue."

She laughed. "Goodness no, not dark blue! I had enough of that when I was in pinafores. My, these are pretty!" There were four large folded pieces of calico: a buff, a light grey with green leaves and white flowers, a rusty brown, and a black sprigged with yellow. There was also a large roll of small pieces. "What's this for?"

"Quilts."

"I must say you got nice colors. They'll make up fine."

"You'll have scraps left from your gowns, too. With something to start on, if you do some sewing now and then, you should have ample material for several quilts. Are you handy enough with a needle to make me some shirts?" He pointed to worn and thin spots in his blue shirt.

"You'll have to let me have an old one to rip up for a pattern. I never made a man's shirt but there ain't as much to it as there is to a lady's gown. I could use some of that blue in my quilts. You ought to have a couple new white shirts, too," she threw over her shoulder. "You didn't get any white for the quilts."

Jonathan grinned. "Seems I'm getting more than I bargained for." But if Castle would make the shirts, he would gladly get extra material for quilts. Nothing like killing two birds. He watched as she felt the texture of the new calicos. A few years ago she would have been less pleased with the finest silk.

"This black is so handsome I'll make it up for second-best." She looked up quickly. "But then, a trustee's wife shouldn't look like she came out of a ragbag."

"I assure you there's no connection between my political career and your new gowns. You've needed them for some time."

"All the same, being trustee is a real honor and you ought to be proud. About time folks showed some appreciation of you."

"You flatter me! But it's no honor and I'm neither pleased nor displeased. The office is a responsibility and will take a certain amount of time and effort. However, I can't begrudge the township my services, since whatever is for the good of the township is for the good of Jonathan Gayle."

"How you talk! You sound like you didn't care two pins. But I'm proud and I think it's an honor."

"Think what you please, Castle, but I warn you: no boasting to the neighbors. Discuss your own affairs as much as you choose, but I forbid you to discuss mine.''

She gathered up the material and laid it carefully in the top of her trunk. ''I think you're mean! What's the good of having my husband a trustee if I can't talk about it?''

As Jonathan rose to go to his chores there was a twinkle of amusement in his eyes. ''That's what I was afraid of. Understand, my dear, I was not elected to make interesting conversation, and if I hear of you making conversation of it, you'll regret it!''

As Jonathan went out the door with the milk pails he heard her chuckle and turned. ''It won't make a mite of difference if I talk about it or not because everyone else will—so there!''

While she cooked supper and laid the table she kept thinking of her new gowns and how she would make them and which colors she would use for what quilts. After supper Jonathan sat on at the table while she cleared up and did the dishes. It was a pleasure to watch her move about from fireplace to table, from table to shelves. She lacked some of Abigail's efficiency but even at her household tasks she had an unconscious dignity and grace that Abigail could never achieve. The day had been hot and the supper fire had further heated the room so when her work was done, Castle washed her face in the tin basin, smoothed back her hair, and went outside to sit on the bench in the cool evening air. Jonathan took his chair and followed her and for a time they sat in silence, listening to the peepers along the creek and watching the fireflies darting about in the rows of young trees.

''Jonathan, I've heard you and Eli talk about Kansas. What's going on out there? They're fighting over slavery, ain't they?''

''Yes. There was a raid on Lawrence and John Brown made an attack on the settlers at Pottawattamie. It's a terrible thing. Everyone thought the question of slavery in the Territories had been settled by the Missouri Compromise until Douglas thought up the idea of 'squatter sovereignty.' Now they're murdering each other in Kansas, and even here in Turkey Grove you can't mention slavery without starting a ruckus. See that you bridle your tongue, my dear. I have no desire to fight either for or against your principles.''

''Can't even speak my own mind!''

''No, you can't. Not at this stage of affairs.''

''But I thought everyone around here was Abolitionist, too?''

''Most are, more or less. Some aren't. And none of them know anything about slavery.''

''Do you?''

''I've at least seen it firsthand in Virginia and Kentucky and Maryland. I don't approve of slavery, and aside from human considerations, it makes no sense economically. Slaves just aren't worth what they cost. White men work for less than it costs to keep slaves and they work harder because they're afraid of losing their jobs.''

''But slaves work for nothing!''

"They represent a large capital investment; they get food, clothing, shelter, and medical care whether they earn it or not. And they get it from the cradle to the grave. Planters don't expect a slave to turn out the same day's work as a white man. I worked harder than any slave from the time I was big enough to swing a hoe. And in London. . . . Castle, did any of the Major's people ever complain that they hadn't had enough to eat where they came from?"

"Why, no, I don't think so. I never heard any of them say . . ."

"I've been hungry, really hungry. For years I was always hungry. I've stood on the streets in the rain and cold looking in the bakeshop windows. . . ." The glow of the hearth fire came from the door and touched Jonathan's dark features. In his eyes was a faraway look as though he were seeing the boy he once had been. "If a slave doesn't want to work, he gets a 'mizrey,' but he eats just the same. If a white factory worker is too sick to work, he goes hungry. A slave isn't sent to the poor farm when he can't earn his keep or gets too old."

"Slavery is *wrong!*"

"I know it's wrong. The system is wrong, but the remedies are wrong, too. Instant abolition would be worse than slavery—for both white and black. It would take years for the necessary adjustments, but nobody wants to wait, nobody wants to adjust. These are sorry times, Miss Castle. You can't begin to know how sorry. And God only knows how it will end." He sighed and looked up at the deep blue star-studded sky. Suddenly he touched his wife's arm. "Whist! a whippoorwill."

9

E I G H T E E N   F I F T Y - S I X   was a presidential year and Turkey Grove, containing nearly a hundred thousand acres of land, polled twenty-seven votes, a majority of them for Fremont.[1] Crops had been good and corn brought a dollar a bushel in Cold Spring, a thriving village of over a hundred inhabitants. Jonathan took his wheat to Stillman's mill on Troublesome Creek and sold the flour for seven dollars a hundred.[2] Everyone was optimistic and Eli Hall talked no more of gold in California, while Abigail congratulated herself that she had stopped at the Gayle house to get a drink of water for the children. When fall came the Indians camped again on Turkey Creek and again the settlers were pestered with their begging and bargaining. But in the spring they broke camp there for the last time and followed their brothers to the Kansas Reservation. Nor were the people of Turkey Grove sorry to see them go. Though they had done no harm, neither had they contributed to the good of the community.

That same spring, Jonathan bought another quarter section to the east of his place and lent Tolly Marker the money to buy a second forty. With eighty acres the boy might have a chance; when he had that under cultivation, more land was available. In the fall when the men sold their grain, they found prices still good, but the county was being settled rapidly and Jonathan feared that when the newcomers had crops to sell, the local market would be glutted, and there was no transportation to eastern markets. So he sold his wheat but kept his corn.

"What's the matter with you, working yourself to death growing corn — for what? If you don't aim to sell it, why raise it?" Castle sputtered. "The critters can't eat *that* much! And me without a new silk dress since I came to Ioway!"

Jonathan bought no silk gowns for his wife. Instead, he took the wagon and drove down to St. Joseph; Tolly went with him, riding one of his little mustangs. They returned three weeks later with fifty young apple trees, six bred sows, and four fresh cows. Hogs would find a ready market since there were few in the county and settlers still depended largely on game for meat. That, Castle could understand. Also, she liked ham and bacon and sausage.

"But what in tarnation are you going to do with four fresh cows? If you think I'm going to take care of all that milk . . .''

"That's exactly what you're going to do. Lew Garrison will buy all the butter you can make."[3]

So the battle was on. For a week, Jonathan brought the milk in and Castle took it out and dumped it in the hog trough. The hogs were happy about it, but Jonathan wasn't. He decided a firm hand was called for, and when he was through his wife had sundry sore spots to remind her that her husband was, after all, the head of the house. So she skimmed the milk and churned the butter and the hogs were equally happy with the skim milk. The second time Jonathan took butter to the Station, Castle went along to visit with Indiana and learned her butter had attained overnight fame.

"How in the world do you make it so sweet? Why, everybody says it's the best butter they ever put in their mouths!"

Castle quoted Abigail, "I'm just careful to churn as soon as the cream is blink." She didn't explain that Jonathan had stood over her with the wagon whip so she had really had little choice as to when she would churn.

Riding home she asked abruptly, "Why can't you dig a cellar? I can't make sweet butter unless the cream is sweet and it's too hot in the house in summer. Besides, there ain't room for us and the milk pans, too. You'll just have to dig a cellar."

Jonathan replied obligingly, "Soon as I'm through setting out the apple trees."

By the time the trees were planted winter was approaching, so Jonathan called on his neighbors to help with the cellar.[4] They dug a wide, deep pit, walled it up with stout logs, roofed it over with a double layer of thick slabs from Crawfords' Mill, set a hollowed out log in the top of the roof for a vent, and heaped the roof around it with earth from the pit. Jonathan tamped the floor smooth and hard, built hanging shelves for the milk pans, shelves against the walls for pickles and preserves, and bins in the corners for potatoes and the apples they would have when the trees came into bearing. Several smaller bins, filled with fine sand from the creek, provided storage for root crops, and with pegs in the roof poles he would be able to hang the hams and bacon they would have when they butchered another year. Castle was immensely proud of her cellar and showed it off at every opportunity. Proud, too, of the rows of gooseberry conserve, plum jam and butter, crab apple jelly, and wild strawberry preserves. Another year she'd have every shelf full and then she'd have something to show! And the cellar would be a fine place to do the churning in summer. Even on the hottest days her butter would come firm and sweet, the finest in all the country 'round.

Though she hated Iowa at any time of year, Castle hated it most in winter. But now that there were roads of a sort, the settlers no longer holed up for the winter as they had done those first years. When the first heavy snow blanketed the prairie in still, breathless white, the men held a husking contest in Crawfords' mill shed. With slab runners on the wagon box, the big greys plowed through the drifts, seeming to enjoy the sport as much as the Halls and Gayles in the sled. Each of the women brought a box supper and Tolly Marker won the husking contest championship and the privilege of eating with the lady of his choice. Nor was there any question as to who the lady would be. Evva Hall was sixteen now, her hair up and her skirts down, and all fall Tolly had been a frequent caller at the Hall homestead. Harriet, too, was beginning to show symptoms of curves where the angles had been, but the boys scorned to notice her, for her hair was still in pigtails and her skirts still short enough to show her pantelets—the pantelets Castle had made for Evva from her ruffled chemise.

Supper over, the women and young folks danced. The mill shed had been cleared and was lighted by lanterns hanging from the rafters, and though the candles flickered fitfully as the wind blew through the chinks between the logs, the wavering light could not slow the pounding feet and swirling skirts. Eli, on a pile of lumber, scraped out the tunes on a dilapidated fiddle, stamping his foot and calling the sets in a singsong that followed the melody.

"Gents to the center, ladies round 'em,
  Form a basket, balance all;
Whirl your gals to where you found 'em,
  Promenade around the hall."

For a time the men watched and clapped, then drifted off behind the machinery to talk. At first they talked of weather and crops and roads and township affairs, but then as always the conversation soon turned to slavery. With each passing season the discussion became more and more heated. Tonight the news was that old John Brown of Kansas fame had come through the county with two of his sons, stopping at the hotel in Indiantown.[5] Rumor had it that he had a group of fugitive slaves with him, but no one knew who the Negroes were, where they had come from, or what had become of them. In fact, no one knew if there were any Negroes, yet no one would believe there were not.

Ed Pettit shook his head ominously. "It's nasty business. Mark my word, this John Brown feller is going to get hisself in trouble if he keeps on."

"He's *got* to keep on!" Solon Crawford insisted. "Slavery has got to be stopped. If they won't free the niggers one way, we got to free them another."

"Freeing a few of them illegal won't do no good," Ed protested.

"Then we got to free them all legal!" Solon folded his arms and his square, stocky body had the look of the immovable object prepared to meet an irresistible force.

"How you figger to do that?" Ed cocked his head and eyed Solon slantwise. "The Supreme Court ruled slavery constitutional."

"We'll change the Constitution!"

"You say true," Axel nodded. "Free country, this. Free for white, for black should be free, too. Slavery, no, it not right."

Jonathan spoke quietly but with deep conviction. "Slavery isn't right, of course, but freeing the slaves isn't as easy as it sounds. Have any of you ever seen slaves on a plantation?" Solon grunted contemptuously, the others remained silent. "Have you ever lived in the slum of a northern city? I've seen both, and I assure you, gentlemen, the majority, not all, but the majority of slaves have more food, better living conditions, less work, and far better treatment than many whites in the North. I've seen white children fighting over refuse in city streets, clad in rags in the bitterest cold. Some men pay hard-earned money for a horse—and abuse it. Some masters abuse their slaves. But a slave is a valuable piece of property and even men of little heart seldom permit a slave to destroy himself by the long hours, heavy work, and poor food that are the lot of the poor in northern cities. The thought of slavery is repugnant to all free people, but let the North heal her own carbuncles before she attempts to lance the boils of the South."

Ed nodded. "Northerners didn't talk Abolition when they was gettin' rich off the slave trade. My Pa told me about the slave ships sailing out of New London. They'd take a cargo of rum and swap for slaves, then bring the slaves over and swap for molasses to make more rum. And they made a neat profit on each deal. I don't like slavery any better than you do, Solon, but you got to look at both sides. Like Jonathan says, the slaves ain't the only ones got it hard. Shucks, we ain't got no bed of roses ourselves!"

"That's got nothing to do with it! The slaves has got to be freed and they're gonna be freed! It ain't Christian to hold human beings in bondage."

"True. But the South is economically dependent on slavery. If the slaves were freed en masse, half this nation would be bankrupt. And it wouldn't be just the southern whites who would suffer. The Negroes would suffer too."

"The niggers suffer if they was freed? You're crazy! Once they're free, their sufferings is over! It's *now* they're suffering."

"Some are, I grant you. I grant you they should be freed. But they're not prepared to fend for themselves. If they were freed now, what would they do? Where would they go? Prepare them for freedom first and free them gradually so that the necessary adjustments can be made, for them as well as for their owners. The planters can't possibly pay wages now . . ."

"Then let them work in the factories!"

"What factories?" Jonathan asked with a wry smile. "There are very few factories in the South. Or are you suggesting we bring the Negroes North and give them the jobs now held by white workers?"

"Of course not! Niggers are used to farming and there's plenty land . . ."

"They know only cotton or cane or rice or tobacco, depending on what is raised in the section where they live. They know nothing of general farming and certainly nothing of farm or money management. They have so much to learn, Solon, and unless you Abolitionists are careful you'll do them more harm than good. If it weren't for the agitation, I think the planters would free them eventually. Most of them don't *like* slavery."

"I don't care what they like!" Solon shouted. "The slaves has got to be freed, all of them, and *now!*"

"And the consequences be damned?" Ed asked.

"And the consequences be damned!"

Ed chuckled. "You're a pig-headed cuss, Solon. Folks like you cause a lot of trouble in this world."

Tempers were getting short and voices loud and Tabitha would have no quarreling at her party. So she shooed the men out on the dance floor with orders to stop talking and start dancing. Seeing Castle across the room, Jonathan waited until the end of the set, then made his way to her. He clicked his heels and presented himself with a bow.

"Miss Castle, may I have this dance?"

She laughed. "You do beat all! Certainly, sir," and she spread her black sprigged skirts in a curtsey.

Jonathan called, "Fiddler, may we have a jig?"[6]

"If the strings hold out!" Eli struck up "Garry Owen" at a clip that set the dancers' feet flying until Castle was breathless, her cheeks flushed, her eyes shining. Whatever had made her think Jonathan couldn't dance?

It was late when they started home, Abigail and the girls in the wagon box, Castle on the seat with her husband. The babies were soon sleeping under the quilts on the hay; the women and girls talked by fits and starts, too weary to keep up their usual chatter. They were swathed in cloaks and shawls and hoods, and the men, bundled to the ears, pulled their bandannas up over their noses and their hats down over their eyes, for the night was clear and the cold intense; the snow squeaked frostily under the slab runners. The greys snorted to free their nostrils of ice; Eli, on little Beauty, followed the wagon to take advantage of the trampled trail. The moon was white on the rolling hills; the trees along Troublesome Creek, black against the sky as they set out, were soon lost to view. There was no wind and the world lay silent under an indigo sky, the stars close and bright. A coyote yipped and another answered, and Jonathan spoke softly.

"Did you like the dance, Miss Castle?"

For a fleeting second she smiled up at him. "What do they know about dancing?"

"But you liked dancing with *me?*"

"Who told you you could dance? Though you did better than the others."

"Then you did like dancing with me?"

"It beat sitting at home with you with your nose in a book."

"I'm not very good company, am I? It's unfortunate our tastes are so at variance. Yet too great similarity might be dull, and life with you is never dull." He paused, then continued thoughtfully. "Basically, we're much alike."

"Us? Alike? Why, we're no more alike . . ."

"You're thinking you're a lady born and bred and I'm the son of a Welsh cottager. You've forgotten that Major Talbot grew up on the Tennessee frontier or he wouldn't have been with General Jackson at the Battle of New Orleans. He didn't become a gentleman until after he became a glassmaker. And you're very like the Major."

"He said I was like Miss Mallory."

"He said you *looked* like Miss Mallory. Did she ever throw a plate?"

"Of course not! She was a perfect lady."

Jonathan laughed. "Your grandmother was a lady but your grandfather isn't."

Castle chuckled. He had her there. Major Hunter was no lady! Maybe she *was* a little like him. Probably if she had a cane she'd thump it as hard as he did.

Snow fell for a week; temperatures were so low that Jonathan was nearly a month without mail, though there was a post office now at Grove City, less than ten miles away.[7] But the distance between the Gayle and Hall homesteads was not prohibitive and communications were maintained. The women did their visiting during the day, but in the long winter evenings Jonathan and Eli sat by the fire with their pipes, debating the pros and cons of crops and gold, for gold was once more a topic of conversation. The previous summer a number of men had left the county for the California goldfields; wild tales were told of those who made fortunes overnight and of those who lost both their fortunes and their lives in barroom brawls.

"If a man's got no better sense than to get drunk and gamble away his money, he deserves what he gits," Eli protested. "What about the ones that strike it rich and git out? The more I hear, the more I wonder if I made a mistake not going on to Californy. Farming won't ever be anything but farming, and who ever heard of a farmer gittin' rich?"

"Farmers don't get rich overnight, it's true, but they have a greater security than those who take their chances in a gold rush. Gold is the most illusive form of wealth, the most perishable of commodities. It's worth only what it will buy in other goods. The land is more enduring than man himself. Gold the world can do without if necessary, but never the land. The soil is the life of the nation and lives on from generation to generation."

Eli leaned toward the fire and knocked out his pipe. Holding it between his teeth, he took out his knife and shaved a fresh pipeful of tobacco. "It's the things gold will buy that I'm interested in. It'll buy most anything and there ain't much of anything you can buy without it—in some form or other."

"What will gold buy that you can't have here?"

"It's Abbie and the girls I'm thinking of. This ain't no country for women and children."

"Abigail and the girls aren't complaining. And it won't always be the way it is now. More settlers are moving in all the time. In a few more years . . ."

Eli was unconvinced, for others were getting rich in a hurry while he plowed and planted and got rheumatism for his pains. Abigail had no regrets and tried to ignore her husband's dissatisfaction. And with the coming of spring there were other things to think about: the red cow had a wobbly-legged red calf; downy, beady-eyed chicks hatched under a dozen hens; and the flowers by the cabin came up thick as hair on a dog's back. Castle, too, was busy. Though she steadfastly refused to work in the garden, she was the one who used the vegetables so she intended to have something to say about what was planted. Having a fine cellar, she wanted more root crops to store, and Berta Olson had told her how to make sauerkraut, so Jonathan must grow cabbage.

"You'll have to start the plants in the house and have them ready to set out when it gets warm or they won't head by frost."

With a flat in the window, Castle planted the seeds and tended the plants, and no young cabbages were ever more carefully tended. Too, she had decided to look after the baby chicks this year. Abigail boasted of her successes and few losses so Castle set herself to raise more chicks with fewer losses than Abigail. One fine spring evening when she was shutting her darlings in the coop she saw Thaddeus racing across the end of the field. Jonathan was coming from the barn with the milk so they waited at the door for Thaddy. Her black eyes were flashing, her face red with rage and running.

"Aunt Castle! Uncle Jonathan! There's a horrid horse trader at our house! He wanted Pa to swap Beauty for an ole plow horse! You gonna swap your team, Uncle Jonathan?''

"No, Thaddy. Your Pa didn't swap Beauty, did he?''

"No siree! He said he'd about as leaf swap Ma or one of us girls. Beauty carried him all the way from Illinoy. Pa says if we're gonna starve, we'll all starve together, us and Beauty and the oxen.''

"I'm glad your Pa feels that way. A man who isn't loyal to his beasts can't be trusted to be loyal to his friends.''

They went in and while Castle strained the milk, Jonathan washed. Thaddeus watched him as he combed his hair and beard.

"Ain't your horses got names?'' she asked, taking her turn at the wash basin.

"I never got around to naming them. Think I should?''

"How can you tell which is which without names?''

"I hadn't thought of that. What should I name them?''

"Hummm,'' Thaddeus studied, twisting her mouth and wrinkling her nose. "They got to have nice names, and big names, 'cause they're such big horses. Don't you know any names?''

Jonathan's eyes twinkled. "How about Archimedes and Alcibiades?''

"Arch . . . Arch . . . My, those are handsome names!''

"Suppose we call them Archie and Al for short?''

"Archie and Al. Now I can tell the girls I named your horses.'' She turned to Castle, "I can stay for supper, can't I? It smells good.''

"We aren't having anything fancy, Thaddy. Just meat and potatoes and greens.''

"I don't think they'll have anything better at home, so I might as well stay.''

Castle laughed. "Nothing like being practical. Lay three places, Thaddy.''

Later Eli came over, for the horse trader had brought news. Two Negro women had been sold and were being taken south by boat, but they had run away and had not been found. A reward of five hundred dollars had been offered by the owner, and all roads and the river were being watched.[8]

Castle burst out indignantly. "Why doesn't somebody *do* something? Jonathan Gayle, are you just going to set there and smoke that pipe while those poor creatures . . . You never take any interest!''

"Not in affairs beyond my control.'' Then to Eli, "What's your opinion?''

"Likely the Underground. There's several fellers around Cold Spring could have had a hand in it, but they didn't have the niggers at their houses. Prob'ly passed 'em on to someone who wouldn't be so apt to be suspected. They're after them hot and heavy with that reward.''

Jonathan puffed his pipe, shook his head, and sighed. "It'll have to end sometime, one way or the other.''

Spring passed and summer came and Jonathan was bringing in his hay. Hearing someone shouting, he leaned on his fork and turned while Eli came pounding past as fast as little Beauty could run.

"The creek! The creek! Get your cows!''[9]

The cows were in the meadow along the creek. If they had crossed to the far side. . . . Jonathan unhooked Archie, threw the traces over his back, and slipped the off line through Al's bridle. Leaving Al with the hay wagon, he grabbed Archie's collar and heaved himself up, harness and all. The big grey was no race horse but he had a stride that covered ground and they reached the creek in time to see Eli plunge Beauty into the flood up to her belly.

Above, where the bank was low, the water had broken over and the cows were stranded on an island between creek and overflow. Eli circled the herd to drive the frightened beasts into the narrow, shallow strip of water separating them from the safety of higher ground. Instead, they trotted the length of their little island and Eli was forced into the rushing waters of the mainsteam to head them back. With Eli urging them away from the swirling confluence of creek and overflow, Jonathan crossed above, swinging between cows and creek, and forced them into the overflow. Once in, the bawling critters took the shortest route to dry ground, but the calves were forced to swim for it and one, only a few days old, was caught by the current and swept past the men. Leaving Jonathan with the others, Eli raced along the water's edge, plunged into the creek below the calf, and caught him by the tail as he came abreast.

"Eli!" Jonathan yelled. "Upstream! Watch out!"

A wall of water was roaring down and Eli, caught in the swift current of the mainstream, was being carried along faster than his horse could swim. He drew the calf across the saddle and urged Beauty on. Just below, the creek turned sharply and Eli watched the bank, gauging the distance, for if he passed the turn he would be swept to the far bank against a high, cut-under spot where he could not hope to get out. Jonathan pounded down to the turn. Snatching off Archie's bridle, he looped one line to a trace chain and threw the other to Eli, bridle and all, trusting the bit and buckles to hold. Eli missed the catch but the water carried the line against Beauty's flank. He seized it and made a quick turn around the saddle horn while Jonathan swung Archie about to take the strain as the line pulled taut. Leading Archie by his mane, Jonathan moved forward slowly, and Beauty, feeling the pull, redoubled her efforts. She was coming into shallow water when the flood struck and she and Eli and the calf went under.

The line held and Archie stood steady, his weight against the collar which had twisted half around his neck under the unequal pull on the single trace. Beauty came up, Eli and the calf still on top, but Eli was bent forward, his head almost in the little mare's mane, clinging to the saddle horn, coughing and choking. Again Jonathan led the big grey slowly forward while Beauty struggled for a footing. Once more they reached shallow water and when Beauty stopped swimming and started to walk, Eli slipped down beside her still holding to the saddle, the calf hanging limply across the mare's withers. Beauty was heaving and staggering so Jonathan went into the water and led her up the bank. Eli came with her, still hanging to the saddle horn, coughing and breathing heavily.

"About done in," he dropped to the ground, head in hands. "A log hit me when that water went over. Be all right soon's I get my breath."

"You hurt?" Jonathan asked sharply.

Eli shook his head. "Winded. Set a minute." He loosened the hat he had pulled down hard on his head for his race across the meadow and pushed the wet hair from his eyes. "Calf all right?"

Jonathan turned and ran a hand over the little fellow's silky head. "He fared better than you did. Come on, Peter Bullet, try your legs." But the legs buckled and the calf stretched on the grass, his sides heaving. "Get your wind boy," Jonathan told him. "Your Ma'll soon be after you. Sure you're all right, Eli?"

"Yeah. That a good calf?"

"Jersey. Make a good bull." He grinned down at Eli. "Since you saved him, you can have the use of him — if he lives long enough." While he talked, Jonathan pulled the saddle off Beauty, who still stood spraddle legged, head hanging. He unbuckled the bridle and slipped the bit from her mouth, tossed it with the saddle, then went over the little mare from stem to stern, finding no obvious injuries. He turned back to Eli. "She seems all right. You feeling better?"

"Most good as new. Here comes Castle. She'll tell you."

Chuckling, Jonathan gathered handfuls of dry grass and began giving Beauty a rubdown while he watched his wife's approach. Castle came at a run, her sunbonnet flapping on her back, her skirts held almost to her knees. Seeing the two men laughing at her she dropped the skirts and slackened her pace. By the time she reached them she had recovered her dignity.

"Eli Hall, what do you mean, getting yourself most drowned like that? You got less gumption than any man I ever saw — except Jonathan. Why did you let him go in the creek?"

"He went after Peter Bullet." Jonathan indicated the calf.

Castle dropped on her knees beside him. "He won't die, will he?" she asked anxiously, her hand on his thumping heart.

"I think he'll be all right. But Beauty took a licking, poor girl."

Leaving the calf, Castle helped rub Beauty, who blew her nose, lifted her head, and shook herself. When they had finished with her Jonathan gave her a final pat and let her go.

"Might as well leave her here in the meadow a few days, Eli. She's no filly and she had a bad time."

"She's a good little mare. Got more sand than some folks."

Eli had gotten to his feet and the calf was trying to do likewise, so Jonathan swung him across Archie's broad back. He submitted meekly, blinking his eyes and looking about placidly. But when they approached his mother and he heard her frantic mooing he answered with a plaintive "Ma-a-a!" Jonathan put him down, and this time the legs held and young Peter threw up his tail and staggered uncertainly toward his mother as she trotted to meet him. She gave him a few reassuring licks with her long tongue and Peter nuzzled her a moment, then began to suck.

Jonathan walked Archie back to the others. "Seems he can sit up and take nourishment so he should be all right. How about your stock, Eli?"

"The cow was on this side and I left the oxen in the field. Abbie and the girls were after the chickens."

"Hope we aren't too late to give them a hand."

Eli shook his head. "Not worth the effort. Abbie and the girls can cover considerable territory. Besides, you'd just scare the hens. They don't know you."

"If the creek comes up any higher it'll get your hay, Jonathan," Castle observed. "Look where it is now."

Water already covered the lower part of the meadow and was creeping up the small rise where they stood. Fearing another breakover from somewhere above, Jonathan went for his hay wagon and brought the load to the stack while Castle made sure the hogs and chickens were safe. Eli, riding the hay wagon with Jonathan, got off at the barn and went home.

When Jonathan had stabled the team he told Castle, "I'm concerned about the Halls. They're closer to the creek than we are and Eli has fields on both sides."

"Maybe we ought to go over." She pushed back her hair and put on her sunbonnet.

They found the Hall family assembled behind the stable watching the creek. Muddy water boiled across half of Eli's wheat field while debris piled against the fence, threatening to carry away the rails at any moment.

"Get the chickens?" Castle asked Abigail.

"Yes, but them young fools is too much for me to chase. I never dreamed the creek. . . . Just look at Eli's wheat!" Abigail was near tears.

Eli patted his wife's shoulder and Evva put an arm around her mother's waist. But Harriet and Thaddeus were watching the water swirling through the fence and shouted in unison, "There it goes!" The corner had collapsed and the churning water swept away almost the entire length of fence. Cressy and Jennifer clutched each other and jumped up and down excitedly but Abigail put the baby in Evva's arms and sat down on a log. Eli sat down beside her and put his head in his hands.

"Them rails will be scattered from hell to breakfast."

"I've a stack by the stable. You can use them to rebuild the fence and next fall we'll cut more," Jonathan offered. "The wheat is still in the milk so if it doesn't come back up you can cut it for hay. Another year you might put this field in hay, then you wouldn't lose more than one cutting in any case."

"There won't be another year! I'm going to Pike's Peak!"

"Oh, no, Eli!" Abigail forgot her doldrums. "That ain't no way! Because you lost a little wheat . . ."

Eli shook his head. "Too much loss and not enough gain."

By sundown the flood had subsided somewhat; when the men went out in the night with lanterns, the creek was almost within its banks. By morning only the debris and destruction showed where the water had been. Eli found Jonathan at the stable saddling Al.

"Still too wet to do anything. Put your saddle on Archie and we'll see how the neighbors fared. Some may need help."

They rode down to Pettits' to cross at the bridge and Grampa met them at the barnyard gate.

"Who be ye? Who be ye?" he demanded.

Jonathan told him but he appeared not to hear. He stood staring from faded eyes, his arms dangling, his body stooped, his mouth half open, in his look and posture the bewilderment of an ancient ape.

"Ed, Ed! Som'uns here. Won't give 'is name. M'self, won't have no truck with folks won't say who they is. Shif'less . . . ridin' round . . . pokin' their noses where they ain't wanted . . ." His voice trailed off into muttered grumbling. Coming out, Ed passed him on the path. "Send 'em packin', Ed! Don't have no truck . . ."

Ed had turned his stock into the pasture and had gone to Crawford's mill for a load of slabs. When the flood came, Patience and the twins had gone into the water up to their necks to get the cows across Jim Branch, but in spite of their efforts a cow and a calf had been lost. Ed had found the cow in the debris above the bridge but the calf had disappeared. Patience had taken a chill and Ed had been up with her all night. He was tired, confused, and alarmed.

"I'll send Castle over," Jonathan assured him.

"Reckon Abbie can spare Evva for a few days. She's a real good hand with housework and young'uns."

"We'll be obliged." Ed drew a sigh of relief. "How'd you folks make out?"

They related their experiences, then Jonathan asked, "Where'd the water come from? We've had no rain."

"Stage driver said they had a cloudburst up in the next county. Bad one."

To save time, Jonathan and Eli headed back the way they had come, but at the bridge they saw the Olson boys riding toward them and waited.

"How are things down your way?" Eli called.

"Lost some crops. Nothing much. They say it was bad farther down toward Cold Spring." When they learned of the Pettits' loss and Patience's illness Knute said, "That's bad. We'll tell Ma," and Hennie added, "We figgered there might be trouble somewheres. We was riding to see did anybody need help." The boys turned their horses and rode off downstream and Jonathan and Eli rode back up the creek.

"Reckon we'd ought to ride on up to Markers'?" Eli suggested. "They're pretty close to the creek . . ." Jonathan nodded and they put the big greys to a trot. At the ford the current was swift and several times the horses sank to their bellies. They found Tolly saddling up and he greeted them with a wide grin.

"Was fixin' to ride over and see was you folks all right. Ma lost half her chicks and she's cryin' her eyes out. Makes me sick myself, but they was gone before we could get near 'em."

"Too bad. I see some of your hay was under."

"Yeah, but like you told me about them fields next the creek, Mr. Gayle, I got the first cutting and what ain't cut this time ain't hurt too much. No great loss."

Again they related the Pettits' misfortunes and Jonathan added, "Want to drive the women over for us?"

"Could I get the wagon across the creek?"

"No, but you can ride over with us and take my team and wagon."

"I'll tell Ma." Tolly ran up to the house and returned and clambered up behind Jonathan. At the Gayles' they left the boy at the stable hitching the greys to Jonathan's wagon, while Jonathan went to the house to tell Castle and Eli went for Evva. Within half an hour they were on the way, Castle on the seat with Tolly, Evva on a chair behind, where Tolly had to turn his head to see her.

"Mind them lines. She ain't going to fall out," Castle chided.

Ed met them at the gate. "Patience is pretty porely, Castle."

"Who's the doctor around here, Ed Pettit? You or me?"

Ed grinned. "That's right. Come on in the house. Patty'll be proud to see you. Come in, Evva girl, you're a sight for sore eyes. You might as well come in, too, Tolly. Maybe Evva can wrastle us up a cup of coffee. I make the gosh-darnedest coffee you ever tried to get out of drinking."

With Laurel and Josie to show her where things were kept, Evva made coffee for the men. Grampa came in, grumbled while he drank his coffee, and still grumbling, wandered back out again. Patience was in the lean-to bedroom and Castle went to work with Jamaica rum and hot mustard steeps, followed by onion poultices. It was sundown when Tolly took her home but she assured Ed his wife was out of danger. Rest was what she needed and Evva would see she got it. That night Evva rocked little Cade to sleep when he cried for his Ma, and by the time Ed took her home some weeks later, Cade cried for Evva. Ed helped the girl down from the wagon and turned to Abigail.

"I sure hope Laurel and Josie grow up like Evva. She's a fine girl, and you can be proud of her."

Abigail kissed her eldest and patted her affectionately.

"She ain't never give me a minute's trouble, Ed. Not since the day she was born."

O V E R in Illinois that summer, Abraham Lincoln and Stephen A. Douglas were campaigning for the post of United States senator, and all over the country their debates were read with interest and discussed with mounting violence. Iowa was the next-door neighbor of Illinois, a Free State, and in many ways economically dependent on the older state, so the problems of Illinois were the problems of Iowa. Yet Eli Hall talked of nothing but gold and Pike's Peak. "Abolition" and "Secession" were fighting words but Eli ignored them and listened only to the tales of gold. The mining camps were booming and western Iowa sent her full quota of adventurers in the quest for fortune.

That year the Butterfield Overland Mail made the first trip from St. Louis to San Francisco,[1] but in Turkey Grove the event of the year was the barn Jonathan built that fall, by far the largest in the township to date.[2] Along one side were stalls for eight horses and an oat bin that would hold feed for as many teams. Opposite were ties for a dozen cows and between was ample space to shelter the new carryall, the wagon, and all the farm equipment. Overhead on three sides were hay mows piled to the roof with prairie hay, timothy, and clover. Across the back was a cattle shed, the lean-to roof reaching up high enough on the barn wall to allow an opening to the hay mow, so that Jonathan could stand in the loft and pitch hay down into the racks in the shed for the steers he planned to fatten for market. The barnlot, too, had been enlarged and grain bunkers set up, and though the hogs were now bedded in the former stable, they would have the run of the barnlot and be able to pick up corn dropped by the steers.

Castle raged that animals should be better housed than she, but Jonathan listened indifferently, if at all. He had come to Iowa with a definite plan and step by step he was carrying it out. The barn was not only part of that plan, it had become an immediate necessity. He had hoped for sons, but had none and apparently would not have. With no prospect of future help, it became doubly important that he have the equipment to accomplish more work with less effort. The barn was essential; a house was a luxury and it would have to wait its turn.

That fall the bottom dropped out of the Cold Spring market and corn went to fifteen cents a bushel.[3] Jonathan and Eli hauled their wheat to Des Moines, a journey of seventy miles, requiring about a week each way. Even there prices had slumped, for transportation to the East was still unreliable. Eli was bitterly disappointed. After losing half his crop to the flood, he had been forced to sell for far less than he had expected. He had farmed before; he should have known better than to homestead again. He'd go to Pike's Peak where there was gold just for picking it up.

"How can you be so sure you'll make a strike?" Jonathan asked as they sat on the barnyard fence on a sunny afternoon.

"The gold's there and I got as good a chance of finding it as anyone else. Why shouldn't I strike it rich?"

"Others get killed. Why shouldn't you?"

"Don't talk foolishness. A man behaves hisself is as safe there as anywheres else."

"Try it another year, Eli. You've got a good start here, and you're making a living. Don't be in such a hurry to catch the bird in the bush. Hold onto the one you've got."

"Save your breath to cool your broth, Jonathan. I'm going to Pike's Peak!"

Abigail, too, pleaded in vain, but her husband went stubbornly on with his plans for the trip west. "It ain't no use," she told Castle as she settled herself with her knitting while Castle bent over the table cutting quilt pieces. "Once Eli's heel starts itching, there ain't no holding him. We had a good farm in Illinoy, only this time I ain't selling. If he strikes gold he can bring it home with him. If he don't, he can come back and go on farming."

"How long does he think he'll be gone?"

"He figgers he'll be back by next summer. He won't stay long away from his family."

Castle's scissors sang through the bright cloth. The day the Halls came in the covered wagon, Abigail had said Eli wouldn't go far without her and the children and she had been right. Perhaps she would be right again. Eli had laid in supplies to feed the family overwinter and ricked up wood enough to last until spring.

"What if he don't get back by summer?" Castle muttered, her mouth full of pins.

"No use crossing bridges ahead of time. The Lord feeds the sparrows and he won't let us starve. I been in a lot of tight spots in my life, but I never been in one yet I didn't get out of somehow."

On a crisp, cold day in November, Eli packed his saddlebags and Castle and Jonathan went over to say good-bye. The men shook hands wordlessly, then Eli bent and kissed Castle, laughing at her shocked expression.

"That's to bind the bargain: you look after my wife and young'uns and I'll bring you a nugget of gold as big as your foot!" Then he caught up little Lucinda, swinging her high over his head while she shouted in glee. "You won't forget your Pa, will you, Redhead?"

Jennifer jerked his pants leg. "I won't forget you, Pa."

" 'Course you won't, honey!" Eli stooped and hugged the child and Cressy sidled over so he drew her, too, into his embrace. For a moment he held his three little girls while his step-daughters, standing in the doorway by their mother, looked on and wept. Thaddeus blew her nose on her petticoat and Abigail neglected to box her ears.

"Won't none of you have time to forget me," Eli laughed as he straightened. "I'll be back 'fore you can say scat. Be good girls, now, and help your Ma." He kissed Abigail and each of the girls in turn. "Say your prayers every night," he admonished them as his glance met that of his wife and she nodded and smiled through her tears. They would all pray for him.

Then Eli mounted little Beauty and waving his hat, rode off down the trail. Beauty whinnied once, then broke into a trot and was soon over the rise. Castle never forgot Eli riding off to Pike's Peak astride the little black mare, his red hair rumpled by the wind, as he waved his old black hat to his family. He was a good man, but he didn't know beans when the bag was open.

A few days later Jonathan left for Missouri, where he sold his hogs and brought back fifty lanky steers.[4] It would mean a hard winter's work, but corn was worth nothing and beef sky-high.

The latter part of December it began to snow and every flake stayed on the ground until the spring thaw. That winter of 1858-1859 the cold was more intense than anything the settlers had yet encountered; herds of half-starved elk drifted down from Dakota and Minnesota, many to die in the snowdrifts which covered the fences. Even in the timber the snow was three feet deep, and underbrush was the only food obtainable. At first a few were killed, but the poor creatures were so emaciated the meat was inedible.[5] Jonathan had several stacks of straw which he used to bed his stock, and though it was not particularly nourishing, it was far better than snowballs. So while the elk remained he pitched straw over the fence for them every day and soon had a considerable herd waiting for their rations at chore time. He knew there had been hard winters before and would be again, but he could not endure to see wild things starve in a land of plenty.

Twice during the winter Abigail had letters from Eli and each time she passed the news on to Castle and Jonathan. He had arrived safely and found the settlement at Denver really booming. He was getting acquainted and learning all he could about prospecting. As soon as he got his bearings he would look for a claim. The second letter had been written more hastily. He had found a partner and they were staking a claim but would not be able to work it until spring. Once they struck gold he'd sell out and come home. There were mining companies ready to pay cash money for a claim that looked good, and it was cash he wanted. They were not to worry if he didn't write again for a while as the camp would be out in the mountains and there would be no way to send mail.

"Don't it beat all?" Abigail said dejectedly, sitting with the letter in her hand, her knitting forgotten in her apron pocket. "All this time and only two letters and no knowing when I'll hear again. Don't look to me like he'll be back by summer."

"At least you'll know he's working his claim, not just sitting around in Denver," Jonathan reminded her.

"That's so, and as long as he went to look for gold, he might as well look. Wouldn't we be surprised if he found it!"

"I should think so!" Castle agreed enviously. If Eli struck gold the Halls would be rich while she. . . . If Jonathan had any sense he'd have stayed in Pittsburgh in the first place. Then she could have lived in a fine house and had parties and balls. . . . Or could she? He couldn't have been doing so all-fired good in Pittsburgh or he wouldn't have come to Iowa to work like a mule. Maybe if they had stayed she couldn't have lived like a fine lady after all. And to live *there* without wealth while Griselda lived at Greenbriar was unthinkable. In Iowa she was no worse off than her neighbors. Unless Eli struck gold . . .

By spring Jonathan's steers were sleek and fat and as soon as the grass was good he drove them by easy stages to Des Moines, returning with a solid roll of greenbacks. However, he only told Castle that the beeves had brought a good price, and she, busy with the affairs of the Hall household, neglected to press him.

Since Eli would not be back in time, Jonathan and Tolly Marker put in some crops for the Halls. The girls worked, too, even eight-year-old Cressy dropping corn and potatoes. Jonathan suspected Tolly put more time on the Hall place than was good for his own, but knowing how he felt about Evva he hesitated to say anything. Even so, unless Eli came home soon, fall would find the Halls with little in the way of salable crops and little money for those things that had to be bought. However, the girls put in a good garden, and since Castle had raised more cabbage plants than all Turkey Grove could use, the Halls would have cabbage. But Castle, backed by Evva, refused to allow Abigail to work in the fields or even in the garden, for she was expecting another child in the late summer. After her success with the cabbage plants, Castle had decided her thumb was as green as Abigail's so she went over to help thin marigolds and heliotrope and bring home plants for a flower bed of her own. Jonathan found them digging like a pair of terriers and dropped a letter in front of Abigail.

"Oh, my!"

"What is it?" Castle sat back on her heels and looked up.

"A letter from Eli!"

"Well, open it! What does he say? Has he struck gold yet?"

Castle was as excited as Abigail and bounced up, dusting her hands on her skirts, while Jonathan drew Abigail to her feet and waited while she tore open the envelope and glanced over the sheet. Turning, she dropped heavily on a bench and sat staring at them as though incapable of speech.

"What does he say?" Castle insisted.

"He struck gold!" Abigail waved the letter at Jonathan. "You read it. I'm that excited I can't see. He says he'll be home soon."

Jonathan read the letter aloud but when he finished his face was grave. "I'm glad for your sake, Abigail. His, too."

"What does he mean, there at the last? Something about his partner. What does he mean, Jonathan?"

"Perhaps he thinks the man isn't entirely honest. But if he sells to a mining company I don't see how his partner could cheat him."

"He's trying to tell me something," Abigail insisted. "Just tacked on like that, I don't know what he means. If the man ain't honest, why don't he say so?" She shook her head, then a smile spread over her face. "Goodness, wonder what it feels like to be rich? Why, we can buy the girls new shoes and dresses . . ."

"Mercy on us, Abigail!" Castle burst out disgustedly. "You don't think you'll go on living *here!* Why, you'll live in the city and have a fine house and carriages and . . . and . . ."

"Oh, no! Not all that! I wouldn't know how to act!"

"You'll live like a fine lady, just you wait and see!"

Castle was wildly, bitterly envious and when she and Jonathan started home she was on the verge of giving him a piece of her mind when he said, "I don't like that postscript."

"Postscript? What are you talking about?"

"The letter was carefully written, carefully worded. Then across the bottom was scrawled, 'I don't trust my partner.' I think Abigail was right when she said he was trying to tell us something. Hummm. . . . The body of the letter was written for the partner's benefit . . . the postscript was scribbled on—at the risk of his life, for all we know! Since the letter was mailed, he didn't get caught at it. Nevertheless, I shall take it upon myself to make inquiries in Denver."

"Good grief! You don't mean . . . ? If anything happened to Eli . . ."

"Mind you, not a word of this to Abigail if you value your hide! I've no proof of anything. I may be jumping to conclusions. But I've seen men hanged on less evidence."

For a time the Halls were jubilant. Eli had said he would be home soon. But how soon? Would he just ride up to the door on little Beauty? A month passed with no further word. Likely he had been delayed. But the sun continued to rise and set, days stretched into weeks, and the weeks added up until that strange postscript hung like a cloud over Abigail's head. She tried to put it from her mind. Eli would come—soon.

Castle dreaded Abigail's coming confinement. Lucinda had been bad enough; then Abigail had been healthy and hearty and happy. Now she walked the floor half the night, ate almost nothing, and under the simmering heat of summer was growing pale and hollow-eyed. She moved about the house listlessly and she and the girls talked less and less of the gay times they would have when Pa came home and they had lots and lots of money. They talked, for silence would have been unbearable, but they talked of everyday things: of crops and weather and chickens and jelly and jam.

Jonathan wrote several letters but could not locate Eli. He was known to have been in Denver during the winter, but beyond that Jonathan could learn nothing. There was no record of his claim, no record of anything. Eli had vanished. Yet it was quite possible he was still out in the mountains, equally possible that he was on his way home.

"You going to tell Abigail?" Castle asked.

"I have nothing to tell her. She knows he was in Denver and that is all I know definitely. The rest is speculation. And if you tell her of my suspicions, you'll regret it!"

Early in July the trustees went to Cold Spring for a meeting with county officials and Lew Garrison brought Indiana over to spend the day with Castle and Abigail.

"Well, now, Indie! What a nice surprise! How'd you ever get away from the Station?"

"This ain't a stage day and a couple weeks ago Lew brought a hired girl up from Cold Spring to help out. She's a flighty piece, but if she can't make out one day without me I might as well find it out now. I ain't been off the place in a dog's age. Castle, that's a mighty handsome quilt you got on the frame there. Sunburst, ain't it? Get us a couple needles and let's see what we can do with it. No sense setting around twiddling our thumbs." So they seated themselves around the quilting frame to enjoy a good gab fest with no men to bother about.

"There ain't nothing I like better'n quilting," Abigail remarked as she bit off a piece of thread and aimed it at the eye of the needle. "It's so sort of soothing. Keeps your hands busy without taxing your mind."

"What have you heard from Eli?" Indiana asked. "I might as well be dead and buried for all I know about what goes on in Turkey Grove. I get all the news from back East and out West, but I never know what my own neighbors are up to. Now, what about Eli?"

"I ain't heard since the letter saying he struck gold," Abigail's voice was expressionless as she knotted her thread with a quick twist.

"He struck gold?" Indiana looked up in astonishment. "Well, I'll be bound!" She shook her head incredulously. "When he comes home you'll be so fine you won't have anything to do with the likes of us. But then, I guess he wouldn't make much more money on a gold mine than Jonathan made on them steers. Ever hear of such a thing? He's a smart one!"

Castle found herself staring at Indiana with her mouth open, coughed, cleared her throat and asked innocently, "What was so smart about it?"

"Why, feeding his corn instead of selling it for next to nothing. He stopped at the Station on the way home from Des Moines and Lew said he had a roll of greenbacks that would choke a cow. Big ones, too. Lew said . . ."

But Castle was no longer listening. The idea! Jonathan bragging to Lew how much money he'd made and not a word to his own wife. She'd have something to say to him! Imagine him selling those steers for all that money. That would show folks. The other men had sold their corn for pennies and look what Jonathan got for his just by feeding it to those walleyed steers! . . . But why wouldn't he build a new house? With all that money. . . . One of these days she'd build a fire that would really set the thatch afire. . . . Well, why not? That would be one way of getting a new house! The more she thought of it, the more feasible the idea appeared. How would he or anyone else know the difference? He was forever yapping at her about fire, telling her the sparks would catch in the thatch. But only when it was hot and dry. If the cabin were to burn accidentally it would have to be during a hot, dry spell. Well, she'd waited this long, she could wait for the proper time. Come fall, she'd have a new house or know the reason why.

A week later Abigail's seventh daughter was born without difficulty and when the baby was tucked in her mother's arms, Abigail smiled more happily than she had in months.

"I'm going to name her Samantha after Eli's Ma. He'll like that."

Castle didn't particularly care what Eli would like. The idea of him going trailing off getting himself killed when Abigail was in the family way! She was still stewing when she went home that evening and since she couldn't very well tell Abigail what she thought of Eli, she told Jonathan.

"Castle, he did what he thought was for the best. He was so carried away by the idea of having limitless wealth for his loved ones that he was blinded to the risks to himself."

"Piffle! He just didn't like farming."

Jonathan could never decide which were the more difficult: the letters Castle sent, or those she received. Major Hunter, Miss Sarah, and Marybelle all wrote from time to time, and after each letter Jonathan was in for several unpleasant days. Then in due course the letters had to be answered and Jonathan wrote more or less at his wife's dictation. They were her family and he felt duty bound to see that she kept in touch with them. But as though family letters were not enough of a problem, Anne Middleton also wrote occasionally, and Jonathan was always tempted to destroy any and all epistles addressed in her handwriting. He never did, but more often than not, he wished he had. In her latest effort, Anne had related at length the delights of the lovely and exciting lawn party the Delacroix family had held at their estate in Greenbriar. If only Castle could have been there! However gay the affair had been, it contributed nothing to Castle's happiness. For days she had been glummer than glum. Sometimes mockery goaded her out of her doldrums, and sometimes teasing brought a laugh, but this time nothing made any impression.

Supper was over and Jonathan sat with his book on the table before him. He saw the printed page but the words did not register. His wife was a conundrum and the answer was not in his book. At Homeplace she had known years of unhappiness and in Iowa she saw only the drudgery. For the other women of the community, their present life was only relatively harder than the life they had known elsewhere, and they could look forward to a future brighter than anything they could have hoped for in their former homes. But Castle could never hope to find in Iowa the ease and luxury she had known in her youth. If she were ever to be content in Iowa, she would have to find new interests, new satisfactions, new values—something sufficiently important to compensate for what she had lost. But what?

T H E more Castle brooded over the difference between her lot and the social whirl of Griselda Delacroix, the more determined she became to force Jonathan to build a new house. Him with all that money and his fancy barn, the finest for miles around, and her living in the shabbiest cabin in the whole township! She'd show him! August was hot and dry and Jonathan was cutting hay. He said it was good haying weather and hoped it would last. Castle hoped so, too, but for another reason.

The last Saturday of the month Jonathan went to Cold Spring, and that was an all-day trip. Abigail and the girls took the oxen and wagon to pick plums along the creek and Castle agreed to join them when she finished her churning. But she had her own plans for the day and they had nothing to do with plums. When her neighbors were safely out of the way and her butter made up in neat pats, she went into action. She emptied Jonathan's bookshelves and stacked the books against the far fence. Making sure all his papers were safe in his brass-bound chest she pushed and hauled until she had it a good distance from the house. Next came her own hide-covered trunk; it proved almost as heavy and hard to move as the chest. Perspiration was trickling down her back and her hair clung damply to her forehead. Apparently she would earn her new house by the time she got it. Suddenly she sat down on the trunk and laughed. She'd let the furniture burn up right along with the cabin so Jonathan would have to build new—and better. Once the trunk was beside the chest she carried out the quilts and pillows and feather bed and piled them on top. The corn shuck mattress could burn. Then came a final check of the cabin. Had she overlooked anything? Jonathan would have her hide if she left anything of his.

Satisfied there was nothing further of value she built up the fire, poking and piling on wood until the blaze roared up the chimney, then went outside to await developments. There were none. Sparks shot high but fell harmlessly to earth some distance from the cabin. She was disgusted. All this time Jonathan had been warning her she'd set the house afire just poking the backlog. Well, she wasn't going to be beat by a stupid fire, not after all her hard work. She returned to the cabin and took a burning stick from the fireplace, carried it out, and threw it as high as she could onto the thatch. In a moment it caught and tongues of red flame danced in a puff of smoke that quickly grew to a rolling cloud. Soon the roof was blazing and she stood laughing as the flames shot higher in widening waves. She'd show Jonathan he couldn't make her live in the same old cabin all her life! However, she was somewhat shaken when she saw Tolly Marker coming bareback and hell-bent for election across the fields much sooner than she had thought possible.

"Mrs. Gayle! Mrs. Gayle! Are you all right?" he shouted as he pulled up and slid down beside her. Relieved at his acceptance of the fire, Castle wanted to laugh but straightened her face.

"Of course I'm all right. You wouldn't expect me to stay in there and let the roof fall on me, would you?"

Tolly tied his heaving mount to the fence and came to stand with her. It was already too late to do anything but watch the cabin burn, for the roof was a roaring inferno and flames were licking the log walls. Then glancing about Tolly saw the pile of bedding.

"You got your things out! You're a brave woman, Mrs. Gayle."

"Hummpf!" was Castle's only comment.

Evva and Harriet came running up from the creek with Thaddeus at their heels. Then came Abigail, whipping the oxen to a shambling trot, Cressy clutching the baby in her small arms, Jennifer and Lucinda clinging to each other with frightened faces. Abigail climbed out of the wagon, panting as though she had pulled the oxen.

"Castle! You're not hurt? Oh, thank God! What if it had happened in the night! You might both have been burned to a crisp! Makes me shudder to think of it."

"Then don't think of it," Castle told her shortly. Such a fuss over a pesky old log cabin. "There's no harm done. Jonathan was fixing to build a new house anyway," she announced grandly.

"He was? Then it ain't so bad. And you saved your valuables. I wish I'd of been here, we might of got everything out. It's a good thing you stayed this morning to do your churning. 'The Lord moves in a mysterious way, His wonders to perform.' "

Ed Pettit and young Luke arrived in time to see the roof fall in and Ed, too, praised Castle for saving her possessions. Soon the heavy logs were burning like kindling wood, the black smoke rolling high while sparks shot in all directions. The barn was far enough away to be in no danger, but the men wet down the roofs of the other outbuildings. By noon the cabin was a smouldering heap and Ed and Tolly departed after reminding Castle to have Jonathan let them know when he was ready to rebuild. She went home with the Halls; Jonathan found her there when he came home that evening. At supper he listened to the tale of his wife's bravery without batting an eye, but at the first opportunity he spoke to her aside.

"My books are all there? And my papers are in the chest?"

"That's where you keep 'em, ain't it?"

"If one is missing you'll remember it the rest of your life."

She gave him a quick, startled look and hastened to help Evva clear the table. Jonathan knew she had set fire to the cabin. Well, let him know it. There was nothing he could do about it now. The rest of them had all been too stupid to catch on, but Jonathan had not been fooled. All the same, he'd have to build a new house. Only right now she had no wish to be left alone with him so she kept close to the others and insisted on staying the night.

As she had expected, Jonathan refused to start the new house until after corn picking, and since she refused to live in the barn, he set up a tent and she took a vacation from housekeeping—though she soon found that camping also had its drawbacks. At first it was rather a lark to cook outdoors and sleep with the feather bed on a pile of straw heaped on the ground. Then came several days of rain. Cooking in the open was impossible, yet when she built a fire in the tent the wet wood smoked and drove her out into the rain to get her breath. After slopping around in the mud all day it was far from pleasant to sleep in a damp bed at night. Wrapped in a shawl, Harriet came over to invite them to come to the house and Castle promptly caught up her cloak, but Jonathan took it from her.

"Tell your Ma we're quite all right. There's no need to upset two households. Run home, child, before you get soaked."

"We could stay there as well as not," Castle protested. "They got room enough."

"We could be quite comfortable in the barn, but since you prefer the tent . . . ," he shrugged indifferently.

"If you once got me living in that barn you'd make me stay there all winter—maybe all my life!" She glanced about their sodden quarters. "I'll make my bed in the cellar. It's dry there."

"There are spiders in the cellar," Jonathan grinned.

"I don't care if there are snakes and snails! It's dry."

So he relented and brought the wagon around and put the canvas over the stays. With their bed in the wagon box they were dry and comfortable until the nights grew chilly. Then Castle complained that the wind came up through the floor and she couldn't get warm all night. With the rain over and the ground dry, Jonathan obligingly raked the coals away and spread their bed where the cook fire had been. Castle went to sleep toasty warm but in the night Jonathan woke to find her sitting up in bed fanning herself with her nightcap. He lay and laughed at her until in exasperation she slapped his face.

"Because I don't want to freeze is no sign you should roast me alive! Get up and move this bed or I'm going to Halls'!"

When his corn was picked and the fodder shocked, Jonathan consented to his wife staying with Abigail while he hauled his wheat and hogs to Des Moines. They were breaking camp when Castle, stowing the three-legged spider in the big pot, turned to her husband impatiently.

"Why can't you build the house before you go? First thing you know it'll be winter and you'll say you can't build the house until spring. Come spring, you won't be able to build it till the crops are in . . ."

"I thought you specified glass windows and a shingle roof," Jonathan said mildly, watching the effect of his words. Castle's eyes opened wide and her brows went up. "Such 'finements' as you are asking for are obtainable only in Des Moines, Miss Castle."

He turned away and his wife stared at his back. There had been a peculiar glint in his eyes; he was up to something. But the thought of glass windows and shingle roof was so overwhelming that she neglected to further consider the significance of her husband's queerness. There was no accounting for him anyway. With Castle visiting, the Hall household took on an air of festivity.

When Jonathan returned with his wagon piled high with siding as well as windows and shingles, Castle was momentarily stunned. A *frame* house!

There wasn't a frame house in the whole of Turkey Grove! Jonathan's eyes were dancing when he came in but Castle was determined to be quite casual about the whole thing and went on helping Evva put supper on the table. She wasn't going to give Jonathan and Abigail the satisfaction of thinking she had been surprised. But Abigail was surprised and delighted. Holding the new baby in her arms, she sat down at the table with Jonathan, leaving Castle and the girls to attend to supper.

"So you're going to build a frame house! My goodness, won't that be fine! What color you aim to paint it?"

"I hadn't thought. Grey, I suppose."

"Grey?" Castle barked. "You'll do no such thing! Think I want to live in a gloomy old grey house?"

"What color would you prefer?" Jonathan asked with amused concern as she set a plate of hot biscuit in front of him.

Castle ran her finger over her nose thoughtfully. Homeplace. The great sprawling Talbot house with its tree-studded lawn had been white. "White," she said with conviction. "I want a white house."

"Then white it shall be," Jonathan agreed.

"A white frame house! How elegant!" Abigail seemed as happy about it as though it would be *her* house. Castle would have been better pleased if Abigail had been a bit envious. After all, her house would be much finer than the Hall house. Theirs was only an overgrown log cabin while hers would be . . .

"When will the new house be done, Aunt Castle? I can't wait!" Thaddeus's black eyes were popping with excitement.

"Well, my land, Uncle Jonathan can't get it up overnight!" Abigail reminded her. "Takes time to build a nice house like that."

"It'll have to stand right where the cabin was on account of the windbreak," Harriet mused. "It'll look just beautiful when the trees are green."

"It'll be the finest house in Turkey Grove!" Cressy announced and Jennifer added, "Ma says so!"

"Don't get impatient," Jonathan warned them. "I have to make another trip to Des Moines before I start the house."

"*Another* trip?" Castle demanded.

"If you want your house painted white."

Jonathan made the second trip to Des Moines and brought back not only paint but hardware, flooring, and other dressed lumber. He and Tolly made endless trips with the pung, bringing stone for the foundation, and still more seemingly endless trips to Crawford's Mill for the structural timbers. Castle was mildly surprised they did not have to wait for it to be sawed out, but with so much to think about it did not occur to her to question a mere trifle. Once done hauling, Jonathan and Tolly laid up the foundation, then butchered a hog; for several days the men worked while the women baked and barbecued and everyone declared there had never been such a house raising. When the heavy work was done and the house enclosed, Tolly stayed on to help Jonathan with the painting and finishing, for Tolly still had debts which wages would help to pay.

Castle inspected her new house frequently. There were two large rooms with a loft over both, and she boasted the loft would bed a dozen people. Should she give a bee, anyone who wished could stay the night. She was a little disappointed her house was not as large as Indie Garrison's, but *she* wasn't keeping a stage station. Each of her rooms had windows of twelve-pane glass,[1] and the house was all of frame and all of a piece, not a log cabin with a frame lean-to like the Pettits', nor a hodgepodge of logs and boards like the Olsons'. And even Indie's rooms were no larger than hers. No doubt about it, it would be the finest house in Turkey Grove.

In the west room there was that luxury of luxuries, the brick fireplace Axel and Knute Olson had laid up so carefully. But in the other room there was no fireplace at all and the men had left a small round hole in the chimney a few feet below the ceiling. While she wandered about admiring her domicile, Jonathan had been checking the windows to be sure they were windproof and weatherproof. Castle was looking at the hole in the chimney when Jonathan came into the room.

"Why in time didn't you have Axel build a fireplace in here? This room won't be a bit of good to us in winter without a fire. And why did they leave that silly hole? The smoke from the fireplace in the other room will come in here and choke us to death. How could they be so stupid? If they think we can sleep in here . . ."

"I doubt that we'll sleep in here, my dear," Jonathan answered casually, inspecting window frames and doorframes.

"With two big rooms I'm not going to sleep in the kitchen! You just close up that hole and build another fireplace."

"We'll see," he told her indifferently. "Tolly and I are leaving for St. Joseph in the morning. You can sleep at Halls' until I get back."

"More steers! Why can't you build the fireplace and make some furniture before you go?"

"I want to get back before bad weather sets in. Abigail enjoys having you—keeps her mind off Eli. And you forget, Miss Castle, the steers paid for your new house."

Jonathan and Tolly drove off in the wagon before daylight. There was nothing unusual about their leaving, but a caravan assembled where Olsons' lane joined the stage road: Sid and Seth Crawford driving their father's wagon and Knute and Hennie Olson with Axel's Conestoga wagon drawn by two teams of mules. By the time they returned, a light snow had fallen and Cressy and Jennifer, bundled up out of all resemblance to anything human, were in the yard scraping up snow for a snowman. Jennifer burst into the house, her nose red, her blue eyes like saucers.

"They're a-comin'," she announced solemnly.

Castle and Abigail caught up their wraps and hurried out. Castle sighed in exasperation, "Great land o' Goshen! He's bought all the steers in Missouri!"

Seth, Sid, Tolly, and Knute herded the cattle into the barn lot and Jonathan followed with the team and wagon. The women walked across the field and were waiting when he pulled in. Once the barn lot gate was closed the boys ambled over to join them.

"I didn't know Jonathan took the whole neighborhood with him. Tolly, your Ma has been fretting about you being gone so long." Then to the Crawford boys, "I thought you worked for your Pa?"

They grinned and looked at each other and Sid said, "He figgered he could make out without us for a spell."

"Everybody but Hennie. What did you do, leave him home to pick corn?"

"The corn's all in," Knute admitted. He looked at the others and they looked at him and they all grinned but offered no further explanation.

"You'd better eat before you go home," Abigail offered. "Go on over to the house and wash up. Evva, Evva! You and Harriet get the supper on."

Girls and boys started across the field and the women went to inspect the wagon. Under the canvas were the usual barrels and boxes of winter provisions. There were also two large burlap rolls which Castle recognized as apple trees.

"Ain't you got enough apple trees?" she demanded.

Jonathan made no reply but climbed into the wagon and handed his wife a small roll. "I thought you might like an osage orange hedge along the fence. With your mansion you'll want your yard in keeping."

"An osage hedge! Won't that be fine!" Abigail sighed. "Keeps the stock out real good, too."

Castle was silent. Her imagination had not yet progressed to the yard of her establishment, but now she caught a swift glimpse of a tall, thick hedge and flower beds and . . . and . . . "I want an apple tree right there at the end of the porch," she announced. No sense asking Jonathan to get her a sycamore, but he could certainly spare an apple tree. An apple tree would not only shade the porch, it would bloom in the spring. Jonathan fetched the spade and the women watched him dig the hole. Castle held the tree in place while he worked in the soil and firmed it down, poured in a bucket of water, finished filling the hole, then pressed it down with his foot.

"There." He smiled at his wife as he leaned on the spade. "There's nothing so good for the human soul as planting a tree and watching it grow. This is an Early Harvest, Miss Castle, the only one I have. So your apples will be different from the others; they'll ripen in late summer, the only yellow apples in Turkey Grove."

When Jonathan had gone to put the spade away and Abigail had gone to see about supper, Castle still stood admiring her new tree. Of course, it wasn't much of a tree, but in a few years it would bloom and in a few more years it would set fruit. And the fruit would be yellow! Someday birds would nest in the branches as they had in the sycamore at Homeplace.

Jonathan said he would sleep in the wagon so he could keep an eye on the steers, but long after the Hall house was dark and quiet the boys drove in the other wagons and Jonathan and the five of them worked half the night by lantern light. In the morning, Castle got breakfast while Abigail and the girls did chores. Jonathan came over, ate, and went back; it was well along in the morning when Castle went to the door to call Thaddeus to get a bucket of water. Glancing across the field she saw considerable commotion around her new house: horses and wagons, men, women, and children swarming about.

"Evva! Harriet! What's going on over there?"

Abigail and the girls came from the stable wearing freshly starched calicos over seldom used hoops. They had sneaked their clothes out when she wasn't looking.

Abigail laughed merrily. "We seen the wagons. They been coming all morning. We might as well go on over. Or do you want to change your dress?"

"What do you mean?" Castle studied Abigail's laughing face.

"Go on, change your clothes. Put on your second best. We'll wait for you if you hurry." Still dazed and uncomprehending, Castle quickly slipped into her rust calico. Abigail called to the girls, "Come along. Bring the baby, Evva. Are all your faces and hands clean?"

The entire Hall tribe ginned mysteriously as they started across the field, Cressy and Jennifer, hand in hand, running ahead. Too bewildered to protest, Castle trailed along, realizing as she approached that the neighbors were all there. Patience Pettit came to meet them.

"Welcome to your housewarming, Castle!"

"Housewarming? Well, I never!" Of course, a housewarming. But they should have waited until Jonathan had made the furniture and she had moved in. How could she entertain in bare rooms? But Patience led her around to the front door where the others had all gathered.

"Now, Jonathan, you got to carry her over the threshold for luck," Patience told him.

Castle protested, but Jonathan picked her up and set her down inside the door as though she had been a bride. For a moment she was too astonished to move. Before a fire in the brick fireplace stood two shiny new rockers; a great braided rug covered the floor and in the middle of it stood a round parlor table and an armchair. At one end of the room was a tall four-poster and nearby stood a handsome bureau. Flanking the fireplace were shelves holding Jonathan's books and below the shelves were cupboards. Jonathan opened them to show her; in one were his papers and writing materials and in the other were her satchel and the chest of remedies. There was even a pewter bowl on the table and candlesticks on the mantel.

"Why . . . why . . ." she faltered and stood silent. The women crowded into the room and the men stood on the porch craning their necks to see over and around each other.

"Well, how do you like it?" Tabitha challenged.

"Ja, so fine you are that you don't know us yet! But in that rug my men's shirts is, and my Karlie's pinafores. And my clothes but what I wear. Your friends' clothes, they make the rug that we all go nekked!"[2]

"Castle, there ain't a rag left in Turkey Grove!"

"Sid and Seth helped me braid but Solon refused to do fancy work— even for you!"

"Martha sewed every stitch of it. She wouldn't let the rest of us touch it for fear we'd pucker it."

"That ain't so! I just wanted to do my share, seeing I'm wearing my rags."

"The kitchen!" Tabitha reminded them.

In the room without a fireplace stood a large table and six chairs and, wonder of wonders, in front of the brick chimney was a black iron cooking stove, the smoke pipe running up to the hole in the chimney. There were shelves and cupboards, too, but Castle hardly noticed them.

"Jonathan Gayle, why didn't you tell me? I've been laying awake nights stewing about this room without a fire. You should be ashamed, letting me fret myself."

"I wanted to surprise you, Miss Castle," Jonathan told her with a bow.

He showed Castle and the other women how to lay the fire and operate the new cooking stove,[3] a luxury all had heard of but never seen. Soon coffee was boiling, chicken and ham heating, and biscuit baking in the oven, which required no coals. In the parlor-bedroom the rag rug was carefully rolled up and laid aside and a trestle table set up. The men adjourned to the barn to ruminate on local gossip until the call came for dinner. While Laurel Pettit waited on the children's table in the kitchen, Evva, Harriet, and Thaddeus hurried back and forth between kitchen and table. Castle was given the armchair at one end of the table, Jonathan and the ladies had the straight chairs from the kitchen, and men and children made do with benches and boxes. Though all the lads were there, Evva had eyes only for Tolly Marker. Not so, Harriet, now a girl of sixteen, her hair up in a knot at the nape of her neck, her skirts as long and her hoops as wide as her mother's. She put a bowl of potatoes between Sid and Hennie and Castle looked up and laughed.

"Which of these young upstarts have you got your eye on, Harry?"

Harriet tossed her head and giggled, blushing as all the boys looked up at her and grinned. "Aunt Castle, you're always funning!"

"Nonsense! You'll marry one of them sooner or later."

Because the stage had been late, Lew and Indiana Garrison had missed the housewarming, but as the guests were leaving Lew rode in with news.

"Couple runaway nigger women come up from Missouri and folks think they was headed for Cold Spring. There's a reward and they're watching the ferry 'crost the 'Botnay. Only place they can cross."

Sid, Seth, Knute, and Hennie rode off at a gallop. Tolly Marker watched them go but remained on the wagon seat with his mother.

"Ain't you goin'?" Solon asked him.

"No, he ain't going!" Martha snapped. "I won't have him chasing runaway niggers!"

"Ach, Martha, they don't ketch!" Berta protested.

"They better not catch them! It's a crying shame . . ."

"Never mind, Castle." The hand that closed on her arm carried conviction.

Everyone knew Castle's sentiments but no one trusted her discretion sufficiently to tell her the boys were not going for the reward but to see that no one collected it. Lest in her ignorance she denounce her friends and disrupt the peace of the community, Lew Garrison hastily changed the subject.

"Me and Indie was real sorry not to be here for your party, Castle. I know everybody had a fine time." There were shouts of, "We sure did!" and "You missed all the fun!" and the others drove off in a babble of greetings to Indiana and farewells to Castle and Jonathan. Then Lew turned back to Castle. "Jonathan sure done himself proud for you, I must say. Mind showing me the innards? Indie would make me sleep in the barn if I come home without seeing everything."

While Castle proudly exhibited her house and furnishings, Jonathan watched and now and then held a hand to his mouth to hide a smile. Had Castle had that same house and furniture when she first came to Iowa she would have hated it all as much as she had hated the cabin with its thatch roof. Now, because she had something a little better than her neighbors, she was so pleased with herself he wondered if he would be able to live with her. When Lew had ridden away, Castle let herself go and expressed her opinion of no-good people who helped catch runaway slaves.

"Last month when John Brown brought slaves through Cold Spring everybody was racing around trying to find them and get the reward! Now a couple poor women are trying to get away and these money-grabbing Ioway folks are raring to get the reward! Ain't this a Free State? Wouldn't you think Ioway people . . ."

"This nation is sitting on a keg of gunpowder, Castle. Pray God no one strikes a match!" He spoke wearily and turned away; something in his manner silenced his wife so that she forgot her anger and looked after him wonderingly.

S O O N after the Gayles moved into their new house, Abigail sold her oxen to Ed Pettit. Standing beside the beasts in their snug stable he made his offer.

"They ain't worth that much," Abigail protested.

"They're good animals and they ain't been overworked," he insisted.

"If we had feed I wouldn't sell 'em, but they eat twict as much as old Sukey and they don't give milk. They hardly been yoked since Eli left, but I can't feed 'em and I can't let 'em go hungry."

"No sense feeding 'em when you got no use for 'em. I can make real good use of them, seeing I got only one team."

"Still no reason you should pay more'n they're worth. I can't take it, Ed."

"Now, Abigail, how do you know what they're worth? You bought 'em back in Illinoy where oxen grows on bushes. Here, good ones costs a pretty penny. I ain't offerin' you no more'n I'd have to pay. You need the money and I need the oxen. What's wrong with that?"

"I do hate to part with them." She stood between them, rubbing first one then the other. "Eli told the horse trader we'd all starve together, but I can't let 'em starve and us eat."

"It ain't like you was selling to a stranger. With me they'll have a dry bed and plenty to eat and I don't overwork my stock."

"I know, Ed, and I'm grateful. I'm just fond of the foolish critters. The girls'll feel turrible. I'll go now, so I won't see you lead 'em away."

She went to the house and busied herself at the fireplace, but the girls gathered at the door to watch and sniffle. "Stop it now!" she told them. "As if it ain't bad enough to have to sell 'em without you crying about it." She laid out the money Ed had given her. "There, Evva. Make out a list and next time your Uncle Jonathan goes to town he can get some things for us."

All fall, whenever they could spare the time, the men of the neighborhood cut wood and ricked it up by the door for Abigail. She hoped there was enough to last until spring, but lest they run short they burned it sparingly, and the girls in the loft room slept between feather ticks and woke each morning with their breath a white frost on the quilts. Though Abigail no longer spoke of Eli, the girls often heard her crying and walking the floor at night. And hearing her, they cried, too.

"Shhh, Thaddy! Ma'll hear you!"

"I can't help it, Evva. We don't know what become of Pa—or *little Beauty!*"

"Pa told us to say our prayers," Harriet reminded them, so Thaddeus dried her tears and they all knelt on the cold floor in their nightdresses. Thaddy put in a special word for Beauty.

A few days before Christmas, Jonathan and Tolly butchered the Halls' hogs along with their own and everyone feasted on fresh pork. Hams and bacon, together with everything that might spoil before it could be consumed, went into the brine barrels to cure. Trimmings were made into sausage, then fried and packed in crocks and the crocks filled and sealed with hot lard. Later, when the meat came out of the brine, the men hung the hams and bacon in Jonathan's smokehouse and the girls watched the fire, feeding it carefully with choice hickory and birch and some of the prunings from Jonathan's apple trees. With wheat and corn for flour and meal and vegetables stored in pits and under the haystacks, the Halls had food for winter.

That winter, Jonathan thought often of Eli. Evenings when he relaxed with his pipe in the comfort of his rocking chair, watching the blazing logs in the new brick fireplace, he remembered other evenings when he and Eli had smoked and talked by the fire, arguing the merits of crops and gold. With Eli he had enjoyed a companionship he had never known with any other man, and with Eli's going, something had gone from his life. Too, he could not but hold himself more or less responsible for the plight of the Hall family, for had he not persuaded Eli to settle in Turkey Grove, they would all have gone on to California together, and might be together even now. Or would they? There was violence in California. Why hadn't Eli been content to stay and farm? He could have made a decent living. Now he was gone without a trace, and what was to become of his family?

Abigail held out until March—then old Sukey went dry long before she was due to freshen. Without milk for the babies, she was helpless. In desperation she sought Jonathan and found him at the barn pitching hay to the steers. When she called he stuck the fork deep into the hay and climbed down the ladder. She told him her story, her face white and drawn, her hands twisting in her apron.

Jonathan nodded. "Sukey should have milked until June. I suppose she's getting old. I can lend you a cow until she comes in."

"Sukey ain't no first-calf heifer, that's a fact, and I'd be obliged for the loan of a cow. But it ain't no use us trying to hang on. Much as I appreciated your generousness, me and the girls can't go on living off our neighbors."

It was the first time Abigail had acknowledged that Eli might not return. Jonathan stroked his beard thoughtfully. "What do you propose to do?"

"Ain't but one thing I can do: farm out the girls and find a place where I can work for my board."

"That's a pretty drastic step. I don't like to see a family broken up. I'd be glad to rent the farm. I could use it."

"What the farm would be worth to you wouldn't be enough for us to live on, and I don't intend to let you support us forever. Evva and Harriet are grown and worth their keep to any woman. Thaddeus is goin' on fourteen and she can do right smart when she has to. It's only Cressy and Jennifer I'm concerned about. I'd have to keep Lucinda and Samantha with me. They're too young to wish off on someone else."

"Have you really made up your mind, Abigail?"

"Been long enough about it. Of course, should Eli come back . . ."

"Of course," Jonathan agreed hastily.

"You'll see the neighbors for me, won't you? With the horse and oxen gone, I got no way to get around. And in a case like this, I couldn't trust myself."

"If you're sure that's what you want to do, I'll do the best I can for you."

Later, when Jonathan went to the house, Castle demanded, "What was Abigail doing at the barn? I never heard tell of such a thing! Why didn't she come to the house?"

"Could you have told her when Sukey was bred?"

"Certainly not! But she could of come here and waited till you come in."

"Abigail was in no mood for conventional niceties." He told her of Abigail's decision, but Castle was not mollified.

"Likely story! I can think of a better one. She's said all along she wouldn't give up the farm."

"She isn't giving up the farm. She's giving up the girls."

"I'll believe it when I see it. But if you think you and Abigail are going to carry on down at the barn . . ." He whirled her about and slapped her face, then walked in by the fireplace and began filling his pipe. "I'll go home, that's what I'll do! And you can *have* Abigail!"

Jonathan was lighting his pipe and between puffs he remarked, "And you'll have . . . Garland . . . if he'll have you."

As he turned, Castle came at him with a headlong rush. The pipe fell from his teeth and with his toe he moved it to the hearth where it would do no harm. Why did it always happen this way? Why must there be violence between them? He caught his wife's hands and pinned her arms at her sides. For a moment she glared at him, then his arms went around her and she struggled wildly. When she pitted her strength against him some deep male instinct rose up and drove him to subdue her. Only in the fierce heat of passion was there any yielding in her, and only her surrender could fulfill his need for domination.

"You . . . pig!" she spat at him before his mouth pressed hers. His arms tightened their embrace and though Castle resisted, her strength was no match for his. She would *not* . . . But a melting softness penetrated her bones and her body went limp against his. She told herself she hated him, but held in his arms, his mouth on hers, her own desires defeated her. Well, anyway, he had not been carrying on with Abigail!

A few days later the trustees held a meeting at Garrison's Station and while the meeting was in progress Solon Crawford stopped in to dicker with Lew about some lumber. When the official business was concluded Lew called Solon to join them and Jonathan told of Abigail's wish to find homes for her girls. Before he had finished speaking, Ed Pettit started the bidding.

"Me and Patience want Evva!"

"I was counting on that," Jonathan said.

"Good thing you were. We'd of . . ."

"Harriet ain't promised, is she? Tabitha took a shine to her."

"No, she isn't promised. Do you want to talk to Tabitha?"

"No, I don't!" Lew Garrison was trying to get a word in edgeways. "Lew will grab her if I don't, and I'd never hear the last of it if I let that girl get away. You can call it a deal right now. That is, if it's all right with Abigail and Harriet."

"I think they'll be glad to call it a deal."

"Shucks," Lew grumbled. "They was too fast for me. I'd of liked to have had one of them girls. I admit Patience has first claim on Evva, but Indie needs help awful bad. She'll make me sleep in the barn for sure. The girls I get down to Cold Spring won't stay. It's too fur from home, or too much work, or they run off with a traveler like that bitch . . ."

"Never mind, Lew. That's over and forgotten."

"Ain't forgotten, there's still talk. Couple more like her and my place'll get a bad name. Sneakin' out in the middle of the night with that critter—and him with a wife in Chicago!"

"You'd be better off with an older, more settled woman. Why don't you offer Abigail the job? Indie couldn't ask for better help, and your worries would be over. Abigail wouldn't run off with a traveler."

Lew laughed. "Ain't that the truth! I hadn't thought of Abigail. She could take charge and give Indie a rest, couldn't she? What about the young'uns?"

"She wants to keep the two youngest with her."

"That'd be the little redhead and the baby. Well, that wouldn't be too bad. Me and Indie are real fond of young'uns. Might be we could manage. Only I couldn't pay cash money and board her and the young'uns."

"I doubt if she would expect cash. I think she'd be satisfied with found. Shall I speak to her?"

"You do that, and I'll see what Indie says. Lately she's in bed more'n she's out and I think she'd be proud to have someone she could depend on."

The next morning at breakfast Jonathan told Castle that Evva and Harriet were promised and Lew was considering hiring Abigail.

"You mean she's really going to let the girls go?" Jonathan nodded. "And you promised Evva and Harriet without saying a word to me about it?"

"I told you . . ."

"You told me! You told me! How did I know what you were talking about? I could have used both those girls . . ."

"What?"

"With a little training they'd make right good servants."

"Servants?"

"And you let them go to the neighbors! Now Patience and Tabitha will have servants . . ."

"*Servants?*"

"Abigail is hiring them out to work for their keep, ain't she?"

"She isn't *hiring* them out, she's *adopting* them out."

"What's the difference?"

"Abigail's girls are no woman's servants. The Pettits and Crawfords are happy to accept Evva and Harriet as daughters."

"They'll expect them to work . . ."

"The same as they worked for their own parents. The same as any child works for his keep as long as he lives with his parents. Because each member of a family contributes to the good of all according to his abilities. The foster-parents will give Abigail's girls the same care, the same affection, the same consideration, and the same respect they accord their own children. You even mention the word 'servant' in connection with those girls and I'll thrash you within an inch of your life! Do I make myself clear? If you want a daughter, ask Abigail for one of the other girls."

"Who wants one of the others? I want someone to do the work."

"Abigail wouldn't allow the girls to come here as servants and you know it. Or you should. And they aren't slaves, so you couldn't buy them. Not at any price."

Castle studied her husband, switched herself over to the stove, lifted the lid, and shoved in a stick of wood. "As long as you've already promised them to Patience and Tabitha, I don't know what you're making such a fuss about. You say Abigail is going to the Station to work for Indie?"

"Possibly."

"Don't you know?"

"I haven't asked her yet."

"Then let's go find out. The dishes can wait. Won't anybody break in and wash'em while I'm gone."

Evva smiled happily when Jonathan told her how eager Ed Pettit was to have her.

"I was hoping they'd want me. If I can't stay with Ma, I'd rather live with Mrs. Pettit than anyone."

"How about you, Harriet? Would you like to live with the Crawfords?"

Harriet giggled and blushed. "I reckon so."

"You reckon!" Castle teased. "You reckon you'd like two big brothers."

Abigail sighed. "My girls have never been around boys, but if Harry has to go, I can't think of a better place than Crawfords'."

"And you, Abigail? Could you manage the Station? They have a good many travelers and with Indie sick most of the time, you'd probably have the whole thing on your shoulders. However, with two babies there won't be many places open to you. At least you know Lew and Indie. It wouldn't be as hard as going among strangers.''

"Indie's been keeping the Station, ain't she? I ain't as old as she is and I ain't got rhumatiz. If they can put up with us, I guess I can do the work and put up with them.''

"Good. I'll be happy to know you and the little ones are provided for. But I rather think Berta will be disappointed.''

"You think she wanted Harriet?''

"She's always wanted a girl.''

"I know.'' Abigail nodded. "Maybe she'd take Thaddy.''

But on Sunday, Berta and Axel drove over in the spring wagon. Berta burst into the house radiating excitement and Axel followed twisting his hat, his broad, weather-beaten face deeply earnest. Berta dispensed with formalities.

"For Cressy we come, if you will give, Abigail. You give her us, ja?''

Abigail motioned them to chairs and sat down abruptly, Samantha on her lap. "Thaddy, get your Uncle Jonathan.'' Then to Berta, "I asked him to make the arrangements for me and I can't do nothing without him knowing about it. But why Cressy? I thought you might like to have Thaddeus.''

"Ach, so jealous I am that you have the lovely Cressy, when others you have and I got none. The age of one I buried, she is, and as fair. Those eyes and hair, mine little girl would have. Kindly please, Abigail, you will give her us, ja?''

"It ain't I wouldn't want you to have her, Berta, but Cressy ain't very big or very strong. Be a long time fore she'd be any help to you.''

"To help ain't what I want! Is for mine little girl I want!''

"But with all the work you got . . .''

"Na, na, the work is nothing! Strong I am, like the ox. Is to keep me from lonesomeness I want the girl. Boys is for the fadder, for the mudder is the girl to stay by the house for company.''

Jonathan had arrived in time to hear Berta's plea, and sitting down with his elbow on the table he turned to Axel. "What do you think of all this?''

Axel smiled broadly. "Is pretty thing, that one. Berta, her heart is set. If she want, for her I want.''

"Cressy isn't strong, you know, and Abigail might not be in a position to take her back later.''

Axel's blue eyes were resentful, then his expression changed. He swallowed and said softly, "Mine they were, too, those be buried.''

Jonathan nodded. "I see.''

"Will you give her me, Yonathan? As mine own she will be, that she be in the place of one I lose?''

"Have you said anything to the boys about it? They might resent a little girl underfoot.''

Berta threw up her hands. "Ja, talk, talk, talk! Knute and Hennie is men already yet. To them little sister be like pet kitten to play with. Nils, he's big boy, smart aleck!'' Berta raised her head, made a face, and gave her shoulders an arrogant, swaggering twist. ''Little sister be to him like little brother. Looks after Karlie, see he don't get hurt. Tease, tease, tease . . . very funny, big joke. Anybody else tease, Whoo! Nils mad, wants fight. Be same with little sister. Karlie . . . ah, Karlie like have little sister to play. Big brudders no fun, pick on him. Little sister, she be company for him.''

Before Berta had finished everyone was laughing, the girls hugging each other, doubled over, holding their sides. They knew the boys—they could just see them!

''All right, Berta,'' Jonathan chuckled. ''Just be sure you and Axel aren't making a mistake.''

''Is no mistake. So much will I luff her!''

Cressy was watching and listening from behind her mother's chair. Abigail bent her head and took Samantha's thumb out of her mouth. Jonathan spoke to Cressy over her mother's shoulder.

''Would you like to live with Mrs. Olson and Mr. Olson and the boys? You don't have to go there if you don't want to, you know.''

''Couldn't I stay with Ma?'' Cressy asked faintly.

''No, Cressy. Your Ma can't keep you. Lucinda and Samantha are babies, but you're a big girl. You'll have to live with someone else, but we won't force you to go with anyone if you think you wouldn't be happy with them.''

''If I can't stay with Ma, I'll go with Mrs. Olson. She makes good buns. And Karlie is . . . nice.''

Again they all laughed and Cressy smiled and hid behind her mother. Berta held out her hand to the child.

''Mine little girl you will be, ja? The good time we have, you and me. I teach you make the buns, all you want, and lots other things we make to the old country. You like that? Karlie, we make him step! He be nice to you. And those big Knute and Hennie and Nils, they step, too. This great Axel, he be your Pa, but he step, too!'' Cressy smiled and slipped over to take Berta's hand and Berta drew the child close and cuddled her against a broad shoulder. ''Ach, the sweet thing she is! Now we take her?'' Berta asked. ''Quick before minds change?''

Jonathan and Abigail exchanged glances. ''It might be just as well. You have nothing to gain by waiting.''

Abigail rose and gave Samantha to Evva. She gathered up Cressy's hand-me-down pinafores and panties, tied them in a bundle, and kissed the child good-bye. They all stood around the wagon while Axel handed up his wife and newly acquired daughter. Berta tucked the child beside her, a mighty arm around the small shoulders, and Cressy snuggled against her and cried because she was leaving her home and her mother and sisters.

Evva had expected to stay with her mother until the last, but Patience Pettit was sick again and when Ed came for her, she went and spared her mother useless tears. So Harriet would stay with Abigail, since Tabitha was in no hurry. Jonathan felt that if the girls must go, the sooner the better.

Because the matter was much on his mind, when he met Elder Bates in Grove City on Saturday, he related Abigail's misfortunes along with the other news of Turkey Grove. The Elder's reply came as a shock.

"Brother Gayle, the Lord has denied me and my wife the blessing of a child and this is the answer. We will serve Him as the spiritual parents of one of that unfortunate woman's children. The God of the fatherless does not forget his own. Tell Mrs. Hall Sophronia and I will gladly take one of her girls."

Unwilling to commit himself, Jonathan was equally unwilling to offend the Elder. "Mrs. Hall will be grateful, Elder Bates. You're living in Grove City now?"

"Yes, like St. Paul, our abode is a tent and we go wherever the Lord calls. I swapped my house in Cold Spring for a bigger one here — and a horse to boot. We've a great work, Brother Gayle. In due time we'll erect a fitting structure for the worship of our God. Right now we meet in the barroom of the hotel. Brother Starkey lets us use it free. He does no business Sunday mornings anyway."

In his preoccupation with matters spiritual the Elder neglected to arrange details as to when and how he was to become the father of the fatherless, but Jonathan knew he had made the offer in good faith and would expect it to be accepted. Yet he disliked subjecting either Thaddeus or Jennifer to the rigors of the Elder's ardent Christianity. The Elder was a good, conscientious man. Too good and far too conscientious. And too generous. He was capable of making a neat profit on a horse trade or a house swapping, but equally capably of handing the profit to the first loafer who appealed to his sympathies. That night Jonathan lay thinking long after he and Castle went to bed. At last she turned over with an impatient flounce and confronted him.

"What's the matter with you? Will you stop grunting and groaning and let a body get some sleep? What ails you, anyway?"

"I don't know if I should tell you. Elder Bates offered to take one of Abigail's girls."

"*Elder Bates!*"

"Yes. Elder Bates."

"Land-a-living! What next? You didn't promise him?"

"No, but I don't know how to refuse. He wouldn't understand. Besides, I can't let the girls go to total strangers. He's a good man, though I don't know much about his wife. Still, I've never heard anything against her. Have you?"

"No, except she's real bossy and so good she hurts all over. Which of the girls you going to give them?"

"I can't make up my mind. Jennifer is such a little tyke . . ."

"You always been partial to Jennifer, though for the life of me I don't know why." Castle lay down. "She's homely as a mud fence and stupid to boot."

"She isn't stupid!" Jonathan protested. "She just doesn't talk much."
He was trying to visualize little Jennifer living with Elder and Sophronia

Bates and all his instincts rebelled at the picture. He couldn't do it. Yet he was fond of Thaddeus, too. She was so lively . . . He shook his head and groaned. Well, Thaddy was older. Perhaps she could survive the Elder and his long-faced better half for the few years remaining before she married. Thaddeus had spirit. She would not be easily broken.

"Maybe Taddeus can handle them," he muttered, then turned on his side and slept.

Castle laughed out loud, for if she knew Thaddy, it would be a battle royal.

When Jonathan told Abigail the Elder would take Thaddeus, she smiled wanly and said, "She ain't likely to be as easy to convert as her Pa."

Thaddeus accepted her fate without protest. She liked the idea of living in town and going to meeting Sundays and sometimes weekdays, too. Saturday, when Jonathan went to town he took Thaddeus with him; Abigail and Harriet were left with only the three younger children. Sunday afternoon Lew Garrison drove up to the gate and Abigail's heart sank. She could no longer postpone the evil day, so she went out to meet Lew.

"Indie's down in bed again, Abigail. If we ever needed you, now's the time. You're about ready, ain't you?"

"As ready as I'll ever be. Let me run over to Gayles' first. Harriet, you watch the young'uns. Jennifer, get that bundle by the door. You're going over to Uncle Jonathan's."

Jonathan had seen the wagon and met her at the door. "Lew came for you?" Abigail nodded, not trusting herself to speak. "Are you ready? I didn't know you were going so soon."

"Indie's sick."

"I see."

Castle called, "Come on in, Abigail. You leaving right away? Come set a minute — you look ready to drop. You ain't sick?" Abigail shook her head and sat down in the rocker, still holding Jennifer's hand. Castle rocked complacently but Jonathan stood watching expectantly. "You taking Jennifer with you?" Castle asked.

Abigail pushed back her slat bonnet and spoke with firm resolve. "Jonathan, you always been real fond of Jennifer so I'm giving her to you and Castle for your own, seeing you got no children and I got no way of taking care of mine. You're the best friends a body ever had. I couldn't bear to give Jenny to just anyone, but I know you'll take care of her same as I would, so she's yours."

Jonathan could not agree with Abigail's optimistic view of Castle as a mother, but he couldn't speak ill of his own wife. Besides, he wanted Jennifer. Now she had been offered he knew this was what he had wanted all along; this was why he had not been able to give Jennifer to Elder Bates. He wanted sturdy, sober little Jennifer for himself.

"We'll do our best for her, Abigail," he promised.

"I know you will. I won't worry about her for a minute. There, Jenny, kiss Aunt Castle and Uncle Jonathan and from now on they'll be your Ma and Pa."

Castle bent and kissed the child, hiding her resentment and indignation behind what she hoped was a gracious smile. What an utterly outrageous thing for Abigail to do! Without so much as a by-your-leave!

"We'll take care of her till you get straightened out . . ."

"No, Castle," Abigail shook her head gently. "I won't ask for her back. Not ever. I owe you and Jonathan too much to expect you to take care of her now when she's little and nothing but a bother, and then take her back when she's big enough to be some good to a body. No, she's yours, same as though she was your own." Abigail wiped her eyes on her apron. "I got to get back. Lew's waiting."

Jonathan went with her and he and Lew piled her belongings in the wagon. They boarded up the windows and nailed the door while Abigail sat on the wagon seat, Lucinda beside her and Samantha on her lap. It was like nailing down the lid on Eli's coffin and shoveling in the dirt, an admission that he would not come back.

"Harriet can stay the night with us, Abigail, and I'll take her to Crawfords' in the morning," Jonathan said as she kissed the girl good-bye. When the wagon was gone he and Harriet crossed the field, Harriet sniffling as she went. "Don't let Jenny see you crying, Harry. She doesn't realize it's an unhappy occasion."

Harriet nodded. "It was just so awful, seeing the house boarded up like that. Must of been turrible for Ma. If we only knowed what become of Pa."

"I know. I miss your Pa, too."

"You do?"

"Yes. He was my friend. I never sit by the fire in the evening without thinking of him. He was a good man."

Harriet dried her eyes. She felt better knowing Uncle Jonathan missed her Pa, too. The evening was like any other when the girls came visiting, and sleeping in the big loft room was a lark for Jennifer. Next morning she rode along when Jonathan took Harriet to her new home. When they returned he told Castle he would build a trundle bed for the little girl so she could sleep in the room with them.

"I won't have it!" Castle flared. "Of all the outrageous . . ."

"Whist!" Jonathan commanded sternly. "This is not the time." He nodded toward Jennifer, who was laying the table.

Castle shoved wood in the stove and slammed the lid back in place. "If you don't want her to hear what I have to say, get her out of here!"

"Watch your tongue, woman! She is *my* daughter! *You* could have given me a child and would not. Out of the goodness of her heart Abigail has given me the child you denied me. Whether you like it or not, you're going to be a mother to her. A good mother. As God is my witness, if you aren't, I won't be responsible for what happens to you!"

JENNIFER followed Jonathan to the shed and while he worked on the trundle bed she built pig pens of bits of board and pinned shaving curls in her hair. She tagged along when he went to the house and watched without comment while he fitted the trundle bed under the four-poster. When he finished and returned to the shed with his tools, she yanked her coat back on and trudged after him. He went to the barn and climbed up in the mow to throw down hay for the stock and for a time Jennifer amused herself climbing up and down the ladder, tumbling about in the hay. When she tired of that she climbed up in the carryall to play going to town. The barn was warm and dim and dusty, the light of the setting sun falling in a long golden beam from the window high in the rear gable. The horses snorted and munched their oats; the cattle in the shed pushed and shoved each other to reach the hay racks; a cow lowed and her calf answered from the pen. Jonathan fed the stock, then fetched the milk pails. Jennifer heard the clatter as he set them down, then the rhythmic spurts as the milk struck the pail. The barn was a wonderful place for a little girl to play and the comfortable, familiar sounds and smells conveyed a sense of warm security.

When Jonathan finished milking he called, "Don't stay too long, Jennifer. It's almost suppertime. I'll carry the milk in and feed the hogs, then we'll go to the house."

Jennifer answered without bothering to listen. "All right, Uncle Jonathan . . . Giddy-ap, giddy-ap . . . 'Most suppertime . . . Come on, boys, up the hill . . . 'Most time for supper . . . Nearly up, now. There. Now you can rest . . . 'Most time for supper . . . 'Most time for supper!'' Suddenly Jennifer's stomach established communications with her brain. "I better find out what Aunt Castle's gonna have. Maybe I'll go home for supper. I ain't been home all day. Wonder what Ma's cooking for supper? See what Aunt Castle's gonna have . . .''

Scrambling down from the carryall she trotted across the barn lot, through the gate with the rock hung on it to pull it shut, and up to the kitchen stoop. Inside she paused to sniff. Turnips. Turnips were all right, but not unusual.

"Guess I'll go home, Aunt Castle," she announced, her hand on the latch.

Castle was moving the pots around on the stove and replied without turning. "You can't go home. You have to stay here."

"Why?"

"Because nobody else wants you!" Castle slammed the oven door.

Jennifer didn't waste words in idle argument. On her way out, she threw a glance in the direction of the barn lot where Jonathan was slopping the hogs but skipped over to the rail fence bordering the south field. "He wouldn't hear me if I said good-bye," she told herself. Only stubble

131

remained in the field now and instead of going around the end, she went straight across. Here and there snow still crusted the ground and with darkness coming on the going was rough. As she approached, the log house on the far side did not look quite right somehow and an intangible doubt nipped at the child's heels. Soon she was running full tilt. Twice she fell, jumped up, and ran on. There was no light in the house, no sound of voices. Evva was at Pettits', Thaddy had gone to Grove City, Cressy was at Olsons', and that morning they had taken Harriet to Crawfords'. But where was Ma? And Lucinda and Samantha? The house was dark and still. She climbed the fence and stopped. There were boards over the windows. The house looked queer. She crossed to the door. The latch string always hung out, but now there was no latch string, no way to open the door. She knocked, then banged, but silence answered her.

"Ma! Open the door! The latch string is in." She listened but there was no sound of footsteps, no answering voice. "It's me, Jenny. Open the door, Ma. I can't get in!" To a child accustomed to noise, the silence was terrifying and she called hysterically. She beat on the door with her fists and kicked with her feet until knuckles and toes hurt. "Open the door, Ma! Let me in!"

Jonathan finished his chores and went to the house. In the kitchen he glanced about. "Where's Jennifer?"

"She said she was going home."

"You didn't let her go?"

"I told her not to. She went out anyway. I don't know where she is and I don't care!" She banged three ironstone plates on the table. That many more dishes to wash. She'd make the brat dry them, that's what.

Jonathan slammed the door behind him, vaulted the fence, and struck out across the field. Then he heard Jennifer crying and ran. She was crouched on the doorstep, sobbing and calling her Ma, her small chapped hands digging at the door that would not open.

"Jennifer!" he dropped down beside her, feeling the coldness of the stone through the seat of his pants. "Didn't you know your Ma went to take care of Mrs. Garrison?" Jennifer continued to cry, her hands still digging at the door. "I though you knew, child. . . . Jenny, I don't know how to talk to a little girl. I never had a little girl. . . ." For a moment he watched the child helplessly in the deepening dusk. "Try to understand, Jenny. Mrs. Garrison is sick and your Ma has gone to look after her. She wants you to stay with Aunt Castle and me while she's gone. Or until your Pa comes home." How did one explain adult affairs to a child of six? An hour ago she had been quite happy. "Don't you like me, Jennifer?" he asked gently. "I thought we were good friends. Does it make you so unhappy to have to stay with me for a while?" The small hands still picked at the door, but listlessly now. "I don't know what to do about it, Jenny dear. Not having a little girl, I don't know how little girls feel. But I was ever so happy when your Ma said you could stay with me. I hoped you'd *want* to stay."

Suddenly Jennifer turned and threw her arms around his neck, clinging to him and crying. Jonathan held her close, stroking her hair and patting her gently. She was *his*. Her mother had given her to him. She was *his* child, *his* daughter. Please God, may she learn to accept me as I have accepted her! When she grew calm he dried her eyes with his bandanna, picked her up, and carrying her across the yard set her down on the other side of the fence. Swinging over, he took her hand.

"Aunt Castle was taking up the supper when I left. Unless we hurry, the food will be cold." He shortened his stride so Jennifer could keep up and they entered the house together, the child still sobbing and hiccoughing softly and clinging to his hand. He looked down at her, then stooped quickly. "There's blood on your cheek!"

For a moment she was blankly silent. In the effort to remember, she forgot to cry. Her hand went to her face and realization came. "I fell crossing the field."

"The stubble," Jonathan nodded. He helped the little girl off with her coat. "Here, Castle, wash her face and see if she's hurt."

"You're as bad as Berta Olson," Castle grumbled as she wet a cloth and washed Jennifer's face more thoroughly than gently. "I suppose from now on it'll be one fool thing after another. It's just a jab. Don't amount to anything."

"Put something on it. It probably hurts."

"She didn't even know it till you made a fuss about it." She dabbed on goose grease. "Next time, watch where you're going. I can't be bothered with you getting hurt all the time. Pull up your chairs. Supper's waited long enough."

Those first days in her new home solemn little Jennifer went about the house crying continuously, and all Castle's threats and Jonathan's awkward kindnesses could not dry her tears. Lonely and forlorn in a strange household, missing the commotion of the crowded cabin, the little girl wandered aimlessly from room to room, inside, then out, talking to herself incoherently through her tears until Castle vowed she was demented.

In the evenings when the candle was lighted, Jonathan took her on his lap and showed her pictures in his books. At first she continued to sniffle, but soon she bagan to ask questions between jerky sobs, and after a few nights she stopped crying. Then he began to read to her: *Aesops Fables* and the stories of Ruth and Esther and Samuel and David. But Jonathan had little in his library for a child and that little was soon exhausted, for he had not the patience to reread endlessly. In the end he read for his own pleasure, and though the words had little meaning for Jennifer, his voice carried a soothing rhythm that was comforting. For him, there was deep happiness in this new relationship, and the first time Jennifer called him "Pa," he felt a thrill of pleasure and pride.

Aside from holding the child on his lap in the evenings, Jonathan was no more demonstrative with her than with Castle, yet Castle was aware of his growing fondness for the girl, and that in no way endeared her to her foster-mother. During the day while Jonathan went about his work, Jennifer trailed Castle about like a puppy with its tail between its legs. Half afraid of Castle, she was yet more afraid of this strange loneliness. Castle taught her that there are worse things than being alone. More than once her shins were bruised, for Castle did not hesitate to use her foot if the youngster got in the way. And the small ears often ached from the back-handers she administered indiscriminately whenever the impulse seized her and Jonathan was out of earshot. And Jennifer learned not to cry, for if she did Castle "gave her something to cry for." Too, she learned not to complain to her mother.

At the first opportunity, Abigail came for a brief visit, and standing beside her mother's chair Jennifer waited for a pause in the adult conversation, then blurted out, "Aunt Castle slaps me!"

Abigail smiled and patted her cheek. "I reckon she don't slap you unless you need it." And she believed she had spoken the truth, for certainly Castle would be the last person on earth to strike a child without reason.

Castle, too, laughed off the accusation and Jennifer's complaint was ignored. But when Abigail had gone, Castle shut Jennifer in the dark cellar until time for Jonathan to come to supper; thereafter Jennifer held her peace in her mother's presence. When Jonathan took butter and eggs to Garrison's Station, Castle and Jennifer rode along to visit, and though Jennifer had a fine time playing with Lucinda, Castle had little opportunity to visit with Abigail. Instead, she visited with Indiana. Obviously, Abigail's new life was not an easy one, yet she accepted what the Lord had put upon her with a cheerfulness Castle found quite maddening. She was still fuming when she started the fire to warm up the leftovers from dinner.

"Abigail does all the work and all Indie Garrison does is nuss her rhumatiz. And with them two young'uns, Abigail certainly has her hands full. And her used to having Evva and Harriet to do most of the work. . . . Ask me, she was better off on the farm. I bet my best bonnet she don't do no more blattin' about when the Lord closes one door He opens another."

Jonathan dried his face and put a dipper of water in the basin. "Wash your face and hands, Jennifer. Seems to me the Lord opened quite a few doors for Abigail and her girls."

Abigail was grateful that her daughters had been made welcome in the homes of her friends, and respecting those friends, it did not occur to her to worry about her children. The foster-parents provided for them and in return were entitled to the same respect and obedience she would have demanded. Should the girls require discipline, it was up to the foster-parents to administer it as they did with their own children. She knew Evva had taken on a considerable burden but it was of her own choosing and she was happy with her new family. Nor was Harriet idle, but Tabitha asked nothing of her she would not have expected of a daughter of her own. Thaddeus needed a firm hand; unless a girl learned to work in her parents' home, it would be that much harder for her when she married. If Sophronia Bates could make Thaddy earn her keep, so much the better. Cressy, the delicate one, had mighty Berta Olson as her shield and protector, and Jennifer, youngest of those she had given up, was with Castle and Jonathan and surely no child could be in better hands. So, though Abigail worked hard at the Station, she was at peace with her own conscience. She had done the best she could; the rest was in the hands of the Lord.

By 1860 the railroad had been built two-thirds of the way from Dubuque to Cedar Rapids and everyone looked forward to the time when it would cross the state. Meanwhile, the Turkey Grove community was growing. Sam Seaman and George Fry, enterprising eastern land grabbers, had overgrabbed and found themselves land poor.[1] The price of land had gone up, but not fast enough, and they were in trouble. Rather than lose their holdings for taxes, they were selling for whatever they could get, and a number of settlers took advantage of the opportunity. Until now, Turkey Grove had been rather proud of itself, for the permanent settlers were all respectable, hardworking, God-fearing men and women.[2] There had been a few less than desirable settlers but they had remained only briefly. Now the Henderson and Jason families settled on Crooked Creek not far from Crawfords' Mill, and they did not go. They stayed, for years a blot upon the escutcheon of the township. They were tribes rather than families — connected by marriages — the men coarse and unkempt, the women foul-mouthed and slatternly, and they were suspected of everything from petty pilfering to horse stealing.

Castle had heard Tabitha Crawford frothing at the mouth over her new neighbors, but it was a while before she saw them. Then Jonathan decided to build an addition to the house so Castle could have a parlor, Jennifer a room of her own, and he a place to store his seeds and the like. On one of his trips to the mill with a load of logs, Castle and Jennifer went along to visit with Tabitha and Harriet. As they crossed Crooked Creek bridge below the mill, some of the Henderson-Jason women were picking firewood off the slab pile. Castle stared and her back stiffened as she sniffed disdainfully. Jonathan laughed and she turned on him indignantly.

"They ought to be run out of the county! It ain't decent to have such filthy creatures living in the same neighborhood with respectable people."

"Jesus Christ had twelve disciples, and one of them was Judas."

"What's that got to do with it?"

"If He could put up with Judas Iscariot, we should be able to put up with the Hendersons and Jasons."

Fortunately, there were other and better additions to the community. To everyone's surprise, Sam Seaman built a house near a small grove and settled down to farm a half section of his own land. George Fry soon followed his partner's example. Among those who had bought land from them were Hiram Radcliff, with a wife and three children, and Dowd Wright and his son Preston. Jonathan, to insure himself against encroachment and to provide ample pasture for his stock, had purchased the half section adjoining his land on the north and had again lent Tolly Marker money for another forty.

With so many families in the neighborhood, a township meeting was called that spring to discuss the need for a school. George Fry, whose children were grown and gone, did not trouble to attend, but Sam Seaman, himself childless, not only attended and voted for the school, but offered a portion of his grove as a site for the schoolhouse. Because the grove was centrally located, the offer was accepted, though reluctantly, for his neighbors had not forgotten his land-grabbing activities, and this magnanimous gesture was viewed with suspicious eyes. However, arriving with their logs on the day appointed for the school raising, the men found that Seaman had rived out enough clapboards for the roof. This was no gesture, for riving clapboards was a slow and tedious task.[3]

Lew Garrison had staked out the site and his oak logs were laid first. Then came the walnut Jonathan had cut along the creek, followed by Axel Olson's chestnut and Ed Pettit's ash. Above were laid Tolly Marker's linden beams and aspen roof poles. But the schoolhouse could not be completed in one day. Solon had brought slabs for the puncheon floor and his smoothest boards for desks and benches. These and the stick-and-clay chimney, the stone hearth, and the oak door remained to be done. Because they had little timber, the Wrights and Radcliffs offered to donate labor instead, and between them the schoolhouse was completed in time for the trustees' meeting called to arrange for hiring a teacher. Heretofore the meetings had been held at the Station, but henceforth the school would serve as the community center. The three men all arrived about the same time and while the others wandered around checking desks and windows, Ed Pettit built a fire to test the chimney and drive out the dampness. With the fire burning cheerfully, they sprawled comfortably on the benches, their feet toward the blaze. Jonathan and Ed filled pipes and Lew brought out his plug and bit off a sizable chew, since Indiana was not there to object.

"Right cozy, ain't it?" Ed remarked, watching the firelight on the rafters.

"Best schoolhouse in Turkey Grove," Lew grinned around his cud.

"But worth little without a teacher," Jonathan reminded them.

"I'd suggest Evva but I don't know how Patience would make out without her."

"And Harriet's kind of young, even if Solon and Tabitha would be willing."

"I hadn't thought about Harriet. She might do at that," Ed nodded. "She's smart enough."

Lew demurred. "Wouldn't be right to ask her to take on them Henderson-Jason young'uns. Sure as shootin' some of 'em'll come to school and we can't stop 'em. But they won't be easy to manage."

"That's so. Looks like we got to go further afield. Jonathan?"

Jonathan took his pipe from between his teeth. "I say, must the teacher be a young lady? Wouldn't a young man do? There's Preston Wright. You met him at the school raising. Seems like a fine young chap. Graduated from the Academy, and last year he attended medical school in Chicago. He has a far better education than any young lady we'd find anywhere around."

"Suppose Dowd would be willing?" Ed mused. "He's got a heap of work cut out."

Jonathan smiled. "He might be willing if it were put to him in just the right light."

Lew chuckled. "Maybe you better do the putting, then. If it's all right with Dowd, it's all right with me and Ed. Preston is big enough to handle them Henderson-Jason upstarts, and if he can't teach 'em anything, it ain't likely anybody else could." Lew rose and stretched. "Might as well go home. I'm tired."

At dinner the next day Jonathan said he was riding over to see Dowd Wright about hiring Preston to teach school.

"Then I'm going along," Castle announced.

"Why?" Jonathan's eyes sparkled.

"Don't be silly! Clean your plate, Jennifer."

There was always a certain amount of curiosity about newcomers, but because Dowd and his son were alone, they had attracted more than their share. The women had thrown up their hands in horror at thought of a bachelor establishment, but the men, who could more easily find an excuse for stopping by, reported that Dowd was a fussy, old-maidish housekeeper. For Castle, this was a chance to find out if what the men said was really true.

"After you see Mr. Wright you'll want to go by Pettits' and tell Ed what he says, and Jennifer and I can visit with Patience and Evva while you and Ed gab. Besides, I got a new tonic for Patience. She's still real poorly."

The Wright cabin was small, but neat and trim. A rail fence enclosed the dooryard and at the side of the house, Dowd was spading a flower bed. He leaned the spade against the wall and came to greet them, a short, dumpy little man with a bald head and blue eyes in a round face as smooth and calm as a mountain pool.

"Get down and come in, neighbors. Suppose it seems foolish planting a flower bed with all the work I got, but my wife always wanted flowers under her window. Come on in, and excuse me while I wash up. I'm real proud to have company."

Jonathan presented Castle and Jennifer, and when Dowd had hung the towel back on the peg he shook hands all around.

"You folks was at my raising and the school raising, but with so many people there, I hadn't quite got all the names and faces together. Glad to know you, Mrs. Gayle. And this is your little girl. My, she's a fine, healthy looking youngster." He set out chairs for them as he talked. "Make yourselves comfortable and I'll put water on for tea."

He swung the iron kettle over the fire, threw on wood for a quick blaze, and while he got down the brown teapot and the blue and white cups and saucers, Castle inspected the cabin. A prairie bed was neatly made up and covered with a bright clean quilt. The floor had been scrubbed with a brush and sand as had the table under the window. On shelves by the fireplace, dishes were carefully arranged; even the mantel held only the clock and candle holders, not the usual clutter of masculine pipes and papers. Not a woman in Turkey Grove had a house so immaculate, and Dowd's shirt was ironed better than Jonathan's.

Dowd spread a cloth and laid the table for tea, then brought a tall blue and grey cookie jar. "My wife always wanted the cookie jar kept full," he beamed. "Here, young lady, help yourself. I got plenty more."

Jennifer accepted a handful of cookies and they disappeared with incredible speed. Dowd filled a plate and put it near her with a wink.

"Did you lose your wife recently?" Castle asked.

"Yes, that's why we come West. Preston stayed to finish his term of school and got here just a few weeks ago." He drew up a chair and poured tea, handing the cups around with a practiced hand. "My wife was an invalid for years and it took all I ever made for doctor bills and such like. Preston and I figgered we'd do better to make a fresh start. He wants to be a doctor." There was pride in his voice and Jonathan nodded approval. "Help yourselves, now. Eat all you want, child. I'm real proud of my son."

"He impressed me as a fine young chap," Jonathan agreed.

"Thank you kindly, Mr. Gayle. I'm hoping we can made enough here to keep going till he gets his degree. It'll be a long haul, but he earns his board and room working in the laboratory so it's only tuition we got to worry about. That's cash in advance and it makes it kind of hard, a lump sum like that. But we got a good farm here and I think we can do it. I hope you like the tea, Mrs. Gayle. It's uncolored Japan, my wife's favorite."

"I never tasted any like it before, but it's delicious. I wonder if you'd give me the receipt for these cookies? They're the best I ever ate."

"I'll be glad to write it out for you. It's my wife's. You see, she couldn't do much so she bossed me around. She was real fussy, Ellie was. Kept me on my toes, I tell you!"

Castle laughed. "She did a good job of training you. I never saw a house as neat and clean. And I hope my cookies will be as good as yours."

"Mighty nice of you to say so. I sort of got in the habit of doing things the way Ellie liked." He refilled the cookie plate and continued. "Me and Preston miss her, but she suffered so much for so long we try to be grateful to the Lord for taking her."

"A sensible way to look at it," Jonathan approved. "Speaking of your son's tuition, I may have the answer for you. The trustees would like to hire him to teach the new school this summer. I know you need his help here, but the teacher's pay would be sure, while crops and prices are always uncertain."

Dowd rose abruptly, his rather womanish manner suddenly gone, his short fat figure seeming taller, more manly. Twice he paced the length of the room, then faced Jonathan.

"You can't know what it would mean to us, Mr. Gayle, to have his tuition provided. It's as though the good Lord had heard our prayers. But I have to be honest with you. Preston has never taught and he's never been around children. He wouldn't know where to begin. I don't know if he could teach the children anything, or if he could make them behave. I just don't know."

"I appreciate your frankness, Mr. Wright, but we aren't prepared to pay the salary of an experienced teacher. No matter whom we hire, we'll be taking a chance on their ability to teach and keep order. I doubt if we could find anyone any better qualified than your son."

Dowd extended his hand. "Then Preston will do his best."

"Fine. Then that's settled."

A few mornings later Jonathan told Castle he was going to Garrisons' Station. "I'll be back for dinner. I'm leaving as soon as I finish at the barn." "But you took butter and eggs when you went to tell Lew about Preston. I haven't enough yet for you to make another trip."

Jonathan went out without bothering to reply.

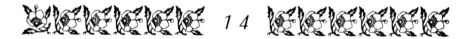 14

T H A T spring Jonathan again drove his steers to Des Moines and when they were disposed of he went on to Illinois and brought back a small herd of breeding stock. In a few years he would be able to raise his own beeves for market. Yet with each addition to the farm, whether land or stock, the work increased and he suspected he might be biting off more than he could chew. He knew he was overworking, for the weariness of the day stayed with him through the night and rose up with him again in the morning. He needed help, but where to get it? A man from town who knew nothing of farming would be worse than useless. So-called hired hands were frequently unstable drifters who came and then went without warning. He needed a dependable man who knew how to farm. Tolly Marker helped out from time to time, but Tolly had a farm of his own and work enough to keep himself busy. Solon Crawford could not get the lumber out fast enough to meet the demand even with the help of his two sons. The Olson boys worked year-round with their father, for Axel had the greater part of his section under cultivation. Yet Axel had a weakness for money, and this year Nils was doing a man's work in the fields. It might be worth trying.

Jonathan saddled young Buck, half of a newly acquired team, and rode through the timber to Olson's ford. Buck splashed in and stopped in the middle of the stream for a drink. Jonathan let him have his fill, then put him up the bank and through the trees to the field where Axel and Hennie were hoeing corn. In the next field, Knute and Nils swung in unison as they walked down the rows. A man with four sons certainly had a lot to be thankful for. Axel looked up and he and Hennie came to the fence and leaned on their hoes.

"Like the gentleman you ride about when there is work yet?"

Jonathan dismounted and climbed up on the rail fence. "Work?" he shook his head. "With three big boys, what do you know about work? Does it take four of you to do what I do single-handed? You ought to be ashamed of yourself, Axel. Aren't you as good a man as I am? Let's see your muscle."

Axel laughed. "Is trick! You try trick me. Vot iss?"

"You're right. I want one of your boys. My place is too much for one man to handle. Do you need *three?*"

"Is not too many. Lots work."

"Your place is no bigger than mine. If I could get along with one boy, why couldn't you get along with two? Cash is handy when it comes every month."

Axel scratched his head thoughtfully and set his hat on the back of his head. "Ja, cash money is good. But boys is good, too. Vich is best — that hard say."

"It's a waste of labor to have more help than you actually need, and you surely don't need them all."

"Now, maybe not. Is harvest yet to come."

"Use the boy's wages to buy a reaper and you can cut more grain in a day than ten men with cradles."

"Vot's this?"

"A reaper. A machine to cut grain, ready to thresh. Hitch a team to it and the machine does the work."[1]

"Have seen?"

"I'll have one in time for harvest. Then if you and the boys will help me with the threshing, I'll bring my reaper over and cut your grain for you. How's that for a deal?"

"If machine works, is good deal for me. About boys, now. Might be Hennie you could have. Nils not smart enough make you a hand. Knute too smart, can't spare."

"I'd be happy to have Hennie." Jonathan and Hennie grinned at each other.

"Vot you pay?" Axel asked suspiciously. He was always suspicious where money was concerned. Jonathan named a wage lower than he expected to pay.

"Na, na!" Jonathan raised his ante. "Is worth more to me." Again Jonathan raised. "Not enough," Axel shook his head.

"Well, I'm sorry. I'd like to have had Hennie. Seems I'll have to get a man from Cold Spring. Shouldn't be difficult. Not many men around here who can pay cash wages."

"Is so. But town man, what he know? My Hennie know how to work good. Not lazy. Not fool like town boy."

"Oh, I wouldn't take a town boy! I'd find someone who wanted a start . . ."

"Know nothings! How much you say you pay?" Jonathan repeated his last offer. "Not much, but cash money is good to have. Hennie, go tell Mamma give you clothes."

As Hennie turned to go he winked at Jonathan. "I'll only be a minute, Mr. Gayle. Unless you don't want to wait."

"I'll wait. Want to bring your pony?"

"Sure, if you don't mind."

"You feed his horse? How much . . ."

"No charge, Axel. He'll want to visit home now and then and it's a long walk."

Axel shook his head. "Feed is money . . ."

Jonathan laughed. "Not when you try to sell it. I've plenty."

Castle was putting dinner on the table when they rode in. Jennifer, watching for her Pa, called, "He's bringin' somebody with him. They stopped at the barn."

"Good land! Who is it?"

"Hennie Olson. Pa's coming in. Hennie's stabling the horses."

"Now what in the world?" Jonathan came in and Castle burst out, "Why did you bring Hennie at dinnertime without telling me? I thought you was hoeing corn."

"No, I was looking for a hired man. And I found one."

"You mean . . . Hennie's going to stay here?"

"He is. This is the best morning's work I've done in years."

"I won't have him! I won't cook and wash and clean for another man! I got enough . . ." She stopped abruptly when she heard the gate slam behind Hennie.

He scraped his feet carefully at the door and came in grinning. "Howdy, Mrs. Gayle. Reckon Mr. Gayle told you I'm working for him now. Ain't I lucky? Ma says you're the best cook in Turkey Grove."

"That's nice of you, Hennie. Come in and I'll lay another place. We ain't got much for dinner. I wasn't expecting company. Jenny, did you wash? Put some water in the basin for Hennie." To Hennie, Castle was cordiality itself and when she spoke to Jennifer her voice was so solicitous the child looked at her in surprise and forgot to answer.

So Castle cooked as she had never cooked before, and Hennie's generous praise kept her fairly smirking, though his appetite would have been sufficient tribute to any woman's cooking. Because he always cleaned his feet so carefully, it was imperative the floor be kept scrubbed and shining. At first Castle was put out that he must occupy her fine loft room, but the boy made his own bed and kept his clothes in such good order she told his mother he was no bother at all. Too, he proved someone to talk to. With Hennie at the table, mealtime was a pleasure, and when he was around she went out of her way to be kind to Jennifer. She wouldn't want him telling his Ma she mistreated the child. He quickly made friends with Jennifer and she followed him about the house and barn asking endless questions and listening in wonder to his equally endless answers. For Hennie's patience was inexhausible and talking never interfered with his work. But both Castle and Jennifer enjoyed the boy most in the evenings. Then he made cornstalk dolls and whittled all manner of toys for the little girl, while Castle extracted the latest news of the neighborhood. Hennie knew everything about everybody without any apparent effort at finding out. He never seemed curious, yet he knew when someone's cow had a calf, and the sex; he knew who went to Cold Spring and for what. He knew, too, who was "slave" and who was "free," and he knew how the Underground operated, though he professed complete ignorance as to who the operators were. Often on the porch in the twilight, Jonathan joined the conversation, and though Hennie could never be led into an argument, he had an unfailing fund of information which he was always willing to pass on.

During one of these evening news fests, Castle sat rocking and knitting while Jonathan smoked and Jennifer sat on the steps with Hennie, watching him whittle tiny animals by what was left of the daylight. When it grew too dark to see he handed her the toys and leaned back against a post.

"Hear Mr. Crawford is going to enlarge the mill. Guess it's about time. They been swamped with work the last couple years. Good thing you had your order in before the cabin burned or you wouldn't of got your house before winter."

"That's why my order was in. And that's why I got out the logs for the addition and took them over ahead of time. But if Solon doesn't make all he can now, he won't have another chance. Once the railroad comes through, his mill won't be worth a tinker's damn."

"Think the railroad will come through soon?"

"Not soon, but eventually. Once it reaches Des Moines, Council Bluffs will be next."

Castle was no longer listening. The railroad was an old story. But Hennie said Jonathan had ordered the timbers *before* the cabin burned, and that meant he had intended to build the house all the time! In her excitement she dropped a stitch in the sock she was knitting and it was too dark to see to pick it up. She dared not speak her mind with Hennie there so all she could do was fidget impatiently and listen to the crickets and katydids until he and Jonathan talked themselves out and Hennie yawned, stretched, and took himself off to bed. Then she took Jennifer in, unbuttoned her, pulled out the trundle bed, and got the child into her nightdress. By the time she was asleep, Jonathan came in to go to bed.

"What did Hennie mean about you ordering the lumber from the mill before the cabin burned?"

Jonathan smiled at her in that maddening way of his. "That your efforts were wasted, Miss Castle. You would have had this house even if you hadn't burned the cabin."

"Why didn't you tell me you aimed to build a new house?"

"I wanted to surprise you, my dear," he told her as he stripped off his shirt. "But I *have* told you I'm building the addition, so don't feel you have to burn *this* house to get a couple of extra rooms."

One of her shoes missed his head. She turned quickly to look at Jennifer but the child was sleeping soundly.

"All them steers you buy dirt cheap and sell sky-high every year—it's about time you did something for me. I want some new dishes like them cups and saucers of Dowd Wright's. And some decent knives and forks. There's no reason we can't live like respectable white people. And I want some silk gowns. I should think you'd be ashamed, your own wife looking like one of them Henderson-Jason women."

"My wife wouldn't look like one of those Henderson-Jason wenches if she wore a squaw's blanket!'' he replied with asperity. "I've never been ashamed of my wife and I never will be, no matter what she wears. As for dishes and silver, I'll see what I can find the next time I go to Des Moines. They have nothing at Cold Spring I'd want on my table.'' He climbed into bed. "If you had a dozen silk gowns, what would you do with them? You have one in your trunk you haven't worn since you came to Iowa — one besides the mull.''

"The mull ain't fit to wear. I tore it.''

"You mend beautifully, my sweet.''

"Don't you sweet me, you . . . you . . .''

"Will polecat do?'' Jonathan asked politely. "I'm too tired to think of anything more original.'' Comfortably settled in bed he snuffed the candle and left Castle in the dark. She lunged at him, but in the darkness missed and fell sprawling. He burst out laughing. She found him and clutched his hair.

"Be quiet, you fool! Hennie'll hear you.'' What if Hennie heard and told his mother? Or the other boys? "Be still, will you? I'll pay you off! I'll burn your barn!''

"You do, and you'll burn with it!'' he hissed between chuckles as he heaved her over onto her own side of the bed. "That barn is your bread and butter, my fair lady, as well as the parlor and the fancy dishes you want.''

"Why did you go to the Station that day?''

"That's a state secret. Good-night, my love.''

"My love, my foot! I'll find out sooner or later.''

"You probably will.''

Now that he had Jennifer, Jonathan thought less of that child he might have had. He would do for Jenny what he would have done for a child of his own, and she would not have to struggle as he had. Nor were his efforts to get a competent teacher for the school entirely unselfish; Jennifer would go to school. With that, Castle was in complete accord. Not that she gave a hoot if the child ever learned to read or write, but she was tired of having the youngster underfoot. Jennifer was just one more thing Castle had to endure, as she endured the housework, the neighbors, and everything else that went with living in Iowa. Iowa! If only she could think of a good excuse for Jonathan to let her go home!

Jennifer went to school the very first day, though most of the boys of the community would not start until the corn was laid by.[2] It was a two-mile walk, but where Gayles' lane met the stage road she saw Preston Wright coming and waited for him. The new teacher waved and smiled in an effort to appear more debonair than he felt. When they fell into step she studied him seriously.

"You don't look like a school teacher.''

"Don't I?'' He flushed but continued to smile at her.

"No. You don't look no different than Hennie or Knute or Sid or Seth or Tolly. Only you got on your Sunday shirt.''

Preston laughed. "Probably the shirt is the only difference.'' Then, wondering how the children felt about school, he asked, "Do you want to go to school?''

"Um-humm. Pa says you'll teach me to read and write. Will you?"

"If you'll try to learn, I'll try to teach you. Will you try?"

"Sure. If I learn to read I can find out what it says in Pa's books. That would be fun."

Having agreed to allow Cressy Olson and Jennifer Gayle to sit together, Preston had no further problems with those two. With Cressy's help at school and her Pa's encouragement at home, Jennifer gave McGuffey's First short shrift. But school meant more than learning to read and write; it meant temporary escape from Castle and reunion with Cressy and Cade Pettit. However, it also involved daily conflicts with the Henderson-Jason progeny, of which there were many, and from them Jennifer learned more than the three R's. They were as rough and tough as their parents, and it was not until Preston had thrashed Jud Henderson, the ringleader of the crowd, that he was able to maintain a semblance of order in his schoolroom. Outside the school, it was something else again. Luke Pettit, with the aid of Karl Olson and Morton Radcliff, managed to keep the older boys at bay. Laurel and Josie Pettit, with Mary Radcliff's assistance, took on the larger girls. But the smaller children quickly found that Cressy would not defend herself, which made her fair game for endless teasing and bullying whenever Teacher was out of earshot. So to Cade and Jennifer fell the chore of protecting Cressy from her peers, the too numerous Henderson-Jason small-fry.

By the time the summer term ended, Jennifer was a battle-hardened veteran who no longer took an occasional back-hander to heart. In that separate world of childhood she had grown a tough little shell and learned not only to give as good as she got, but to avoid the issue when she was out-matched. She had learned to accept the pain of a blow without flinching, but she had also acquired considerable agility in ducking and dodging a blow if she saw it coming. By summer's end, Castle seldom did more than graze her swiftly moving shoulder, and since to strike *at* the youngster relieved Castle's anger as much as hitting her, both were satisfied. By the time school was out, crabapples and wild plums were ripe and Jennifer was too busy to be lonely. She shinnied up the crab trees to pick the scarlet fruit, and with her small pail, penetrated plum thickets, heedless of scratched legs and arms, though on occasion Castle boxed her soundly for her torn clothing.

However, Castle was both surprised and gratified, for Jennifer was certainly a far better worker than she would have believed possible, and once started, picked steadily until her pail was full. Yet each time she emptied it into the big basket, she found some excuse to dawdle before beginning again. She must go to the creek for a drink, or to wash her perspiring face, or to bathe her scratched and stinging legs. Argument was useless, and always there was some temporary diversion, yet by the end of the day her basket would be nearly as full as Castle's. Jonathan would stop for them in the wagon and find Castle with her gown soiled and her bonnet askew and Jennifer with her brown pigtails half unbraided, her face smeared, and her underwear in tatters. But oh, the fine jam and preserves they would have to put on the cellar shelves! Jennifer was as enthusiastic as Castle; perched on her high stool, chattering like a magpie, she stirred the steaming pots while

Castle seeded more plums for more preserves, her own tongue wagging as fast as the child's.

That fall Jonathan built the addition to the house. The main structure was a story and a half and Jonathan continued the roof down over the one-story addition, then extended the porch halfway across the end of the parlor so it could have its own door opening onto the porch. Castle was elated that guests would be able to enter the parlor directly from the porch. That parlor was not only her private preserve, but heavily posted. In due time it would be used for weddings, funerals, and christenings, but woe be to the reckless soul who dared set foot in its sacred precincts on lesser occasions.

Jennifer's room was small, but it was a room of her own and she was delighted, while Castle was equally happy to be rid of the nuisance of the trundle bed. To Jonathan, Castle's pride and Jennifer's pleasure were worth the cost—and the cost had amounted to a pretty penny. For the new rooms required new furniture: a bed, a bureau, and a chair for the small bedroom; a curved, carved walnut settee and matching chairs and a marble-topped center table for the parlor, to say nothing of ingrain carpet for the floor. And on every item the freight had amounted to almost as much as the purchase price. While he was about it, Jonathan bought silver and Staffordshire for his wife, new checked cotton cloths for everyday, and a piece of Irish damask for special occasions. Though she reminded him they had used Lowestoft everyday at Homeplace, no Sevres was ever more cherished than her blue Staffordshire with its handsome pictures of famous places back East.

While Castle and Jennifer bustled about arranging and rearranging, Jonathan watched and listened and smiled. Too, there was his own small seed room, as heavily posted as Castle's parlor, where he could hang his best ears of corn and spread his vegetable seed to dry, safe from mice and mould.

Though to Castle 1860 was the Year of the Parlor, to others it was the year Abraham Lincoln was elected President. During the summer Jonathan had had little to say about politics, and whenever Hennie brought up the subject, Jonathan merely assured him Lincoln would be elected. Castle ridiculed the idea. With three important men running against him, Lincoln didn't have a chance. But Lincoln was elected and a month later South Carolina seceded. In February the Confederacy was formed and Castle said it was the best thing that ever happened; now slave owners couldn't make anybody send back runaway slaves and there'd be no more slave catchers.

But in March events nearer home pushed national affairs into the background. Patience Pettit had not been herself since her wetting when Turkey Creek flooded, and during the long stormy winter, cold had followed cold and her cough had grown steadily worse. Both Castle and Evva had done all they could for her, but when Patience came down with pleurisy her resistance was gone and blistering mustard steeps, sizzling onion poultices, and steaming toddies failed to ward off pneumonia. Castle had been at her bedside night and day, but at dawn one morning, Luke brought her home. Jonathan climbed out of bed and lighted a candle when he heard the wagon. Castle came in and plopped down on a chair, exhausted, baffled, and in-dignant.

"She's gone!" she announced angrily. "Nothing did any good. It ain't right! There ain't no sense to it. There's Grampa, over eighty, hobbling around with a stick, blind as a bat and deef as a post. Why couldn't it have been him? He'd be no loss."

"Castle! That's blasphemy!" Jonathan's tone was stern but his eyes were gentle.

"I don't care! That old hellion raises more Cain than any ten people, and Patience was too young to die."

"My dear, you have no right to question God's wisdom."

"Haven't I, though! I watched her die, didn't I? I got a right to my opinion." Then, arms on table, head on arms, for the first time Jonathan saw his wife cry. Castle in a rage and throwing things he could face, but how cope with Castle in tears? Yet, watching from across the table, he wondered if she wept in grief for her friend or in impotent fury at the blind Providence that had beaten her. She had accepted her victories easily; defeat came hard.

"Evva is with them," he reassured her.

"How long will she stay? Her and Tolly are fixing to get married as soon as they can."

"That won't be for a while yet. By then Laurel will be able to look after the others. She's a capable girl, and even Cade is no baby. He's older than Jennifer."

Castle straightened and wiped her eyes. "Luke went to get Martha to lay Patience out. They want you should read the burial service."

Jonathan nodded. It was ten miles to Grove City and Elder Bates, the muddy roads all but impassable in places. Too, he had buried the four who already lay in the Turkey Grove burying ground: Josh Marker, two of Old Man Henderson's grandchildren, and a stranger who had accidentally shot himself on the way to California. So the neighbors stood bareheaded in the March drizzle while Jonathan read the burial service for Patience Pettit. Evva Hall stood with Ed and the children and when Cade hid his face in her cape and cried, her own tears fell as she tried to comfort him.

Jennifer had not had an attack of croup for so long, both her mothers thought she had outgrown that baby ailment. But at the burying ground the rain and half-melted snow had seeped through her shoes and her feet were soaked. After the service the Gayles went home with the Pettits, and all evening Castle was busy helping Evva with the funeral supper. That night they drove home in the carryall with Jennifer wrapped in a quilt in the back. The rain had stopped but the night air was raw and clouds scudded across the sky. Jennifer, weary from the day's excitement, slept on, not even waking when Jonathan carried her into the house. Undressing the youngster, Castle discovered the wet shoes, but even then she was too tired and distraught to consider the consequences. In the night, the child's hoarse breathing wakened Jonathan and he roused Castle from the heavy sleep of near exhaustion. Jennifer had had croup before, but never like this. Jonathan put her in the big bed and Castle worked over her frantically while he built up the fire and set the kettle boiling on the stove.

"It'll be a miracle if she don't have pneumonia," Castle declared. "Her feet was wet all day. Looks like you could have kept an eye on her, seeing I had so much else on my mind." She expected Jonathan to deny responsibility; instead he accepted it.

"Yes, I should have looked after her. You had enough to do." He did what he could to help, but when not otherwise occupied, he paced the floor.

"Will you set down and be quiet? You're enough to drive a body to drink!"

He sat down in the rocker by the fireside and propped his head on his hands. "I wouldn't have had this happen for the world."

"The way you take on, she might as well be your own flesh and blood."

"If she were, I'd only be responsible to myself and my Maker. As it is, I am also responsible to her mother."

"Her mother . . . Jonathan! Quick! She's choking! Hold her till I get my finger down her throat! I got to get that phlegm. Hell fire and damnation! She'll be dead before morning!" However, her throat cleared for breathing, Jennifer relaxed and Castle looked at her husband with wide eyes. "God help me! I never would have believed I could do it, but I did, and it worked!"

"You've done a great many things you didn't know you could do, Miss Castle," Jonathan told her quietly. He laid a hand on her shoulder and turned her about. His rough hand brushed the stray locks of bright hair from her forehead. "Didn't you know that was why I married you? Because I knew you could do things you had never done."

"You do beat all!" was her only comment, but the look that went with it made him smile.

Toward dawn, Jennifer fell asleep. Castle sat beside her watching and Jonathan dozed in the rocker by the fire, now and then rousing to throw on more wood, then standing for a moment looking down on the child. If Jennifer had died . . . He could think no further. He had not fully realized how very much the child meant to him. He had loved her, planned for her future—yet he had still regarded her as the child of Abigail and Eli Hall. Now he knew she had, in truth, replaced the child he had been denied. If Jennifer had died . . . He recoiled from the thought. He dared not even imagine his desolation.

Around sunup, the little girl opened her eyes and looked up at Castle. "I ain't dead yet, Ma!"[3]

"You better hadn't be dead, young lady! I'd tan your hide good if you up and died on my hands!"

15

"I declare, Jonathan, that child is growing out of all her clothes. I've let down hems and let out seams 'till she ain't got a stitch fit to wear. It's a disgrace! If you're that set on keeping her, the least you can do is dress her so she doesn't look like something out of a ragbag."

"I'm going to Cold Spring tomorrow. Give me a pencil and paper and tell me what you need. I'll see what I can do."

Castle rattled off the list of materials she would need for pinafores, pantalets, and petticoats. If she had to put up with Abigail's stupid, homely brat, at least she shouldn't have to be ashamed of her clothes. She expected Jonathan to protest the length of the list, but he wrote it all down without comment.

Next morning Jonathan left as soon as he finished his chores; the afternoon passed and he had not come home. He had never been so late and Castle could not make up her mind whether to go ahead and get supper, or wait, so she sat on the porch looking across at the Hall house, standing empty and forlorn, the dooryard grown up to weeds. When the Halls were there it had always seemed so bursting with life. Now the boarded-up windows stared at her like the eyes of the dead. Maybe someday one of the girls would marry and live there. Evva and Tolly would marry eventually, but likely they would live on the Marker place. Hennie said Harriet was keeping company with Seth Crawford, and if she married him, she certainly wouldn't live on the Hall farm. Unless, of course, Sid took the Crawford place. Thaddeus was only fifteen, and it would be a wonder if she ever married with Sophronia Bates on her tail all the time — though Sophronia had her hands full right now, according to recent gossip. With that nephew of hers coming to live with them she was likely in stitches. Jordan Pierce had been kicked out of a couple of colleges back East, so his folks had sent him out to Sophronia and the Elder, hoping they could slow him down a bit. He was supposed to be reading law with Judge Duncan, who had moved to Grove City and given up politics to practice law — though folks said he had given up politics the way a drunkard gives up liquor. And from what Hennie said, Jordan was reading law about the way he went to college. Of course, if he weren't Sophronia's nephew, what he did wouldn't be such a scandal.

Jennifer was perched on the big gate that opened on the lane, watching for her Pa. Castle called and told her to fetch the lantern. Like as not Jonathan had got chewing the rag with the men at the store and forgotten the time. Hennie, doing the chores alone, was late getting done and it was almost dark. She lighted the lantern and sent Jennifer to the barn with it.

"Mind you don't set it down! Your Pa would skin you alive if you burnt his barn. Run on, now. Hennie can't see much longer."

Jennifer skipped off in the gathering dusk, the tallow candle flickering as the lantern swung from her hand. She liked waiting at the gate for Pa, but holding the lantern for Hennie would be even better. Castle went in and started the supper, then came out and sat on the back stoop. Couldn't be anything serious keeping Jonathan. Other men let their teams run away or an axle break, but not Jonathan. He had left Buck and Jerry for Hennie and taken old Archie and Al. He'd been favoring them lately, but he said a trip to town would be good exercise for them. Al and Archie had never cut any capers in the heyday of their youth so she could not imagine them acting up now. But what could be keeping him? Hennie and Jennifer came to the house with the milk and Castle strained it into the milk pans while Hennie washed, then he carried them to the cellar for her. He was such an obliging boy, always willing and cheerful. When he came back, supper was ready.

"If Jonathan hasn't sense enough to know when to come home, he'll just have to eat what's left. Jenny, did you wash?"

"Yessum."

"Then wash again. And don't just dip your fingers and run them over your face. You're as streaked as a painted Injun."

Jennifer washed energetically, then mounted her stool. Castle was putting the food on her plate when they heard wheels. Instead of driving on down to the barn, Jonathan had stopped the team at the yard gate and in a moment he came in. His shoulders drooped, his face was grey and his black hair rumpled. When he spoke his voice held a terrible weariness.

"It's started."

"What's started?" Castle asked in bewilderment.

"War."

"War!" Castle and Hennie exclaimed in unison, and Hennie's chair scraped back as he leaped from the table.

"Yes. Fort Sumter was bombarded. Anderson had agreed to surrender, but the Confederates wouldn't wait. They fired on United States property." He moved wearily to hang up his hat, then turned and spoke in angry frustration. "They've forced us into a war the North didn't want. They're insane! They *have* to be insane. What can they hope to gain by a war? Why? *Why?* Officers of the Army and Navy resigned and went home to their own states; nobody tried to stop them. Senators and congressmen went home; nobody bothered them. They seized all the government property within their own states — military posts, arsenals, everything — why wasn't that enough? Fort Sumter isn't *in* South Carolina. It's on an island that belongs to the Federal Government. Why deliberately provoke us? Now they've pushed us too far." He sat down heavily, ran his hand through his hair, shook his head, and spoke to Hennie. "When you finish supper I'd be obliged if you'd take care of the team. I'm tired."

Castle hardly knew which was more astounding, war or Jonathan asking Hennie to put up his team. It was the first time he had ever failed to stable the horses before coming to the house. But what was Fort Sumter? What was Jonathan talking about? Hennie, as stunned as Castle, still stood by the table, his eyes wide, his arms hanging limply as though his body had forgotten them.

"War!" he repeated softly. Then, "What'll happen, Mr. Gayle?"

"God knows. War is an avalanche. Any fool can start one, but once started, no one can control it. Sit down and eat, boy." Then to Castle, "I have a letter from Marybelle. We'll read it after supper."

Castle brought the coffeepot and filled the cups while Jonathan washed. "I declare, Jonathan, you act like you was a hundred years old. You tell the others to eat, maybe you'd feel better if you had your victuals. Set up, now, so I can get done and find out what Marybelle has to say."

Marybelle had much to say, most of it regarding secession and the Confederacy. She had written in near panic; Baltimore was swarming with Secessionists and there were rumors that President Lincoln and his cabinet would be kidnapped and the capital captured. Virginia and Maryland were both threatening to secede and if they did, the Unionists would find themselves surrounded in enemy territory with Washington in enemy hands. She had tried to persuade Drew to pack up and go home while they could, but he said if they did they would lose everything. He couldn't believe that if Maryland joined the Confederacy they could even lose their lives! He insisted that they wait and see. But what about Miss Sarah and Major Hunter? If Virginia seceded they might try to take Pittsburgh, because Drew said they would need the mills and foundries if there was to be any fighting. And Kentucky might secede and then the Ohio River wouldn't be safe any more. Couldn't Castle and Jonathan go home right away? If there should be trouble in Allegheny County the Major would be sure to get mixed up in it somehow and someone should be there to look after him and Miss Sarah.

By the time Jonathan finished reading the letter, Castle had her trunk open and was flinging the contents on the floor. "How long you reckon it'll take us to get ready to go?"

"We aren't going," Jonathan told her quietly as he folded the letter.

"What do you mean, we aren't going? Of course we're going!" She stood staring at him, her hands fussing with the knot of hair now loosened and askew from hanging her head in the trunk.

Jonathan chuckled. "My dear, Miss Sarah and the Major are in no more danger today then they were yesterday. Nor is Pittsburgh."

Castle was again submerged in the trunk. "You read Marybelle's letter, you know what she said! I'm going home!"

"Are you?" Jonathan turned and the candlelight fell across his face revealing the lines of weariness. "Are you?" he repeated softly, his dark eyes studying his wife as she confronted him.

"Yes, I am, and you're not going to stop me, so don't try it. You can stay here till you rot if you want to, but I'm going home where I belong—if I have to walk every step of the way to Council Bluffs!"

"Very well, my dear, If you're sure you want to go, I'll drive you to Council Bluffs and put you on the boat. But understand me, Castle. If you go now, you aren't coming back—ever."

"Come back?" she laughed mockingly. "You bet your bottom dollar I'm not coming back—ever! Have you ever given me any reason to want to come back?"

For once Castle's barbed words struck home and Jonathan slumped in his chair, chin on chest, gazing moodily into the fire he had lighted to drive out the dampness of evening. Had he really given her no reason to want to come back? He had tried. How had he failed? Would he lose her now? Would she go back to Homeplace—and her lost love? For several days the sitting room was littered with Castle's clothing and knickknacks. Then on Saturday Jonathan brought a letter from Major Hunter ordering them both home immediately. "If there is to be a war you are much too far away to be of help to anyone, and you will most certainly be needed."

"There!" Castle exclaimed. "Didn't I tell you? We got to go home right away."

"*This* is our home, Castle. We're both needed here."

"This ain't *my* home and it never will be! I belong . . ."

Jonathan shrugged. "I'm not going, Castle. I'm staying here."

"Stay, then! I'm going home just as fast as I can!"

This was her chance, her golden opportunity! Now she could go home without Jonathan and the Major would not disown her for leaving her husband. He'd disown her if she didn't! He'd hate Jonathan for staying where he was no help instead of coming home like he should. There was nothing to stop her from going home now. But when she started repacking her trunk she found she had far more than it would hold.

"I got to have another trunk, Jonathan. Unless you'll let me take your chest."

Jonathan filled his pipe and shook his head. "Take only what you'll need for the trip. It may not be as simple going back as it was coming. Should Missouri or Kentucky secede, the borders will be closed by the time you get there and you may not find transportation. Take only what you can carry in case you do have to walk."

"Walk? Why should I walk? If I take the boat at Council Bluffs, when I get to St. Louis I'll get Captain Tim . . ."

"Captain Tim's steamboats may not be running. In fact, he may not even have any steamboats. Everybody knows the Talbots are antislavery. If Missouri secedes . . ."

"What do I care about Missouri?"

"St. Joseph and St. Louis are both in Missouri and the Missouri River runs all the way across the state. If Missouri secedes, the river will be in the Confederacy. The Secessionists will grab every boat on the river—and they won't let them go to Pittsburgh."

"Good land! But there must be some way. . . . Ain't there a stage or a train?"

"Probably. But the same thing applies. If Missouri leaves the Union, *nobody* will be going from there to Pittsburgh—unless they go afoot or horseback." Jonathan laughed. "I can't quite see you riding that distance horseback, even if you could buy a horse. You'd be better off to wait and see what Missouri and Kentucky do. If they stay quietly in the Union, your trip will be no problem. But if either goes with the Confederacy . . ."

"All right, all right! I'll wait. But I'm going to get all ready for when the time comes. I'll have to figure what to take."

But sorting her cherished possessions was not easy. Where had all the stuff come from? And if she couldn't take her things, what would become of them? Every item of her dearly hoarded treasures required separate consideration: would she need it? Or should she leave it to an uncertain fate? The process seemed endless and for days she stood on an island surrounded by clothing, boxes, bundles, and odds and ends of this and that.

Once Jennifer asked, "Ma, if you go home to Pittsburgh, who's going to take care of Pa and Hennie and me? And folks that get sick?"

"I don't know!" she snapped, but she paused in her frantic picking up and putting down and looked at the child. Who would take care of them? Well, why should she care? Let them take care of themselves. "There's a doctor at Grove City. He can look after anybody gets sick."

"Not when the roads are bad. Anyway, folks would rather have you."

"Out of the mouths of babes . . . ," Castle murmured. Jennifer wasn't so dumb. What would the neighbors think of her—leaving her family? What if somebody died because it took too long to get a doctor? Never mind, she'd be at Homeplace and it wouldn't matter what the neighbors thought of her.

At mealtime Jonathan and Hennie talked of war and rumors of war and in spite of herself, Castle was oppressed by her husband's attitude of foreboding. Nor could she guess that much of his dejection was due to her determination to go home. For he kept asking himself: *had* he given her no reason to want to come back? Since she really seemed resolved to go, his masculine pride deeply hurt, he would not attempt to prevent her going. This time the choice must be her own. Nor could there be any doubt now that they faced a war of some sort. There had been skirmishing along the Potomac and the fighting had come dangerously close to the capital. The county had not been included in the President's first call for volunteers,[1] but with the second call, Sid and Seth Crawford enlisted, and a few days later Hennie announced that he had signed up, too. Jonathan took it calmly, his fork only pausing between bites.

"So that's why you're late. Well, wash up and come to supper. Better eat while you can. Army food isn't always the best even when there's enough of it."

Castle wasn't so calm. "If you weren't so all-fired big I'd take you across my checked apron! What do you mean, joining the Army? Ain't folks got enough to worry about? How do you know you won't get yourself killed? You boys are enough to try the patience of Job! Did you join up without telling your Ma and Pa?"

"Good Lord, no! Pa'd have the hide off me if I done that. I ast, and he argued some, but Knute had already out-talked him so he was too beat down to put up much of a fight against me. Once we was signed up and all, I think he was kinda proud of us."

Castle gave her chair an angry hitch as she rose to get more potatoes from the pot on the stove. "Looks like your Pa ought to have better sense, even if you and Knute don't know any better than to get mixed up in anything that looks like a fight. You two go packing off, leaving your Pa and Jonathan without help — you're out of your minds. What's it all about, anyhow? Makes no sense to me.''

Hennie only laughed at her and Jonathan made no comment.

Such a commotion! But if it gave her a chance to go home . . . Next day she was back at her trunk, this time packing the things she could not hope to take with her. Even so, trying to make up her mind about everything . . . She was standing there when Jennifer popped in to say they were getting company. Castle glanced out the window and saw the Crawford horse and buggy. The sitting room was in an uproar and there was no time to redd up.

''Here, Jenny, set chairs on the porch. It's cooler outside.''

Tabitha and Harriet had come to tell her that Harriet and Seth were to be married in July, and they had brought the material for the wedding gown.

''You'll make it for me, won't you Aunt Castle?''

''Why, of course, Harry!'' Castle answered automatically, but she was thinking that Harriet was going to be married while Evva would have to go on waiting. And Evva had waited so long already. Seemed Tolly would never get out of debt. But she wasn't too surprised about Harriet and Seth. Castle accepted the material and lifted a fold to examine the texture as the three women settled themselves, spreading their skirts and fanning themselves as they talked.

''Seth is set on marrying before he goes,'' Tabitha explained. ''And I ain't sorry, either. Don't know how I'll stand it with the boys away, but if Seth and Harry get married I won't have to worry about losing her.''

Harriet smiled, her round, freckled face glowing with happiness, that inner illumination of the woman who knows she is loved. Then her expression changed. ''Sort of scares me, though, when I think of Seth going off with the Army.''

Castle's thoughts had been of Evva rather than Harriet, but at the word ''Army'' the gears clicked. ''You mean to set there and tell me you aim to marry a man who's going prancing off to this silly war?''

Harriet's eyes widened in astonishment. ''I'm marrying Seth!''

''If he goes off fighting Rebels, he can get himself killed, then what's going to happen to you? Just tell him he's got to stay home or you won't marry him. Him and Sid and Knute and Hennie — the whole lot of them are crazy! Bands and parades! That's all they're thinking about. The Rebels got *guns* and they already started using them! Don't you *let* Seth go off to war!''

Tabitha flared up indignantly. ''You ought to be ashamed talking like that! What would you think of the boys if they refused to fight for their country? You want slavery here in Ioway? Who's going to protect *us* from the Rebels if the boys don't do it? You, of all people, to talk that way! Why, you were the fourth woman in Turkey Grove, and the whole township depending on you ever since!'' Tabitha was crying and Harriet was crying and Castle felt tears stinging her own eyes.

After they had dried their eyes, Harriet giggled. ''Remember when you dressed us all for the camp meeting, Aunt Castle? You've been cutting and pinning for all of us ever since, and if you didn't make my gown, I wouldn't feel properly married!''

"Well, there ain't much time, Harry. I don't know if I can get it done by then. How do you want it made?''

Style, material, and labor were discussed, and by the time Tabitha and Harriet left, Castle had not only agreed to make the gown but had offered to bake the wedding cake. She waved good-bye as the wagon went out the lane, then with a comfortable sigh turned to go into the house. With one foot in the doorway she stopped.

"Glory be to Gideon! I plum forgot I was going home!" She surveyed the littered room and her open trunk. "Now what?" she asked herself. "I can't very well go piking after them and tell them I forgot I was going home and wouldn't even be here for the wedding. And if I don't make Harriet's gown, who in tarnation will? There ain't one of the others knows the first thing about cutting out. And the cake! I bet none of 'em ever even seen a proper wedding cake. Blast! The things I get myself into! I don't see any way out of it now. Does look like I'm going to have to stay till after the wedding.''

Well, the room had to be redd up. She couldn't work in such a mess. She crammed as much as she could in the trunk, then began putting the rest of the things back in their usual places. When Jonathan went to the sitting room after supper, there was no evidence of packing. Had she finished? Or decided not to go? He knew better than to ask; in due time he would be told. He went out onto the porch, filled his pipe, and prepared to await developments. When the supper dishes were done, Castle and Jennifer joined him.

"I got to cool off and rest my feet." Castle sat down and fanned herself with the corner of her apron. "Jonathan, when you go in, I wish you'd set up the trestle table. I can't do all that cutting on the bed.''

"What cutting?" he asked, poking his pipe with a twig off the little apple tree.

"Didn't I tell you?'' She sounded as innocent as the purring cat who had just consumed the canary. "Harriet and Seth are getting married, and she wants me to make her wedding gown. Tabitha is real disappointed in the goods, but she ordered it from Des Moines and there ain't time to order again. Harriet wants six flounces and to make it look right, they got to be at least eight . . . ten yards at the top and maybe twelve at the bottom. I don't like to trust 'em, but I can't whip lace on all the flounces and get it done in time, so Tabitha and Abigail and Berta and Martha and Evva will each whip one and I'll only have to do the bodice and top flounce. But with all the lace and tucks on the bodice . . . Stop breaking twigs off my tree! Break 'em off your own trees.''

Jonathan grinned and studied his wife in the shadowed dusk. Apparently she would not be leaving immediately. Harriet's wedding and wedding gown would hold her a while longer. Perhaps Iowa would not let her go. Could Iowa hold her, even if he could not? The apple tree was still hers. She had not relinquished her claim on it. Or its claim on her, whichever it might be. When he went to town, he took Castle and Jennifer to Olsons' to visit and leave the flounce for Berta to whip. When he went to Garrisons'

Station the process was repeated—a flounce was left for Abigail. On the way home they stopped at Markers' with still another flounce, but when Castle asked if Tolly had joined up, Martha exploded.

"He ain't joined and he ain't going to! There's enough young fools in a hurry to get killed. He's staying home where he belongs."

Tolly had not been allowed to chase runaway slaves, and now he was not to be allowed to join the Army with the other boys. For Castle, the shoe was unaccountably on the other foot and she rather resented Martha's attitude. That the other boys had made their own choices and were, in fact, risking their lives, seemed not to matter to Martha as long as Tolly stayed at home and did his work. As if he had ever done anything but work! And Tolly was evidently mortified, for he hung his head and the more his mother protested her dependence on him as her sole support, the more he blushed and fidgeted.

"Besides, Tolly and Evva are fixing to get married next year; then he'll have two of us to think about."

"Aw, Ma, the war'll be over by then."

"All the more reason you should stay home and tend your crops."

It required a special trip to get the final flounce to Evva. While they were visiting, Castle caught snatches of conversation between Jonathan and Ed and thanked her lucky stars she had postponed her trip home. That evening she asked Jonathan what was going on and he explained that although the state of Missouri had refused to secede, the governor had seceded. He and his troops were engaged in a civil war of their own with Captain Lyon, commander of the Arsenal at St. Louis. There had been fighting in and around the city, and later at Jefferson City. Bridges, railroads, and telegraph lines had been destroyed in the retreat to Booneville, where there had been a pitched battle.[2] Had she left home, she might have met a warmer reception in St. Louis than she would have enjoyed.

"Why didn't you tell me?"

"You were still packing. At the rate you were going, the fighting might have been over before you were ready to go."

In the excitement of preparing for Harriet's wedding, Castle forgot Missouri. Harriet's would be the first real wedding in Turkey Grove, with the first real wedding gown and the first real wedding cake. Remembering the cake Cookie had baked for her to share with Garland, she determined to show the others how it should be done. For two whole days she stirred and beat and baked while Jonathan groaned when he saw the frosting and thought of all the white sugar it had required. Well, his wife was still in Iowa. If cake frosting would keep her, he would buy the sugar.

On the day of the wedding he carried the cake into Tabitha's kitchen, with Castle at his heels. The women stood about and exclaimed, "Oh!" and "Ah!" and she was properly gratified—and Jonathan said a silent prayer for more weddings. Leaving the cake to be admired, Castle went to the parlor-bedroom. Harriet's gown was spread on the bed in billowing folds. Tabitha had curled the girl's straight hair on the heated poker, and with stays laced tighter than she had ever worn them, Harriet was almost breathless. From her trunk Castle had brought a watered silk ribbon of softest blue for the sash, but Tabitha protested it should be white.

"Something old, something new, something borrowed, something blue," Castle quoted the old luck rune. "The gown is new, the sash is blue, and I brought a pair of earrings to lend her. Now all she needs is something old."

Tabitha brought her "trinklet box" and took out a gold filigree brooch wrapped in a linen handkerchief. "Ma Crawford give me this when I married Solon. By good rights it ought to go to Sid's wife, but he's waiting on a girl down to Grove City and I don't like her. I ain't met her, but with Seth marrying first . . . Here, Harry."

Harriet and Tabitha hugged each other across the flounces and both grew tearful. Abigail went for her handkerchief and Sophronia Bates sniffed loudly.

"Here, here! Don't start crying yet!" Castle admonished them. "You don't want the bride going to the altar with her eyes all red. There, Harry, you do look handsome. But be careful not to muss your curls. They ain't in very tight."

More than a hundred guests had been invited for *her* wedding, and Castle had thought it a pity there should be so few for Harriet's, but when they had all gathered, there were more than a few: not only all the "family connections," but also the Wrights, the Radcliffs, the Seamans, and the Frys. Jordan Pierce, too, had come with the Bateses—he was the only stranger. Tabitha had set a day when there was no stage, so Lew had brought Indiana and Abigail and the youngsters. This was the first time Abigail and all her girls had been together since she gave up her home. Jennifer and Cressy were assigned the task of keeping the little ones clean and out of the way, for Harriet was the first of the girls to marry and her mother determined to enjoy her cry in peace.

The boys had cleared the mill shed and decorated it with flowers and greenery gathered from all over the neighborhood. There, under a canopy of boughs, Harriet and Seth were to be married. Evva would stand with Harriet, Sid with Seth. It was all quite proper, yet Castle still felt it wasn't right for the younger sister to marry before the elder. When the time came for the nuptials, Harriet was blushing and all a-flutter, but Evva carried herself with even more than her usual calm. She glanced quickly at Tolly, and he grinned and nodded. Behind him stood Jordan Pierce. Castle would have looked at him twice even if she hadn't heard rumors of his escapades. He was not as handsome, and there was no actual resemblance, yet he reminded her of Garland. This wedding raised the ghosts of so many memories.

Elder Bates came forward and took his place. Before him, the bridal party stood solemnly silent while he eulogized the young couple about to embark together on life's stormy sea. It occurred to Castle that the Elder had probably never seen the sea and knew no more about its storms than she did. However, his little sermon served its purpose and before he was half done, the women were all weeping into their cambric handkerchiefs. Only Thaddeus remained dry eyed, and she was not yet counted as a woman. Besides, this was Harriet's day, and no one noticed the younger sister.

After Seth kissed his bride, she turned and hugged her mother. "You're the best Ma a girl ever had," she whispered, and Abigail sniffled happily. Then it was Tabitha's turn, and more tears. "You been good to me, Ma."

"I've waited a long time for my own daughter," Tabitha wept.

"Aunt Castle?" Harriet looked over Tabitha's shoulder at Castle, and she, too, kissed the bride while a kaleidoscope of memories flashed through her mind: Harriet washing dishes by the covered wagon; Harriet beside her, watching that awful storm; Harriet standing with tears on her cheeks watching her Pa ride away; and last, Harriet with eyes swollen with weeping the day her Ma closed the house. Now Harriet was married and would have children of her own. She had grown up.

The men were shaking hands with Seth, but Castle was astonished when Jonathan bent his head and kissed Harriet. Jonathan, of all people! Yet Harriet threw her arms around his neck and exclaimed, "Uncle Jonathan, you been so good to us all!" And he brought out his linen handkerchief and dried her eyes — and his own. He had been strangely quiet since the war started. Castle often wondered if he might have something on his mind she didn't know about.

The wedding over, everyone relaxed and Castle returned to her packing. She wanted to be ready to leave as soon as the Rebels were driven out of Missouri. That there was an alternate route, Jonathan had not told her. True, he didn't want her to go, but more than that, he wanted her to get there safely if she did go. It would be one thing to put her on the boat at Council Bluffs, where, for an extra stipend, he could place her under the care of the boat's captain. Under normal circumstances, the possibility of a foul-up was remote. It would be quite another thing for her to take the eastbound stage from Garrisons' Station to Cedar Rapids, and thence to Pittsburgh by train. That would be a long, slow, and grueling trip, the weariness and discomfort of travel by rail beyond Castle's imagining. There would be numerous layovers, numerous changes from train to train, from railroad to railroad. With Castle's inability to read, her utter ignorance of geography and complete lack of all sense of direction, the opportunities to get lost were beyond counting. It was possible, of course, that she could survive the trip and reach Pittsburgh eventually, but Jonathan very much doubted that he could survive the anxiety and suspense for the fortnight or so she would be en route. So he did not tell her there was another way to go.

Each time Castle spoke of going home, Jonathan assured her his promise held: as soon as Missouri was safe for travelers, he would take her to Council Bluffs. She should have been pleased, but was not. Why was he so willing for her to go? Did he want her to go?

On the Sunday following Harriet's wedding, Castle was starting supper when Jennifer dropped the knives and forks on the table with a clatter and ran to the window.

"We're getting company. There's a buggy at the gate."

Castle hurried to look over the girl's shoulder. "Why, it's Elder Bates! Whatever is he coming here for? Quick, Jenny, redd up the setting room while I put the kitchen to rights." She dashed about hanging up dish towels and stacking pots and pans, then smoothed her hair, straightened her bodice, and tied on a white apron never intended for kitchen use. The Elder was coming up the path. "He looks like he's been pulled through a knothole. Something must of happened." She opened the door and greeted him with apparent delight. "What a nice surprise, Elder! How are you? And where's Sophronia? You should of brought her and Thaddy."

He made a gesture as though to brush her remarks aside and dropping into a rocker, leaned back wearily. "Is Jonathan home? I must see him."

"Yes, he's home. Jenny, run fetch your Pa. He's down at the feedlot. There ain't anything wrong, is there?"

Again the Elder stalled. "I must talk to Jonathan."

"But Elder Bates!" Castle was becoming alarmed. "Is . . . is anybody . . . dead?"

"No, no! . . . I almost wish she was!"

"Why, Elder! What on earth . . . ?"

"I *must* speak to Jonathan!" he repeated doggedly, and Castle went to the door. Seeing her, Jonathan broke into a run.

"What is it?"

"I don't know. He won't tell me. Must be something dreadful." At the door she stopped him. "Clean your feet. You been tramping around the lot. Jennifer, you play outside."

Jonathan cleaned his feet and went in. The Elder was pacing the floor wringing his hands, his Adam's apple jerking emotionally. "Good evening, Elder," Jonathan said quietly.

The Elder started. "Jonathan!" Then taking a deep breath. "What have I done to deserve this? I cannot understand why God should so punish me! Thaddeus is married!"

"Thaddeus married!" Jonathan was incredulous and Castle began to laugh.

"Sister Gayle! This is no laughing matter!"

She continued to laugh. "I thought something awful had happened."

"Ain't it enough a child should marry without the knowledge and consent of her rightful guardians? What will her mother say? I have failed in my duty. The girl was entrusted to my care. . . . That this should happen to *me* . . ."

"It didn't happen to *you*, Elder. Thaddy is the one got married," Castle told him tartly, but Jonathan silenced her with a look.

"Whom did she marry?" he asked mildly.

Elder Bates glanced up, then down, and for a moment seemed unable to answer. Then speaking painfully in a low voice, "My wife's nephew, Jordan Pierce." A blank silence followed, then he added, "I'd ruther it was anybody else."

Jonathan cleared his throat. "The boy is not of age, is he?"

"Lacking a few months."

"The marriage of minors is not legal without the consent of the parents. It can be annulled."

The Elder shook his head dolefully. Jonathan raised his brows in interrogation. "They went to a box supper at the church last night. Sophronia had a bilious attack and was in bed all day. I went home from the party early and left Jordan to bring Thaddeus. I looked upon them as my children, as brother and sister. This morning Sophronia found their beds had not been slept in." He groaned. "Judge Duncan married 'em and they spent the night at the Center House! I'll never forgive the Judge. The whole affair is common knowledge. It can't be annulled. . . . Thaddeus's reputation . . ."

"I see," Jonathan nodded and leaned back in his chair. "Then there's nothing to do but make the best of it. Jordan is reading law with the Judge?"

"He has been, yes. The Judge says he has possibilities. Can't say I agree."

"Judge Duncan is no fool. And he's a fair man. If he condoned this marriage, he'll give Jordan every chance."

"Jordan has volunteered!" Added to the shock of Thaddy's marriage, this information left both Castle and Jonathan speechless. "How can I ever face Abigail?" Again the Elder groaned and Castle lost patience.

"Such a fuss! There ain't no harm in a girl getting married. Sophronia married you, didn't she?"

"That's different!"

"How? If the Judge married them, it's legal. Think how much worse it would of been if they'd stayed at the hotel without getting married."

"Sister Gayle! I'm surprised at you! To say such a thing . . ."

"All the same, young folks have been known to do such things, so I say it's a good thing they got married first."

"But Jordan! If she'd married anyone but Sophronia's nephew!"

"You ashamed to claim kin with Thaddy?"

"You don't understand." The elder tried to be patient. "Jordan is a black sheep . . ."

"So is Thaddy. If she can't handle him, I don't know who can. My, what a handsome couple they'll make. Jonathan, we'll have to give them a wedding dinner, seeing they had no wedding. Abigail can't do it, that's sure. Sort of welcome the groom into the family, so to speak."

Elder Bates was past protesting. He turned from Castle as if she were beyond help. "Jonathan, will you go with me to break the news to her mother?"

"Certainly. But we'll have supper first. You'll feel more up to it after you eat. And Castle had better go with us. This is a matter a woman can handle better than a man." The Elder threw Castle a look of dismay, but seeing that Jonathan was smiling he subsided. "It'll be all right," Jonathan assured him.

They ate supper and Castle stacked the dishes and left them. Elder Bates felt it his duty to tell Abigail personally, but Castle had her own ideas. When they drew up at the Station, Abigail came to the door and Castle called gaily, "Guess what? Thaddy's married!"

Abigail dropped on the doorstep as though her knees had given way. "Thaddy . . . married?" she repeated in bewilderment.

Jonathan grinned as he handed his wife from the carryall. "Cut off a dog's tail with one quick stroke!" he thought. "Let the shock deaden the pain." Castle ignored both men and brushing down her skirts went to Abigail, who stared up in stunned silence. Castle drew her to her feet.

"Come on in so I can tell Indie, too. No use telling it twict . . . and I'm that excited! Jenny, run on and find Lucinda and Samantha." Jennifer looked after her two mothers curiously, but forgot them when Lucinda and Samantha came running around the house.

Indiana Garrison called from the bedroom where she lay propped among her pillows. "Castle! Come in here! Did I hear you say someone got married?" Indiana's hair was white but her eyes were sparkling, her cheeks plump and pink. Castle sat beside her and taking off her sunbonnet, used it for a fan.

"Thaddeus is married, and you'll never guess who to! Sophronia's nephew, Jordan Pierce!" Abigail sank into a chair and began to cry into her apron. Castle and Indiana exchanged a glance, then Castle went on with the story, ending with, "They give 'em the slip! I always said Thaddy could look after herself."

"But it ain't possible," Abigail protested. "Thaddy's only fifteen!"

"She is young, but she's always been strong-headed and if she didn't marry young, she wouldn't be fit for a man to live with. Don't you worry, them young'uns got spirit. They'll make out."

Abigail wiped her eyes and straightened her apron. "I just don't know what to think."

"What's to think about?" Indiana asked matter-of-factly. "The girl's married and you might as well make up your mind to it. Being married is like being dead—you stay that way."

"But she's only a child!"

"How old were you when you married her Pa?"

"Going on seventeen!"

"Practically an old maid. A good year older than Thaddy."

Abigail smiled. "You know good and well she shouldn't of done it, Castle. You're just trying to keep me from feeling bad."

"If you'd seen the Elder . . ." By the time Castle finished her takeoff on the poor man, even Abigail was laughing. "I told Jonathan we'd give a dinner for them. Sophronia won't be in the mood for it."

"I only seen Jordan at Harriet's wedding, and I didn't pay him any mind. Does seem they could give me a chance to get acquainted with him a little."

"That's right. Castle, you tell the Elder them young'uns has got to come up here and make their peace with Abigail."

Thaddeus and Jordan made their peace with Abigail—but once more Castle's packing was postponed. For days she bustled about getting ready, then the whole clan gathered for the dinner. Indiana came with a cane and once settled in a rocker, stayed there for the day. Seth and Harriet blushed whenever they were spoken to; even a stranger would have guessed they were newlyweds. But finding herself in the limelight, Thaddeus was shy and all but tongue-tied. Jordan laughed and took his punishment like a gentleman, and Castle kept thinking how much he reminded her of Garland. As they were leaving the table, he paused by Jonathan's bookshelves.

"You have a good library, Mr. Gayle."

"Fair. You're welcome to borrow anything you wish."

"Thank you, sir. When I come back. There are few books around here."

"And fewer readers. My law books are on the bottom shelf. Do you like the law?"

"I don't know yet. I admit I haven't taken it very seriously—till now. Judge Duncan hasn't despaired of me, though. You know him, don't you, sir?"

"Yes, he's a good man. You may as well call me Uncle Jonathan."

Jordan smiled. "With your permission, I will, sir."

To Jonathan, the boy's speech and manner were as refreshing as a cool breeze on a summer's day. He hoped Jordan would come back safely from the war. It would be a pleasure to spend an occasional evening with someone who could discuss things other than crops and weather. But the guests were crop-and-weather men with chores to do, preferably before dark, so Castle and Jonathan stood on the porch saying good-bye well before sundown. Watching as Jordan slipped his arm through Thaddy's, Castle sighed.

"He does so remind me of Garland!"

Jonathan glanced at her in quick anger. "I hadn't heard of his jilting anyone to run off with Thaddeus. And he *did* marry her."

Castle whirled and slapped her husband's face so hard she left the print of her fingers on his cheek. But the mark he left on her backside was no fingerprint.

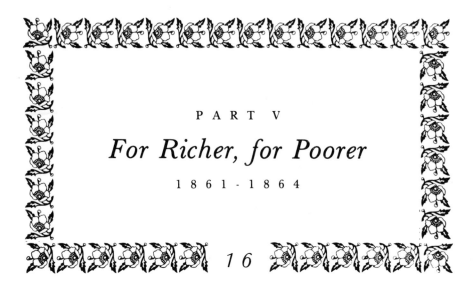

PART V

For Richer, for Poorer

1 8 6 1 - 1 8 6 4

16

B Y 1861, Cold Spring, the county seat, was a thriving little town of nearly three hundred inhabitants, with two hotels, two schools, a church, a printing office, and a number of stores.[1] In January the first newspaper had been established and called *The County Gazette;*[2] this small paper became the most important publication in the world to many county residents, for it gave not only news of major developments in the war, but followed closely the movements of the Iowa regiments.

The Fourth Iowa was mustered in at Council Bluffs[3] and on the ninth of August left for Jefferson Barracks, Missouri. Sid and Seth Crawford, Knute and Hennie Olson, Repp Radcliff, and Jordan Pierce went with the Fourth, as did many of the other county men. When they were gone, life settled back to routine, but with a difference, for there was a sense of emptiness that went deeper than the mere fact that it was harvesttime and everyone was short handed.

But the peace that descended on Turkey Grove did not bring peace to Castle. There had been a bloody battle at Wilson's Creek in Missouri,[4] and she was still in Iowa. If she ever expected to escape, she could not forever postpone her going. Jonathan came in to dinner and found her back at her trunk.

"You've decided to go?"

"My home is at Homeplace, and that's where I'm going. And you'll be glad when I'm gone. You might as well admit it."

Jonathan shrugged, "No, I won't be glad when you're gone. It's your decision, not mine. I only hope you get there safely." He had lost his appetite. He laid his knife and fork on his plate and rolled his napkin. "Clean your plate, Jennifer," he told her from force of habit.

163

"You didn't clean yours, Pa. Ain't you hungry?"

"No. I'm not hungry. Castle, if you must make this foolish trip, don't pack today. I have to get the hay in. Whether you go or stay, the stock will have to eat next winter."

"How long will it take you?"

"A few days. I'll get it done as quickly as possible. If you must go, the sooner you go the better your chances of getting there alive and in one piece."

"Think you can scare me? No decent man would hurt a woman."

"They are *not* 'decent' men, Castle. And they might do worse than shoot you."

Castle considered that remark as she went about her work. Once past the Missouri bushwhackers the men would be gentlemen and she'd have nothing to fear from them. Only a no-good bushwhacker would harm a woman.

"Ma?" Jennifer asked soberly. "What if you was captured and took by the Rebels?"

"Now you shut up! You're as bad as your Pa. You're just trying to scare me out of going."

Sometimes the wind blew endlessly, roaring in the trees along the creek until Castle almost went out of her mind. Now for a week or more the air had been still and hot and heavy, with a dry, dusty smell. The leaves hung limp and tired, rustling only occasionally with a vagrant whisp of breeze. Good haying weather. But Jonathan had had no help since Hennie enlisted and once more was overworked and bone weary. Yet, as he had told his wife, the stock would have to eat, and the hay would have to be brought in. For three days he was in the field before sunup and worked until it was too dark to see. The afternoon of the fourth day he staggered into the kitchen white and shaking. "Get the rum," was all he said, but Castle ran to the cupboard.

"What ails you?" she demanded, pouring a stiff drink.

Jonathan drank and lay back in the rocker, his eyes closed, his hands pressed to his abdomen. Castle touched his forehead and found it wet and clammy. She put her finger on his pulse and heard her own pulse pounding in her ears, but could feel no pulse in Jonathan's limp wrist. She tried again; it was there—but slow, weak, and irregular. A touch of sun? His heart? She didn't know, but common sense told her she had to get his heart beating properly, his blood circulating.

"You'd best get to bed. You won't do no more work today."

Half lifting him, she helped him to the bed. Getting his clothes off was a task, for he was big and heavy and seemed unable to help himself. Once in bed, he lay still and white, perspiration beading his forehead. Castle filled a jug with hot water, wrapped it in a towel, and put it to his feet while she plastered him with hot mustard steeps. She dosed him liberally with rum, and by the time his chest and belly were bright red, his pulse had steadied though it was still not all it should be. Before long he was resting more quietly, his forehead no longer damp, a little color back in his cheeks.

"Jonathan! Where did you leave the team? They can't stand out in the sun all day. I'll send Jenny to unhook them and bring them in."

"West field. This end."

Castle called from the back stoop, but there was no answer. Pesky brat! Underfoot when she wasn't wanted, nowhere about when she was needed. Castle went to the gate and called again and Jennifer answered.

"Come here this minute! Your Pa's took sick."

Jennifer came running, her eyes wide and frightened. "Pa's sick? But he was just in the field. He ain't bad sick, is he?"

"Why didn't you come when I called? Yell my lungs out . . ." She gave the girl a thump on the back that staggered her.

Jennifer swung out of reach, choking back her tears. "Pa . . .?"

"He ain't dead yet, but no thanks to you. He left the team and wagon in the field. See if you can unhook them off the wagon."

"Can't I see Pa first?"

"No, you can't. Now git! No, wait. Could you ride old Al up to Markers'?" Jennifer nodded. "All right. After you bring Buck and Jerry to the barn, take Al and go ask Tolly to come over and do the chores. Your Pa won't be able to." Jennifer, still dazed and frightened, stood waiting. "Go on, go on! Didn't I say git?"

She struck at the child again, but this time Jennifer was on guard. Once out of her Ma's hearing, she began to cry. Was Pa so bad sick she couldn't even see him? What if Pa was to die, like Aunt Patience? And Ma was going away. . . . She'd be an orphan! She couldn't stand it for Pa to die. She'd ruther die, too!

While she worked over Jonathan, Castle had been too busy to think, but Jennifer's misgivings had set her wondering. How sick was Jonathan? His heart had nearly stopped, that she knew, but she didn't know why. If anything happened to him, what would she do? What *could* she do? She couldn't run the farm. Would she have to work out, like Abigail? Then she remembered: she was going home.

Yet the thought brought no sense of pleasure or release. Without conscious direction, her feet carried her around the house where she stood looking at her little apple tree. Globes of pale yellow were scattered among the branches, only a few, for the tree was young. Someday it would be a nice big tree, big enough to shade the porch. Birds and blossoms in the spring, apples for sauce and pies in late summer. . . . She must go in to Jonathan. She couldn't go home with him sick-abed. She'd have to wait again.

Jonathan looked up at her. "Feel better?" she asked, and he nodded. She took the jug from his feet to refill it. No, she couldn't leave until Jonathan . . . What would the neighbors think? Once Jonathan was well, they could think what they pleased. But she'd have to wait—until Jonathan was well enough to drive her to Council Bluffs.

When Jennifer returned, Martha and Tolly came with her. At the sight of Martha, Castle drew a sigh of relief. She wasn't sure how bad off Jonathan was, and she felt more easy when Martha said likely he was working too hard, or maybe got a touch of the sun. For a week she came every day to help with him, and she and Tolly and Jennifer did the chores at both places. For another week Jonathan did little more than help Jennifer with the chores and garden. Castle was uneasy that he sat on the porch when the hay was not all in yet. He had never neglected his work, but if the hay stayed much longer in the field, it would be fit for nothing but bedding for the stock. Then Tolly came and cut the hay and Ed and Luke Pettit helped him bring it in, and Jonathan only watched. He was certainly taking his time about getting well. Castle was growing impatient, for Missouri was once more in an uproar. When and how was she going home?

In September, after a week of rain, Turkey Creek flooded again, the water rising even higher than before. Castle stood in the drizzle and watched the waters eat away the foundation of the old log stable that had been the Halls' first home. Slowly the structure tilted, then crumbled. The roof, now almost bare of sod, caved in and the timbers were tumbled away in the hurrying brown water. The flood covered Abigail's once carefully tended garden, now grown up to weeds. Here and there a stalk of wild mustard raised its head above the water, nodding with the current. That other time, the creek had swept over Eli's wheat and carried away his confidence in Iowa. Where was he now? In some unmarked grave? And Abigail and the girls scattered like the rails of his fence. Only the tall log house with its boarded-up windows remained of the Hall homestead.

The Turkey Grove boys were in Missouri, but they were still in training. Maybe the war would be over before they got into the fighting that was going on down there. Rascally Rebels! Trudging back to the house she thought how hard it must be for Harriet and Thaddeus, knowing their husbands were down there with bushwhackers all around. And Thaddy, having to stay on with the Elder and Sophronia.

She didn't have to stay there, did she? Why couldn't she come for a visit? Castle stopped short. She was going home, but she couldn't leave until Jonathan was well. Saturday, he was going to Grove City for his mail. Maybe he could bring Thaddy back with him, and she could stay until he was well enough for the trip to Council Bluffs. Castle moved toward the house, but at the gate she stopped again, gasped, and clapped her hand over her mouth. Thaddeus could stay and keep house for Jonathan and Jennifer! Then nobody could say she was a deserter for leaving. The Bateses didn't need Thaddy, and she'd probably jump at the chance to get away. She'd get Jonathan to bring Thaddeus for a visit, then work it out.

But he returned alone from Grove City on Saturday. Thaddeus wasn't real pert and Sophronia was afraid the trip would be too much for her. Jonathan washed and he and Jennifer took their places at the table.

"Ain't that just like Sophronia! As if a few miles would hurt the girl. As if I couldn't take just as good care of Thaddy as she can. What did she say was wrong with her?"

"Sophronia didn't say. But when I drove up, Thaddy was out behind the house heaving Jonah."

"You don't mean it!" Castle's plans had gone up like a pricked balloon, but her professional instincts were hot on the trail.

"Seems a shame. She's only a child herself."

Castle did some rapid finger counting. "Hummm. Early May. You going to Crawfords' any time soon?"

Jonathan threw back his head and laughed. "Now you must investigate Harriet!"

"I can't be in two places to onct."

"I hadn't thought of that. Though I suppose Sophronia could manage."

"*Sophronia Bates?*" Castle stared at him incredulously. "She's got less sense than God gives a goose. I'd sooner trust Tabitha." She laid her fork on her plate and looked across the table at her husband. "Jonathan, what am I going to do? How can I go home if Thaddy's in the family way? And maybe Harriet, too. What would Abigail think of me if I left right when her girls needed me? Everybody will expect me to look after them girls. Seems I can't call my soul my own no more!"

Jonathan reached over and covered his wife's hand with his own. "Miss Castle, when other people depend on you, your soul is *not* your own." He smiled at her crookedly. "If it's safe for you to go, I'll take you to Council Bluffs after this is over."

So Castle decided to wait until after Harriet and Thaddeus had their babies. Only Thaddeus didn't have hers. Early in November, the Elder came for Castle. She tied up Jennifer's nightdress and a clean pinafore and sent her to Markers', and Jonathan hitched up Buck and Jerry, for the Elder's horse was spent. They went as fast as they could, but by the time they reached Grove City Thaddeus had already miscarried, and all Castle could do was make the girl comfortable. She was frightened and miserable, and Sophronia was half hysterical and wholly incoherent.

"She was eating breakfast and I said . . . she wasn't doing a thing! I watched her like a hawk and I don't see . . . she was just eating and she dropped her fork. I don't see . . . She shouldn't of done it!"

"Done what?" Castle snapped.

"Got married!"

"Oh, for heaven's sake, Sophronia, shut up and get out of here!" Sophronia put her nose in the air and stalked out of the room. Then they heard her banging and slamming pots in the kitchen. "Wooden swearing," Castle told Thaddeus with a chuckle. "Aunt Lucy always said banging things around when you got mad was the same as swearing. For my part, I'd rather she'd go ahead and cuss and get it out of her system without all that clatter."

Thaddeus giggled. "Ma always slams things when she gets mad. Guess nobody ever told her it was the same as swearing. She scolds if I say 'darn'."

"Makes a difference whose dog's tail is being stepped on. Feel better?"

"Some. Am I awful sick, Aunt Castle?"

"Land no! You ain't sick at all. You just had a bad gut ache. A few days in bed will fix you up fine. Soon as you get your strength you'll be good as new, and you won't be sick at your stomach any more, either."

"That's good. I been so hungry I could eat a dead horse, and I couldn't keep anything down. Ma said I should just eat crackers and milk."

Castle snorted. "Next time, eat what you want. If it comes up, go back and start over. No sense starving yourself when there's nothing the matter with your stomach. Now, if you have a bilious attack, you have to take a through of calomel and some salts and then give your innards a rest. But you can't rest your stomach for nine months, so you might as well go ahead and eat."

"Maybe there won't be no next time," Thaddy whimpered.

"Don't be stupid. Of course there will be."

Sophronia's miff was short-lived, and once the excitement was over, Castle endured her visit. But three days of the Bates's unmitigated piety brought her to the verge of apoplexy and she was glad to see her husband when he came for her. Riding home in the carryall, Jonathan studied his wife out of the corner of his eye. With Thaddeus off her hands, would Castle again start talking of going home? Or would he gain another reprieve because Harriet was still expecting? Did Castle really want to go, or was she unconsciously looking for excuses to stay? He doubted if she knew.

It was a brisk fall day with bright sun and blue sky, but the snap in the air warned that winter was not far off. The trees along the creeks were mostly bare; only the oaks and maples held their leaves, the colors faded now to gold and russet and crimson. On the rolling hills, summer's green had already turned to winter's dun. Castle took it all in with a certain satisfaction. In Ioway the seasons followed each other much the same as they had done in Allegheny County. But what was happening there? It had been weeks since she had heard. Had the war brought changes the seasons failed to mark? Or were they still untouched, secure and unaware of armies and battles? She had expected to be there with her own kith and kin long before this. But if she went home, who would look after Harriet? She shook herself as though trying to shake off the bonds that held her. Like creeping vines her friends clung about her, the tendrils of their dependence holding her in a grip she lacked the courage to break. She couldn't leave Harriet and her unborn child and trust to luck that someone else would be willing and able to do what everyone assumed she would be there to do. It would only be a few more months. Maybe by then the war would be over and Jonathan would take her home.

Jonathan swung the team off the stage road and into the lane. He let Castle off at the house, put the carryall in the barn, and hitched old Al and Archie to the wagon. They needed the exercise and the carryall was too light to ford the creek when it was high. He had brought a few groceries for Martha, and he would have to think up an excuse for them since he couldn't tell her they were in payment for his and Jennifer's board. He had taken most of his meals there while Castle was gone, using his inability to cook as an excuse. The truth was, the house was unendurably empty with Castle and Jennifer both away. Jennifer had enjoyed her visit with the Markers and was in no hurry to go home. Riding back, Jonathan let her hold the whip the lively old horses had never needed. Once across the creek and headed for home, she jerked his sleeve.

"Pa, could I ride with you sometime when you go to town? Not when Ma goes to visit, but when you go to town."

Jonathan laughed. "You wouldn't want to visit Thaddy?"

"Yes, I would. I ain't seen her in a long time. But *You* don't go to town to go visiting. You . . . go to town!"

He smiled down at her. "I see. There is a difference, is that it? I suppose you could go to town with me, and just stop in and see Thaddy while you were there. Is that what you mean?" Jennifer nodded. "Thaddy would like that, too."

"Could I, Pa?" She searched for words. "It would be just plum awful wonderful!"

"Jenny, it's hard for a man to know what a little girl would like. So when there's something you want very much, will you tell me? I may not give you everything you ask for, because sometimes little girls ask for the impossible, or for things they are better off without. But I do want to give you whatever happiness I can." She smiled up at him and nodded. "Some pleasant Saturday, I'll take you to town with me."

But winter set in and it was a long time before there was a pleasant Saturday. Whenever the roads were passable, Jonathan went to town. Castle accused him of going to sit around the stove in Freeman's store, fighting the war with the men. Actually, he made those long cold drives for his papers and mail. He always got home in time to do the chores, but after supper he settled himself with the newspapers, feet to the fire, the candle at his elbow. When the dishes were done and the milk strained, Castle and Jennifer joined him. Jonathan obligingly read aloud, not only the news of the war, but any items he thought would interest his wife, even the fashion notes. Those she carefully tucked away in the storehouse of her memory against the day when she would be making herself some new gowns. Too, Jonathan answered their questions and explained about places and events, for Castle's ideas of geography, history, and politics were as hazy as Jennifer's. Not a week passed without news of important happenings, here, there, or yonder, for armies faced each other on a battlefront two thousand miles long. Neither Marybelle nor Major Hunter had said anything further about Castle and Jonathan coming home, for Maryland had not seceded and Pittsburgh had not been attacked.

O N   a Saturday in early March of 1862, Jonathan had not come home by chore time. Castle waited until after dark, then lighted a lantern and she and Jennifer went to the barn. The cows were bawling to be milked, and she worried almost as much about them as she did about Jonathan. Jennifer had watched her Pa do the chores often enough to know the routine. After showing her Ma how to dole out the corn and oats, she attempted to milk, and though she made slow work of it, she kept at it until she had relieved the cows' udders and stopped their bawling. Then, while Castle held the lantern, Jennifer went up into the loft and threw hay down into the various racks. When they got back to the house, Jonathan still had not come, and the supper on the back of the stove was dried to nothing. Castle put the food aside and she and Jennifer went to wait by the sitting room fire. Jennifer fell asleep on the floor and Castle bundled her into bed, clothes and all, then returned to her rocker. Never before had Jonathan been so late. Her knitting needles stopped and started as her mind wandered.

It was nearly midnight. Unable to endure inactivity any longer, she threw the half-finished sock aside, lighted the lantern again, and put on her cloak and went out. A light snow had been falling most of the day and the sky was heavy and overcast. It was impossible to see for any distance and the snow would muffle the sound of wheels. Perhaps Jonathan had come and she had not heard him. She went down to the barn and opened the upper half of the door leading to the aisle in front of the horse stalls. Old Al whinnied softly and Archie craned his neck. The new Belgians, Ginger and Spice, snorted their annoyance at being disturbed. But Buck and Jerry were not there. Jonathan had not come.

She closed the door and turned away. Should she go for Tolly and send him to look for Jonathan? No, that wouldn't do. Jonathan might come while she was gone; then he'd set out to look for her. What if Jonathan had had another spell? He'd only had the one. He might never have another. Or he might . . . Gathering up her skirts she trudged back to the house, hesitated, then went to the big gate that opened on the lane. Should she leave it open? She might as well; the stock were shut up for the night. She started down the lane but she could see nothing, and though she listened intently, she could hear no sound other than her own heartbeat and the faint rustle of the falling snow. The wind was light, but raw, and her teeth were chattering. She turned and looked back at the warm shelter of her home, candlelight and firelight glowing in the window. Across the south field the Hall house was a barely discernible blur. The sight of it always depressed her; now it seemed so desolate and eerie she felt the hackles rise on the back of her neck. What if Jonathan, like Eli, never came home?

She shook herself. She was letting her imagination run away with her. If Jonathan didn't come by morning, she'd get word to the men to go and look for him. Meanwhile, there was nothing to do but wait—for Jonathan or morning—whichever came first. She returned to her rocker by the fire and an hour later she heard his, "Whoa, whoa, boys," as he stopped the team to close the lane gate. The idea of him staying out half the night! She'd tell him a thing or two! The wagon moved off toward the barn and she fumed with impatience until she heard his step on the stoop. Or was it his step?

He crossed the kitchen to the fire and bending forward spread his hands to the blaze. Castle rarely thought of her husband's age, but now it occurred to her that he was no longer young. There was grey at his temples and threads of silver in the roach above his forehead. His bronzed face was lean and lined, his shoulders drooped, and the hands he held to the fire were knotted, the fingers calloused and bent to the plow and the hayfork. She forgot her anger, forgot the sharp words she had prepared, and sat watching him as she might have watched a stranger, a tall, black-bearded stranger on a moonlit verandah.

"There was fighting at Pea Ridge today," Jonathan remarked. "Colonel Dodge and the Fourth were there. General Carr was wounded."

"There's fighting every day." Then the words penetrated. "The Fourth? You mean the boys . . .?"

"Yes. They've been in a few skirmishes, but this was a real battle. The report said General Carr lost a quarter of his command. One man out of every four." Jonathan dropped heavily into his rocker while Castle stared at him blankly.

"Are our boys . . . all right?"

"I don't know. When we heard there was a battle, some of us drove down to Cold Spring where there's a telegraph.[2] I stayed til after eight, but the casualty lists had not started coming in yet. They should have them by Monday."

"Did you eat?"

"Yes. We had supper at the hotel. There were quite a few of us waiting for news. Nobody even knows if the fighting is over yet."

It was nearly dawn when they went to bed and all day Sunday Jonathan was deeply depressed. Why should he be so concerned for his neighbors' sons? There was no logical reason, yet the refrain repeated itself over and over: One out of four in General Carr's division. Knute, Hennie, Sid, Seth, Jordan . . . One out of four! Monday when his chores were done, he hitched Buck and Jerry to the carryall. Seeing it, instead of the wagon, Castle suggested that she and Jennifer ride along. Jonathan shook his head and she let it pass. Ordinarily his refusal would have brought on a storm, but she felt no inclination to argue. War and its consequences were men's affairs, and this would be no pleasure trip. From dinnertime on, she and Jennifer watched the lane, but it was late afternoon before the team came over the rise. They were moving slowly, as befitted the bearers of ill tidings, and Jonathan left the carryall at the gate, coming silently to the house.

"Which one?" Castle asked, her hands twisting in her apron, while on Jennifer's face the freckles stood out as though painted on paper.

"Hennie."

Hennie, with his pleasant grin, his obliging ways. Hennie, unfailing source of local gossip, would whittle no more for Jennifer. Never again would she trail him about, never again watch him at his work. The grave would close over another of Berta's children. Or so they thought. But this time Berta would be denied even the scant comfort of burying her dead. Axel, too, had been in town that day, and when the Gayle carryall drew up at his gate, he and Jonathan shook hands wordlessly. Cressy met Jennifer at the door, her pale face streaked with tears, and the two little girls crept under the kitchen table to crouch and cry softly. Berta sat by the fireplace, her body slumped against the wall. She held her hand to Castle without lifting her head.

"Two graves I leave in Pennsy'wany, and now anudder yet! Mine little Hennie! Oh, God, why such things should be?"

"The Lord giveth, and the Lord taketh away, Berta," Castle said gently. "You got to have faith. Only the Lord can help you in times like this."

Worse was yet to come, for Knute wrote blindly, out of his own deep pain, without thought of the anguish to his parents. On the morning of the battle they had been camped at Elkhorn Tavern, with a light snow falling. When the attack came, they were outnumbered and outflanked, and forced to change fronts. The Fourth ran out of ammunition, and General Carr ordered a bayonet charge.[3] It was then Hennie fell. Knute had dragged him back through the lines and left him beside a tree while he started to locate a dressing station. He had gone only a few rods when he heard a shell coming and threw himself to the ground. He was covered with mud and debris and got a few cuts and bruises, but when he looked around, Hennie was gone and the tree was gone. There was a big hole in the ground where the tree had been and only fragments of blue cloth. Later, he had found himself back in the fighting, and he thought they had won the battle, though he didn't know and didn't much care. After what had happened to Hennie, he didn't much care about anything.

Over an unopened grave, Axel placed a headstone with his son's name, Henrik Olson, and the dates of his birth and death. On Palm Sunday, Jonathan read the burial service while family and friends stood weeping under the bright April sky.

"I am the resurrection and the life. . . ." Denied the joy of having a son, Jonathan was spared the sorrow of losing him. But Hennie had been a member of his household, and he would have been proud of such a son. . . . "He that believeth on me, though he were dead, yet shall he live." Were the other sons of his neighbors still alive? And for how long?

So many men were in the army; so many families waited and hoped. Nobody had any money, and shinplasters were all but worthless. Farms were growing up to weeds.[4] The Rebels held the Missouri River south of St. Joseph, and supplies were not to be had even in Council Bluffs or Des Moines. Corn was worth nothing in cash, wheat scarcely worth the effort to haul it to town. At the outbreak of the war, Jonathan had tightened his belt. In the fall he had stored his corn rather than sell it on a glutted market. In the spring he had bred only two sows. Why raise hogs he couldn't sell? Meanwhile, his beef herd was increasing, and when there was again a market, his beeves would be ready. He had numerous other investments of which Castle knew nothing, but for the present, with the entire county in financial straits, he foreclosed no mortgages and asked no interest of those who could not afford to pay. Everyone had to live, and there would be time enough to think of profit when the war was over.

While storekeepers had been able to replenish their stocks, he had filled the cellar and seed room with provisions but warned his wife to draw on their reserves sparingly since they could not be replaced. When he had set out the orchard, Jonathan had built a row of hives along the fence and searched up and down the creek for bee trees until he captured enough swarms to start his hives. Buckwheat honey and buckwheat cakes were a treat while they were a novelty, but now both had become a monotonous part of their regular diet, and Castle longed for white flannel cakes and white sugar. But white sugar was all but unobtainable, and even brown sugar and molasses were scarce and expensive. So honey served as "long sweetening" in everything she cooked and baked.

Then there were the apples. Most of the trees were beginning to bear, though so far the crop had been light. Jonathan had been very proud of his first apples, and Castle delighted with her first apple pies. But all winter they had eaten stewed apples, baked apples, fried apples, apple fritters, apple turnovers, and apple dumplings until apples had become a burden rather than a pleasure.

"Apples! What in tarnation are you going to do with all of them this fall?" Castle asked in disgust. "You might as well let them rot on the ground. You can't sell them and we certainly can't eat them all."

"Barter, my dear, is an ancient and honorable medium of exchange," Jonathan grinned at her, spreading apple butter on his bread. "I can swap apples for whatever the stores have in stock, and the neighbors can always use a few and pay for them with an extra day's work at harvesttime. Also, the market for cider vinegar is almost unlimited. All I need is a cider press."

"I don't care what you do with them, so long as I don't have to eat them three times everyday and Sundays."

On a morning in early May, Solon came for Castle before breakfast. When he finished his chores, Jonathan drove over to the Station and took Abigail to Crawfords'. It was her daughter and her grandchild and he felt she should be there. When not otherwise occupied, he and Solon sat in the mill shed door and watched the house and talked. Now and then someone called for wood or water, but for all the women's bustling about, nothing seemed to be happening. Jonathan was unperturbed, but Solon was restless and uneasy.

"She's all right," Castle assured him each time he went to the house to question her. "She's just slow. Some babies come quick and some take their own sweet time." Harriet, too, questioned Castle. "How should I know how bad it hurts? Ask your Ma. She ought to know."

Abigail smiled. "It ain't no picnic, Harry, but there are worse things."

Once after a hard pain, Harriet whimpered, "I wish Seth was here." A few minutes later Castle found Abigail at the kitchen window, her eyes wet with tears.

"I was alone whan Samantha was born. Eli was gone . . ."

"He was away when Lucinda was born. A man ain't no help."

"It's just awful lonely having a baby and not knowing if your man is dead or alive. I can feel for Harry, 'cause I know what it's like. And not a thing anybody can do about it."

"Don't you go talking like that around Harriet! You keep a grin on your face."

"Oh, I wouldn't add my troubles to hers."

Tabitha, who was with Harriet, called and Castle hurried back to the bedroom. But again, nothing much happened.

At the mill, Solon and Jonathan were killing time, wandering about checking the machinery for damage due to long disuse. But they, too, were thinking of Seth.

"Too bad he couldn't be here," Jonathan remarked.

"Can't understand how the war just goes on and on. What's Lincoln thinking of, letting it drag on like this? If he'd free the slaves the war'd be over in no time," Solon nodded wisely. "Once free, the niggers would rise up and overthrow the Rebel government and put an end to it."

"I suppose the field hands would quit work, but I doubt there'd be any revolt. The Negroes have no organization and no leadership, and they're accustomed to taking orders from their masters. They have to be told what to do and how to do it, or they do nothing. To do anything they hadn't been told to do could get them in serious trouble."

"I swear, Jonathan, you're damn near a Southerner!"

"Far from it, but I do know something of the slaves and the conditions of their lives. They aren't taught to think or act for themselves." Jonathan shook his head. "Solon, thinking for themselves is the last thing the owners want them to do. They keep them ignorant and treat them like children; and most of them behave like children — thoughtless, irresponsible children. Wisdom, judgment, and common sense come only with experience, with maturity. The slaves are treated the way you treat your horses; they work and eat and sleep and do as they are told. They've never had a chance."

Harriet's son was born in the middle of the afternoon and the men got no dinner until nearly chore time. Solon offered to take Abigail back to the Station, so Castle and Jonathan set out for home. In the carryall she leaned back wearily.

"I'm that tired I could sleep for a week, only I better get my satchel packed before something else happens."

"Castle, something *has* happened. There's a war, remember?"

She flared up angrily. "You said you'd take me to Council Bluffs and put me on the boat after Harry had her baby. Now you're trying to back out!"

"The boats aren't running. You know that. That's why we can't get sugar or calico or a dozen other things. There *are* no boats. The Rebels hold the Missouri between St. Joseph and St. Louis and the boats can't get through.[5] That's why we can't sell corn or hogs. The troops go on foot, and that's the way you'd have to go. It's a thousand miles to Pittsburgh, and fighting at every crossroad. Strange as it may seem, I don't want you killed. Or stranded among cutthroats and ruffians. It would be insane to let you try to go to Pittsburgh now."

Next morning, Jonathan let his wife sleep while he did his barn work, then went over to Markers' in time to join them at breakfast and give them word of Harriet's new son. He took Jennifer home and went on to his work. When he came in at noon, the dinner was ready. It was not until a few days later that he realized Castle was spending little time in the kitchen, while Jennifer seemed to be doing the cooking.

"Where's your Ma? What's she doing?" he asked when he came in with the water bucket and found Jennifer putting the food on the table.

"She's piecing a quilt."

"Who cooked the dinner?"

"I did. Ain't it all right?"

"How did you get home from school in time to cook dinner?"

"I didn't go."

"Why not?"

"Time the breakfast dishes are done and the house redd up, I can't get there in time. And I couldn't get home in time to cook dinner."

"Are you going to school this afternoon?"

"I can't, Pa. The noon hour will be over. I guess I'm too slow."

"When did you go last?"

"The day Harriet had her baby."

"Why haven't you gone since?"

Jennifer was near tears. "Ma says I got to do the work, and I can't do it and go to school. I just can't, Pa."

"What's your Ma been doing all this time?"

"Piecing a quilt, like I said."

"I see." Jonathan strode into the sitting room where Castle sat by the window with a stack of quilt blocks on the table beside her, a half-finished block on her lap. "Why have you been keeping Jennifer out of school?"

"I ain't been well. If you can be sick-abed, so can I."

"You aren't sick-abed. You're well enough to eat and sleep and piece quilts and do what you like. Why do you suppose I wanted Preston Wright to teach again this year if not to give Jennifer a chance for an education?"

"What do I care about her education? I've worked my fingers to the bone for the worthless little trollop, and now she's big enough to be some use, I'm going to use her!" The scissors slipped from her lap with a clatter and she bent to retrieve them. "You won't let me go home where I can be waited on like a lady, so I aim to see Jennifer waits on me, and waits on me proper!"

Jonathan caught her shoulder and hoisted her out of the chair with one hand while with the other he slapped her face, one side coming, the other side going. He was white to the lips, his eyes black sparks of fury. "You harridan! Make a servant of my daughter, will you! I'll teach you!"

Castle would have clawed his face but he struck her hand so hard the wrist went limp. Catching her other shoulder, he shook her in fury until her long hair fell down her back. "Make a servant of my daughter! I'll break every bone in your body! I'll tear you limb from limb!" Losing her balance, she went to her knees and he let her fall. As she went down, she clutched his hand and sank her teeth into the flesh so the blood ran. He yelled and slapped her fiercely, then kicked her and sent her sprawling.

Castle lay gasping, but managed to laugh mockingly, "*Your* daughter! She's Abigail's brat."

"Abigail gave her to *me! You* wouldn't give me a child, but Abigail did! And she doesn't expect her to be a servant to you! She expects her to be brought up and educated as though she were my own, and I intend to do it! Make no mistake, my daughter is going to school every day there is school, and she's going in the morning and taking her lunch, and staying all day. I told you before that if you mistreated her, I wouldn't be responsible, and before God, I meant it! Try anything with her again and you won't live long enough to regret it!"

Castle still sat on the floor, but she was no longer laughing. Her eyes were wide and a little frightened. "I believe you mean it."

"You better believe I mean it!" Jonathan lunged, caught her by the hair and dragged her to the kitchen. Jerking her to her feet, he shoved her toward the stove. "You stupid, lazy cow! If I catch you making Jennifer . . ." The girl was cowering behind the stove, sobbing in terror. Still panting, Jonathan straightened and gazed at her and his anger drained away, leaving him cold and shaken.

"Come outside, child," he said quietly. Jennifer followed him reluctantly, fearfully, sobbing as she went. "Come on down to the barn with me. I want to talk to you."

She followed him through the yard and down to the barn. Once inside, he pulled himself up on a manger and motioned her to do the same. For a time they were silent, except for the little girl's stifled sobs. Jonathan drew out his bandanna and wrapped it around his still bleeding hand.

"If you haven't a handkerchief, blow your nose on your petticoat; then stop crying. I want you to listen to what I say."

Jennifer turned up her blue calico skirt and blew her nose, then dried her eyes, but she continued to watch her Pa fearfully. He studied her sadly. After all Castle had done to her, he had only made matters worse.

"Don't be afraid of me, Jenny. I won't hurt you. I'm sorry you should have witnessed such a scene. I should have remembered you were there." He ran his fingers through his hair. He was so often at a loss with the child. Yet she must understand. "Jenny, your Ma is a good woman. Always believe that, no matter what she does. But there are times when she is possessed of a devil, and there are times when she arouses a devil in me. I suppose there's a devil in every man." He shook his head and tried again. "You know how she cares for the sick. She goes anywhere, and everywhere, at all hours of the day and night. You know she missed her last chance to go home to her own people when she stayed to take care of Harry."

"I asked her once who'd take care of people, if she went away."

"You did?"

Jennifer nodded. "She said she didn't know, but she looked kind of worried."

"Your Ma isn't always good to you, or to me, but it hasn't been easy for her to get used to living in Iowa after growing up the way she did. She's told you about her home and her family. You know how different it is here. She had never even picked up her own clothes; she just dropped them on the floor."

"I know. She told me. Amanda took care of her."

"No one is perfect, Jennifer, and no one is all good or all bad. The most we can ask of anyone is to be more good than bad, and your Ma is. She can be ruthless, even cruel, but never spineless or cowardly. Remember when you had croup, how she sat with you all night long? How she took care of me when I was sick? And she'd do it again—and again. She might be mean between times, but in time of trouble, she'd be there, and you could depend on her. Try to see the good in her, and overlook the bad for the sake of the good. Believe me, your Ma is worthy of your respect. I've admired her from the moment we met, though I know her faults, and she has often hurt me deeply. Those we love most have the power to hurt us most, and they don't even know it." His voice was low and he spoke as though he were explaining to himself.

"You love her, don't you, Pa?"

Jonathan glanced down at the child with a startled expression, then smiled, his lips drawn down a little at the corners. "Yes, Jenny, I love her. More than she will ever know."

"Does she love you, Pa?"

He laughed. "Now you're asking questions, and that isn't what we're here for. I want to talk to you about school. You mustn't stay at home without a good reason, you know. I doubt if your Ma will interfere again, but don't stay at home to help her unless it's really necessary. You're old enough to know when she does need you, aren't you? Anytime you aren't sure, ask me."

"Yes, Pa. Like if Ma was sure-enough sick-abed, or somebody died, or something important . . ."

"That's right. But you must get an education, child. It's man's best weapon against adversity, and if it cannot cure poverty, it can make it endurable. I've read to you from books you didn't understand in the hope that someday you would want to understand. I'll see that you go to school. The rest is up to you."

"I have to study, don't I?"

"Yes. You have to do your own learning. No one else can do it for you. Now about your Ma. We don't talk about family affairs with anyone outside the family. Do you understand?"

"Yes, sir. I ain't no tattletale, Pa."

No, Jennifer was no tattletale, but her Ma was one of the family, and when she asked, "What did your Pa say to you at the barn?" Jennifer told her.

"He said you're a good woman, even if you ain't always good to him and me. He said you're strong and brave . . .''

"Is that the truth?" Castle's grip tightened on the child's arm and she squirmed. "Don't lie to me, Jennifer."

"I wouldn't lie to you, Ma! Pa said he loves you more'n you'll ever know. But you do know, don't you?"

Castle released the girl and stepped back. "You sure that's what he said?"

"A-course. Only you do know he loves you, don't you, Ma?"

"Yes, certainly. You run along now and study your lessons so you won't be behind the others when you go to school tomorrow."

 *18*

O N a bright Saturday in June, Jennifer went to town with her Pa. Castle dressed her in stiffly starched calico over a small pair of hoops, and below the calico were ruffled pantalets. When they started, a clean blue sunbonnet shaded her face, but before they had gone a mile it was hanging down her back. Neither threats nor appeals to her vanity could arouse in the child a proper regard for her complexion. When they drew up at the Bates's gate, Thaddeus came running to meet them, her curls bouncing, her eyes dancing.

"Jenny, baby! You finally got here!"

Jennifer scrambled over the wheel and threw her arms around her sister. Sophronia came trotting down the path like a thin, grey exclamation point.

"How'd do, Jonathan. My sakes, that child has growed! Why, she's most up to Thaddeus's shoulder. Get down and come in. Noah's away right now, but you might like a glass of fresh buttermilk. I can't offer you tea or coffee. We ain't had either in months. Noah says it's wicked to pay so much for creature comforts when so many folks is bad off."

"Thank you, Sophronia, but I won't stop now. I have some business to attend to. I'll be back later."

He hitched the team in front of Freeman's store and went across to Judge Duncan's office. The Judge, grey-haired and portly, pushed a pile of books and papers aside and rose to shake hands.

"Good to see you, Mr. Gayle. Sit down. Been wanting to talk to you."

"Not about the war, I hope," Jonathan grinned as he sat down and the two men proceeded to fill their pipes and lean back at ease.

The Judge waved a fat, freckled hand. "War's talked about too much.

Too many people think they know how to run it. Something else on my mind. War'll end sometime, and when it does, the railroad will be built on across the state. It'll cross the county, and what I want to know is, where? Moved to Grove City because it's a better location for the county seat than Cold Spring.[1] But if we don't get the railroad, we don't get the county seat."

"I have no objection to either," Jonathan shrugged.

"You wouldn't have!" the Judge laughed. "But what will happen to your property if the railroad passes us by? Ever think of that?"

"I can guess."

"Exactly! You're a big taxpayer. Use your influence."

"Judge, when the railroad comes through, you and I will have nothing to say about where. So far, Grove City isn't important enough for them to go out of their way, and my influence wouldn't make a particle of difference."

"What of your property, man?"

Jonathan shrugged. "Move the town to the railroad. The land will always be valuable for farming."

"You mean move the buildings?"

"Why not?"

The Judge shook his head. "Wouldn't have thought of it, myself, but sounds feasible. By golly, it could be done!"

Jonathan nodded. "Now we've settled that, I have a bit of business for you. I've drawn my will, and I want you to go over it and see that it is in accordance with Iowa law."

"Your will? Good God, Gayle, there isn't anything wrong with you is there?"

"No, I just want to have my affairs in order." He handed over a sheaf of foolscap and the Judge put on his spectacles. Once or twice he slid them down his nose and peered at Jonathan over the steel rims, then laid the sheets down and looked at him curiously.

"Sure this is the way you want it?"

"Quite."

"This Jennifer Hall. You speak of her as your foster-daughter. Is it legal?"

"Not yet." Jonathan explained the circumstances. "I can't ask her mother to give the child up legally until she's convinced of her husband's death."

"You think he's dead?"

"I can't think anything else."

"You're willing to provide for this child, even though there's a chance her father might come back and claim her?"

"Her father was an honest man, and my friend."

"And your wife?"

"She is amply provided for."

"Supposing the child dies without issue? Do you realize her share, under present circumstances, would go to her mother and sisters?"

"Certainly. They'd make good use of it. They're fine people. Jordan Pierce married one of the sisters. You performed the ceremony."

"The Bates girl?"

"That's right. Thaddeus Bates is my daughter's sister."

"I didn't know that. That Thaddy is a fine girl. Best thing ever happened to Jordan. Hope he makes it back." The Judge heaved himself up out of his chair and went to the door. "Hey, Sam, you there? Go fetch Jesse Freeman and Joe Starkey, that's a good boy."

The witnessing completed, Jonathan walked back to the store with Jesse Freeman, feeling almost young again. He intended to live his three score years and ten and something over if possible, but it was a good feeling to know Jennifer was provided for. It made her seem more truly his own, knowing she would share the rewards of his labors. While Jonathan made his purchases, Jesse Freeman told his own tale of woe.

"I just got back from Des Moines, and I tell you, Mr. Gayle, things are something fierce. Never seen the like. Why, I paid two dollars a pound for tea; rice, eighteen cents a pound; dried apples, twenty cents. Reminds me, you going to have some apples this fall? I'll be glad to take 'em in trade if you'll bring 'em a few bushels at a time. Apples is mighty scarce around here. Saleratus? Yeah, I got some, but I paid two bits for two pounds. Couldn't get much white sugar, and had to pay thirty-five cents a pound. And I paid thirteen-fifty for half a barrel of mackeral, and ten-fifty for a keg of nails. Calico? No use you looking at it, Mr. Gayle. It ain't the kind you buy. Paid sixty-five cents a yard for it, too. Cost me sixty-five for unbleached muslin, and mighty poor stuff it is. And a dollar a yard for denim. I don't know what folks are going to do for clothes. If this keeps up we'll all be running around nekked as jaybirds. I got to make a little profit if I aim to stay in business, and freight's a dollar a hundred. I'm ashamed to charge such prices, but I got no choice. Anything else?"

Jonathan glanced about and noticed a small pair of shoes. Jennifer had complained her shoes hurt her toes, though shoes always hurt when a child had been going barefoot. But Jennifer was growing and it was quite possible her shoes were too small for her now. He might as well get her a new pair while she was in town to try them on. He examined the shoes. The leather was not the best and the workmanship poor. However, she would wear them little before winter, and by spring she would outgrow them. They should last that long. Too, she would enjoy buying them. If she came to the store for shoes, she would feel she had "been to town." He turned to Freeman.

"My daughter is at Elder Bates's. I'll bring her in and see if you can fit her with a pair of shoes."

Thaddeus came along with them, almost as excited as Jennifer. Jonathan bought the shoes, and Jennifer wanted to wear them, so Jesse wrapped the old ones and as he gave her the package he pinched her cheek.

"Give me a kiss and I'll give you that doll up there on the shelf," he told her, pointing to a doll with a china head and a faded pink dress.

Jennifer backed away and took hold of her Pa's hand. She had never had a real doll, and the new shoes were not half so fine as that doll in the pink dress. But Jesse Freeman chewed tobacco, and his stringy yellow mustache was stained with the juice. Jennifer could not have kissed him if her life had depended on it. Gazing in fascinated desire at the doll, she shook her head resolutely.

"Aw, come on! Just one little kiss!" Jesse coaxed. "Don't you like the doll?"

Jennifer pressed close to her Pa. "Um-humm. I like the doll. But I don't kiss men. Only Pa."

Thaddeus hugged her in mingled pride and disappointment, but Jonathan straightened his shoulders and smiled broadly. "Give us a bag of peppermint candy, Jesse."

Jonathan and Jennifer had dinner with the Bateses, and afterward the men talked war and politics on the porch, while the girls helped Sophronia with her Saturday baking. When it was time to go, Jennifer climbed over onto the seat with her sack of candy, while Jonathan paused to say good-bye to Thaddeus.

"I'm going to make Jennifer a doll," she whispered. "It won't be as elegant as the one in the store, but I'll do the best I can."

"You're a good girl, Thaddy."

Thaddeus rose on tiptoe and kissed his cheek. "Nobody else thinks I'm good."

"Nonsense. Everybody knows you're good. Ask your Ma or Aunt Castle."

"You really think so? Ma Bates says . . ."

"Don't take her too seriously, child. The milk of human kindness soured on her stomach years ago. She means well, but she has spiritual indigestion."

Thaddeus laughed. "You mean it ain't just me? I do try, but I don't think I can ever be like her. What's the matter with me, Uncle Jonathan?"

"Heaven forbid you should ever be like Sophronia! You're young and full of life, and I wouldn't change a hair of your sweet head. If a filly didn't kick up her heels, you'd worry about her. But the filly that kicks up in the pasture will settle down and pull when she's in harness. Isn't that right?"

Thaddeus looked up at him seriously. "Yes, that's right. When Jordan comes home, I'll pull like a mule."

"Good!" Jonathan climbed up on the wagon seat, then bent down and Thaddeus came close. "Another thing, I like that young husband of yours. I'm glad you married him. He's a fine lad."

On the way home, Jennifer carefully licked the stripes off the candy, and what was left at the end of the trip she hoarded for weeks. True to her word, Thaddeus made a doll for Jennifer, a rag doll of rather peculiar anatomy with sawdust filling. The face was not especially pretty, but it was clearly intended as a face. The eyes were worked in blue thread, the nose and mouth in red. The dress was pink, the pantalets made of white flour sacking, and though Castle shook her head and deplored Thaddy's careless workmanship, Jennifer was in ecstasy. She clutched her treasure to her heart and thereafter Betsy Bobbit was seldom out of her sight as long as the poor creature held together. In time the sawdust filling oozed out and the face faded to a blur, but when at last Cressy and Cade conducted funeral services for her darling, Jennifer's childhood was interred with the remains.

After the death of Hennie Olson, Preston Wright and Tolly Marker became acutely aware that they were the only young men left in the neighborhood. Though his father's place in the community was well established, Preston, as a medical student and schoolmaster, never quite fit the pattern in Turkey Grove. The boys his own age had stood in awe of his superior education, and even his elders remembered their lack of schooling in his presence. Only with Jonathan could the boy be wholly at ease, and now, lonely and restless, it was to him Preston turned, dropping in frequently in the evening when the Gayles sat on the porch, Jonathan with his pipe, Castle with her knitting, Jennifer in quiet conversation with her doll. Often he found Tolly there, too, for Tolly had long since grown weary of his mother's endless harping on his duty to her and the farm. With Jonathan as the catalytic agent, the two young men soon became friends, even going together to Pettits' when Tolly called on Evva, though more often than not they talked war with Ed and Luke while Evva and the Pettit girls listened.

Early in July, both boys enlisted, and after keeping company for five years, Evva and Tolly were married in haste at last. Once more there was a furor of preparation, and only Evva remained calm and composed as she went about her work, putting the house in order and their best clothes in readiness. Laurel and Josie helped, and though Josie joked and teased, Laurel wiped her eyes with suspicious frequency. She said it was a touch of hay fever, but Evva knew better, for she, too, was torn between her natural duty to make her home henceforth with Martha Marker and the knowledge that she was still needed at Pettits'. Laurel was not yet fifteen, and Grampa was becoming more difficult every day. Lately, to top it all off, he messed his pants with disgusting frequency.

Martha Marker made Evva's decision for her. "I'm an able-bodied woman and I can look after myself. Wouldn't be right for Laurel to have so much put on her when she ain't even got her growth yet. My land! Patience Pettit would haunt me to my dying day if I took you from Ed and the children."

Castle contributed a bit of reassurance. "Just you look after the Pettits, Evva. Jonathan and me can keep an eye on Martha. If she gets too lonesome, Jennifer can go visit her a while."

Evva was to wear Harriet's wedding gown since a new one would cost a fortune, even if material could be had at any price. The gown had to be fitted, for Evva was taller and slimmer than Harriet. Martha had come along to lend a hand generally, and while Castle pinched and pinned, Martha ironed curtains and Laurel and Josie hung them.

"Aunt Castle, did you know Aunt Berta isn't coming to my wedding?" Evva asked, trying to stand straight and hold still.

Castle looked up at her quickly, then back to her pins. "Hummm. We'll see about that. Turn a little now—that's right." Castle stood back and studied the girl. "I'll have to let the hem clear out and face it. You must be a good three inches taller than Harriet. Martha, see what you think; is the bodice took in enough?"

Once satisfied with the gown, Castle was in a hurry to get home and Jonathan was nowhere about; She put the carefully wrapped gown in the carryall and stood wondering where the men were. Hens clucked and sang about the yard and down toward the barn a rooster crowed. Then she heard the screech of the grindstone and following the sound, found the men sharpening an ax.

"Ready?" Jonathan asked.

"I been ready. Come on, Jonathan, I'm in a hurry."

Once in the carryall, Castle announced that they were going to Olsons' but she did consent to stop at the house long enough to give Jonathan his dinner. Nor did she mince matters when she confronted Berta.

"What do you mean, you ain't going to Evva's wedding? I never heard of such a thing! Ain't it on account of Hennie that Tolly and Preston are joining up? How can you insult Evva like that?"

"But only these few months my Hennie is dead, and no fit mourning clothes I got, and can't get nohow," Berta protested tearfully.

"Nonsense! I know folks in mourning ain't supposed to go to parties and such, but this is different. And I got a black silk you can have. I ain't had it out of the trunk since I came to Ioway. I'll open the seams and let down the hem. You've lost twenty pounds, I'll be bound."

"Ja, my clothes don't stay on so good no more."

Evva had made no complaint at having to wear a second-hand wedding gown, but Castle grumbled as she worked. "As if it ain't enough for Harriet to marry first, now Evva can't even have her own gown. I never did approve of the younger sister marrying first."

"Not even when Marybelle married before you did?"

"You shut up! I got no time for your smart talk. If Evva can't have a new gown, the one she wears is going to fit proper. And I got to fix that black silk for Berta, with little enough time to do it." She gave the white muslin an impatient jerk. "Don't get me riled, that's all. I got enough as it is."

"I'm sorry, Miss Castle. I shouldn't tease you." She looked up at her husband in astonishment. It was the first time he had ever apologized for anything he had said to her, and he had said far worse. He turned to light his pipe, then continued between puffs. "You're . . . a good woman, Miss Castle . . . and a good . . . neighbor." He grinned down at her as he turned away.

Caught off guard by her husband's praise, it was not until days afterward that she thought of all the things she should have said. Why hadn't she had her wits about her? For once, Jonathan had admitted he was wrong, and she had failed to take advantage of her opportunity. She had just been so pushed with work. . . . Could it be Jennifer had told the truth about what Jonathan said that day at the barn? He had said she was a good woman, and that was what Jennifer said he told her. Maybe he did say it. . . . But the rest of Jennifer's tale was a bit too hard to swallow. Why would he tell Jennifer he loved her? He had certainly never told her! Maybe Jennifer had just made it all up. If he loved her he wouldn't make her work like a nigger and wear calico.

With the two gowns to remodel in a hurry, Castle pressed Jennifer into service doing the cooking and cleaning, while she sewed. As excited as her Ma over the wedding, Jennifer bustled about with an air of importance, and the two chattered in complete amity, each busy and a little pompous in her own sphere. Puzzled but pleased, Jonathan watched and went about his business. So much the better if there could be peace between them.

Yet for all the excitement and commotion, Evva's wedding was not the gay occasion Harriet's had been. Too many faces were missing, and Berta, in Castle's black silk, was a reminder that at least one would not return. When the ceremony was over, Cressy and Cade and Jennifer wandered down along the garden fence, uncomfortable because they dared not play in their best clothes.

"If I was older, I'd join up," Cade announced.

"You might get killed, same as Hennie," Cressy reminded him.

"Maybe they'll all get killed," he jerked his head in the direction of the house.

"Don't say it, Cade! It's bad luck," Jennifer warned.

"If you girls start crying, I'm going off."

"Don't go, Cade. We ain't played together . . ."

"I don't feel like playing."

"I don't either. I don't like weddings. They're sad. Everybody cries. I guess I won't get married." Jennifer chewed a blade of grass.

"Sure you'll get married. Want to be an old maid?"

"Wonder who I'll marry?" Cressy giggled. "Who you going to marry, Cade?"

"I don't know. You or Jenny. Ain't made up my mind." Cade slid down off the fence. "They got cake, ain't they? Let's go see . . ."

The Twenty-Third Iowa Regiment was mustered in at Des Moines on the tenth of September, 1862, with Company I composed entirely of Cass County men.[2] With Tolly and Preston went Roe and Jud Henderson and Tanner Jason. Township sentiment was divided between horror that members of the Henderson-Jason tribes were associating with Preston and Tolly, and approbation of the boys for having the spunk to join up. No one doubted either their willingness or ability to do a fair share of fighting.

It had been bad enough before, but now few county homes were untouched by the war. Hay rotted in the field for lack of hands, but in Turkey Grove the men worked as a team, going from farm to farm and field to field. Tolly's hay was cut and stacked with the rest, and when his corn had been picked, Martha gave a husking bee so the labor could be shared and a little fun added to give zest to the task. Martha had held out as long as she could against her son enlisting, but once the deed was done, she never complained. With sighing and head shaking, she told Castle it was almost a relief when he was gone.

"I'd been hanging by my toenails wiggling myself to death, knowing he'd go sooner or later if it kept on. I tell you, it took all the sand right out of my craw trying to keep him home. Now I'm that worried I can't sleep nights, but my conscience is clear.''

Jonathan had long since turned old Archie and Al to pasture, and in the summer, Archie had quietly laid down and died. Jennifer had wept for her old friend, and when she was concerned about Al, Jonathan assured her he had been retired on a veteran's pension of corn and oats and hay. When Castle's temper got out of bounds, Jennifer slipped away to climb on old Al's fat back, swayed to the shape of a saddle, and played riding into combat with a host of imaginary comrades. That fall, Jennifer sought Al's company frequently, for Castle's temper was uncertain. Marybelle had written that Lee had crossed the Potomac into Maryland, promising to ''free'' the state, and everyone was terrified lest he attack Baltimore. But General Lee failed to free Maryland. He and McClellan met near a small town called Sharpsburg, and in the end it was Lee who retired back across the Potomac. The battle had been a bloody stalemate, but on his way up the Potomac to join Lee, Jackson had captured Harper's Ferry with eleven thousand Union troops and quantities of much needed supplies. However, though the Union troops were a loss to the one side, they were of no great benefit to the other.

Castle could make no sense of Jonathan's talk of prisoners. He had been reading the paper and now folded it carefully and laid it aside, watching while she continued to knit, her hands moving swiftly and gracefully. Worn and calloused by work, they had lost none of their shapeliness. Jennifer sat in her favorite place on the hearth, her back against the chimney breast, her knees drawn up to her chin — near enough to the crackling fire for warmth, yet safe from occasional sparks. Jonathan regarded the newspaper accounts of the war as history in the making, and it was largely for his daughter's benefit that he read and explained the reports, for his efforts to educate his wife sometimes seemed a bit misplaced.

''All this business about prisoners — what's the matter with that stupid Lincoln? Refusing to swap those no-good Rebels for our men. What's he mean, they ain't equal? Ain't our men as good as Rebels? That's the craziest thing I ever heard of.''

''The Confederacy is not the equal of the Union, Castle. The United States is a recognized nation, the Confederacy is a group of states in rebellion. It's a matter of international law. Lincoln refuses to talk to representatives of the Confederacy because he denies there is a Confederacy. He says the southern states are still part of the Union, and not a separate country. To exchange prisoners would be to admit that the Confederacy is a nation.[3] And that's what the fighting is about in the first place: whether or not the states can leave the Union and set up a country of their own.''

''The Confederacy was formed, wasn't it? What's the sense beating about the bush? I thought the fighting was about the slaves.''

''No, the issue is secession. There was no question of slavery where it existed. The Constitution and the Supreme Court guaranteed the rights of slave owners in the slave states. The argument was over the territories.[4]

Remember the fighting in Kansas over whether it would be "slave" or "free"? Because Lincoln and the Republicans object to slavery in the territories, the southern states seceded and lost all claim to the territories for the Confederacy. Figure that out if you can."

"That's as crazy as Lincoln not knowing there's a Confederacy. But the South already seceded, so what's the fighting about?"

Jonathan sighed. "The South will be compelled to return to the Union."

"I'd like to know how! The way they're fighting . . ."

"Castle, they haven't the men or the materials of war. They lost the war when they fired on Fort Sumter, and any man of intelligence should have known it. It's so incredibly stupid . . ."

But that fall of 1862, there seemed little reason to believe the South was defeated, or would be. Again and again the Army of the Potomac had been outgeneraled, outmaneuvered, and outfought. Just before Christmas, Sherman and the Fourth Iowa moved to reinforce the attackers at Vicksburg. Vicksburg would not be easily taken, and with that threat hanging over them, no one wanted to spend Christmas alone. Elder Bates was holding services in town and couldn't come, but the Pettits and Garrisons and Abigail and the two little girls went to Crawfords', while Evva and Martha, Dowd Wright, and the Olsons had dinner with the Gayles. The women all helped, and Berta was in better spirits than in months. Dowd Wright made an effort to be gay and witty, though Jonathan noticed that his hand shook when he lifted his cup. Dinner over, the men sat by the fire talking while the women did the dishes. With more help than she could use, Castle sent Cressy and Jennifer to play, and they skipped down to the barn to ride to battle on old Al. But without Cade, the game seemed dull.

This time the men found a topic of conversation that was a mere side issue of the war. With Preston gone, they must find another teacher. Twelve-year-old Karl Olson, scorning to play with the girls, stayed with the men and offered his suggestion for their benefit.

"Let's have Evva for our teacher. She'd be a good teacher."

"So much you know . . . ," Axel began angrily, but Jonathan laughed.

"We'll ask her," he told Karl, and when Evva came in he said, "I understand you haven't enough to do to keep busy." Evva stared at him and Jonathan laughed again. "Karl thought you might like to teach school."

Evva sat down abruptly. "I couldn't, Uncle Jonathan. You know that. But why can't Ma Marker teach? She's alone now."

Martha squealed and clapped her hand over her mouth. Everybody laughed, but Jonathan looked at her questioningly. "Good land! I don't know as much as the young'uns!" she protested.

"You can read and write and cipher, can't you?"

"Yes, but that ain't all there is to teaching school."

"The children had better learn that much than nothing at all. Finding a qualified teacher is out of the question this year, Martha. I'm only one trustee, I can't offer you the job. But if it were offered, would you refuse?"

"You can't be serious! Oh, I don't know what to say! How could I teach when I got no education? But I couldn't refuse, because I need the money."

"Think it over, Martha," he told her. He had done considerable thinking, and Evva's suggestion would solve two problems: a reasonable facsimile of a teacher for the children and a means of livelihood for Martha.

The day after Christmas the attack on Vicksburg began. Then came the president's Emancipation Proclamation; contrary to Solon's prophecy, the Negroes did not rise up and overthrow the Confederate government. Instead, Grant continued to hammer at Vicksburg, and Solon learned to his sorrow that freeing the slaves was not enough.

Newspapers were days old when they arrived and the nearest telegraph was at Cold Spring. Drawn by that magnet, the men twice made the trip in spite of bitter cold, for anything was better than the deadly waiting. On the first trip they learned only that the attempt to take Vicksburg by assault had failed. On the second trip the casualty lists were in, and Solon drove home with bowed head, for Sid had been killed in the action. In time a letter from Seth told the circumstances. They had waded across Chickasaw Bayou in the face of heavy fire, but after capturing the first line of the enemy works, they found the rest of the brigade had remained behind, and they were shot to pieces—the whole bloody mess so much wasted effort.[6] At roll call, Seth learned Sid had not returned, and when the stretcher bearers brought him in, he was dead. The Fourth Iowa had lost a third of their men and been instructed to inscribe on their banners, "First at Chickasaw Bayou." But what good was that when Sid was dead? He had been buried with military honors. "God only knows when I'll be home. These Rebels know how to fight."

Tabitha and Solon bore their loss with grim fortitude, and Harriet's grief was genuine, for Sid had been a good brother to her. Yet again and again she caught herself thinking, "Thank God it wasn't Seth!" She felt guilty to be so heartless but could not help being grateful Seth had been spared. The baby was so sweet and pretty, and he would need his father. Nor was there any question now as to his name. Sid was dead, but there would still be a Sid Crawford. She wanted him christened properly, but for that she would wait until Seth came home.

T H E trustees held a meeting and hired Martha Marker to teach the school. Though both state and county had voted relief for families of volunteers,[1] she would need more than that to keep the farm going until Tolly came home. Rather than ask her to teach in summer, when she would have farm and garden work to do and young chickens and pigs to tend, the school term was held during the late winter and early spring, and for it the men banked and chinked the schoolhouse and filled the woodshed. Jennifer stayed with Martha during the week, and Jonathan rigged a box sled for them. Martha would have used her one remaining mustang, but Jonathan persuaded her to take old Al, so once more the great beast plowed his way through snowdrifts, snorting and blowing with all his usual enthusiasm. And Jonathan's mind was at rest, for even in a blizzard, old Al would find his way home.

During the three months of school, Martha had little time to worry or feel lonely. Together she and Jennifer did the housework, milked the cow, and cared for the stock. To Jennifer, those were happy times, the days filled with the excitement of being with the other children, while in the evenings she and Martha read and ciphered by the light of a tallow dip, the firelight filling the room with dancing shadows, their questions and answers punctuated by the gentle ticking of the clock and the snap and crackle of burning wood. If Martha's grammar was sometimes faulty, her curiosity was great, and the children studied if only to inform her of what they learned. Then spring came once more, and the men plowed and planted, and Jennifer dropped corn while Martha made her garden.

At Anderson's Hill, Preston Wright got a minnie ball in his leg, but his father seemed more relieved than alarmed by the news. He leaned on the counter at Freeman's store and rubbed his nose thoughtfully.

"Does seem a hospital tent ain't quite so exposed as the front lines. I'll sleep easier tonight, knowing he's in a bed instead of a ditch."

However, Preston was not long in bed nor long out of the fighting. Next came word that Jud Henderson had been wounded, though not seriously. Then the first week of June, Axel Olson received a letter from Knute saying Seth Crawford had got a piece of shrapnel in his arm, nothing much, and he'd be back on duty soon enough. As usual, the men were gathered at the post office in Freeman's store, and after Axel read the letter, he handed it to Solon. Solon glanced over it hastily and dashed out of the store, scrambled into his wagon and turning on three wheels, set out full tilt for home.

"I be damn!" Axel remarked solemnly. "So quiet he take it when Sid get killed, now Seth ain't bad hurt, off he go, bang!"

"There's a finality about death that leaves a man stunned," Jonathan mused and Dowd Wright nodded.

"He was afraid of all the things that might have happened. Now for a little while he can relax. Like when Preston got hit, I was just so god-awful glad it wasn't worse.''

For the first time, Jonathan felt out of place among his neighbors. All these men had sons in the army; he alone would have nothing personal at stake when Grant made his next move. For now the Twenty-Third was in the vicinity of Vicksburg, too, and that city on the bluffs above the Mississippi had become the most important post on earth to many residents of western Iowa. While the others were still talking of Solon and Seth, someone shouted, and they all suddenly stood silent and listening. A horse was coming at a gallop; they glanced at each other uneasily and moved out onto the board-walk. No man would ride a horse like that unless he had urgent business. Jesse Freeman stepped out into the road and hailed the rider, who slowed his heaving beast, then pulled him up sharply.

''The Twenty-Third . . . Milliken's Bend . . . Surprised!''

''Tommy! Take the horse and get a fresh one from the livery stable, and be quick about it!'' Jesse called.

Men came running, and horse and rider were surrounded in a confusion of crowding, pushing men. But the Turkey Grove men still stood under the store awning, a tight, mute group, until Dowd Wright gasped, ''The Twenty-Third!'' Turning he called over his shoulder, ''I'm going to Cold Spring,'' and started for his wagon with a purposeful swing of his fat body.

With long strides, Jonathan came abreast of him. ''We'd better take my team. They're faster and the carryall is easier riding than the wagon.''

''You're going?'' Dowd asked in surprise as he paused at the hitch rack.

''Tolly Marker is with Preston. Martha and Evva will want to know.''

''I'd forgotten.''

''Behind my wagon I take your horses,'' Axel shouted and Dowd waved agreement.

Jonathan clucked to the team. He kept Buck and Jerry at a brisk trot, and Dowd braced his feet against the dashboard and tried to be patient. He wanted to gallop madly as the rider had done, but he knew nothing would be gained by winding the horses at the outset. They would get there soon enough. Perhaps, too soon. Bad news always came too soon. Or there might be no news at all—yet. Even the telegraph was not magic; it took time to learn the details of a battle, time to get the reports to the telegraph station, time to send the message through. Everything took time, and after a battle there were many messages to be sent many places. Someone had to wait. And Dowd had to wait, though it was well past noon when they reached Cold Spring, and the ambush had taken place the previous day. When at last the operator gave out the lists, Dowd ran his eye down the long columns of names.

''Wright . . . Wright . . . Wright . . . I don't see it.'' He sat down and handed the paper to Jonathan. ''You look. My eyes aren't so good.''

Jonathan looked. ''No, Preston's name isn't here. H . . . Henderson . . . no. J . . . Jason . . . no. M . . . Marker . . .''

It was a moment before Dowd became aware of the silence, then he looked up quickly, alarm in his kind blue eyes. "Well, well, what is it, man?"

"Marker."

"Marker? Tolly Marker? His name's there?"

"Yes."

"Dead?"

"Yes."

Castle heard the sound of wheels late in the afternoon, and when Jonathan left the carryall at the gate, she knew something was wrong. She stood waiting at the back stoop and when she saw his face asked, "Who is it?"

Jonathan looked at her and some remote corner of his brain registered the fact that her raven wing brows were startlingly black against the pale triangle of her face. He sank down on the stoop and sat a moment before he spoke. "Tolly."

"Tolly!" Castle turned and looked up the creek toward the Marker farm. "He was such a good boy, and he worked so hard. . . . His Ma didn't want him to go. Oh, Jonathan, how'll you ever tell her? And Evva! Poor, poor Evva! They waited so long, and then got married in such a rush, and he left right after, and now . . . ."

She slid down on the stoop beside her husband and he put his arm around her and drew her head to his shoulder absentmindedly. Castle had sought the comfort of her husband's arms, and he, dreading his task as the bearer of sad tidings, failed to realize the significance of her act. He held her gently, instinctively, yet all but unconsciously while she leaned on his shoulder and wept.

"Get your bonnet and we'll go over to Markers'," he said at last.

She shook her head. "We'd best go to Pettits' first. Evva can come back with us to Markers'." Then she added, "Laurel will have to get along somehow."

Jonathan nodded. With Josie's help, Laurel would have to get along. Evva's place would be with Martha, now. Evva, who was a widow before she had known what it was to be a wife. Jennifer came up from the garden where she had been weeding. Her freckled face was flushed, her hair mussed, and her sunbonnet hanging down her back. Yet Castle did not reproach her, and seeing her Ma and Pa sitting together so dejectedly, she slipped between Jonathan's knees and asked soberly, "Who got killed, Pa?"

Jonathan smoothed the stray locks of straight brown hair from her hot little forehead and spoke quietly. "Tolly."

Jennifer leaned forward and pressed her face against his. "He shouldn't of got killed. Not after Evva married him."

"We have to go tell Evva. Wash your face and come with us." Perhaps Jennifer could break the news better than he.

But Evva needed no telling. Coming to meet them she looked in their faces and understood. She helped Jennifer down and held the girl close in her arms, pressing her cheek against the child's face. But her eyes were dry when she straightened and spoke to Castle and Jonathan.

"I'll get my bonnet and tell Laurel I'm going."

Like Evva, Laurel needed no telling. She had come to the door but stopped on the stone doorstep when she saw Evva coming back up the path, her head high and her shoulders straight. Laurel bit her lip, but said nothing. Her Pa and the boys were at the barn and Josie was feeding the chickens. She was glad they were not around. It would be easier for Evva.

"You'll have to finish the jam." Evva spoke quietly. "There are cold potatoes to slice and fry for supper. Open a jar of apple sass, Pa likes it right well. I'll come tomorrow for my things."

As she tied on her bonnet, Evva looked quickly at Laurel, then away, and Laurel understood. A word of sympathy, and Evva would have broken down, but Laurel was silent and Evva went out and climbed into the waiting carryall. As they started, she looked back. Laurel's head was bowed against the doorframe, her shoulders shaking. Evva was leaving her second home, and Laurel was losing her second mother. When they reached the Marker place, Martha was at the cow stable. Hearing wheels, she rose with the milking stool in her hand and called a greeting. When there was no response, she hung up the milk pail and went running. The others got down from the carryall and walked to meet her. Martha hesitated, paused irresolute, her hands working in her apron. Then she came on more slowly and when Evva came to her, their hands reached out and clung, heads bent, not looking at each other.

"He's dead. I knowed it would happen. That's why I tried so hard to keep him. But he was too proud. Tell me, Jonathan."

There was little to tell. Company I had been taken by surprise: an ambush, a brief skirmish, swift slaughter, with more than thirty killed and wounded.

"He didn't even die in a big battle, like heroes in the history books," Martha said sadly. "He was just shot from the bushes like a Injun. He wouldn't of wanted it that way. He'd of wanted to die in a real big fight." She bowed her head and Evva slipped her arm around her mother-in-law's waist. But Martha's head came up. "Go on home and do your chores, Jonathan. Your cows'll be bawling their heads off."

"I'll be over tomorrow," Castle told them. "Come, Jennifer."

"Let her stay the night," Martha suggested. "She'll be company for us."

Jennifer looked up at her Ma, then moved over and took Evva's hand. When her parents had gone, she helped Martha finish the chores while Evva got supper. They all sat down at the table and both women made a pretense of eating. When the dishes were done, Jennifer asked, "We going to read tonight, Aunt Martha?"

"Might as well. No sense getting out of practice," Martha agreed, and brought out the books they had used during the school term. So they sat around the candle until bedtime, taking turns reading out of McGuffey's Fourth. But long after Jennifer was in bed and asleep, the two women sat on while the candle burned down and at last sputtered and went out unnoticed.

War, war, war! Every day brought news of battles, and places no one had ever heard of became familiar and horrible. In those months of 1863, war had lost its last vestige of glory. The years of suffering had been too long and too bitter. In June General Lee moved North: across the Potomac, across Maryland, and into Pennsylvania. After long months on short rations, the Confederates found themselves in an untouched land of huge, bulging barns. For a time Lee's men lived "high on the hog," though for the most part they paid for what they took—in Confederate currency. If the Pennsylvania farmers were apathetic in the face of invasion, Castle was not.

"There! You see? The Rebels are in Harrisburg and next they'll be in Pittsburgh! We should of gone home."

"Do you think our being there would stop Lee's army? Even if he hopes to take Pittsburgh, he'll still have a long way to go."

It had rained all day and Jonathan had come from Grove City wet and chilled. Before settling down with the papers, he built a fire and Castle drew her rocker near the hearth where the firelight touched her bright hair, her hands clasped over the sock she had been knitting. As usual, Jennifer sat on the floor, arms wound around her bare knees, her brown pigtails dangling across her shoulders.

"What if they got to Homeplace, Ma? What would they do?"

"Burn all the houses and everybody in them!" Castle snapped.

"Don't be ridiculous. They aren't barbarians. Besides, they are nowhere near Pittsburgh. And if they were, there's no reason to suppose your family would be molested."

"When I say my prayers, I'll tell God about it," Jennifer said.

"Seems to me He don't much care what happens to folks or He wouldn't let wars get started in the first place."

"Castle, Castle! Man is a free moral agent. Because we can distinguish between right and wrong, we're responsible for the consequences of our own acts. But we're cowards. We can't face our own guilt. So we say it's God's will, and thereby clear ourselves. We say, 'Thy will be done,' then do as we please. To expect God to take care of us when we don't take care of ourselves is the way of the parasite."

"Am I a parasite, Pa?"

Jonathan laughed. "A very charming young parasite, my dear. But someday you'll be old enough to take care of yourself. Then you won't be a parasite any more."

"I hope I live to see the day," Castle grunted.

"In Iowa?"

"No!" she snapped. "I'm going home first chance I get." Did he want her to stay? If he did, why didn't he plain out say so?

The Army of the Potomac had crossed the river and Maryland, then headed west into Pennsylvania. Then Lee turned east, and the two armies inadvertently bumped into each other at a little town called Gettysburg. By the time that was over and the two armies had parted company, the Confederates were in no condition to harass Homeplace. On the Fourth of July,

Vicksburg surrendered, the Mississippi was open to the Gulf, and Turkey Grove heaved a sigh of thanksgiving.

In August the Twenty-Third was transferred to the Department of the Gulf and steamed down the river to camp above New Orleans. In September they were in the attack on Sabine City, and a week later a letter from Major Hunter reported that Captain Tim had lost three of his steamboats: one had burned and two had sunk when they hit snags.

Throughout the summer and fall, the Fourth Iowa had remained with Sherman, making the long, muddy march from Memphis to Chattanooga, and battle followed battle in swift succession, while again the men of the township haunted the telegraph office.

"I don't see why *you* have to go," Castle complained when Jonathan came home late for supper.

"I don't either," he admitted. Nevertheless, he continued to go. Then one day he returned and left the carryall at the gate. Knute Olson was missing at Lookout Mountain.

"But it ain't dead," Berta insisted pathetically. "It ain't dead. Missing is, but not dead."

She looked an old woman, now, her pale hair dull and lifeless, her cheeks sagging, and the blue eyes that had twinkled so merrily were haunted by sorrow. Axel, too, had aged. He had been hard on the boys, but he had loved them. When Berta brought out her handkerchief and wiped her eyes, he went to her and patted her shoulder.

"No, it ain't dead, Mamma. It ain't dead."

Castle and Jonathan rode half way home in silence. The other neighbors, all with offerings of food or the like, had come and gone in the course of the evening. They had said little, but words had not been needed. Jonathan clucked to the team and sighed.

"Berta could toss Martha or Evva or even Tabitha right over her shoulder. Yet the others have the greater endurance. They all show the effects of their losses, but none of them have gone to pieces the way Berta has."

"I been thinking about it all evening. Seems Berta is like the dahlias at home: so big and beautiful, but a hard frost and they're finished."

"An apt comparison." Jonathan nodded and fell silent again. The others were more like . . . well, goldenrod. He wondered into which category Castle would fall under similar circumstances.

In December Castle was wakened in the night by a loud pounding on the door.

"Jonathan! Jonathan, get up! Somebody's at the door."

"Huh? What? Oh! . . . Yes, who's there?"

"It's me, Luke Pettit, Uncle Jonathan. Grampa's took bad."

"Go around back and I'll let you in, Luke."

They could hear the snow squeak as he clomped around the house. Jonathan pulled on his pants and lighted a candle. Castle dragged herself out of bed and started dressing.

"Wouldn't you know Grampa couldn't get sick in the daytime, when a body was up and about. No, he has to wait till the middle of the night, the ornery old fool!"

It was the middle of the morning when Luke brought her home, and she was still fuming when Jonathan came in to dinner.

"Making me lose a night's sleep for nothing! The old galoot is as good today as he was six months ago. . . . Jenny, stir the gravy."

"What was the trouble?" Jonathan bent over the washpan and sloshed handfuls of water over his face. "Laurel wouldn't have sent for you if she hadn't been worried."

"She was worried enough. Old ijit was heaving like a steam engine. Scared the girl out of a year's growth."

"What did you do?"

"Mustard steeps and a jigger of rum. . . . Take up the gravy and get a bowl for the potatoes, Jennifer."

"You and your mustard steeps! Poor old soul is probably as red as a lobster even now."

"Well, he's alive. More or less."

"And you're disappointed."

"What's the good of him wearing everybody out? He's helpless as a newborn babe and no more brains. Laying there in the bed for months, messing himself, don't know one person from another. Like as not, don't know his own name. No good to himself and a burden to everybody else. Shame to waste good rum. . . . Come on, the dinner's on the table."

Less than a week later, Luke came for Castle again in the dead of night. Again she went and again returned with the same report.

"Land o'Goshen! Why don't he make up his mind to live or die?"

Twice more Luke came for her in the night; twice more she went. Two nights later, Luke was back.

"I'm awful sorry, Aunt Castle, but Laurel's real scared. She said you wouldn't mind."

"Much good it does if I do mind! Is he going to keep this up all winter?"

"Laurel's plum wore out. She's hardly slept since he's been taken sick. If Josie sets up with him, she falls asleep in the chair, and I'm no better. Pa and Laurel take turns, but she don't trust him either."

"All right! All right! Great guns! Such a fuss over dying."

Early the next morning, Castle came home smiling and complacent. "The funeral is tomorrow and Ed wants you to read the service."

"So Grampa is dead?"

"Would there be a funeral if he wasn't?"

"What did you do this time?"

"Same as before," she threw over her shoulder as she hung up her cloak.

"How much rum . . . hummm . . . a good bit judging from the bottle."

"Laurel had it over there. She give him some, too."

"How much did you give him last night?"

"Two . . . three jiggers. Put some wood in the stove while you're there. The fire's most out."

Jonathan put wood in the stove. "How much rum had Laurel given Grampa before you got there?"

"Two . . . three jiggers. What're you driving at? You a lawyer?"

"If I were, I might have to try you for murder."

"Murder! You're crazy! After all I done for Grampa . . ."

"Giving him more rum than his weak old heart could stand."

"You make me sick! Grampa *liked* rum. He died real happy, too. Suppose I did give him a little boost into heaven, what's the difference? He was going anyhow."

"Castle, you're incorrigible! That was more liquor than that old man had had in years. No wonder he died happy!"

"He'd been on the brink for months. I'm going in and take a good nap."

 2 0

T H E long, weary year of 1863 came to an end, but Knute Olson was still missing when the Fourth Iowa came home on a veterans' furlough in February of 1864.[1] Thaddeus and Jordan Pierce planned to visit in Turkey Grove for a week and Castle decided to hold a family reunion. The others could not be expected to entertain; Crawfords and Markers and Olsons were all in mourning and Laurel had enough on her hands. That evening when Jonathan went to the sitting room, he found the place looking as though a cyclone had struck it. White linen billowed over the bed and lace-edged ruffles draped the chairs.

"Castle, get this stuff out of the way so I can sit down."

"Don't touch it!" she shrieked.

"What is it? I didn't know there was that much lace and frumpery left in the county."

"That's *all* the lace and frumpery that's left. It's my very best white linen petticoat, the only good one I got left."

"But it's all ripped apart."

"I can't make a christening robe for Little Sid without ripping it apart, can I?"

"Christening robe?"

"Lord love me! Why are men so stupid? Harriet's been waiting till Seth come home to have Little Sid christened, and now Seth is home. We might as well have the christening at the reunion. Everybody will be here anyway. The Elder and Sophronia are coming, too."

"You're making a christening robe out of your petticoat?"

"What else would I make it out of? Can you buy anything better?"

Jonathan leaned back in his chair and studied his wife. "Why are you doing this? Why sacrifice your last good petticoat . . ."

"You make me tired. Little Sid is Abigail's first grandchild. Harriet wants him christened proper, 'specially seeing he's named for Sid. If he's going to be christened at my reunion, he's going to have a decent christening robe."

"Isn't Little Sid a rather husky youngster for a christening robe?"

"Yes, he is. He's near two. But Harriet couldn't help it if Seth was gone so long the baby is half growed before she could get him christened."

For the women, what to wear was no problem: they wore what they had. Castle dug down in her trunk and brought out the mull and mended it, and though the mends were plainly visible, she settled it about her hips with an exasperated jerk.

"First time in my life I ever wore a mended gown in public!"

"Ain't you got no other, Ma?" Jennifer asked sympathetically.

"Only the black, and don't seem fitting I should wear it when the others are in mourning and I'm not. If this war don't end soon, none of us will have a dud to our backs." She hitched the bodice in place. "Here, Jenny, button me up the back. I wonder what the fashion is now? I ain't seen a fashion plate. . . . Mind you keep clean. You're Little Sid's aunt and you got to look neat."

Jonathan had dressed in his broadcloth and ruffled shirt, but Castle tied his cravat because he never got it straight.

"Why can't a man dress himself?"

"Did you button yourself up the back, Miss Castle?"

She grunted and turned to the mirror to see if Jennifer had the buttons and buttonholes matched up right. Jonathan had buttoned that bodice a time or two. But Jennifer was clever with her fingers and made no such fuss as Jonathan had.

Abigail and the Garrisons were the first arrivals. Lew lifted Indiana from the wagon and set her on her feet, hoops and all. Abigail climbed down and taking Indiana's arm piloted her to the house where Castle waited at the door.

"So you got here, Indie! It's been so long, I can't remember when I seen you last. How's she been, Abigail? And you don't get around much more than Indie. Here, take the rocker."

"She ain't been too well," Abigail reported, easing Indiana into the chair.

"I keep Abigail that busy looking after me and the Station, she don't have time to go gadding around getting into mischief." Indiana groaned as she arranged herself. "Now, this is fine. I can see and be seen and talk till my tongue hangs out. Good thing it's my limbs that's afflicted. I'd hate to stop talking."

Lucinda and Samantha had followed their mother in, but now they and Jennifer stood looking at each other uncertainly, until Abigail turned to them in annoyance.

"What's this? You've seen each other before. Don't just stand there—go find something to do. Play, if you want, but keep clean." When the girls ducked out of the kitchen, she returned to the others. "I hope the Bateses get here early. Seems I never see Thaddy any more. But the Elder is so busy. Just about everybody that comes on the stage is either going to a funeral or coming from one. How can the war just go on and on?"

"Does seem there's no end to it. But let's not talk about it today. I don't want Berta thinking about Knute or Dowd worrying about Preston."

"That's right," Indiana nodded. "A christening should be happy."

On the whole, the day was happy. Once the big trestle table was set up in the sitting room and the guests had taken their places for dinner, Castle felt she was living an event over again. Yet there had been so many changes in so few years. At the children's table in the kitchen, Cressy and Jennifer presided, and Laurel and Josie Pettit waited table for the adults. Jordan Pierce was "family" now, yet Castle knew him so little he still seemed a stranger, a tall, rather handsome stranger who reminded her of Garland. Dowd Wright was not a "connection," but with Preston away he was alone, and it seemed somehow fitting to include him with the rest. Glancing about, Castle saw the mark of years on the faces of all her friends, and Martha Marker, in her scanty black calico, suddenly reminded her of Aunt Lucy. That was it! Aunt Lucy had known sorrow and grief and hardship, and she had carried it with her head high, just as high as Martha's. Evva, for all her gentle sweetness, was growing a little prim and school-teacherish since she had taken over Martha's job.

At the housewarming, Harriet had blushed when Castle teased her about the boys, and Thaddy had giggled at her sister's embarrassment. Now Harriet talked and ate with one eye on the bed where her son slept, and Thaddeus glanced again and again at the husband beside her. Luke Pettit, sixteen now, had taken his place with the men with quiet assurance, and his father looked his way often enough for Castle to know Ed was wondering how long the war would continue. Nils Olson, as tall as his father and almost as broad, was nineteen. Please God, no more of Berta's boys! Karl, at least, was still safe. This time he ate with Cade in the kitchen, sitting beside eight-year-old Lucinda, his one and only love.

Once the edge was off their appetites, everyone chattered.

"I'm thinking of buying a new shirt this year," Jonathan announced, and even Elder Bates laughed. "I'm serious. Now that Union troops are in control of the Missouri, wholesalers will be back in business."[2]

"What you figger to use for money?" Ed Pettit asked.

"Greenbacks! I've seen several since the first of the year."

"The sight of one would be real refreshing," Dowd nodded.

"You'll be seeing them before long, I'll warrant. Farms have been idle and we've had no transportation, but the demand is greater than ever. The East will be willing to pay the price to get what they need. With the boats running to St. Louis, we'll be able to sell anything we can raise. Believe me, I really do expect to have the price of a shirt before many moons."

"If you get a new shirt, I'm going to have a new gown!" Castle declared.

"You shall have it," Jonathan promised, bowing to his wife.

"Jonathan, Jonathan! You're starting a revolution! If Castle has a new gown, every woman in the township will want a new gown. Think what you're doing, man!" Solon protested.

"Jordan's already bought me goods for a new gown," Thaddeus told them proudly.

Sophronia sniffed. "Jordan paid a fortune for that silk. Does seem wicked to spend so much on vanity when folks is starving."

"No one should go hungry in the midst of plenty, Sophronia. You and the Elder should report needy families," Jonathan told her anxiously. Thaddeus threw him a grateful glance and he raised one eyebrow in acknowledgment.

Later the guests gathered in the parlor, Harriet with Little Sid in her arms and Seth beside her. The Elder, holding Castle's pewter bowl with water from the well, read the baptismal service in his best ministerial manner. But Little Sid robbed the occasion of its proper dignity by jabbering during the reading then kicking and screaming when the Elder attempted to place a wet and dripping hand on the child's semibald head.

When the guests had gone, Castle turned to her husband. "Well, I'd better get my trunk packed before anything else happens."

"Your trunk . . . packed?"

"You said the boats are running, so there's no reason I can't go home."

"The packets are running as far as St. Louis, but at the moment, there's fighting on the Ohio. It was in last week's paper. I read it to you. So far as we know, they're still at it."

Castle stood in the middle of the room and confronted her husband angrily. "First it's bushwhackers in Missouri, now it's gunboats on the Ohio! You just don't want me to go home!"

Jonathan pulled off his white shirt and slipped into a work shirt. "I don't want you to start, unless I'm sure you can get there, Castle."

"Jennifer! Jennifer, come unbutton me. . . . If there's fighting on the Ohio, I'll take a train from St. Louis."

Jonathan folded his broadcloth pants and laid them carefully in his chest, then turned to his wife. "For God's sake, woman, be reasonable! Why this unseemly haste? You're in no danger here, your family's in no danger in Pittsburgh, and if they were, what could you do about it if you were there? Wait! Wait! You've waited this long, wait until you can make the trip in comfort—and safety. Castle, I give you my word of honor, if you'll wait till the fighting is over, I'll take you all the way home and make sure you get there in one piece."

Castle paused, half out of her bodice. "That a promise? You mean it?"

"Yes, yes! That's a promise!"

In April, the Fourth Iowa returned to duty with Sherman. Jonathan's atlas was worn and shabby, the maps defaced by lines following the marches of the Iowa men: from Iowa to Missouri, to Arkansas, to Memphis, to Vicksburg. The Twenty-Third had gone down the Mississippi to fight in Louisiana, then to Texas, and back to Louisiana. The Fourth had marched the length of Tennessee, from Memphis to Chattanooga, then down into Georgia, fighting along the railroad toward Atlanta.[3] At Dallas, Jordan Pierce was hit in the foot by shrapnel. That had been in May and now it was June, summer again and hot, and still no one knew how seriously he had been injured. Supper over, Castle and Jonathan were sitting on the porch waiting for the house to cool enough for them to be able to sleep. Jennifer sat on the steps wriggling her toes in the dust of the path. The wind had gone down with the sun and no breath of air stirred the trees where katydids shrilled in a continuous chorus.

"Reckon he'll be crippled?" Castle mused.

"I don't know. I'm thankful he wasn't killed." He knocked the ashes from his pipe into his hand and scattered them beyond the edge of the porch. "Keep the bugs off your flowers," he told her as she watched with a censorious eye lest he drop ashes on her porch. "I wouldn't want Thaddy widowed. She's taken enough punishment. If Jordan is crippled, his fighting days are over, and a man can be a lawyer with one leg. Not that I want him crippled—heaven forbid! But it would be a relief to have one of them out of the war."

Jonathan shaved fresh tobacco and Castle gazed off across the prairie toward the west. The sun was gone, but there was still a rosy glow in the sky, and up in the deepening blue of the evening firmament, a star was shining.

"It's gone on so long, I can't remember what it was like when there wasn't a war. Can't anybody stop it?" Jonathan shook his head but made no answer as he puffed to get his pipe going. "I feel real sorry for Dowd Wright, living all alone like that. He was at Markers' the other day, and Evva says he looks real poorly. Next time you see him, tell him to come to dinner. He ain't got a soul but Preston . . ."

"Martha had no one but Tolly."

"She's got Evva. Besides, a woman can stand more than a man."

Jonathan studied his wife thoughtfully. "You may be right. Sometimes you show insight remarkable for a person of your ignorance. Or are they related: ignorance and insight. Perhaps a person who relies too strongly on reason loses contact with the primal instincts."

"How dare you sit there and call me ignorant! If I wasn't so plagued tired, I'd take you apart for that. I know more about the war than any woman around here."

"She does, Pa," Jennifer piped up. "Evva teaches school, but her and Aunt Martha don't know the first thing about what's going on."

Jonathan grinned and his eyes twinkled. He had always relished his wife's spunk, and the fact that he could still draw fire was proof the steel had not lost its temper. Too, he liked Jennifer's defense of her Ma. From a man's eye view, the two of them seemed to be getting along much better lately.

Then out of the dusk came the pound of hooves and Elder Bates brought his lathered horse to a halt at the gate. "It's Thaddeus!" he shouted and Jonathan started around the house calling over his shoulder, "Bring your horse to the barn. Rub him down while I harness the team."

Castle dashed into the sitting room and scurried around getting her things together, flinging instructions at Jennifer as she went. "Get your nightdress and a clean pinafore, and go over and stay with Evva and Aunt Martha. It ain't good dark yet, but light the lantern and take it so you won't stub your toe. Call when you get to the ford and Evva'll come meet you. Thaddy's sick, but it ain't anything to get excited about. Your Pa'll let Evva know tomorrow." As Jennifer closed the kitchen door behind her, Castle called, "Take your bonnet!" But Jennifer didn't come back.

Under other circumstances, Castle would have enjoyed the ride, with only the sound of the wheels and the rhythmic clop-clop of the horses' hooves to break the silence. But again and again the Elder urged Jonathan to go faster, and each time Jonathan assured the distraught man they were making good time. Not until she saw Thaddy did Castle understand the Elder's urgency. Sophronia stood beside the bed wringing her hands and crying. Castle shoved her out the door and closed it firmly behind her. It was after midnight before Thaddeus lay quiet and spent, her eyes closed.

"Ma says it's the judgment of God," she whispered.

In sudden anger, Castle banged her fist on the small table. Startled by the thump, Thaddeus opened her eyes.

"Jesus Christ have mercy on us! The things folks say about God! Does that old hatch-hen think He's got nothing better to do than chase around making trouble for folks? Ain't the good Lord got enough on His hands as it is? She ought to be burned as a witch!" Castle straightened and brushed a hand across her forehead. "Thaddy, if a man was as stinking mean as folks try to make out God is, he'd be run out of town on a rail. I ain't as pious as Sophronia, but I got a better opinion of God than she has. I figger if He wasn't better than me, He wouldn't be God very long. You ask me, I'd say He's just as sorry about this as I am. Judgment, my foot! You just ain't got your growth yet. Wait a few years and you'll have the strappingest young'uns in the county."

Thaddeus smiled and fell asleep. Castle sat in a rocker by the bed, sleeping when Thaddy slept, yet each time the girl roused, Castle was as wide awake as though she had not been snoring with her mouth open the moment before. Not until morning did she permit Sophronia in the room, and she fixed the good sister with an implacable eye which kept her on her good behavior.

"I'm all right, Ma," Thaddeus told her. "Just weak and sore."

"A cup of tea would do her good," Castle remarked.

Sophronia drew herself up haughtily. "We got no tea. It's wicked to indulge . . ."

"Never mind the sermon! The girl is sick and a cup of tea would be good for her, and war or no war, she's going to have it. Jonathan, Jonathan! Hustle down to Freeman's and get some tea. And I don't care what it costs. Shake yourself, now, I'm in no waiting mood."

Jonathan stuck his head in the door, nodded agreement with his wife's orders, winked at Thaddeus, and was gone.

"Ain't he the nicest man?" Thaddy smiled.

Castle grunted noncommittally and swept out to the kitchen to put the kettle on. Later, when Thaddeus had had tea and toast, Castle went back to Sophronia's bleak kitchen and poured a cup for herself while she munched on cold cornbread left from the Elder's breakfast. She hoped Jonathan had got enough to eat. Sophronia set a rather thin table. She had dreamed of living at Greenbrier, and here she sat in Sophronia Bates's kitchen in faded calico, eating cold corn pone. . . . She had dreamed of Greenbrier, and this was where she had ended up . . .

Then came another thought: how old were Garland's sons? Ten years she and Jonathan had been married, eleven years before that . . . Why, one would be about twenty and the other near eighteen, both old enough to be in the army. Devil take the war and whoever started it! Why couldn't somebody put a stop to it? She drained her cup and pushed it aside. Suddenly, overwhelmingly, she wanted to go home to her own white house on Turkey Creek, sit on her own porch in the twilight and watch the stars come out, and know there was not a single, solitary Bates within miles of her. Thaddeus was in no danger. All she needed was rest. That, at least, Sophronia should be capable of handling. She was going right back home with Jonathan.

Whenever Castle received a letter, Jonathan read it to her, but only after she had opened it herself. That, he insisted, was her right and privilege, and though she could not read, she could recognize her own name and identify any familiar handwriting. When, in August, he brought her a letter, she glanced at it, stuffed it behind the kitchen clock, and went on dishing up the supper.

"Marybelle. It'll keep. I wish I'd hear from Anne Middleton. It's been so long I'm beginning to wonder. 'Spose anything could have happened to her?''

"Probably busy. But Marybelle's letter is postmarked Pittsburgh.''

"She must of gone home for a visit. Come on Jennifer. Get the coffee, and after supper your Pa can read the letter here at the table while you do dishes.''

"I wish Aunt Marybelle would bring Susan and Rebecca for a visit,'' Jennifer remarked as she passed the potatoes to her Pa so he could help himself first.

"Heaven forbid! Those girls are a pair of fiends.''

"You're remembering them as they were ten or eleven years ago. They've probably changed.''

"Good grief! That's so. Why, they're most growed up! You've got me anxious to find out what Marybelle has to say.''

Jennifer made slow work of the dishes, for she kept stopping to listen to the letter. When General Early raided Maryland in July, Drew Coleman, who was working for the Quartermaster Corps, had gone out to General Lew Wallace with supplies. Suspecting Early would attack Washington, Wallace had attempted to delay him, and there had been some fierce fighting. [4] Drew had not returned. She had waited and waited, and after Early had moved on, she had appealed to General Wallace, who had done what he could to try to locate Drew. He had not been found among the dead or wounded, but he might have been taken prisoner.

Marybelle knew nothing whatever of her husband's business—though he had been doing little enough of late—and she had found she was not capable of giving the necessary orders or making essential decisions. She had done the best she could for as long as she could, then had sold out for what she could get and had gone home to Pittsburgh with the two girls. She had found everything all right at Homeplace, though Miss Sarah seemed frail, and the Major limped badly and complained of his leg. She felt they needed her and hoped when Drew came back—if he did—that he would consent to stay and help the Major at the glasshouse. The glasshouse wasn't doing much business, either, though the Major was trying to keep the place going in the hope of better times once the war ended.

"There now! I should have gone home. I told you . . ."

"What could you do if you were there?" Jonathan folded the letter and gave it to Castle. "Now Marybelle is there, she'll do what she can. But she's in a difficult position. I suppose Drew could have been taken prisoner, though that isn't exactly an enviable fate."

"He might as well be dead. Those Rebels . . ."

"The prisoners don't all die, Ma. Some of them stay alive and some even get exchanged. Pa read it in the paper, remember?"

Marybelle's letter received confirmation from the Major, who wrote a few weeks later. He was both worried about Drew Coleman and concerned about his business. There was almost no market now for the fine cut and engraved glass in which he had always taken so much pride. And with Captain Tim carrying government troops and cargo, the less expensive glass had the warehouses bulging at the seams for lack of transportation. But glassblowers and cutters, the Talbot kind, were scarce and hard to find, and they were the company's greatest asset. The older men, craftsmen whose experience made them irreplaceable, he must keep somehow. The younger men who had not already enlisted, he had fired and told them where their duty lay. Then the Major repeated the story of Marybelle's troubles and expressed his pleasure at having her and the girls at home.

In the fall, the long-awaited letter from Anne Middleton arrived, and among the various items of news and gossip, she remarked that Garland Delacroix had sold some of his canal boats and was so short handed he was forced to captain one of them himself. Later, when she thought about it, Castle couldn't stop laughing. It had taken a war to force Garland to do a little work!

Sherman and the Fourth Iowa pushed closer and closer to Atlanta, and in September word came of its surrender. Soon after Sherman started his march to the sea, Thaddeus had had a letter from Jordan warning her she might not hear from him for a while. Too lame for full duty, Captain Pierce had been placed in charge of foraging parties. Provisioning the troops from barns and corncribs of hostile farmers was not the safest job in the world, but it seemed less dangerous than fighting, and Jordan's family and friends relaxed a little. However, when news of the surrender of Savannah came a few days after Christmas, it created hardly a ripple, for by that time the neighborhood had other things to think about.

When Jonathan rode over to invite Dowd Wright to Christmas dinner, he found him so ill that for days he had had neither fire nor food.

"I'll take you and your stock to my place," Jonathan told him. "Castle will fix you up."

"I don't want to trouble you."

"Nonsense! Castle likes nothing better than playing doctor."

Jonathan took quilts from Dowd's bed and made a pallet in the wagon, then got Dowd into it and covered him warmly. Before leaving, he closed the cabin securely, never guessing how long it would remain closed. Castle's Christmas dinner was called off; only Evva came that day, though she came not to dine but to help care for Dowd. She stayed three weeks. helping with the housework and taking turns with Castle sitting up nights with their patient. Then one cold grey dawn, rousing from a doze, Castle found Dowd dead. She hurried to the kitchen where Jonathan was sleeping to be near in case of need. She shook him and he sat up and pushed his hair out of his eyes, only half awake.

"He's dead, Jonathan. Come on, get up. Dowd's dead."

"Dead?" He stared at her blankly, uncomprehending. "Dead, you say? You mean Dowd. Good God!" He got up, went in, and looked down at his friend. Castle had folded his hands and put pennies on his eyelids. "Make a pot of coffee, Castle, but don't call Evva yet. There's nothing she can do. Let her sleep."

Castle went back to the kitchen and Jonathan pulled the sheet over Dowd's face and sat down by the fire. It had burned low, and leaning forward he threw on lightwood. Dowd could not have been much older than he, but at the moment he felt old and tired himself. He ran his fingers through his hair. Castle had done her best, but it had not been enough. Even she met defeat now and then. He would have to write to Preston. A letter would reach him eventually. His father's death would be a blow. He threw on heavier wood and went to the kitchen. The coffee smelled good. Castle filled a cup and set it before him and he sipped with satisfaction.

"He's got to be buried decent," Castle reminded him.

"Yes. I'll get word to the neighbors."

"Not many can come. Harriet's expecting any minute. She can't come and Tabitha won't dare leave her. I don't think Berta should come."

"No reason she should. The men will come, and Evva and Martha and the Pettits. The roads are bad. I won't ask Elder Bates to make the trip."

"Who you going to get to help with the digging? The ground will be hard . . ."

"Yes. Ed and Luke are nearest. We'll lay him over in the northeast corner."

"Off by himself?"

"He's used to being alone. Eventually there'll be other graves. We have to allow for keeping families together."

"Burying folks before they're dead! I'm going to call Evva and Jennifer and make breakfast. Evva and I can wash Dowd and lay him out. What about the funeral? You'll make the coffin?"

Jonathan nodded. "I have some good boards. Might as well have the funeral tomorrow. There's no one to wait for and the roads won't get any better. We can have the service here, then only the men will have to go to the burying ground."

"Then I got to clean house."

That afternoon the coffin was placed in the parlor and Dowd laid in it. Next day the neighbors came for the service. To Castle, it seemed a shame Dowd should be buried without kith or kin, and his only son not even knowing he was dead. A terrible thing to die alone with no one of your own blood. Should she die in Ioway, there would be no one of her own. She wouldn't die in Ioway. Soon as the war was over, she'd go home. When her time came, she'd die in her own home and be buried with her own family. Jonathan needn't save a place for her in the Turkey Grove burying ground!

The following day it turned bitterly cold and snow fell steadily. The storm had barely blown itself out when Solon came for Castle. Her satchel was ready and she put on her cloak and climbed in the wagon, instructing Jennifer about the housework and cooking as she tucked her skirts about her on the wagon seat.

"You ought to be big enough to look after your Pa till I get back tomorrow. Now, go on back inside before you get your feet wet and catch cold. Don't forget to keep the fires going while your Pa is out. He won't want to build a fresh one . . ."

Back the next day, she told Jonathan, "No trouble at all." Then to Jennifer, "Harriet's got the nicest new baby boy you ever set eyes on. Soon's the roads are fit, we'll go over and you can see your new nephew. Did you dust? And make the beds up proper? What did you cook for your Pa?"

Jonathan grinned. Time was when Castle would neither have known nor cared about such housewifely matters. "Jennifer isn't a bad cook, and she's as good a housekeeper as you are. Wonder who taught her so much?"

Castle sniffed. "One guess."

T H E first Sunday of April, Ed Pettit brought Abigail over, and Castle tried to hide her astonishment that they had come together and without the children. She kissed Abigail and said she would call Jennifer.

"Don't call Jenny yet," Ed told her. "We want to talk to you and Jonathan." He straddled a chair and sat with his arms folded on the back, grinning at Castle while he flushed brick red under his permanent tan. "I asked Abigail to marry me, but she says she can't. What's the legal situation, Jonathan? Is Abigail married or widowed?"

Castle plopped in the rocking chair and stared at Abigail, who in turn rocked nervously, fussing with her hair in embarrassment.

Smiling broadly, Jonathan explained. "Abigail is a married woman until she has proof of her husband's death. Failing material evidence, the fact must be established by law."

Ed unfolded one arm and scratched his head. "Mind translating?"

"When a person's whereabouts have been unknown for a period of seven years, if he cannot be located after diligent search, he can be declared legally dead."

"Eli's been gone longer'n that, ain't he?"

"Yes, but Abigail heard from him in the spring of 1859. He can't be declared dead for another year. I didn't tell Abigail, but I tried to trace him when he failed to return. I have letters in proof that his whereabouts have not been known since he was in Denver." Then to Abigail, "Did you keep his last letter?"

"Yes, I did."

"Good. It will corroborate our assumption of foul play. I was convinced Eli was in danger when I saw that letter."

"Why didn't you say so?" Abigail asked in amazement.

"No proof. But time has proved I was right. It'll work out."

"Then Abigail can marry again?"

"Certainly."

"Think she'd ought to?"

"That would depend on whom she married," Jonathan laughed.

The others joined in, but Castle burst out impetuously, "Of course she ought to! And she'll have to be married here; Indie couldn't manage a wedding, and neither could Laurel. But what's Indie going to do for help without Abigail?"

"Lew's talking of selling out. Indie ain't getting any better or any younger. Only Lew don't like to admit he ain't either."

"Not an easy admission," Jonathan agreed with a wry face. "I'm thinking of going to China where my grey hairs will be appreciated."

That same Sunday, Richmond was evacuated,[1] and a week later General Lee surrendered. The news reached Turkey Grove on the Tuesday stage, and Lew Garrison did a Paul Revere of his own. Castle was churning in the cellar when she heard him shouting and came up the steps at a run, her skirts almost to her knees, her hoops tilted sideways.

"What is it? Is Indie took bad?" she called, hurrying to the gate.

"Lee surrendered!"

"Lee surrendered?" she repeated blankly. *"Lee surrendered!"*

"He sure did! Sunday. Grant caught him in a trap."

"You mean *we* won? The war's over?"

"Won't be long, Castle. Lee's a real fine general, but if licking him will help end the war, then I'm glad he's licked. Been enough killing—on both sides."

Castle had no answer. There had been enough killing. If the war ended, she could go home. Jonathan had promised to take her. When he came home from town Saturday night, he told her President Lincoln had been shot.

"So he's dead," she said slowly, lifting the stove lid and setting the pot of potatoes over the fire. "I never had any use for him. If he hadn't been elected, there might not of been a war. But it ain't right to just up and shoot him in the back like that. Don't seem right the boys should get killed, either. Hennie was such a nice boy, and Tolly worked so hard. Sid, and Knute . . . none of 'em ever done any harm . . ."

Jonathan spent Sunday with newspapers edged in black. But the fighting was not over. Mobile had been attacked by land and sea, and the Twenty-Third had been part of the brigade that reduced the Spanish fort.

Jonathan pushed the papers aside and filled his pipe. Telegraph lines would be jammed, it would take time for casualty lists to come through. Since his father's death, there was no one to watch for Preston's name. On Monday the casualty lists were posted at Grove City, and to Jonathan's relief, Preston's name did not appear.

While the President's body lay in state at the capital, fighting continued in Georgia, but before the funeral train reached Springfield, Johnston had surrendered to Sherman. Then Montgomery, Macon, and Columbus were captured and the scattered remnants of the Confederacy surrendered—now here, now there—and at last General Kirby Smith surrendered to General Canby in Texas and the war was over.[3] On the night Jonathan came home with that news, he caught his wife by the shoulders, swung her around, and kissed her soundly as she stood by the stove with a spoon in her hand.

"It's over, Miss Castle! No more fighting!" He whirled her in a little jig. "Now the boys can come home!"

"When will they get home, Pa?" Jennifer asked as Jonathan started to wash for supper. "Seth ain't seen the new baby yet." She sliced the bread and put it on the table and when her parents had seated themselves she poured the coffee before taking her place.

"Yes, Seth has a new son. But the men won't be mustered out for a while yet. They're scattered all over the country. It'll take time to get them rounded up and accounted for."

"Anyway, now the fighting is over, you can take me home."

Jonathan studied her for a moment, then shook his head. "Castle, Castle! I wish to God I could take you home tomorrow and have done with it! You don't *think!* There are thousands and thousands of men in the various armies, spread over thousands of miles of country—and every one of them in a bigger hurry to get home than you are. And the government equally anxious to get them home—and off the payroll. The government will take over whole cars, whole trains, whole steamboats, so they can send the men back where they came from as fast as possible. You wouldn't be able to get passage for love nor money. If you did, you'd be jam-packed in with a bunch of strange men."

"I knew it, I knew it! You *promised.* Now you're making excuses."

"I fully expect to keep my promise, but don't demand the impossible. Would you want to sleep on the deck of a steamboat with hundreds of soldiers? Or in a railroad car with you the only woman? Not all soldiers are gentlemen, believe me, Castle. You wouldn't enjoy their company. Be patient, my dear. I want you to go home and visit your family, but I want you to enjoy the trip in comfort. I want it to be pleasant, something to remember, to look back on."

Castle searched her husband's face. Was he putting her off, or did he really mean what he said? "All right. I'll take your word this time. But so help me Hannah, when the men have come home and things have settled down, I'm going home—and you aren't going to stop me!"

In June, Jonathan had a letter from Preston Wright. He read it sitting on the back stoop, sat smoking for a time, then rose and went into the house.

"Who you going to write to?" Castle asked when he got out paper and sharpened a quill.

"Preston. I think we should invite him to come here for a few days when he gets home. It would be hard for him to go directly to that empty cabin."

"Mercy yes! Then I'll have a young man coming home from the war, too. Tabitha and Sophronia needn't think they're the only ones. I'll clean the house . . ."

"Don't start tonight. He's still in Texas."

"And I'll go over and clean the cabin and set things to rights."

Jonathan nodded. "Bound to be thick with dust."

"You can go over with me and help clean," Castle told Jennifer "Your Pa'll have to take us over with the scrub pails and such."

"Will Mr. Wright teach school again when he gets home, Pa?"

"I don't like taking the position from Evva. She needs the job."

Castle looked up from her mending, her brows drawn together in concentration. "Didn't Elder Bates say they was looking for another teacher at Grove City?"

Jonathan laid down the quill and took his pipe from his mouth. "You're right! Exactly the place for Preston. They want a teacher for the upper grades, to prepare them for Academy. Miss Castle, I sometimes think you have more sense than I have."

"Shouldn't strain you none to figger that out."

The Fourth was mustered out at Davenport,[4] and Solon Crawford met the stage at Des Moines. Castle would have given her eye teeth to be at Crawfords' when Seth and Jordan got home, but Jonathan was adamant.

"This is a family affair. Even Abigail will stay at the Station until she's wanted. None of us are any kin to Seth or Jordan. You turn will come when Preston gets here." Jonathan went through the house to the porch.

Castle went out, wiping her hands on her apron along the way. "You going to meet Preston in Des Moines?"

"Preston is in the West. I think he'll probably come by way of Council Bluffs. And he may prefer to come by stage."

"Well, he ain't a-going to. You can go to Council Bluffs and meet him." Castle plopped in a chair and wiped her face with the corner of her apron. It had been a hot day.

"Why?" Jonathan asked, between puffs on his pipe.

" 'Cause if he comes on the stage, he'll get off at the Station and Abigail and Indie will see him before I do!"

Jonathan shrugged. "We're no more to him than they are."

"We are so! His Pa died at our house, didn't he? The others ain't written to him, or invited him to come to visit, and they didn't go over and clean his cabin for him, either."

"Let's not kill him with kindness, Castle," Jonathan knocked out his pipe. "However, I want a horse-drawn drill, and I can make the trip to Council Bluffs for less than the cost of having it freighted to Grove City. If he does come by way of Council Bluffs and I have business there, he shouldn't feel embarrassed at riding back with me."

"Another of your contraptions! You always have money for what *you* want."

"I'm no longer young, Castle, and I have no help on the farm." Jonathan rose and went toward the barn; his wife watched him in silence.

So in August, Jonathan went to Council Bluffs. The roads were graded now and he hoped to be back in about ten days. Castle had made up her mind Preston should not be able to say his father had been a better housekeeper than she, so everything was scrubbed until it hurt. Among other things, Jennifer was sent to make up the bed in the loft room, and Castle hoped Preston wouldn't remember Hennie had slept there.

It was hot the afternoon Preston arrived with Jonathan and the drill. Castle went to the gate and he leaped down and took her hand.

"You've no idea how good it is to be coming home," he told her. "And it's most kind of you to put me up, Mrs. Gayle."

"We're proud to have you, Preston. My, you look handsome in your uniform!"

He smiled. "I bought other clothes in Council Bluffs, but Mr. Gayle thought you'd like to see me in uniform. For my part, I'm heartily tired of it."

"You do look tired, and not just tired of the uniform. You had a long trip. Come in and have a bite to eat."

"Thank you, but I'll help Mr. Gayle first."

Sensing that their guest was not yet ready to sit down and gossip with Castle, Jonathan made no protest, and Preston swung back up and rode to the barn. Castle stood for a moment looking after them. Preston was thin. No, it was more than that. He had been slender as a lad; now he was a man, lean and hard with a new manner and bearing. Coming home, under the circumstances, would not be easy for him; best let him have a little time to himself. She turned back and went into the kitchen.

They were getting the supper when the men came in. Jennifer, mashing potatoes, looked up shyly but did not speak, and Preston stopped in the doorway and stared.

"You're . . . you're Jennifer! I wouldn't have known you. Have I been gone *that* long?" Laughing, he crossed the kitchen, hand out.

Jennifer put down the potato ponner, wiped her hands on her apron, and shook hands gravely. "I wouldn't have known you, either."

"Had you forgotten me?"

"No, but you look different."

Preston grinned. "It's the uniform. I used to wear a white shirt. Remember?"

Jennifer giggled and ducked her head. "I didn't know any better."

Jonathan had been nearly two weeks without mail, so the following morning he and Preston went to Grove City. All day Castle and Jennifer cooked and baked, yet at supper that evening, though Preston ate heartily, he scarcely seemed to notice the food and failed to compliment her on her cooking as Hennie had always done. Instead, he and Jonathan talked of men they had met in town, of men who had come home from the war, and those who had not. When they finished, Jonathan stood up, replaced his chair, and began fumbling in his pockets.

"A letter from Marybelle." He laid it on the table and her fork clattered on her plate. The envelope was edged in black.

"Why didn't you tell me?"

"If you've finished, come into the sitting room. Jennifer, the dishes."

"But Pa!"

"Jennifer."

"Yes, sir." Disappointed, she rose and began clearing the table.

"I'll dry for you," Preston offered. "I used to dry for Pa, so I'm an experienced hand, though a bit out of practice." Then more seriously, "It is your Ma's letter, you know. They'll tell you about it afterward."

"I know. And it isn't good news."

The dishes were done and the kitchen swept and in order by the time Jonathan came to the door and invited them into the sitting room. Castle was in the rocker, her eyes red, sniffling into her handkerchief, the heavy knot of hair slightly askew.

"Get the palm leaf and fan your Ma, Jenny. She's had a blow and this heat is no help. Come in, Preston. The news is bad but not private. Castle's grandfather and great-uncle are both dead. Captain Timothy Talbot had several steamboats, and he and Major Hunter Talbot were taking a new one down to Louisville on a trial run. The boilers blew up and they were killed."

"How awful! I'm terribly sorry, Mrs. Gayle."

"Fortunately there's good news, too. Castle's sister, Marybelle, has heard from her husband. He was captured just outside Baltimore, but he's alive and he'll get to Pittsburgh as soon as he can."

Castle blew her nose. "Major Hunter and Captain Tim . . ."

"My dear, they died as they lived: proudly, courageously, and with their best boots on. They would have wanted it that way."

"I'm going into mourning tomorrow, and I'll mourn for a whole year."

Later, Castle was still sniffling when Jonathan got into bed beside her. In spite of the heat, he slipped his arm around her and drew her head to his shoulder. "Do you want me to take you home, Miss Castle?"

She turned and pressed her face against his neck. "No, Jonathan, no. Not now. I couldn't stand it. I couldn't face Homeplace without Major Hunter and Captain Tim."

With his wife in his arms, Jonathan barely breathed lest he break the spell. Grieved though he was by the deaths of men he had much admired and respected, he was deeply grateful his wife did not want to go home. Too, there was one bit of news in Marybelle's letter that he had not passed on to his wife. He had told her privately that Garland Delacroix's elder son had been killed in the fighting around Richmond and that the other boy had married in Texas and was staying there. But he had not told her that Griselda was dead, probably of a fever.

In the morning Castle built a fire under the big pot in the yard that Jonathan used for butchering, and into it, with ample black dye, went every gown she owned except the one she had on. She would mourn Major Hunter and Captain Tim, and while she was about it, she might as well mourn Garland's son, too. However, that was something she did not tell her husband.

In November Jonathan had a letter from Drew Coleman. After his unpleasant experience as a Confederate prisoner, he had reached Pittsburgh in October. Since then, he had been trying to straighten out the affairs of Major Hunter and Captain Tim and was finding it a considerable undertaking. Both had left wills, and other than bequests to servants and provision for Miss Sarah, everything went to Castle and Marybelle, "share and share alike," with Jonathan and Drew as executors. He hoped Jonathan would be able to come to Pittsburgh and go over the books and accounts with him. If not, he would do the best he could. The glasshouse had been operating at a loss for some time, and the Major had liquidated his other holdings to keep it going. Apparently, most of Captain Tim's profits on his government contracts had also gone into the glasshouse. Probably both men had felt there was a better future in glass than steamboats since the railroads were already cutting heavily into the riverboat trade.

Drew had been trying to learn as much as possible about the glass business as he seemed to be stuck with it. He had talked to other glasshouse owners in the vicinity and with the older men at the Talbot factory and had come to the conclusion that it would be advisable to put out a line of cheaper pressed glass, using the new lime formula.[5] They should, of course, continue the lead crystal on which the firm's reputation had been built, but a piece of the lower priced market might help them to get back on a paying basis. He would appreciate any advice and would await Jonathan's reply. Jonathan's reply was brief: do the best he could and use his own judgement. If Drew did the work of managing, he, Jonathan, should share the costs. And he suggested Drew pay himself a reasonable salary.

Jonathan had still not told his wife of Griselda's death. The longer he postponed the telling, the more difficult—and unnecessary—it seemed. What good would it do to tell her? What harm in not telling her? If he could be sure Garland no longer mattered to her. . . . But if she still clung to her girlish illusions, what would she do if she knew he was now a widower? She had declined his offer to take her home; but if he told her about Griselda, would she still stay in Iowa? Or would she fight tooth and nail to go home—to Garland? To have allowed her to go home to her family during the war would have been one thing. To permit her to go now for the sole purpose of making a fool of herself over a man who had never loved her was something else again. It was too chancey, telling her. He could not bring himself to take the gamble. He told himself he was a coward, then shrugged and answered himself, "All right. So I'm a coward."

L E W and Indiana Garrison had definitely decided to sell the Station, and Solon Crawford was elected to replace Lew on the Board of Trustees. Though they were aware of Evva's limited education, she did seem to do a fair job of teaching the children, and certainly she and Martha would not be able to get along without her salary, small as it was. Jonathan had passed the schoolhouse on the way home from the grist mill, and he was thinking of Evva when Jennifer came to open the gate for him. He carried the flour and meal in and stacked it in the seed room, then turned to Jennifer.

"What sort of teacher is Evva? Are you learning anything at school? I want the truth, Jenny. Never mind Evva is your sister."

"Yes, Pa, Evva is a good teacher. She studies harder than any of us. She says teaching us gives her a chance to get an education, too. Want me to show you my books and papers? Evva says I'll be ready for the Academy in a couple more years."

"All right, child. I just wanted to know."

"Funny you asking about Evva," Castle remarked. "She walked home with Jenny this afternoon and left just a little while ago. She says Josie told her that when school lets out in Grove City, Preston is going back to medical college again, and that him and Laurel have an 'understanding.' "

"And what might that be, pray?" Jonathan took the lid off the cookie jar and brought out a handful. He gave Jennifer one and they both munched.

"Sort of like an engagement, only no announcement or anything."

"That's fine, though I can't see them marrying anytime soon."

"If Laurel gets married, Josie will have to quit school and stay home and keep house," Jennifer protested, turning her head from side to side so her braids swung to and fro across her back.

"Stop that, Jenny. You make me dizzy. They got to wait till your Ma and Uncle Ed get married, so don't worry about Josie. How much longer will it be, Jonathan?"

"Judge Duncan will take care of it this summer. You can't hurry the law."

That summer, Thaddeus was expecting again, and several times Castle and Jennifer went to town with Jonathan to make sure all was well. This time Castle was taking no chances. She'd put the girl to bed and keep her there if she had to; Thaddy was going to have this baby or she'd know the reason why. With school out, Evva went to Grove City and stayed with Thaddeus the last few weeks, and Castle went in a few days before she was needed. Thaddy had no trouble at all. When she came home, Castle was bursting to tell the news, so Jonathan obligingly drove her over to the Station after supper. The children were sent out to play in the dusk, while the grown-ups gathered around Indiana's bed.

"Nicest baby you ever seen, Abigail. Great big nine-pound boy. And

Jordan was that proud he went right out and bought a house! Sophronia was so mad, she ain't spoke to him since. But I'd hate to see Thaddy try to bring up a baby in the same house with Sophronia Bates.''

"Thaddy ain't had it easy," Abigail admitted. "But the Bateses been awful good to her.''

"Sure they been good to her," Indiana snorted. "But who could live with them? I'd have taken to drink long ago.''

Jonathan cleared his throat and smiled broadly at the ladies.

"Now that my wife has given her news, I have an announcement to make. Abigail, you have been declared a widow under the law. You and Ed can marry whenever you care to.''

The following Saturday Jennifer waited for her Pa at the gate and rode down to the barn with him to help put up the horses. When they came to the house, both were loaded with bundles.

"Now what?'' Castle demanded when they came in. The way Jonathan was grinning made her highly suspicious. "You're up to something.''

"Come to the sitting room. Some of these are for you.'' When the bundles were dumped on the bed, Castle began pawing them open. "I was in the store when Jesse was ordering stock the first of the month, so I asked him to get a few things for me. Only the best, and never mind the price. I wouldn't want your expert workmanship wasted on inferior materials. Incidentally, would you like to have one of the new sewing machines?''

"A sewing machine?''

"Yes, a sewing machine. You've heard of them. Do more work in less time. I could get one for you if you'd use it.''

"Of course I'd use it! Think I like to sit and prick my fingers? When can you get it?''

"I can order it next time I go to town. Don't know how long it will take to get here. Go ahead with your packages.''

There were six calicos and a silk, each prettier than the other. Castle exclaimed over them in delight, then turned abruptly in mingled anger and disappointment. "I'm in mourning and you know it!''

"Not any more, you aren't. The year is almost up, and you don't want to mourn at Abigail's wedding, do you?''

"I hadn't thought of that. I couldn't give her a wedding at all if I was still in mourning. Wouldn't be fitting. Folks in mourning don't entertain.''

"Pa got goods for me, too,'' Jennifer announced.

"Jennifer's skirts are up to her knees, and her cuffs are up to her elbows. You'll want her respectable for the wedding.''

"That's right. She ain't got a thing fit to wear. Jenny, you'll have to help, or I'll never get gowns done for both of us in time.''

Abigail and Ed were married in August, with all the family and family connections gathered in the Gayle parlor. But Lew and Indiana Garrison shared the honors of the day, for this was their farewell to Turkey Grove. They had sold the Station to Sam Seaman and were going to Council Bluffs to live with their daughter, their pioneer days at an end. Pioneer days were at an end for all of Turkey Grove. Only Indians inhabited the township when

Lew had built his first cabin. Now, the Indians were gone; most of the township was under fence; and roads replaced the trails. Iowa was no longer a wilderness, and settlers had become prosperous farmers.

It had been a long, hot day. Jennifer, who had done more than her share of the work so her Ma could have time for her guests, went to bed as soon as the dishes were finished, and Castle joined her husband on the porch. For a time they sat in the silence that graces long years of intimacy. Castle was tired, but it had been a good day. Everything had gone off just right. Now Abigail's problems were solved, and so were Ed's. Josie could stay in school, Laurel and Preston could be married. Then a new thought came and she wondered it had not occurred to her before.

"Now Abigail is married and has a home, you reckon she'll want Jennifer?"

"Possibly."

"If she does, will you let Jenny go?"

"I'd have no choice. Abigail is her mother."

"You'd let her go? I thought you was so fond of Jenny?"

"I am."

"Then why?" She studied her husband, her rocker stilled.

"No matter how fond I am of the girl, I have no right to stand between her and her natural mother. I've been happy to regard Jennifer as a God-given replacement for the child I might have had, but Abigail has her rights, and Jennifer hers. I intend to speak to Abigail and Ed, and if they want Jennifer, they shall have her."

"You're crazy!" Castle snapped, but let the matter drop. So Jonathan still held it against her that she had had no children. It had been her doing the one time, but there had never been another time, and that wasn't her fault. Or was it? Was it the result of what she had done the first time? No matter. She had never wanted children anyhow. But the idea of Jonathan offering to let Abigail have Jennifer back! After she'd worked her fingers to the bone for the young'un, to let her go when she was big enough to be some help. . . . And good company, too. Jenny had been such a stupid, owlish brat, but she'd turned out real smart. Wasn't much around the house she couldn't do, and she was sensible to talk to. Abigail just hadn't better want her back!

A few weeks later, Jonathan took Castle and Jennifer to call on the bride and groom. Lucinda and Samantha were playing under a tree, setting a stone table with bits of broken crockery. Jennifer stopped to say hello, then went in search of Cade. She had loved Lucinda as a baby, but she had seen little of Samantha since her infancy. In the years since, the relationship with them both had become more one of casual friendship, while the shared experiences of school life had made Cade her comrade.

Abigail and Ed were sitting in the shade at the side of the house, and Laurel brought chairs for Castle and Jonathan. While commenting on the heat, they made themselves comfortable, Ed straddling a splint-bottom chair, Jonathan with an ankle over a knee, the women with their skirts spread about them, their palm-leaf fans waving busily.

"Ma, suppose Josie and I make some punch?" Laurel suggested.

"Go ahead," Abigail nodded, and the girls raced each other to the house.

Jonathan and Ed talked crops and weather while Abigail admired Castle's new sprigged calico. But Jonathan had come for a purpose, and as soon as he could he turned to Abigail.

"Now that you are married and settled, do you want Jennifer?"

"Jonathan, I told you when I give her to you I'd never ask for her back. You're the best friends I ever had, and I ain't mean enough to take advantage of your goodness that way. Liké I said then, she's yours. Same as your own child."

"You're sure of that, Abigail?"

"Yes, I'm sure."

"You won't change your mind later?"

"What are you driving at?" Castle broke in impatiently. Was he trying to persuade Abigail to take the girl?

"Just this: if Abigail is sure she wants us to have Jennifer permanently, I'd like to make the adoption legal. A verbal agreement made in good faith does not always hold in a court of law. Would you object to legal adoption, Abigail?"

"No, of course not."

"I would like very much for Jennifer to have legal status as my daughter."

"I think that would be just fine, don't you, Ed?"

"If that's the way you want it," he shrugged, noncommittally.

"Then I'll draw up the papers and have them ready for your signatures. Meanwhile, think it over, and talk it over together. Once the adoption is recorded, it will be too late to reconsider."

"I won't reconsider," Abigail assured him.

Laurel and Josie brought the punch; Abigail said the others smelled it, for they all arrived for a share: Jennifer, Cade, Lucinda, Samantha, and Luke.

"It's good to see you with a home and family again, Abigail."

"It's good to be here,'" Abigail said complacently.

Jonathan glanced at the sun. "Getting along toward chore time. We'd better get started. Castle? Come Jennifer. Say good-bye."

When their guests had gone, Abigail and Ed returned to their chairs. He reached over and took his wife's hand.

"You sure you want to let Jonathan adopt Jennifer? I'd rather take her."

"Now you listen to me, Ed. Jonathan come to the Station once—a long time ago it's been—but he knew Lew and Indie were going to town and I'd be alone. He asked me would I mind if he named Jenny in his will. Said he wouldn't do anything long as there was a chance Eli might come back, but if he didn't come, he'd like to be sure Jennifer was provided for. I told him it was all right with me. Then the morning Little Sid was born, Jonathan come for me and took me to Crawfords' and on the way he told me he'd written his will and Jenny was to have a share of everything he's got."

"Did you see the will?"

"I seen it, I read it, I approved it. Jonathan wouldn't do nothing without me knowing about it."

"Is it legal?"

"It is. Judge Duncan has it."

"Well I be drawed on! I never heard of such a thing!" Ed marvelled, shaking his head. "Jenny ain't even any kin to him."

"She's the only child he has or ever will have. That's why he wants it all sewed up legal, so there can't be any question of her rights. You still think we should take her away from him? You think he don't deserve to keep her?" Abigail leaned back and fanned herself, but her usually placid face was grim and her eyes bright.

Ed stared at his wife, this still new wife of his. "I got to admit, if he thinks that much of her, he's sure got a right to keep her. Legal, too."

So Ed signed his name under Abigail's and Jonathan wrote his wife's name under his and she made her mark. When it was all signed, Judge Duncan leaned back in his swivel chair, shaking the folded foolscap at Jonathan.

"Now, I feel better!"

"So do I," Jonathan admitted.

When Preston Wright returned from Chicago that fall, he and Laurel Pettit were married, and Abigail gave their wedding the full treatment. Ed's sprawling, unplanned house had grown with his family, and Abigail had done wonders with it, from flower beds to whitewashed walls. The day was mild and bright with a blue October sky, and when the ceremony was over, Cressy, Cade, and Jennifer again wandered down along the fence, restless and uneasy in their best clothes.

"How long is it since Evva got married?" Cressy mused, holding her long skirts above the weeds.

Cade considered. "Six years." Hands crammed in pockets, he propped himself against the rail fence.

"Seems ages ago," Jennifer remarked thoughtfully. Then, "But this time it doesn't seem sad."

"Of course not. The war's over and Laurel has nothing to worry about."

"Here comes Luke," Cressy nodded at them and moved off to meet him, and the two strolled away together.

"What do you know about that! Josie said Luke had a girl. You reckon it's Cressy?"

"She never left us to go off with him before."

Cade shook his head. "Couple weeks ago Josie shined Luke's boots for him and he was sort of suspicious. Didn't seem natural, her going to all that trouble for him. Sure enough, he said the flies swarmed around his feet all afternoon. Found out afterwards Josie put molasses in the blacking. Wonder if it was Cressy he went to see? Say, if Luke married Cressy, and I married you, what kin would our children be?"

"Goodness! I don't know. But it would be fun, wouldn't it?"

"Come on. No use us hanging around here. Might as well go back to the house and see if there's anything to eat."

In 1868, circuit courts were established in the county,[1] and Jonathan tried his first case in the state of Iowa. Castle was elated. How fine it would be if Jonathan could be a lawyer instead of a farmer. Then they could live in town and she could ride about in a carriage, and they would have a fine big house, and she could wear silk everyday. But Jonathan dashed her hopes promptly and completely.

"I have no intention of opening a law office, and I have no intention of accepting fees."

"What's the sense of going to all that work, setting up nights until all hours, if you ain't going to get paid for it?"

"Because occasionally there'll be cases that interest me, or people who need legal counsel and can't pay for it."

"You're the stupidest man alive! Think of all the money you could make as a lawyer!"

"Few lawyers get rich, Castle."

"Look at Judge Duncan."

Jonathan laughed. "I could buy him out with my small change."

"That's crazy. Look at the fine house he lives in!"

Again Jonathan laughed, but said nothing further, and Castle's wrath burned itself out in fruitless sputtering. It would never do to tell her he held a mortgage on the Judge's house for far more than it was worth. But the Judge paid his interest regularly, and Jonathan considered him a good risk, even if the house should prove a white elephant. Jonathan had never discussed business affairs with his wife and seldom mentioned money in her hearing. She knew he had sold the north half section, the greater part of his beef herd, and most of his hogs, and she assumed it was because he needed the cash. However, Jonathan was not liquidating his capital, but reinvesting where the returns would involve less effort on his part.

During the war, he had marked time, but at its conclusion, with prices soaring, he had built up his operations until he again had more work than one man could handle. Then it came to him that he was no longer master of the farm, but its servant, and he had called a halt, gradually whittling down both the acreage and the stock to his own size. Now he was waiting for the railroad. When he knew where it would cross the county, he would know where his investments would do the most good. The farm had served its purpose. Without sons, it was not as important as it had once seemed. He had other plans now. In a few years he would build a house in town — which town depended on the railroad. But it would be a house elegant enough to please, if not entirely satisfy, his wife. Jennifer would go to the Academy, perhaps later to Des Moines. On that score he had not yet made up his mind. It would be lonely without the girl.

When he built his house, he would have front and back parlors for Castle and a study for himself: a place for his books, a desk, a comfortable chair or two. He would practice a little law for his own pleasure and to keep from growing stale. He would have a garden and an orchard, a cow and a few chickens to keep himself busy, for he knew he would never be content without the feel of earth on his hands, without animals and growing things about him, without trees he had planted and tended. Life would be pleasant in a few more years. He would be able to do so many things he had long wanted to do, things for which there was no time while he carried a heavy load of farm work. Castle would have a little buggy of her own and a gentle mare to drive, enough gowns to keep her from grumbling more than she would whatever the circumstances. A few more years and they would be done with hard work and frugal living. And he would be free of the specter of poverty that had haunted him all his life.

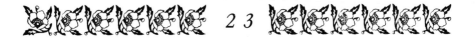 2 3

I T was April, and though it had been sunny during the day, the evening air was raw and chilly. Jonathan made a fire in the sitting room and arranged his papers on the table, while Jennifer washed the dishes, and Castle, in the cellar, skimmed the milk and got her cream ready to churn in the morning. When she came up, she stood a moment looking at the first stars twinkling faintly overhead, while the western sky was still bathed in the golden afterglow of the sun. All day the wind had roared in the trees, but it seemed to be going down with the sun. Castle hoped it would. The wind tired her, as though it lashed her body as it lashed the tops of the trees. And when the wind blew in the night, she heard it even in her sleep. There were peepers along the creek; that meant spring had come at last. While she speculated on tomorrow's weather, she heard hoof beats coming down the lane from the stage road. Someone was riding hard. Either he was drunk or someone was bad sick. She set the milk pail on the back stoop and hurried around to the big gate, calling as she passed the house.

"Jonathan! Jennifer! Somebody's coming—fast!"

They came out the back way, through the yard gate, and joined her at the lane gate. "Can you tell who it is?" Jonathan asked.

"No, he's yelling so . . ."

The horseman was in sight, now, but in the dusk it was difficult to see. "It's Seth!" Jennifer exclaimed. "I know his horse. It's that blaze face."

"Get your things, Castle. It must be Harriet."

"She ain't due . . ."

"Don't argue, woman! He wouldn't ride like that . . ."

Castle ran to the house and Jonathan opened the gate and stepped out. He could hear now. Seth was shouting, "Aunt Castle! Aunt Castle! Come quick!"

"She's getting ready," Jonathan shouted in return.

Seth slowed as he approached, then pulled up and tumbled from the lathered, exhausted horse. Jennifer caught the bridle and trotted the animal toward the barn. She could blanket him, walk him, and rub him down. No one else would have time, and it would be a shame for such a good horse to be foundered.

Seth sucked in a deep breath and tried to speak. "Ma's . . . dead. Pa's . . . burned. Bad. Harriet's . . ."

"Harriet's what?"

"Started. The baby . . ."

"Can you walk? Come on to the house. Tell Castle about it while I hitch up. She'll have to know what to take. What happened?"

"House burned. Ma must of . . . upset the lamp. Or something. Pa . . . went after her . . ." He broke down and began to sob.

Jonathan caught him by the shoulder and shook him. "Stop it, lad! Pull yourself together. You've no time for tears now." He pushed Seth up the steps and into the sitting room. "Castle?" She answered from the kitchen and he called to her. "The house burned. Tabitha is dead, Solon is burned, and Harriet is in labor."

"My God!" She stood in the doorway and stared blankly at the two men. Then passing her hand over her eyes, "I got to think what I'll need."

"I'll get the carryall," Jonathan told them and went out through the kitchen.

"Seth, you folks got vinegar?"

"Yes. In the cellar."

"How much?"

"Half a barrel? Why?"

"Set down and tell me about it while I get my things together. Your Pa bad?"

"Clothes most burned off."

"House gone?"

"Yes."

"Hummm. Have to take everything from here. I'll be back." She went to the back stoop, got the milk pail, washed and scalded it. A pile of sheets from the cupboard went into it. Quilts. She pulled the quilts and pillows from her own bed, then went in and took the quilts from Jennifer's bed, folded them and stacked them by the front door. She took out her medicine satchel and checked the contents. Rum. Not much left. Jonathan had bought a new bottle . . . where? Yes, the shelves. Coffee. And the pot and cups. They'd all need coffee. A loaf of bread. The children would have to eat.

"Got any milk?"

Seth looked blank but answered. "Yes. Down cellar."

"What did you say happened?"

"Pa was doing chores. He came out of the barn and the house was blazing. He went after Ma . . ."

"Did he get her?"

"Yes, but too late. She must of spilled the lamp. He was setting by her when I found him. Setting there moaning. She . . . she . . . Oh, God!'' He hid his face in his hands as though to shut out the memory. ''I threw a horse blanket over her and got Pa in the mill shed. And Harriet . . .''

''She ain't due for two . . . three weeks yet.''

''She's started.''

''What started her?''

''We was in Grove City. She and the boys spent the day with Thaddy. Harriet figgered it was her last chance to go visiting. We were late starting home . . .''

''Go on, go on,'' Castle was checking and rechecking, adding this and that to her satchel or to the pile by the door.

Seth drew a breath, shook his head, and continued. ''Coming home we saw the smoke against the sky. I drove as fast as I could.'' He ran his hand over his face. ''Maybe I shouldn't of, but I was too scared to think. The roads are rough. . . . Then finding the house burned and Ma . . .''

''Harriet didn't see your Ma?''

Seth stared at her incredulously. ''No, no! Of course not.''

''There's Jonathan with the carryall. Get the quilts, Seth.''

Jonathan came in. ''I sent Jennifer on Buck to tell Evva and Martha to come. You'll need help.'' Castle threw him a grateful glance. ''She'll ride on down and stay with her Ma. Ed and the boys will see that our stock is cared for.'' Castle nodded. Jonathan would stay with her. He had hitched up the rather skittish new team, Kit and Kate. Butch and Jerry were too old for such a trip and Ginger and Spice too heavy-footed and slow. Jonathan was usually careful of his horses, but this time he didn't spare them. As long as she lived, Castle never forgot that wild ride. Seth, in the back, clung to the sides of the carryall, Castle clutched the metal arm on her side of the seat, while Jonathan braced his feet against the dashboard, the carryall careening drunkenly at every rut and bump. At the bridge, Seth shouted, ''The mill shed!'' Jonathan made the turn on three wheels and drew to a halt. Throwing the lines aside, he lifted Castle down with scant regard for hoops or skirts.

''Take care of them mares!'' she reminded him, and he nodded, unhooked the lathered team and led them toward the barn. Castle took her satchel and the milk pail full of sheets. ''Bring the quilts,'' she told Seth, then entering the shed and seeing the single lantern swung from a rafter she called back, ''Get the lantern from under the seat. I got to have light enough to see what I'm doing.'' Following the sound of Harriet's hysterical screaming, she found her on a pallet of straw, the two little boys crying beside her. Solon sat humped over on a horse blanket spread on the floor, moaning wordlessly, his face and hands puffed beyond recognition.

Standing over Harriet, Castle made herself heard. ''Shut up!'' she commanded sternly. ''Stop that yelling. And you too,'' she told the little boys. ''Keep quiet and don't bother me.''

Surprised to sudden silence, Harriet looked up and whispered, ''The baby . . .''

''You had two before without any such fuss. Save your strength. You'll need it. Lay down and keep quiet. The baby ain't here yet.''

"The pains have started!"

"All right, all right! You've got all night and nothing else to do. I got to take care of your Pa. He's worse off than you are." She moved over to Solon and he muttered through swollen lips," Tabitha . . ."

"Never mind Tabitha. The dead can wait. They ain't in no hurry. I got to get them rags off you and see how bad you're burned. And none of your stupid modesty. I've seen nekked men before."

With her scissors Castle slashed the remnants of Solon's clothing and lifted the pieces off one by one to avoid breaking blisters unnecessarily. Dirt couldn't get in if the skin wasn't broken. His shoes were heat twisted, but they had protected his feet. His hands and face were the worst, though his back and shoulders and the calves of his legs were painfully burned. His chest, belly, and thighs were only somewhat reddened. It was his hands Castle was most concerned about. A man needed his hands.

"Seth, get a bed ready for your Pa. Spread one of them quilts on some straw, then put a sheet over it. We got to get him bandaged and covered before he takes a chill. I don't think the burns will kill him, but a chill could."

Jonathan reached the shed in time to help put Solon on the clean pallet. When that was done, Castle told him, "We got to have heat in here. Fire the boiler and close the shed up somehow to keep the wind out. And while you're about it, get the coffeepot. The coffee's in it; fill it with water and set it on the boiler. Seth, take that pail and get me some vinegar. I'm going to need a lot."

Jonathan got a good fire going in the boiler and put the coffeepot where it would heat. Then he found a wagon sheet, and with his penknife, slit it in pieces to cover the door and windows. While Castle waited for the vinegar, she selected a couple of old, soft sheets and ripped them into strips for bandages. When Seth came, she dipped them in the vinegar and began to bandage one of Solon's arms—from the shoulder down.

"Get to work on his other arm, Seth. You can do it. It don't have to be fancy. Law, that vinegar smells to high heaven!" Seth went to work and soon Solon's arms were bandaged. "Where's that rum? Here, Solon, take a good swig."

"I don't drink," he muttered.

"Tonight you do! Drink it! That ain't enough. Come on, are you a man or a mouse? Get enough of it down you to warm your innards. That's more like it."

"Can't keep liquor down," he protested.

"You keep it down! I won't have good Jamaica rum wasted. Seth, get the pillows. Now, Solon, on your belly with the pillow under your chest. Good. Bend your knees and hold your feet up. There. Seth, you do his legs. Jonathan, Jonathan! Hand me that piece of sheet—no, the other piece." She tore off a section, folded it and dipped it in the vinegar, then spread it across Solon's shoulders as a compress. Then to Seth, "His legs done? Bring the sheet. Open it and spread it over him. Now a couple of quilts. There. Solon, let me get another dose of rum down you. Drink it! You want to live or die? I ain't doing this for the fun of it, you know. That's better. Now for your head." She had to cover the burns, yet leave holes for eyes and nose and mouth. Then a thought struck her. "Solon, you can see? Your eyes ain't. . . ."

"I can see," he mumbled. "Hat on . . . lost it . . ."

"Thank God you had it on—and didn't lose it too soon."

The head was a slow process, but once done, Seth placed a pillow so his Pa could rest his head and ease his aching neck. Castle's knees felt as though they would come up through the top of her head. She twisted around, hoops and all, and sat down on the floor, then started on his hands, bandaging each finger separately. Harriet moaned now and then and Castle glanced at her from time to time. She would be slow this time, as she had been with Little Sid. The boys were still huddled beside her, but they were watching Castle and the others and were no longer crying.

"Jonathan! I need splints for his fingers—ten of 'em. Seth, you're going to have to keep them bandages wet. Don't uncover your Pa any more'n you have to, but don't let them bandages dry out."

Evva and Martha arrived and Castle barked her orders over her shoulder. "Get a bed made for Harriet."

"We brought a feather tick and quilts," Martha told her.

"Good! I want the tick for Solon. Jonathan, you and Seth lift him—get him around the middle where he ain't burned much. Evva, you push the tick under from that side and I'll pull from here. That's fine. That'll keep the cold from coming up from the ground. There's plenty of quilts for Harriet. Seth, fetch a pan of milk from the cellar. Martha, I brought a loaf of bread. Give the boys some bread and milk and put them to bed. They're plum wore out. Evva, you stay by Harriet."

Jonathan brought the splints and Castle added one to each bandaged finger, the one on the middle finger extending well up the wrist and secured the entire length. The palms of his hands were blistered and when they healed, they might draw. She had to prevent it. A man needed his hands.

"There, Seth. Wet his hands good. . . . I smell coffee. Did you find the cups?"

"I have them." Jonathan brought a cup of strong black coffee and raised Solon while Castle held the cup. Solon drank slowly through thickened lips.

"Good," he said. "Hurts . . . to drink . . . but good."

"There. Help me up, Jonathan. Seth, stay with your Pa. Give him coffee and all the water he'll drink. Try to get some more rum down him. If he's a little drunk, he won't hurt so much. Keep the bandages wet . . . mind now!"

"Shouldn't I take care of Ma?"

"No, you shouldn't. I'll take care of your Ma." Then to Evva, "Harriet all right?"

"I guess so," Evva replied uncertainly, stroking Harriet's hand.

"Great guns, girl, this ain't the first time you've attended a lying-in! You must of been married, or you wouldn't be a widow, so don't act like an old maid. When I need help, I got to have someone I can depend on, and that's Martha and you." Evva smiled sheepishly, and Harriet, relaxing between pains, snickered at her sister's discomfiture. "Is she all right, or ain't she?"

The two girls looked at each other. "She's all right for now."

Castle nodded. She had been watching Harriet and asked, "Pains pretty far apart, ain't they?" Harriet admitted they were. "You got lots of time. Take it easy. There ain't no rush." She could hear Martha over behind a pile of lumber talking quietly to the little boys. Martha had a way with young'uns. They'd be all right. "Call me if you need me," she told Evva. "Where's your Ma, Seth?"

"By the currant bush."

"Look after your Pa."

Taking Jonathan's lantern, Castle left the shed. Jonathan followed. A well-worn path marked the way from the shed to the house, but when she reached the place where the house had been, she found only blackened, smouldering ruins. Skirting the debris, she made her way to the currant bush Tabitha had planted in her dooryard. A form lay beside the bush, a horse blanket covering the head and torso, the legs extending beyond, bare and blackened, and ending in shapeless, heat-twisted shoes. For a moment Castle stood uncertainly. What could she do?" Why must *she* do anything? She was tired. Why couldn't she go back to the mill shed and go to sleep and let somebody else worry about Tabitha? Why must she stand there shaking, knowing that what lay under the blanket would be unbearable? Then she heard footsteps.

"Castle?" Jonathan called softly.

"What is it?" she snapped.

"Go back. I'll take care of Tabitha."

"You can't take care of her."

"You can't carry her, Castle."

"I don't aim to try."

"You can't dress her here."

"I can't dress her anywhere. Bring me a sheet."

"As bad as that?"

"Looks so. Bring the rest of those strips I tore for bandages."

"I'll be back in a minute."

By the time she got through, she wouldn't have sheets for the beds. Jonathan would have to get muslin. . . . She had done the best she knew how for Solon. She hoped his hands wouldn't draw. His face would likely be scarred, but that couldn't be helped. His arms and legs weren't too bad. At least, she didn't think they were. She had doctored burns, but nothing like this. Jonathan came with the sheet and bandages.

"Go away," she told him.

"You can't do this alone."

"I can and I will!" she declared determinedly. "Go away, blast you! You got no right to see Tabitha with half her clothes gone, even if she is dead."

Jonathan moved away reluctantly, but only as far as the path. Castle hung the lantern on the currant bush, and he watched her shadowy form by its pale radiance. The lantern light blurred and he saw her standing in the light from tall ballroom windows, gowned in dull gold brocade, her copper hair, the black brows, the wide full lips. . . . He had thought her a handsome woman then. Now . . .

Castle untied her hoops, let them drop to the ground, and stepped out of them. She pulled the back of her skirts between her legs and tucked the hem into the front of her belt. With her skirts confined, she spread the sheet on the ground, and clinching her teeth, slowly and carefully lifted the blanket from what had been Tabitha Crawford. For all her care, bits of flesh clung to the cloth, and she went around the currant bush and was sick. Again she stood irresolute. Must she do this? Seth had offered, and so had Jonathan. But it would be inhuman to ask Seth to do what she could not bring herself to do. Tabitha had been his mother. But Jonathan could do anything. . . . Jonathan, prepare Tabitha for burial? No, Tabitha wouldn't like that. She would have to do it herself. No one else could. Like it or not, it was her responsibility.

She went back and put the blanket aside. She wouldn't think of this "thing" as Tabitha. It was just a dirty job to be done. She couldn't work with her eyes closed, and even with them closed she could not shut out the horror that must somehow be wrapped securely in the sheet. The long hair was burned off close to the scalp except for a few spots where singed remnants remained. Only fragments of scorched cloth clung to the seared flesh. The face was an almost featureless mass, the bone of the nose laid bare when the blanket was removed, the hands and arms seemingly ready to break at a touch. God! She must have upset the lamp all over herself. How could she have done such a stupid thing? She had been so proud of that lamp![1]

Cursing, Castle knelt on her already sore knees. She couldn't touch that oozing flesh. . . . She wrapped her hands in strips of bandage, then pushing and shoving, she rolled the body onto the sheet and folded the edges over, tucking the corners in carefully. Then she unwrapped her hands and flung the pieces of bandage on the smouldering embers of the house. A blaze flared up and she knew that bit of evidence would not confront the Crawford family. Tearing the wide bandages into strips, she tied them around the mummy figure, then spreading the blanket, rolled the body onto it catty-cornered, folded the corners over, and again wound the bandages around to hold the blanket in place. The coverings must not come off when the body was placed in the coffin—enough that she and Solon and Seth knew what it contained.

When she was done, Castle loosened her skirts, picked up her hoops, and made her way to the barn. Jonathan watched her go, then returned to the mill shed and sat down on the doorstep. An owl hooted, peepers were out along Crooked Creek, and the pungent odor of vinegar drifted around the canvas over the door. He could hear Evva soothing Harriet. He would go for Castle when Harriet needed her. And Castle would come. For so many years, Castle had come when she was needed. But this time something was different. With this business of Tabitha the pattern was somehow changed. He could not quite put his finger on it. A vague recollection of something from the Bible flitted through his mind. What was it? It was there, yet he couldn't pin it down. The upper room . . . the last supper. . . . That was it. But what? "He took a towel and girded himself . . . poured water . . . washed the disciples' feet." Yes. For the first time in her life, Castle had humbled herself. For the first time, she had done something without pride, with no glory to herself—something that was not expected of her, for which she would receive neither praise nor admiration. Only her own inner integrity had demanded she do this. And because it was something she required of herself, no one could help her.

At the barn, Castle had thrown herself on the straw in an empty stall, but her overwrought mind wouldn't let her rest. Again and again she saw the thing that had been Tabitha. She lay in the straw and wept until exhaustion blotted out memory and she fell asleep. It was there, her hoops beside her, that her husband found her in the dim light of early dawn. He smiled as he looked down on her in mingled sympathy and amusement: his wife in a calico gown, without hoops.

"Castle!" he called softly. "Castle, Evva wants you. You'll have to come."

"God above me! If it ain't death, it's birth! Can't you let me be?"

"No. Evva and Martha can't bring the baby."

"That's so," she admitted, and rolling over she heaved herself to her knees. "Help me up. Don't just stand there. I'm stiff."

Jonathan took her hands and drew her to her feet. "You're a great lady, Miss Castle," he told her and she stared at him in blank astonishment while he smiled broadly.

"I never felt less like a lady, or looked a worse hag. You certainly picked a fine time to poke fun at me." She glanced down at her hoopless skirts, then gathered them up and draped them over her arm. At the door she said over her shoulder, "Bring my hoops. I'll need 'em again someday." Grinning, Jonathan picked up the hoops and followed his wife.

It was well along in the morning when Harriet's daughter was born. After the baby had been washed and fed and Little Sid and small Eli had been allowed to see their new sister, Harriet consented to drink a cup of milk, then closed her eyes and fell asleep. Meanwhile, Jonathan kept the fire going and the coffee hot and brought such food as he could find, so they could eat by turns. When he could, he selected boards and took them outside where he made the coffin, and he and Seth laid Tabitha in it. He sent the boy back to the mill shed, then nailed the lid on as tightly as possible. For the moment, that was all he could do. The demands of the living took precedence over the needs of the dead.

That afternoon, Ed Pettit drove over with a load of food, clothing, bedding, pots, pans, and crockery collected from the various households of the neighborhood. When he left, he took the body of Tabitha Crawford with him in the wagon, and he and Luke set the coffin on sawhorses in the lean-to bedroom. Abigail kept the door shut, and they tiptoed past gingerly, for in spite of Castle's care in wrapping the body and Jonathan's thoroughness in nailing the lid, the room exuded a faint but sickening odor. To Castle, hoopless now while she nursed both Harriet and Solon, the odor of vinegar became equally sickening, and she hated it for the rest of her life.

When Evva fainted from exhaustion, Castle put her to bed on the children's pallet, but Martha seemed tireless, doing what needed to be done without waiting for instructions. Once, in passing, Castle paused to lay a grateful hand on her thin shoulder. Martha turned, smiled, brushed the hair from Castle's forehead, and patted her cheek. Neither spoke; both understood. When Ed came the second time, Jonathan went back with him to conduct the funeral services.

When the patients were definitely on the road to recovery, the men gathered to build a new house for the Crawfords. Seth told them to put it over on the far side of the barn, but Ed and Jonathan shook their heads.

"The trees are here, and the fence," Ed reminded him.

"You don't want the ghost of the old house haunting you," Jonathan told him. "Build on the same foundation and lay the specter once and for all."

So with lumber from the mill, they built a sturdy new house where the old one had stood, with the same windbreak, the same fence, and the same currant bush in the dooryard. Then one morning Castle came out and the currant bush was gone. It had been pulled out by the roots. Seth had hitched onto it with the team; the hoof prints were cut deep in the sod where the horses had laid into their collars and pulled. Castle said nothing, for she knew how Seth felt. If she had lived a hundred years she could never have faced that currant bush without a feeling of nausea.

Evva stayed on with Harriet, Seth, and Solon for several weeks, while Jennifer went to stay with Martha to keep her company and to help with the garden and baby chicks. Each time Jonathan asked when the girl was coming home, Castle protested she was glad to have her out of the way for a while. Yet a dozen times a day she caught herself on the point of calling Jennifer and was annoyed when she remembered the girl was not there. If anybody had told her she would miss her that much. . . . And the evenings were endlessly long with no one to talk to, for Jonathan sat with his nose in a book or went early to bed—something he had done few enough times in their married life. Maybe he missed Jenny as much as she did.

 *24*

A T last the Union Pacific Railroad had been completed coast to coast, and celebrated with national fanfare. Without fanfare, the shining rails had been creeping slowly and laboriously across the state of Iowa over a period of years. This link with the East was the most important thing that had happened to Iowa since it was opened to white settlement. Only transportation could provide a market for the products of Iowa farms; only a reliable market could provide money to buy those refinements of civilization which, in turn, only transportation could bring to the farmers of Iowa.

However, the railroad had passed a few miles north of Grove City;[1] within six months the town was deserted, the buildings torn down or moved to the site of the new town of Atlantic, which had sprung up almost spontaneously beside the tracks and station. Nor was there any longer a question of the location of the new county seat, for Cold Spring was down in the southwest corner, while Atlantic was almost in the center of the county, an unbeatable combination of commerce and geography.[2] Furthermore, the railroad had passed almost through the dooryard of the Stage Station, and Sam Seaman was not the man to miss so obvious an opportunity. Before the ink was dry on the deed to the right-of-way, he had a town [Anita] surveyed and platted, arranged for a railroad station, and began selling lots.[3] By the time the surveyors had run the last line, a boarding house was in operation, and before the first train came through, Jesse Freeman and Otis Young had stores open for business. A blacksmith shop, a livery stable, a lumberyard, and a drugstore sprang up like mushrooms, and the town became a reality.

Jonathan promptly bought several acres on the hill overlooking the new town. There, in the near future, he would build his new home, within sight of Lew Garrison's old house. There, he and his family could enjoy the comforts and conveniences of town life and still be in the neighborhood where they had lived so many years. That fall, he shipped his beeves from the freight yard at Anita,[4] only a couple of miles from home, instead of driving them seventy miles to Des Moines. And as Sam Seaman had been commissioned postmaster, in good weather he or Jennifer could walk to town for the mail. The former residents of Grove City found new homes in Atlantic. Assuming it would become the county seat, both Judge Duncan and Jordan Pierce built houses there. Laurel and Preston Wright, too, moved to Atlantic, where Preston became both principal and superintendent of schools. Elder Bates, envisioning a wider field of activities and a larger congregation, did a bit of house swapping and ended up with lots for church and parsonage in the new town, and the townspeople obligingly erected the required buildings.

Anita was near enough for Castle to find ample opportunity to visit Laurel and Thaddy. She was pleased that Jennifer could attend the larger school in Anita instead of the old log school in Turkey Grove. After all, it was time for the girl to get acquainted with some of the other young people. Jenny was growing up, and a girl should have a chance to look around a little. Sooner or later she'd get married. And sooner or later she'd have children, and Castle would be a grandmother—like Abigail. Only it did seem Abigail would never stop being a mother. She was in the family way again. And at her age! Castle was trying to keep an eye on her, for it had been a long time since she had had a baby. Samantha was eleven, and it might not be so easy for Abigail this time. Maybe she'd have a boy. Castle knew she was hoping for a boy, though Ed didn't seem much concerned. But Ed had two sons.

The last few weeks before Abigail was due, Castle kept her satchel by the bed, and toward the end of May, Cade came for her. That night Abigail bore her first and only son and named him Benjamin. Castle was jubilant, Abigail incredulous, and Ed grinned from ear to ear. So great was the excitment over little Benji, that for a time the approaching marriage of Cressy and Luke Pettit was almost forgotten.

Luke had taken a job at the newspaper office in Atlantic, and he and Cressy would live there, for he felt she was not strong enough for the heavy work on a farm. Berta had thrown off her lethergy and the house fairly hummed with preparations for the wedding.

"It'll be a wonder if Axel don't die of a stroke," Castle told her husband. "The way Berta is spending money is a caution. Look at this satin. Ain't it handsome? It'll be the first white satin wedding gown in the township."

"What's Jennifer wearing?"

"Hummm. I hadn't thought."

"She's maid of honor, isn't she?"

"Yes, and I guess she'd ought to have a new gown, what with Cressy being so fine. As if I didn't have enough to do! Even the sewing machine can't cut or baste or do a lot of things has to be done. And on this satin, the stitching would show."

"I'll get material for Jennifer when I go to Atlantic Saturday. Jenny, you'd better come along and help pick it out. You'll have to help make it, too, you know."

"Maybe I better go with you," Castle offered.

"You stick to Cressy's gown. Jenny and I can manage." He was smiling behind his wife's back, and Jennifer caught that gleam in her Pa's eye that meant he was up to no good. "How many yards will you need?" he asked her. "You'll want plenty of fullness in the skirt."

"I know how much Ma uses for her gowns."

"You don't need as much as I do, Jenny."

"I do this time, Ma. I'm sixteen."

"So you want to let your skirts down and put your hair up. You needn't be in such a sweat about it. Next year will be soon enough."

"All the other girls let their skirts down when they were sixteen."

"Yours can stay up another year."

"Not if she's to stand up with Cressy. Wouldn't it look rather foolish for the maid of honor to wear pantalets and her hair down her back when she's as tall as the bride?"

"Oh, all right! Just this once. But don't think you're going to have a whole new outfit of clothes just because you're going to wear long skirts for the wedding."

By Saturday, Jennifer could scarcely contain her excitement. She would have a new gown, her hair would go up and her skirts down, and she would be a young lady! The day was cloudy and threatening, but she was too happy to mind. In the brand new surrey they fairly flew to town, where they pulled up and stopped with a flourish in front of McGeehon's General Store. Jonathan tied the team at the hitch rail and they went in together.

A clerk approached and Jennifer drew herself up and said, "Dimities, please," with all the dignity of an almost young lady.

Jonathan caught the clerk's eye. "Silks," he corrected, and Jennifer looked at him and laughed. So that was what he had been up to when he had left her Ma at home. The clerk handed down bolt after bolt and Jonathan pushed each aside. "Too sleezy. No body. Too dark. Poor texture." Annoyed, he asked, "Haven't you anything of reasonably good quality that's pretty enough for a young lady?" The clerk checked the shelves and brought out a bolt of light blue watered silk.

"Oh! Isn't that beautiful!" Jennifer sighed.

"You like it?" Jonathan asked and Jennifer nodded. He felt the material. "It could be better, but I suppose it will do. Very well, a lady's dress length off that piece. Measure it later. Now, show us the calicos."

"Pa-a-a!" Jennifer cocked her head at him. "What did Ma say?"

"Your Ma says a great many things. How well can you sew? Can you do most of the work on everyday gowns?"

"I think so."

"Then don't argue. When a young lady's skirts go down, they don't go back up. Your Ma knows it as well as I do. Pick out half a dozen pieces. No, no, not those drab things! You're not that old. Light colors, or bright colors. There's a nice blue. How about that pink? I'm the one who has to look at them, so they might as well be to my taste. Three more, now. You're only sixteen once, so make the most of it." He turned to the clerk. "Do you have fashion plates?"

"No, sir, but we have the new Butterick patterns."

"What are they?"

"Paper patterns. The lady pins the pattern on the material and cuts around it. The pieces are designed to fit together properly. The ladies like them very much."

"Hummm. Let's have a look. I believe your Ma would be interested."

Several styles were offered. Jonathan found a couple he thought Castle would like, and Jennifer selected one she thought would not be too difficult to make. Then he selected a half a dozen calicos for Castle and two silks: a dull gold and an olive green. That should be a sufficient bribe to assure her help with Jennifer's gowns. It took a bit of doing, but by the day of the wedding, Castle and Jennifer, as well as Cressy, were properly gowned.

"Happy is the bride the sun shines on," Castle thought, as the guests gathered. Luke Pettit was a fine boy, and Berta wouldn't have to worry about

Cressy. She would miss her, but it was only a few miles from the Olson place to Atlantic. Not like it was in the early days when it was twenty miles to the nearest town and no roads. Times certainly had changed.

She reflected on her friends and neighbors. Ed Pettit and Abigail were much the same — Abigail still held a baby on her knee. Glancing about at the others, she wondered about Evva. Not yet thirty, was there nothing for her but long years of widowhood, when she had scarcely been a wife? Berta was in good spirits for the wedding, and though she would never be the same, she was still a handsome woman when she put aside her grief and held her head up. Thaddy Bates had paid dearly for her runaway marriage, but she had a good man, and Judge Duncan was trying to persuade Jordan Pierce to run for the state legislature. Solon's face showed the marks of the fire, though they would fade in time. His hands had not drawn or puckered enough to interfere with their use, a matter of no small satisfaction to Castle. Now that there was a lumberyard in Anita, Seth had few calls to saw out logs and devoted himself mostly to the farm. Harriet, of all Abigail's girls, was most like her mother: round, rosy, and cheerful. Near her stood Lucinda with her mop of red curls and Samantha, all legs and arms, still a dark brown child, and plainer than even Jennifer had ever been. Sophronia and the Elder had changed hardly at all, and he gave his little sermon about the stormy sea of matrimony with the same gusto as he had at Harriet's wedding.

That day of the camp meeting, Cressy had slept with her head on her Pa's coat, and Luke had been a little boy slapping flies off his bare legs, while Jennifer and Cade had played together on Patience Pettit's quilt. Now they all stood before the Elder while Cressy and Luke made their vows. Luke's dark head was high and proud, with Cressy's pale gold near his shoulder. And Cade, the first white child born in Turkey Grove, was as tall as his older brother. How fine they all looked! Cressy's white satin and Jenny's blue were both as pretty as pictures. Jennifer had turned out a fine looking girl and a credit to her family. She'd done well with the gown, too, for Castle had had little time to help her. With the bride's gown and her new gold silk, she'd had her hands full. Jonathan had not only admired her new gown, he'd said, "Why, Miss Castle, when the bride sees you, she'll be jealous!" And him the handsomest man in the township even now.

After the bride had cut the cake and Berta had served the refreshments, Cade and Jennifer strolled out to the shade of the windbreak. Cade wiped his forehead on his cotton handkerchief and Jennifer waved a palm-leaf fan to and fro, stopping now and then to twirl it between her palms.

"Now there are only two of us, Cade."

"Yes. Probably the next wedding will be ours." He looked down at her earnestly as they stood side by side. "I never thought to ask you if you'd marry me, Jenny. I've just always taken it for granted you would."

"So have I."

Cade searched her face, a dust of freckles across her nose, her blue eyes serious beneath the dark brows and brown hair. "You mean you always wanted to marry me, or you were resigned to the inevitable?"

"Both," Jennifer laughed.

"There isn't anyone else you'd rather marry?"

"There isn't anyone else I'd even consider. If I didn't marry you, I'd end up an old maid."

Cade smiled and put his hand over hers. "I'm glad, Jenny. It hasn't been a very romantic courtship, but it saves a lot of bother not to have to worry or wonder about things. I always knew I'd marry you when I grew up, but if you hadn't felt that way about me . . . if you'd married someone else . . . I couldn't be happy with anyone but you, Jenny. It wouldn't seem natural, or right. Will you miss me while I'm gone?"

"You going away, Cade?"

"Yes. Des Moines. To the Academy."

"Yes, I'll miss you. It'll be lonely with you away."

Cade slipped his arm around her and kissed her for the first time. "I'll be lonely, too. When I come back and get a position, I'll ask Uncle Jonathan for you. We're too young to marry yet, and I couldn't ask him to bind himself by a promise until I've proved I'm worth it."

"Pa will understand."

"And you, Jenny?"

"Yes, Cade. I understand."

When Jonathan received a letter from Drew Coleman marked "Personal," he read it at the post office. Garland Delacroix had lost his shirt. Almost from the beginning the canal had been forced to compete with the railroad, and the railroad was winning the battle. Garland had come to Drew, homeless and penniless, asking for work. Drew, struggling to run the glasshouse, sell the glass, and see that it was delivered, grabbed the chance to get an experienced freight man to take charge of the office and handle the shipping. He hoped the arrangement would meet with Jonathan's approval.

Jonathan approved, but he was not sure his wife would. She might feel that working for Drew was too much of a comedown for the gentlemanly Garland. So when he reached home and Jennifer met him at the gate, he told her, "I have some business to discuss with your Ma, and it may not be altogether pleasant. Would you mind doing the chores tonight, child?"

"Sure, Pa. That's all right. You go on in. Supper's ready. I'll stable the team, do the milking and feeding, and eat later. That way I'll be through at the barn before dark."

As soon as he went in Jonathan announced, "Castle, I have a letter from Drew, and you have one from Marybelle. I can tell you about Drew's letter at the table. I've already read it. It was addressed to me." He washed up and Castle put supper on the table, and when they were settled he dropped his bomb. "Garland Delacroix has lost the house at Greenbrier . . ."

"Now wait a minute! You can't misplace a house. What do you mean, 'lost'?"

"He was in debt and his creditors took everything he had: house, canal boats, business, every red cent."

"Well, in heaven's name! How could any one person be that stupid?

Can't even keep a roof over his wife's head! A fine place like that, all those canal boats, the whole thing handed to him on a silver platter, and he can't even hang onto it!''

"But Castle . . .''

"But me no buts!'' Castle snorted. "Nobody left you this farm, you made it yourself. There was nothing here when we come, and nobody give you anything. You done the whole thing yourself, and I never once heard you complain you didn't have money to run the place. That Garland hasn't the brains God gives a fat goose. He was a sickening little swine when he was ten, and he didn't improve with age.''

"Castle! Listen to me! It isn't his fault. Not entirely, anyway. He can't help it if people would rather ship their goods by fast train than by slow canal boat. And who's going to travel on a canal boat when they can get where they want faster by train? His only fault was hanging on too long. He didn't know he was licked and get out soon enough.''

Castle looked up in quick suspicion. "And why did Drew feel called upon to tell you of Garland's idiocy?''

"Because Drew has hired Garland to manage the office and the shipping department.''

"He's out of his mind! If Garland could lose his own business, what's to stop him losing ours?''

"Drew Coleman.''

"What do you mean?''

"Garland will take his orders from Drew. Drew isn't just turning the business over to him, you know. Drew will give the orders; Garland will do the work.''

At that Castle began to laugh. When she had choked and taken a drink of water, she said, "That's the best I ever heard. Marybelle and I own the glasshouse, so Garland is working for us. That comes about as close to justice as you'll ever get.''

"Now you're being spiteful.''

"What if I am? Give me Marybelle's letter.'' She slit the envelope with her knife and gave it back to Jonathan. "Come into the sitting room. I'm not as hungry as I thought I was, and I want to enjoy this in comfort. Maybe Marybelle will tell us more about what happened.''

Jonathan lighted the candle and sat down by the table while Castle leaned back in her rocker. Marybelle related news even more astounding than Drew's brief statement. Miss Sarah, upon learning of Garland's business trouble, had inquired about his mother. When she was told that the court had kindly permitted them to occupy the servants' house at Greenbrier until they could find suitable quarters elsewhere, she had positively exploded. Quiet, self-effacing little Miss Sarah had raised the roof. Sylvia Delacroix was her friend! They had been friends for years—since they were girls! Nothing would do but she and Drew must take the carriage immediately and fetch Mrs. Delacroix to Homeplace. And since there was no sense in Garland living alone in some hole in Pittsburgh, she had brought him along, too. Marybelle was sorry for poor old Mrs. Delacroix, who didn't seem quite right in the head. No telling how long it had been since she had combed her hair or put on a clean garment. Miss Sarah and Aunt Lucy had cleaned her up, and Callie and Amanda had washed for days, doing the piled up laundry brought from Greenbrier. Marybelle hoped Castle wouldn't mind, but there had been no stopping Miss Sarah. And Mrs. Delacroix, poor soul, certainly couldn't look after herself and Garland. Didn't seem right to separate them, either.

"I should be mad as hops, but somehow I just feel sorry for that poor old woman. God forbid, I should ever go out of my head! Does seem that's the very worst thing that could happen to a person. But Marybelle doesn't say a word about Griselda."

"Griselda is dead."

"What?" Castle looked up incredulously. "Griselda . . . dead? When?"

"Quite a while ago. I didn't tell you, because I was afraid you'd want to go home and . . ."

"That sissified . . . I always hated that snooty Delacroix family. Including that bitch sister of old Mrs. Delacroix."

"Watch your language, woman! I'll wash your mouth with lye soap . . ."

"Lye soap, my foot! Washing my mouth wouldn't change that bunch. That fancy floosey saying Marybelle would get a fine husband, and I could teach school. Marybelle always thought she was so smart, just because she was pretty. I do hate to think of them living at Homeplace. It was so beautiful. And I cared so little for it . . . then."

"Were you happy there, Castle?"

She threw her husband a startled look. He had asked her a question like that before. "When I was little, I suppose I was happy enough. Amanda and Little Lief and Bo and I—we all ran wild. But I always hated Marybelle so, and sometimes I almost hated Miss Sarah. Because she loved Marybelle better than me."

"Miss Sarah didn't love Marybelle better, she just understood her better. Marybelle was like Miss Sarah, you weren't. After she had you, she didn't know what to do with you. Like a biddy-hen with a duckling."

Castle studied her husband's face. "Was that it? Was that why she kept out of my way? Because she didn't know what to do with me?"

"I think so. She couldn't cope with you, so she left you to Aunt Lucy. Aunt Lucy could manage you. Miss Sarah couldn't."

"Well, that's so, all right. Maybe that was it. I just couldn't behave the way Miss Sarah thought I should. Marybelle could, but I just couldn't 'ack lak a lil lady.' "

Jonathan chuckled as he lighted his pipe. "You acted like Major Hunter."

A flicker of amusement touched her eyes. "I suppose I did at that," she admitted, rocking complacently.

"That's why I married you."

"You mean that? You said something like that once before."

"Certainly I mean it. If you had been like Marybelle, I would never have bothered to ask you to dance a second time. The world is overflowing with perfect ladies. You were one in a million."

"And Marybelle always thought she was such a much!"

Jonathan took his pipe from between his teeth and laughed. "You mean it's taken you all these years to find out you're a better woman than Marybelle? I could have told you that the first time I saw you."

"I was always so jealous of her," she admitted. "I guess Aunt Lucy knew it, because she tried to sort of comfort me, telling me how I'd be a great lady someday. And I believed her."

"You *are* a great lady, Miss Castle. I told you . . ."

"You told me! And I looked a worse fright then than I do now. A fine lady, I must say!" She smiled wryly, tucking a stray lock of hair behind her ear and brushing a hand over her calico skirt.

"My dearest, it isn't how you look, but what you *are* that makes a great lady. And you *are* a great lady. By the way, while I'm about it, may I tell you how very much I love you, Miss Castle? I believe I did promise to tell you someday."

"Heavenly days! This is so sudden!" And Castle threw back her head and laughed.

Notes

1

1. "During this year [1846] the Mormons were driven from Nauvoo, . . . several thousand scattered up and down the river making settlements in several places. The largest body of them founded a town on the present site of Council Bluffs calling it Kanesville." *Compendium of History and Biog* ʸ *ɪy of Cass County, Iowa* (hereafter referred to as *History of Cass County*), p. 39.

2. "As early as June, 1830, the Longworthy brothers of Galena, Ill., with several other miners, had settled upon the site of Dubuque in order to work the lead mines. . . . " Ibid., p. 39.

3. Eleven million dollars worth of glass was manufactured in Pittsburgh in 1878. John A Kouwenhoven, *Adventures of America, 1857-1900, A Pictorial Record from Harper's Weekly* (hereafter referred to as *Adventures of America*), Fig. 187. The first glasshouses were established in the Pittsburgh area in 1797.

4. "Steamboat owners . . . up to the Civil War, spent fortunes in the decoration and equipment of their boats. . . . The public rooms were often overdecorated so that the effect was vulgar and blatant. In the hey-day of river travel there were dozens of so-called 'floating palaces' on the Mississippi and Ohio." W. E. Woodward, *The Way Our People Lived*, p. 263.

5. "The Indian inhabitants of the County were the Pottawattamie tribe and some of the early pioneers who are still living have good cause to remember the precious beggars. . . . [they] were quite numerous and during the years they were here had encampments on the streams in various parts of the County. . . . The main body of Indians left prior to 1847 although stragglers and small squads could be seen as late as 1856." *History of Cass County*, p. 42.

2

1. "In September 1833, a few months after the Black Hawk treaty went into effect, the Chippawas, Ottawas and Pottawattamies were granted a 5,000,000 acre hunting ground, which included the territory within the limits of Cass County. . . . the western part of the State was still Indian territory and was to remain so until the final treaty with the Sacs and Foxes in 1846." *History of Cass County*, p. 42.

2. "As a rule all were good neighbors and everybody living within ten or fifteen miles was considered a neighbor. If a new settler came in and wanted help to put up his cabin he let people know what day he wanted them and everybody for ten miles or more around would turn out and help him." Ibid., p. 62.

3

1. "In the spring of 1852, the government established a mail route from Des Moines to Council Bluffs, running once a week. The route was as follows: From Indiantown [Cold Spring] up the 'Botny [Nishnabotna River] to Ballard's Grove; there it forded the river and followed the trail to Hamlin's Grove; thence to Morrisburg on the Coon River, thirty-five miles and no house in all that distance; thence to Redfield, to Adel and Des Moines. The journey to Bloomington [from Des Moines eastward] was made with a light canvas covered wagon; thence to Oskaloosa in a two horse hack; to Peoria in an old fashioned Concord coach; from Peoria in a one horse buggy. The distance was four hundred miles each way, the time four weeks to the nearest railroad." *History of Cass County*, p. 59.

2. "The post office was called Cold Spring although the settlement was then known as Indiantown, and the mail was received weekly from the main camp at Kanesville, . . ." Ibid., p. 46.

3. "The nearest point at which we could procure provisions was Council Bluffs." Ibid., p. 60.

4

1. ". . . a fire was kept burning twenty-four hours a day, in summer and winter, for the purpose of supplying coals for lighting. This was a common practice. (If) the constant fire went out from neglect the family usually borrowed coals from a neighbor rather than depend on the uncertain results of flint and steel." W. E. Woodward, *The Way Our People Lived*, p. 126.

2. ". . . the establishment of the four horse coach line between Des Moines and Council Bluffs . . . was one of the greatest things which happened to southwest Iowa and Cass County. In May, 1855, the Western Stage Company commenced running these grand coaches which, as they swept through the country, aroused more pride than the advent of two or three railroads." *History of Cass County*, p. 224.

3. "In the fall and winter of 1854, Doc Morrison, Peter Kanawyer and I bridged the streams and staked the road. . . . In the preceding winter, Dr. Morrison, R. D. McGeeon, Peter Kanawyer and J. R. Kirk spent about two months staking out the road and bridging the streams for a distance of about forty miles from Dalmanutha, in Guthrie County, to the Nishnabotna River about two miles from Indiantown." Ibid., p. 151. The Indiantown settlement eventually became the town of Lewis, which was the first county seat.

5

1. "While the main body of the Pottawattamie Indians were leaving their hunting grounds in Cass County, the Mormon refugees from Nauvoo, Illinois, on their way to far distant Utah, found a temporary haven near the deserted Indiantown. In the summer of 1846 a large body of 16,000 . . . scattered up and down the Missouri River from Council Bluffs and about twenty families settled on the Nishnabotna River and Indian Creek, near Indiantown, . . . they secured the establishment of a post office at their settlement. . . ." *History of Cass County*, pp. 45, 46.

6

1. "The patchwork quilt was the product of long winter evenings when the bad roads bound the family to the confines of the house. Conceived in thrift it became in time an artistic outlet, a means of self-expression. . . . Designs tended to become standardized within the family and within the community." R. J. McGinnis, ed., *The Good Old Days*, p. 63.

2. I have no published authority, though books have been written on folk medicine. The remedies I mention are those of my childhood, handed down from Grandmother to Mother to me.

7

1. "The first camp meeting ever held in the County was . . . in the fall of 1855 in a grove near the 'Botny river. Elder Shinn was the preacher and he made a great success. . . ." *History of Cass County,* p. 56.

2. "Fashionable clothing was not known and the good wives cut and made our clothes as best they could. . . . If a garment was warm and comfortable for winter, or cool and comfortable in summer, it was satisfactory. Fine clothes and fashion cut little figure in those days." Ibid., p. 65.

3. "Great-grandfather's church has been condemned as embodying too much 'hell fire and brimstone.' . . . When Sunday came the preacher forgot all business and politics of the week and became an ardent revivalist. There were few quiet preachers." Eric Sloane, *American Yesterday,* p. 33.

4. " . . . monthly magazines with colored plates of the latest fashions were published in London and Paris and sent regularly to America." W. E. Woodward, *The Way Our People Lived,* p. 181.

8

1. "During the fall of 1856, David A. Barnett and I bought a sawmill in St. Louis and had it shipped by steamboat to Council Bluffs. When the boat reached St. Joseph, it was unloaded there. . . ." *History of Cass County,* p. 223. The trip for the sawmill is taken almost entirely from this account.

2. "In 1856, Grove City was surveyed and platted . . . it was about three miles east of the present site of Atlantic. . . . A few small buildings were at once erected in one of which A. T. Drake displayed a small stock of goods. . . . Mr. Kirk built a . . . hotel. . . ." Ibid., p. 224.

3. "Grant Township held an election . . . following officers were chosen: J. C. Morrison, Edward Griffith and William Peters, Trustees. . . ." Ibid., p. 152.

9

1. "From the time the County was organized there was but one voting precinct, first at Indiantown, then at Lewis. During that fall Turkey Grove Township was organized. . . . Turkey Grove polled twenty-seven votes, a majority for Fremont." *History of Cass County,* p. 63.

2. "The next spring I sowed about thirty acres of wheat and had a good crop—about twenty-five bushels to the acre. I tramped out some in the fall and took some to West Nishnabotna—to what was called Stutman's mill—and brought the flour home and sold it for seven dollars a hundred pounds. Corn was then a dollar a bushel." Ibid., p. 127.

3. "The next spring we got Frink, Walker & Company to put their four-horse coaches on it [the road] from Des Moines to Council Bluffs. This brought the emigrants for California to our doors and gave us a market for corn, hay, potatoes, butter. . . ." Ibid., p. 61.

4. "The first cellars were not under the house. . . . They were underground rooms . . . cellars served as storage and pantries." Eric Sloane, *American Yesterday,* p. 62.

5. "Sometime during the winter of 1857, old John Brown, of Kansas fame, accompanied by two of his sons and one other white man, stopped all night with Mr. Barnett at the 'Grove City House.' Brown and his party had in charge about eighteen runaway negroes—men, women and children—whom they were taking from Missouri to Canada." *History of Cass County,* p. 75.

6. "The waltz was unknown. . . . It did not take its place among the dances until after the Civil War. . . . The jig, a comparatively simple dance, was performed with much clatter and laughter by everybody who was not too old and infirm to lift a foot." W. E. Woodward, *The Way Our People Lived,* p. 195.

7. "A post office was established in Grove City in 1857, but there was already an office by that name so it was christened Turkey Grove." *History of Cass County,* p. 225.

8. "In the first week of November, 1858, . . . a government contractor in Nebraska City, Neb., owned and held slaves at that place. Two black girls whom he had sold were to be sent in

the charge of the steamboat captain to the extreme South. Two men brought the fugitives to Lewis. . . . The owner followed and offered a reward of $500.'' Ibid., p. 108.

9. ''On the 5th of July, 1858, the water in Turkey Creek rose 23 feet in 3 hours at Wakefield's Mill, just below Jim Branch.'' Ibid., p. 226.

10

1. ''But it was not until 1859 that the mails reached California overland. In that year, Butterfield's Overland Mail . . . began its semi-weekly service from St. Louis to San Francisco. . . .'' John A. Kowenhoven, *Adventures of America*, Fig. 42.

2. ''The barns of the west were not without the dignity and romance of American farm life. The flat country became a proving ground for many new ideas in barn building. When a farmer builds a house he draws a rough sketch for the carpenter, but when he builds a barn, you will find him sitting up nights planning. . . . He knows the welfare of his family depends upon the comfort of his cattle.'' Eric Sloane, *American Barns and Covered Bridges*, p. 76.

3. ''. . . but within a few years corn was only worth fifteen cents and wheat twenty-five cents a bushel. As soon as we broke up the virgin soil and it brought forth abundantly we overstocked the market, and as we had no outlet except by team to Council Bluffs or Des Moines, prices fell. I have hauled wheat to both these markets.'' *History of Cass County*, p. 127.

4. ''I bought hogs that fall to be driven to Iowa City and there shipped to Chicago. I paid six cents a pound and some of the farmers got as high as $1,000 for their hog crop. . . . Cattle were driven into the country and fed, which made a market for our corn.'' Ibid., p. 64.

5. ''. . . about 1858, when thousands of elk were forced south from Minnesota and Dakota, and poured into Cass County . . . many were killed in the snowdrifts but they were very poor in flesh.'' Ibid., p. 127.

11

1. ''The people thought I was very aristocratic, as it was the first house in the County with twelve-light windows, made of sawed lumber.'' *History of Cass County*, p. 58.

2. ''. . . the women of the family sewed strips of fabric end to end for rag carpet. No old clothing was ever thrown away. . . .'' R. J. McGinnis, ed., *The Good Old Days*, p. 128.

3. ''Millard Filmore became President in 1850 and set out to modernize the White House. One of his innovations was a cooking stove for the kitchen.'' W. E. Woodward, *The Way Our People Lived*, p. 174.

13

1. ''Mr. Ludley located in Cass County [1855] . . . he was what might be called a land-grabber . . . although he secured much real estate he became land poor. . . . John W. Russel who came in 1857, invaded the township more as a land investor than as a home seeker. . . .'' *History of Cass County*, p. 128.

2. ''The first settlers were comparatively poor people . . . most of them had been brought up on farms in eastern Iowa, Illinois, Indiana, Ohio, Pennsylvania and New York with now and then one from the New England States. . . . It took men and women of heroic and obstinate courage to live here . . . yet they lived a happy life. All were free and equal. . . .'' Ibid., p. 65.

3. ''Clapboards were rived with a froe, those used for siding were cut in pie-shaped wedges toward the center of the log so that one edge was thicker than the other. Roof clapboards were cut from a squared log and were of uniform thickness.'' Eric Sloane, *American Yesterday*, pp. 42-43.

14

1. "Ninety-five different machines [reapers] were tested. More than 20,000 of these machines were made in 1857 and sold at an average price of one hundred dollars." John A. Kouwenhoven, *Adventures of America*, Fig. 32.

2. "The first week of the term I had only two scholars as every child who was large enough had to drop corn. . . ." *History of Cass County*, p. 110.

3. This incident happened. It was one of my mother's early recollections.

15

1. "Because of its distance from the seat of Government, however, its citizens were not included in the President's first call for volunteers, issued in April, 1861; but they responded to the second and every succeeding call with alacrity. . . ." *History of Cass County*, p. 77.

2. "Governor Jackson having taken position there at Jefferson City, he [Lyon] moved against him. Jackson fled, burning and destroying bridges, railroads and telegraph lines in his retreat." J. T. Headly, *The Great Rebellion, A History of the Civil War in the United States* (hereafter referred to as *The Great Rebellion*), vol. 1, p. 86.

16

1. ". . . which is truly a handsome village of from 300 to 500 inhabitants, with good stores, hotels and industrious, enterprising class of citizens. In Lewis are two good schools, a printing office and one magnificent church house of the Methodist denomination. . . ." *History of Cass County*, pp. 102, 103.

2. "The first newspaper published in the County was the 'Cass County Gazette,' established at Lewis in January of 1861, . . ." Ibid., p. 102.

3. "Although the Fourth Iowa was raised in a dozen different counties in the State, because of the large contingent from Cass County its movements and fortunes were watched with breathless interest by the people at home. . . . It was mustered into service at Council Bluffs in August, 1861, under command of Granville B. Dodge, . . ." Ibid., p. 78.

4. ". . . Captain Lyon of the regular army in command of the arsenal at St. Louis refused to obey the order of the police commissioner . . . Governor Jackson and General Price took the field against him. . . . On August 9, at Wilson's Creek, Lyon was killed. Union losses, 1,236, or more." J. T. Headly, *The Great Rebellion*, vol. 1, pp. 86, 136.

17

1. The account of the battle of Pea Ridge is given in *History of Cass County*, pp. 78, 79. A more detailed account is given in J. T. Headly, *The Great Rebellion*, vol. 1, pp. 302-10.

2. "During the Civil War the telegraph was used for the first time for communicating battle news and inter-army information. Though it did a tremendous job, it was not as efficient as it is now and each side tore the others wires and poles down at every opportunity." John A. Kouwenhoven, *Adventures of America*, Fig. 58.

3. "Although General Carr was severely wounded and thus outmatched in numbers, he yielded ground only slowly and stubbornly. As Curtis came up he saw the Fourth Iowa falling back in good order. Colonel Dodge explained that it was entirely out of ammunition. Curtis thereupon ordered a bayonet charge. . . ." *History of Cass County*, p. 78.

4. ". . . but in 1861 the war commenced and everything seemed to stop. The most of our able bodied men went in the army. . . . Immigration ceased. So many men being away to the war left most of the farming to be done by their wives, children and cripples who were unfit for service; consequently, many farms grew up to weeds." Ibid., p. 63.

5. "The Rebels got possession of the Missouri below St. Joseph and we could get nothing

from St. Louis. Corn was worth nothing in money. I hauled two loads of wheat to Council Bluffs and sold it for thirty-seven and one half cents a bushel, store pay.'' Ibid., p. 63.

18

1. ''Grove City made two determined efforts to snatch the county seat from Lewis but both failed.'' *History of Cass County*, p. 225.

2. ''Company I of the Twenty-Third Regiment [Iowa] was composed entirely of Cass County men.'' Ibid., p. 82.

3. ''The exchange of prisoners is a matter very easily adjusted between two belligerent nations, but in a civil war, between the established government and that portion of it in revolt it becomes very complicated. In the former case it is only necessary to follow the established law of nations which gives equal rights and privileges to both. In the latter, by the same law, the rebellious government is supposed to have no rights except those of a common humanity. Theoretically, the moment they are treated as equals on this point, independent national rights are conceded. . . . So at the outset of the war we could not consent to put ourselves on an equality with rebels by entering negotiations on the subject of the exchange of prisoners. They had no right to take or hold prisoners, but to treat with them admitted that they had. . . .'' J. T. Headly, *The Great Rebellion*, vol. 1, pp. 503-6.

4. ''. . . the Free Soil party . . . which put forth a candidate first in 1844 did not demand the abolition of slavery. The central point of its program was the exclusion of slavery from the territories. . . .'' Charles A. and Mary Beard, *The Beards' Basic History of the United States*, p. 262; ''The entire North, including the Republican party, had repeatedly declared in the most emphatic manner, that it had no intention to interfere with slavery in the States where it already existed; for they had no right to do so under the Constitution. Its *perpetuity there was guaranteed* until the States themselves should get rid of it. Hence the Southern conspirators had no fear on that point. . . . They desired to *extend* slavery, because in that way alone could they extend their power.'' J. T. Headly, *The Great Rebellion*, Preface.

5. ''The Army of the Southwest [including the Fourth Iowa] marched across Arkansas to Helena, on the Mississippi, . . . and on the 22nd of December embarked on transports with the right wing of the Army of the Tennessee under General W. T. Sherman.'' *History of Cass County*, p. 79; ''Sherman left Memphis on the 20th day of December and the day after Christmas, . . . and moved down toward Vicksburg.'' *The Great Rebellion*, vol. 2, p. 117.

6. Detailed accounts of the assault at Chickasaw Bayou are given in *History of Cass County*, p. 79; *The Great Rebellion*, vol. 2, pp. 117, 118.

19

1. ''In October [1861] on a motion made by E. B. Bell, the board of Supervisors appropriated $1200. for the relief of the families of volunteers.'' *History of Cass County*, p. 69.

20

1. ''When the remains of the Fourth Iowa reached Des Moines in February [1864] the members of the legislature honored the returned heroes with an impromptu reception.'' *History of Cass County*, p. 81.

2. ''In 1864 times began to improve. The Missouri came into the possession of Union Troops and boats could bring goods to Council Bluffs. Greenbacks became plentiful and the price of farm products rose rapidly.'' Ibid., p. 64.

3. An account of the Fourth's participation in the fighting in Georgia is given in *History of Cass County*, p. 81. The account of Sherman's activities, including the Army of the Tennessee, is given in J. T. Headly, *The Great Rebellion*, vol. 2, pp. 324-29, 521, 522.

4. ''Commanding at Baltimore was General Lew Wallace, the Indiana officer who would

one day write a novel called 'Ben Hur.' He had a small body of troops. . . . An Army, apparently of twenty-thousand men, had crossed the upper Potomac, and was moving towards the gaps of South Mountain. Wallace promptly moved out to meet the enemy. . . . Wallace had little hope of defeating the Confederates, but he suspected that they meant to march on Washington, and he thought he might delay them." Margaret Leech, *Reveille in Washington, 1860-1865,* p. 390.

21

1. Richmond was evacuated on Sunday and the Confederates fired the city to destroy its usefulness to the Union troops under Weitzel, who did not reach that city until Monday. J. T. Headly, *The Great Rebellion,* vol. 2, p. 593.

2. "But while the closing scenes were being enacted on the Atlantic Coast, events were transpiring on the Gulf of Mexico which, under ordinary circumstances would have awakened the keenest interest. Grant designed that the attack against Mobile should keep a large rebel force in Alabama which otherwise would have reinforced Lee. . . . Two brigades of Carr's division moved gallantly to the assault. It was one of the most remarkable raids of the war, but its success and results not being known until after the surrender of Lee and Johnston, it excited little interest." Ibid., vol. 2, p. 612.

3. "Johnston contacted Sherman on April 15th requesting a truce. They met the next day and terms of the surrender were arranged. . . . General Wilson with 12,000 cavalry spent the month of April polishing off the remains of the Confederate Army in Georgia and Alabama. . . . On the 4th of May, General Dick Taylor surrendered to General Canby all the remaining Rebel forces East of the Mississippi River. . . . but on the 26th of May . . . General Kirby Smith surrendered his entire command [Texas] to Major General Canby." Ibid., vol. 2, pp. 601, 611, 613.

4. "The Fourth Iowa was mustered out at Davenport, Iowa." *History of Cass County,* p. 82.

5. Pressed glass had been made for some years. The earliest was with a lead formula, made in imitation of and to compete with British cut glass. Later, pressing was tried with both soda and potash formulas. The lime formula, introduced around the time of the Civil War, was the beginning of the "Pattern Glass" era, which continued until around the turn of the century.

22

1. "Circuit courts were not established until 1868." *History of Cass County,* p. 67.

23

1. "[in 1855] Dr. Abraham Gesner, of Newtown Creek, Long Island, made the first kerosene. . . . He did not sell much of it as there was no lamp in existence in which it could be burned efficiently." W. E. Woodward, *The Way Our People Lived,* p. 298; "Oil was successfully drilled . . . near Titusville, Pa., 1859, leading to an oil boom as petroleum quickly ousted whale oil and burning fluids as an illuminant." Richard B. Morris, *Encyclopedia of American History,* p. 524. I have not been able to find the date of the invention of the kerosene lamp, but I gather they were coming into use by this time.

24

1. "But when the railroad coolly cut through one corner of the plat and passed on to the new city of Atlantic, the residents of Grove City understood that their case was hopeless. . . . Buildings and people moved almost en masse to Atlantic." *History of Cass County,* p. 225.

2. ''On the 20th of October, 1869, after a canvass of the vote on the relocation of the County Seat, the board declared in favor of Atlantic. . . .'' Ibid., p. 232.

3. ''The site of Anita . . . was originally the property of Lewis Beason who caused a town to be surveyed and platted and named, in 1869 . . . a station was established and from that time, Anita was a fact. Mrs. Beason suggested the town be named in honor of her niece, Anita Cowles. . . .'' Ibid., p. 152.

4. ''The first carload of stock was shipped from the Anita freight yards in 1869.'' Ibid., p. 154.

5. ''Patterns for ladies dresses were first manufactured in 1863, by Ebenezer Butterick of Massachusetts.'' W. E. Woodward, *The Way Our People Lived,* p. 181.